Directors' Duties During Insolvency

HEAD OFFICE: 100 Harris Street PYRMONT, NSW 2009
Tel: (02) 8587 7000 FAX: (02) 8587 7100

For all sales inquiries please ring 1800 650 522
(for calls within Australia only)

INTERNATIONAL AGENTS & DISTRIBUTORS

CANADA
Carswell Co
Ontario, Montreal, Vancouver, Calgary

HONG KONG
Sweet & Maxwell Asia
Hennessy Road, Wanchai

Bloomsbury Books Ltd
Charter Road, Central

MALAYSIA
Sweet & Maxwell Asia
Petaling Jaya, Selangor

NEW ZEALAND
Brooker's Ltd,
Wellington

SINGAPORE
Sweet & Maxwell Asia
Albert Street

UNITED KINGDOM & EUROPE
Sweet & Maxwell Ltd
London

UNITED STATES
Wm W Gaunt & Sons, Inc
Holmes Beach, Florida

William S Hein Co Inc
Buffalo New York

JAPAN
Maruzen Company Ltd
Tokyo

Directors' Duties During Insolvency

by

HELEN HORSINGTON

Solicitor
Allens Arthur Robinson
Sydney Office

LAWBOOK CO.
2001

Published in Sydney by

Lawbook Co.
100 Harris Street, Pyrmont, NSW 2009
lbccustomer@thomson.com.au

First edition 2001

National Library of Australia
Cataloguing-in-Publication entry

Horsington, Helen

Directors' Duties During Insolvency

Includes index.

ISBN 0 455 21808 0.

1. Directors of corporations—Law and legislation—Australia. 2. Bankruptcy—Australia. I. Title.

346.9406642

Typeset using 11 on 13.5 Bembo

Printed by Ligare Pty Ltd, Riverwood, NSW

Foreword

In the present climate of a number of high profile corporate financial failures, any text dealing with the responsibilities of directors for the financial misfortunes of their companies is timely. As recent experiences demonstrate, the insolvency of any corporate entity, or for that matter an individual, will often bring distress and anger among those affected, not least the creditors who are left without any or only some recompense for their claims, and then at some delayed time later.

Limited liability

The nature of a corporate entity and limited liability for those involved with it has been part of our legal system for some time. These arrangements are something that society tends to take for granted. But limited liability (in its various forms) is an extraordinary privilege that can only be justified on the assumption that its existence tends on the whole to lead to an increase in the common good. Of course, limited liability is not an open-ended privilege. Its existence assumes that companies will be governed in a responsible manner, by diligent and faithful directors and officers.

Personal liability

It may have in earlier times been the case that this limitation of liability meant that those behind the company were rarely fully exposed outside the corporate veil by way of being required to explain and account to the company's creditors when the company failed. Whatever may have been the case in the past, the increasing trend, reinforced by judicial extension of the law and by legislative change, has seen the directors of the company brought to the fore in any corporate collapse. Directors are now increasingly expected not only to explain and account but in many cases to also compensate creditors for their losses.

Retribution?

In such circumstances, there is to a degree some element of retribution sought by society, a retribution that cannot be effectively applied against an inanimate corporate entity but which at least requires the directors to come forth from behind the veil and explain the reasons for their company's demise. The naming of directors in the press and the displaying of their own personal fortunes, in contrast to those creditors left wanting, is an increasing trend, however much this will often be an unfair pre-judgment.

Insolvent trading and other liabilities

The concept of insolvent trading represents the ultimate statement of a director's personal civil liability, but its full leverage against directors has only been extended in the last decades. It relies on the legal and moral view that for a company to incur a debt which its corporate mind knows it is unable to repay, involves such a degree of culpability that the directors involved should take personal responsibility for the company's acts and account themselves to the creditor that has been left unpaid. That civil liability has then progressed by way of legislative change to a civil penalty level of liability, and more recently to a criminal liability for more serious dishonesty of the directors involved. Indeed, because of these changes or otherwise, the term and the concept of insolvent trading has so much entered the awareness of the business community, and the consumer community, that it is invariably raised early in time on a company announcing its liquidation. Creditors who traded with the company, perhaps for some time, will feel particularly aggrieved and concerned to know the circumstances of their debts being incurred.

Directors of insolvent companies are also exposed in respect of other liabilities. Major amendments in 1993 eliminated the Commissioner of Taxation's priority in insolvency but instead imposed personal liabilities on directors for certain of their company's tax debts. Unpaid employee entitlements, an issue that often excites public and media attention, is another area where directors have more recently been exposed to personal responsibility; and indeed to an expected moral responsibility to ensure the company's employees are fully paid. On that issue, we can observe the more recent focus on retrieval of directors' (inaptly named) "performance" bonuses paid to them by their insolvent company.

Legal incentives

But apart from the pursuit of retributive justice, the law also sees the potential for using these liabilities as incentives for directors to either properly manage their companies, or, if they cannot do so, to put them in the hands of an insolvency administrator. Thus a primary focus of the voluntary administration regime for insolvent companies, also introduced in 1993, is to prompt directors to take early action in respect of actual or likely insolvency, thus preventing or limiting losses to its creditors. Even apart from any expected regard by the directors for creditors' interests, the regime provides the incentive to directors that any potential personal liability – for insolvent trading, tax or other liabilities – might be avoided. This would be assured if the creditors are persuaded to accept the more immediate return usually available under a deed of company arrangement than the uncertain return through pursuit of the directors in liquidation.

While creditors will often shy away from the prospect of relying on recoveries from directors in favour of a more certain return under a deed, the introduction of litigation funding and its judicial imprimatur, has given creditors a more real choice of options to consider. This is coupled with, in the case of some of the high profile failures, a greater readiness to pursue directors rather than take a token amount under a deed.

Directors of straw

However, even if the directors are successfully pursued to judgment, creditors will often find that directors of insolvent companies are insolvent themselves, if only as a consequence of their personal guarantees of the company's liabilities. This situation is exacerbated by the relatively common practice of directors, and others, arranging their financial affairs in a manner designed to minimise the extent of their personal assets. Whilst the courts have shown themselves willing to review arrangements that may seem to have been contrived solely or principally for this purpose, it does add another layer of disincentive and uncertainty for a creditor in seeking to recoup its financial loss. The availability of directors' and officers' liability insurance may assist although that in itself can be limited in scope, assuming that such insurance is in fact maintained.

Shareholder and lender liability

Accountability and recoupment of creditors' losses through directors is therefore problematic. But there are others involved in the insolvency process to which the law may well have regard. Should a secured lender who provides funds to a company itself take some responsibility for the company's ultimate demise, in particular where the company has not only left financial losses but environmental, or public health or other such problems behind? As well, the shareholders themselves are absolved in the process and it is not beyond contemplation that their responsibility might need to be considered.

Indeed, given the size of the "footprint" left by some companies on the natural and social environment, it is conceivable that there will be growing pressure for a review of the relative liabilities of shareholders, directors and officers. In turn, this might lead to a more fundamental review of the ethical foundations for corporate law. For example, we need to determine the extent to which it remains true that company directors have a primary, fiduciary duty to increase the wealth of shareholders. Was it ever so? Is it so today? If so, then to which shareholders does the duty apply – current shareholders, future shareholders, those wanting to enter the market today? More importantly, to what extent should the interests of shareholders be held superior to others such as employees, creditors or the community as a whole? Should shareholders be held more directly responsible for how they vote on matters affecting the overall governance of the companies they own – not least in their selection of directors to act on their behalf?

Competing demands

Company directors are often given mixed signals as to what is expected of them. There are, of course, formal legal obligations. However, there are also the demands of the market – some of which act to encourage corporate conduct of a kind that may be harmful to the interests of the wider society; perhaps only a shade beyond compliance with the "business judgment rule", perceived by some as lowering the level of ethical corporate conduct. And one of the temptations likely to challenge directors struggling to balance these competing demands, is to keep on trading beyond the point dictated by prudence and a proper regard for the interests of those unable to make an informed decision about whether or not to rely on a company's promise to pay.

None of this is to say that these are easy concepts to which a director should adhere. Insolvency may be a sudden or a gradual process, well recognised in retrospect, but difficult to assess at the time. From a personal and psychological viewpoint, it may be hard for directors to acknowledge that their once prosperous company is seriously in decline, that it is not only temporary, and that the upturn in its fortunes is not around the corner.

Law vs ethics

Difficult dilemmas abound for a director in many circumstances of a company's demise. It is to be hoped that this book will be a continuing source of assistance for those inclined to meet the twin standards set by the law on one hand and a proper regard for ethical conduct on the other.

DR SIMON LONGSTAFF	MICHAEL MURRAY
St James Ethics Centre	Editor
Sydney	*Insolvency Law Bulletin*

Preface

The onset of worldwide recession in the late 1980s and the consequential insolvent collapse of a significant number of major Australian companies increased the significance of company directors' duties during insolvency. Legislators in Australia took note of the changed financial environment and sought to alter the nature of company law to increase directors' responsibility for the overall management of their company.

Australian law has traditionally recognised companies as separate legal entities. The concept of limited liability has often been seen as a method for encouraging entrepreneurial activity and promoting economic growth. However, limited liability is open to abuse by directors. To avoid abuse of their position, Australian law has imposed a number of duties on directors. These include fiduciary duties, a duty not to mislead or deceive, common law and statutory duties of care and diligence, good faith and proper use of position and information. The most significant duty imposed on directors in the context of insolvency is the statutory duty to prevent insolvent trading contained in s 588G of the *Corporations Law* (the Law). With Australia moving into uncertain economic times these duties warrant careful attention by directors and officers.

Importantly, many of the duties outlined in this book, other than the duty to prevent insolvent trading, are imposed on officers as well as directors. In this way company secretaries, receivers, administrators, administrators of a Deed of Company Arrangement and liquidators are also bound by a number of duties which are owed to the company.

A number of directors' statutory duties as contained in the Law were amended by the *Corporate Law Economic Reform Program Act* 1999 (Cth) (CLERP) which came into effect on 13 March 1999. This book reflects the post-CLERP position of directors' duties in insolvency.

Under the auspices of the new ASIC Chairman, Mr David Knott, ASIC has recently taken a tough stance on insolvent trading. Clearly it is an area of company law which ASIC intends "to crack down" on.

This book is intended to provide practical assistance to insolvency practitioners in understanding the nature of directors' duties in the ways in which such duties may be utilised to recover money for distribution to unsatisfied creditors of an insolvent company. It seeks to provide an overview of the theoretical framework of each relevant duty and provide a guide to exploiting them for the benefit of unsecured creditors of an insolvent company. It will also be a useful resource for directors and officers who wish to understand the nature of their duties.

This book is current as at May 2001. It is intended as a guide to the practicalities of bringing an action against company directors and officers for a breach of duty, particularly a breach of the duty to prevent insolvent trading. The publication should not be treated as providing any definitive advice on the law. Matters differ according to their facts. The law changes. You should seek specific legal advice on specific fact situations as they arise.

Helen Horsington
April 2001

Acknowledgements

The author and Allens Arthur Robinson would like to extend their thanks to Lampros Vassiliou, partner of Allens Arthur Robinson and Head of Insolvency and Reorganisation in the firm's associated Bangkok office, for providing the initial support and encouragement for this manuscript and from whom the idea to write the manuscript grew.

Gratitude and thanks is also given to Michael Quinlan, partner of Allens Arthur Robinson and convenor of the firm's Insolvency and Reconstruction Practice Group, for thoroughly reviewing and editing the manuscript during various drafts.

Thanks is also given to the staff of Thomson Legal & Regulatory Publishing Group, particularly James Davidson, James Jarvis and Kirsten McNeill, who have provided so much support and assistance and exhibited so much patience during the preparation of this manuscript.

The author would also like the thank Mr Damien Considine, Senior Lecturer in Law at the University of Wollongong, who gave so willingly of his time to discuss corporate law and regulation and corporate governance issues.

The author would also like to thank her parents, Mary and Raymond Condon, her husband Colin, and her friends who have all been a constant source of encouragement during the course of the writing of the book and a great support and inspiration during the last few difficult months.

Table of Contents

Table of Checklists

Table of Abbreviations

ASC	Australian Securities Commission
ASIC	Australian Securities and Investments Commission
ATO	Australian Taxation Office
CASAC	Companies and Securities Advisory Committee
CSLRC	Companies and Securities Law Review Committee
CEO	Chief Executive Officer
CLERP	Corporate Law Economic Reform Program
CLERP ACT	*Corporate Law Economic Reform Program Act* 1999 (Cth)
Cooney Report	Senate Standing Committee on Legal and Constitutional Affairs, *Report on the Social and Fiduciary Duties and Obligations of Company Directors: Company Directors' Duties* (AGPS, Canberra, 1989).
Harmer Report	Australian Law Reform Commission, *General Insolvency Inquiry* (AGPS, Canberra, 1988).
ITAA	*Income Tax Assessment Act* 1936 (Cth)
The Commissioner	The Commissioner of Taxation
The Law	*Corporations Law*
VLRC	Victorian Law Reform Commission

Unless otherwise stated, all references in sections are to the *Corporations Law*.

PART A

Definitions and Elements

Overview of Directors' Duties

1

OBJECTIVES

This Chapter will:

- provide an overview of the general nature of directors' duties;
- outline the various categories of duties imposed on directors and other company officers;
- introduce the basic features of each duty imposed on directors and other company officers.

[1.1] Introduction

A wide range of duties are imposed on directors. These duties take on a special significance when the company is, or may be, insolvent.

Directors' duties are owed to the company generally. No duty is owed to individual shareholders or groups of shareholders of the company. When a company is solvent the shareholders as a general body are entitled to be regarded as "the company" in the context of directors' duties. However, where a company is insolvent, directors must have regard to the interests of creditors of the company. Directors' duties fall into four general categories, discussed below.

[1.2] Contractual duty

The contracts under which directors and other officers are employed will often stipulate conditions of employment.

[1.3] Common law duty

Case law has progressively developed a number of legal duties by which directors are bound. These include the common law duty of care, skill and diligence.

[1.3.1] COMMON LAW DUTY OF CARE, SKILL AND DILIGENCE

The common law duty of care, skill and diligence stems from the law of negligence and the relationship of proximity between the director and the corporation.[1]

A director must exercise the degree of care that a reasonable person would exercise.[2] Although directors are not expected to bring any particular qualifications to their office, they should have at least a minimal understanding of financial affairs,[3] and if any special qualifications are possessed these must be used.[4] Although directors are not bound to give continuous attention to the affairs of the corporation[5] they are expected to place themselves in a position to guide and monitor the management of the corporation.[6] The business judgment rule applies to this common law duty of care, skill and diligence: see s 180(2).

---

1 *Daniels v AWA Ltd* (1995) 13 ACLC 614 at 655 per Clarke and Sheller JJA.
2 *Daniels t/as Deloitte Haskins & Sells v AWA Ltd* (1995) 13 ACLC 614.
3 *Commonwealth Bank of Australia v Friedrich* (1991) 9 ACLC 946 per Tadgell J.
4 *Re Brazillian Rubber Plantations and Estates Ltd* [1911] 1 Ch 425.
5 *Re City Equitable Fire Insurance* [1925] Ch 407 per Romer J.
6 *Daniels t/as Deloitte Haskins & Sells v AWA Ltd* (1995) 13 ACLC 614 at 664.

[1.4] Equitable/fiduciary duty

The rules of equity impose a number of duties on directors by virtue of the fiduciary relationship between directors and the company. A liquidator is able to bring proceedings for breach by a director of a duty owed to the company which, but for the insolvency of the company, would otherwise be exercisable by the company.

A fiduciary relationship is formed when a fiduciary undertakes or agrees to act for or on behalf of, or in the interests of, another person in the exercise of a power or discretion which will affect the interests of that other person.[7] A fiduciary refers to the person undertaking to act on behalf of another. Equity imposes special duties and obligations on fiduciaries.

These duties stem from the central duty of loyalty a director owes to the company.

Equitable duties include the duty to act in good faith for the benefit of the company as a whole, the duty to avoid fettering discretions, the duty to exercise powers only for a proper purpose and the duty to avoid conflicts of interest.

[1.4.1] DUTY TO ACT IN GOOD FAITH FOR THE BENEFIT OF THE COMPANY AS A WHOLE

A subjective duty of good faith is imposed on directors under which they must act "bona fide in what they consider – not what the court may consider – is in the interests of the company".[8] Directors must also give proper consideration to the interests of the company. Knowledge that they are not acting in the best interests of the company acting without these interests in mind will result in a breach of the duty.

[1.4.2] DUTY TO AVOID FETTERING DISCRETIONS

Directors often have many discretions and functions conferred by the constitution of the company. Because these duties must be exercised for the benefit of the company as a whole, directors generally cannot fetter discretions conferred on them. Directors must give adequate consideration when they are exercising discretions and must not delegate their discretions without proper authority.

[1.4.3] DUTY TO EXERCISE POWERS FOR PROPER PURPOSE

Directors' discretions and powers cannot be used arbitrarily for any purpose. The fiduciary relationship between the company and the director implies that discretions and powers must be used in the interests of the company rather than the

7 P Nygh and P Butt, *Butterworths Concise Australian Legal Dictionary* (Butterworths, Sydney, 1997), p 157.
8 *Re Smith & Fawcett Ltd* [1942] Ch 304 at 306 per Lord Greene MR.

personal interests of the director. Directors must exercise these discretions and powers for a "proper purpose".

A director can breach their duty of good faith if the law objectively considers that what they are doing is improper, even if they subjectively believe that what they are doing is in the best interests of the company.[9] The personal views of the director or executive officer as to whether or not their actions are for a proper purpose are not relevant.

[1.4.4] DUTY TO AVOID CONFLICTS OF INTEREST

Directors are granted discretions and powers that must be exercised in the best interests of the company. When a director has a personal interest that may conflict with the best interests of the company, it is possible that he or she will not exercise her or his discretions and powers to advance the company's best interests but will rather seek to advance her or his own personal interest. Directors have a fiduciary duty to avoid conflicts of interests.[10]

A director should not be placed in a situation where their interest and their duty to the corporation may conflict.[11]

[1.5] Statutory duty

There are a number of statutory duties imposed on directors and other officers. Many of these encapsulate fiduciary duties, although there are often important differences between common law and statutory duties of the same nature. Where a compensation order is sought under the civil penalty provisions, a company's liquidator will have standing to bring proceedings.[12]

[1.5.1] DUTY TO PREVENT INSOLVENT TRADING

Directors are under a positive duty to ensure that the company does not incur a debt whilst it is insolvent, or does not become insolvent by incurring that debt. This duty is imposed by s 588G of the *Corporations Law* (the Law). The duty under s 588G only applies to debts incurred after 23 June 1993. If a debt was incurred prior to this time, the director will be bound by the duty contained in s 592(1) of the Law. It is beyond the scope of this book to discuss in detail the elements of the duty in s 592(1).

Importantly, the duty under s 588G to prevent a company incurring a debt arises only if the company is insolvent when the debt is incurred, becomes

9 *Australian Growth Resources Corp Pty Ltd v van Reesema* (1988) 6 ACLC 529.

10 *Keech v Sandford* (1726) 25 ER 223; *Phipps v Boardman* [1967] 2 AC 46; *New Zealand Netherlands Society "Oranje" Inc v Kuys* [1973] 1 WLR 1126 at 1129; *Guinness plc v Saunders* [1990] 2 AC 663.

11 *Phipps v Boardman* [1967] 2 AC 46.

12 Section 1317J(2).

insolvent by incurring that debt, or by incurring debts at that time including that debt: s 588G(1)(b). This limits the operation of the insolvent trading provisions to companies who have failed financially or which are at least under the threat of such failure. In contrast to the position under s 592, the duty in s 588G is not limited to companies which have entered or which subsequently enter external administration. Whilst s 588G can apply to companies under external administration, it can also apply to companies which never enter it and to those which do enter external administration but are subsequently restored to solvency. The rationale for this extension is that:

> ... if directors no longer have to consider whether their company will or may enter external administration in order to predict liability, they will have a greater incentive to monitor the company's financial fortunes on an ongoing basis.[13]

Although it is possible for s 588G to apply to companies in a form of external administration other than liquidation, such as a deed of company arrangement under Pt 5.3A, in practice this will prove difficult. Due to the standing rights reserved for liquidators under the insolvent trading provisions, unless ASIC brings a claim or the Minister authorises it, a claim may only be brought against a director under these provisions after the commencement of winding-up of the company. Accordingly, where it is intended to prosecute a director under s 588G creditors will often choose to place the company into liquidation.

Section 588G also applies to companies that enter external administration but which are subsequently restored to solvency. For example, a company that enters voluntary administration but enters into a Deed of Company Arrangement under Pt 5.3A may be restored to solvency. Creditors who enter into a Deed of Company Arrangement are bound by it and may be wise to consider whether the proposed Deed contains a release of the directors personally as they would otherwise be bound by any release which may thwart their ability to bring an action for insolvent trading.

There has been debate as to whether the insolvent trading provisions may be of particular concern to directors of incorporated associations.[14] Such associations are usually constituted by unqualified but well-intentioned volunteers with minimal financial expertise or understanding of the Law. Section 9 of the Law defines a company to include Pt 5.7 bodies for the purpose of, inter alia, Pt 5.7B of the Law (which includes the insolvent trading provisions). Part 5.7 bodies are

---

13 S M Pollard, "Fear and Loathing in the Boardroom: Directors Confront the New Insolvent Trading Provisions" (1994) 22(6) ABLR 392.

14 For a discussion of the applicability of the insolvent trading provisions to incorporated associations see A S Sievers, "The Meaning of 'Association' or 'other Body' for the Purposes of Part s 7B and s 8 of the *Corporations Law*" (1995) 13 CSLJ 65; C Huntly, "Dionsyius, Damocles and the Unseen Perils of Insolvency for Officers of Incorporated Associations" (2000) 18(4) CSLJ 262.

defined to include partnerships, associations or other bodies that consist of more than five members. Importantly, a "body" does not need to be a body corporate In addition, s 18 of the Law which states that a reference to "carrying on business" includes non-profit activities. Of particular concern may be the presumption of insolvency on the basis of inadequate accounting records as such bodies often have poor records or no records at all. However, the extension of the Law to incorporated associations is unlikely given that s 6 of the *Associations Incorporation Act* 1984 (NSW) specifically excludes the application of the Law to incorporated associations.

The application of s 588G to a wide range of companies is consistent with the general policy of the insolvent trading provisions to increase incentives for directors to monitor the financial affairs of their company. A number of elements of liability must be fulfilled for this duty to be imposed:

- The person must be a director at the time the company incurred a debt. The term "director" has the meaning given to it under s 9 of the Law, and includes de facto and shadow directors.
- The company must be insolvent at the time the debt is incurred, or become insolvent by incurring that debt. The term "insolvent" has the meaning given to it under s 95A of the Law. Insolvency will be determined by looking at the whole of the financial assets available to the company, including credit resources. It generally means an endemic shortfall of working capital, and not merely a temporary lack of liquidity. There is no simple definition of the term "debt". Generally a company incurs a debt when by its choice, it does or omits to do something which, as a matter of substance and commercial reality, renders it liable for a debt for which it otherwise would not have been liable.
- At the time the debt was incurred there must have been reasonable grounds for suspecting that the company was insolvent or may become insolvent. To suspect means a positive feeling of apprehension or mistrust reasonable grounds are assessed by the objective standard of a director of ordinary competence. The Court will determine what a reasonable director of ordinary competence would have done in the circumstances and then determine whether the actions or omissions of the particular director were reasonable in the circumstances.[15]

Breach of the duty to prevent insolvent trading can have both civil and criminal consequences.

Under s 588G(2), if the director failed to prevent the incurring of the debt and he or she knew that there were reasonable grounds for suspecting insolvency,

15 Corporate Law Reform Bill 1992, Public Exposure Draft and Explanatory Paper (1992), para 101.

or a reasonable person in their position would have been so aware, then a civil penalty may be imposed.

Under s 588G(3), if this failure is done with a dishonest intent a criminal offence will have been committed and a criminal penalty may be imposed.

There are a number of defences available to directors. These defences only apply to the civil penalty provision under s 588G(2). If a criminal offence is committed under s 588G(3), there are no defences available to a director. The only way the director can escape liability is to rebut the elements of liability.

The defences are that:

- There were reasonable grounds to suspect that the company was solvent and would remain solvent even if it incurred the debt.
- The director relied on a competent and reliable person who was responsible for providing information as to the solvency of the company. On the basis of this information they expected that the company was solvent.
- Through illness or other good reason the director did not take part in the management of the company.
- The director took all reasonable steps to prevent the company incurring the debt.

The Court also has the power under s 1317S and s 1318 to excuse a director from liability under s 588G(2).

A holding company can be liable for the debts of its insolvent subsidiary.

[1.5.2] MISLEADING AND DECEPTIVE CONDUCT

Under the *Trade Practices Act* 1974 (Cth), the *Australian Securities and Investments Commission Act* 1989 (Cth) and the *Fair Trading Act* 1987 (NSW) (and equivalent legislation in other States) directors can be personally liable for misleading and deceptive conduct.

[1.5.3] DUTY OF CARE AND DILIGENCE

Section 180 of the Law provides that directors and officers of a corporation must exercise their powers and discharge their duties with the degree of care and diligence that a reasonable person would exercise if they:

- were a director or officer of a corporation in the circumstances of the corporation;
- occupied the office held by, and had the same responsibilities within the corporation, the director or officer; and
- had the same experience as the director or officer.

The business judgment rule applies in relation to decisions regarding the business operations of the corporation. This has the effect that the degree of care and diligence will be satisfied if the director or officer makes the relevant decision:

- in good faith for a proper purpose;
- without any personal interest in the subject matter of the decision;
- informed about the subject matter of the decision to the extent they reasonably believed to be appropriate; and
- with a rational belief that the decision is in the best interests of the corporation.

[1.5.4] DUTY OF GOOD FAITH

A director or officer of a corporation must exercise their powers and discharge their duties in what they believe to be the best interests of the corporation and for a proper purpose: s 181. Failure to do so could lead to the imposition of a civil penalty. If the director or officer is dishonest in failing to fulfil this requirement, and does so intentionally or recklessly, then a criminal offence will have been committed: s 184(1).

[1.5.5] USE OF POSITION AND USE OF INFORMATION

Under ss 182, 183 and 184(2) and (3), directors and officers of corporations have a duty to make proper use of their position and the information they acquire through their position.

[1.5.6] LIABILITY FOR UNPAID GROUP TAXES

Under the *Income Tax Assessment Act* 1936 (Cth) directors can be made personally liable for unremitted PAYE tax deductions.

[1.5.7] DELEGATION AND RELIANCE

There is explicit statutory recognition that directors can delegate functions to others and rely on any information provide by others in the performance of their duties under s 189, s 190 and s 198D of the Law.

[1.5.8] OTHER STATUTORY DUTIES

In addition to the duties imposed on directors' outline above, directors can be made personally liable under a number of various statutes.[16] These include:

Animal Research Act (NSW) 1985 (section 58)
Banana Industry Act (NSW) 1987 (section 28)
Boxing and Wrestling Control Act (NSW) 1986 (section 70)
Building and Constructions Industry Long Service Payments Act (NSW) 1986 (section 63)
Casino Control Act (NSW) 1992 (section 167)
Charitable Fundraising Act (NSW) 1991 (section 51)

16 See D James, "Boardroom Liabilities are Still Piling Up" (1997) 19(3) *Business Review Weekly* 56 for a full listing of applicable statutes.

Classification (Publications, Films and Computer Games) Enforcement Act (NSW) 1995 (section 62)
Commercial Vessels Act (NSW) 1979 (section 51C)
Consumer Credit Administration Act (NSW) 1995 (section 41)
Corporations Law
Crown Lands Act (NSW) 1989 (section 176)
District Court Act (NSW) 1973 (section 154)
Employment Protection Act (NSW) 1982 (section 22)
Environmentally Hazardous Chemicals Act (NSW) 1985 (section 53)
Exotic Diseases of Animals Act (NSW) 1991 (section 73)
Farm Debt Mediation Act (NSW) 1994 (section 28)
Fertilisers Act (NSW) 1985 (section 36)
Firearms Act (NSW) 1989 (section 83)
Fisheries Management Act (NSW) 1989 (section 279)
Food Act (NSW) 1989 (section 76)
Heritage Act (NSW) 1977 (section 159)
Listening Devices Act (NSW) 1984 (section 29)
Lotteries and Art Unions Act (NSW) 1994 (section 22C)
Maritime Pollution Act (NSW) 1987 (section 56)
Marketing of Primary Products Act (NSW) 1983 (section 157)
Medical Practice Act (NSW) 1992 (section 187)
Mining Act (NSW) 1992 (section 376)
Motor Accidents Act (NSW) 1988 (section 134)
National Parks and Wildlife Act (NSW) 1974 (section 175B)
Noxious Weeds Act (NSW) 1990 (section 62)
Nursing Homes Act (NSW) 1988 (section 50)
Occupational Health and Safety Act (NSW) 1983 (section 50)
Ozone Protection Act (NSW) 1989 (section 22)
Passenger Transport Act (NSW) 1990 (section 57)
Poisons and Therapeutic Goods Act (NSW) 1996 (section 36D)
Ports Corporatisation and Waterways Management Act (NSW) 1995 (section 104)
Poultry Meat Industry Act (NSW) 1986 (section 21)
Private Hospitals and Day Procedures Centres Act (NSW) 1990 (section 53)
Public Health Act (NSW) 1991 (section 78)
Radiation Control Act (NSW) 1990 (section 23)
Rail Safety Act (NSW) 1993 (sections 82 and 83)
Residential Tenancies Act (NSW) 1987 (section 127)
Retirement Villages Act (NSW) 1999 (section 186)
Stock (Artificial Breeding) Act (NSW) 1985 (section 38)
Theatres and Public Halls Act (NSW) 1908 (section 34)
Tow Truck Industry Act (NSW) 1998 (section 88)
Therapeutic Goods Act (Cth) 1989 (section 55)

Continued ... /

Trade Practices Act (Cth) 1974
Unhealthy Building Land Act (NSW) 1990 (section 12)
Uranium Mining and Nuclear Facilities (Prohibitions) Act (NSW) 1986 (section 11)
Veterinary Surgeons Act (NSW) 1986 (section 69)

What Is Insolvency and How Can It Be Proved?

2

"*The conclusion of insolvency ought to be clear from a consideration of the debtor's financial position in its entirety and generally speaking ought not to be drawn simply from evidence of a temporary lack of liquidity.*"[1]

1 *Sandell v Porter* (1966) 115 CLR 666 at 670 per Barwick CJ.

OBJECTIVES

This Chapter will:

- discuss the statutory definition of insolvency and its elements;
- analyse the cash flow test of insolvency and the balance sheet test of insolvency and identify the main differences between these two tests and the way in which they are applied;
- summarise the rebuttable presumptions of insolvency which can be used to establish the insolvency of the company at a particular point in time.

[2.1] General overview

[2.1.1] STATUTORY DEFINITION OF INSOLVENCY

The definition of insolvency is central to the operation of the insolvent trading provisions. Liability is not triggered under the insolvent trading provisions unless the company was insolvent at the time the particular debt was incurred, or became insolvent by incurring that debt: s 588G(1)(b).

Prior to 23 June 1993, no statutory definition of insolvency existed. The Law now contains s 95A which provides a definition of insolvency. Section 95A is not limited to the insolvent trading provisions or Pt 5.7B generally, but has application throughout the Law. However:

> ... it represents a particularly important reform ... in relation to Pt 5.7B because it refines and partially codifies the complex law surrounding the situation which arises when a company is insolvent.[2]

Under s 95A a person is deemed solvent if, and only if, it is able to pay all its debts as and when they become due and payable: s 95A(1). A person that is not solvent is deemed insolvent: s 95A(2). Section 85A of the Law states that the term "person" includes a body corporate as well as an individual natural person.

The definition in s 95A suggests that a cash flow test is intended rather than a simple balance of assets over liabilities.[3] However, companies will often experience both types of insolvency and the Courts increasingly adopt a flexible consideration of "insolvency" and will often consider both types of insolvency.[4]

The primary cash flow test of insolvency was epitomised recently by Prior J in *Powell v Fryer*:[5]

> The commercial solvency of a company is not proved by merely looking at its accounts and making a mechanical comparison of its assets and liabilities. Insolvency is a question of fact falling to be decided as a matter of commercial reality in the light of all the circumstances with things being viewed as it would by someone operating in a practical business environment. The statutory focus is on solvency, not liquidity. Thus it is appropriate to consider the terms of credit or financial support available to the company with which to defray any debts owed to creditors. The question is not to be answered merely by looking at the financial statements.

---

2 S M Pollard, "Fear and Loathing in the Boardroom: Directors Confront New Insolvent Trading Provisions" (1994) 22(6) ABLR 399.

3 *Leslie v Howship Holdings Pty Ltd* (1997) 15 ACLC 459.

4 *Powell v Fryer* (unreported, Sup Ct, SA, Prior J, 14 April 2000).

5 Unreported, Sup Ct, SA, Prior J, 14 April 2000.

The definition introduced by s 95A does not differ significantly from the traditional definition of insolvency in s 122(1) of the *Bankruptcy Act* 1966 (Cth). However, s 122(1) of the *Bankruptcy Act* provides for insolvency where a person is "unable to pay his debts as they become due from his own money". Despite the omission of the "from his own money" requirement under s 95A, cases indicate that a similar requirement will nevertheless be imposed, requiring the company to be able to pay its debts from its own resources.[6] This is supported by *Stargard Security Systems Pty Ltd v Goldie*,[7] the primary case considering the meaning of s 95A within the context of the new insolvent trading provisions.

However, the statutory definition of insolvency contained in s 95A will only be relied upon when the statutory presumptions of insolvency in s 588E(3) and (4) are unable to be relied upon or are able to be rebutted.

[2.1.2] REBUTTABLE PRESUMPTIONS OF INSOLVENCY

A major difficulty in finding directors liable under the insolvent trading provisions has been proof of insolvency on the day that the particular debt was incurred. Often the financial records of the company are inadequate or they enable proof of insolvency on dates other than the one required. In many situations, the liquidator is "... a stranger to the past business operations of a company, [and] is often confronted with considerable difficulty in affirmatively establishing that a company was insolvent at a time prior to the winding up, even though there may be every indication that this was the case".[8]

In order to overcome this problem, two rebuttable presumptions of insolvency have been introduced into the Law. These presumptions of insolvency effectively reverse the onus of proof. The presumptions operate in relation to civil recovery proceedings and are not applicable for the purposes of criminal prosecution.

---

6 See *Geraldton Building Co Pty Ltd v Woodmore* (1992) 8 ACSR 585, where Master Bredmeyer interpreted the definition of insolvency in s 95A as importing a restriction on the source of money for payment of the company's debts. This restriction meant that the company must be able to pay its debts as they fell due from its own resources. Contrast the opinion of S M Pollard in "Fear and Loathing in the Boardroom" (1994) 22(6) ABLR 399 at 403, who argues that the section means that regard must be made to whether the person was unable to pay her or his debts from any available resources. He argues that if the "from his own money" requirement had been included within s 95A, directors would be entitled to feel "hard done by" as it would mean that the company would be unable to rely on reasonable expectations of forthcoming financial support from a parent company, increased revenue from advertising, or other similar sources. However, under the case law indicating that a similar "from his own money" requirement is imported into s 95A, it is clear that such sources of money available from the company's own resources, assets, and expected cash flows can be relied on. This is further supported by recent cases such as *TCN Channel Nine Pty Ltd v Scotney* (1995) 17 ACSR 116; and *Khoury v Rosemist Holdings Pty Ltd* (unreported, Fed Ct, Aust, Boon JA, 15 April 1999).

7 (1994) 13 ACSR 805 (see para [2.4.3] below).

8 Australian Law Reform Commission, *General Insolvency Inquiry* Report No 45, Vol 1 (1988), para 290.

The presumptions are appropriate because they can be rebutted and they apply to directors who should stay involved with the financial affairs of the company and thus have access to the means of rebuttal.

(a) Presumption as to continuing insolvency upon proof of insolvency at a specific date

Under the presumption in s 588E(3), where it is proved that a company which is being wound up was insolvent at a particular time during the 12 months prior to the relation-back day (most often the date an application to wind up the company is filed or an administrator was appointed), it is presumed that the company was insolvent from that time until the relation-back day.

This presumption has been applied by the Court in numerous cases recently, indicating that it provides an increasingly useful tool for establishing insolvency for the purpose of the insolvent trading provisions. For example in *Powell v Fryer*[9] the Court looked to the presumption of continuing insolvency to establish the insolvency of a company at the time the relevant debts were incurred, namely within the period between 23 June 1993 and April 1995. In the words of Prior J:

> It is not disputed that the company was insolvent on 2 April 1995. The bank's demand of 24 June 1994 clearly establishes that the company was unable to pay its debts as and when they fell due and payable soon after that. Therefore it must be presumed that the company was insolvent throughout the period beginning 30 June 1994 and [ending 12 months later].

(b) Presumption of insolvency based on insufficient accounting records

Under the presumption in s 588E(4), where it is proved that the company failed to keep proper accounting records which correctly explain and record its transactions and financial position, and which enable true and fair financial statements to be prepared and audited or has failed to keep them for seven years after the completion of the transaction to which they relate (s 286(1) and (2)), it is presumed that the company was insolvent during that period.

This presumption does not arise where the failure to maintain accounting records was minor or technical: s 588E(5). It also does not arise where the accounting records have been removed, destroyed or concealed by a person other than the defendant director and the defendant director was not implicated in those activities: s 588E(6).

9 Unreported, Sup Ct, SA, Prior J, 14 April 2000.

[2.1.3] ABILITY TO PAY "ALL" OF THE COMPANY'S DEBTS

The test of insolvency in s 95A is directed towards the company's ability to pay *all* its debts as and when they become due and payable. The inquiry under s 95A, and consequently the inquiry under s 588G(1)(b), is the company's ability to discharge all its debts rather than merely particular debts, on their respective dates for payment, at the time when a particular debt is incurred. Accordingly, liability can be established under s 588G(1)(b) without reference to the particular debt incurred if, at the time the particular debt was incurred, the company was unable to pay other debts. In this way, liability can be triggered if the company cannot pay a debt or an installment of a debt despite its ability to pay other debts.

[2.1.4] PAYING DEBTS AS THEY "BECOME DUE"

For a debt to fall due it must at least be recoverable by legal action.[10] Generally whether or not a debt has become due is determined by reference to the legal agreement between the parties. Mere inaction by a creditor in enforcing its rights against a debtor does not usually influence whether or not the debt has become due,[11] although if the creditor has allowed, or created a reasonable expectation, for a period of grace for repayment, this may impact upon the determination of whether the debt has become due.[12] In this way, a course of dealing between the parties can be used to indicate that a debt becomes due and payable on a date other than that originally stipulated for by its repayment.[13] In the absence of trading terms the Court will look to the custom of the industry.[14]

The inclusion of the words "as they become due" also indicates that insolvency must be determined with reference to a consideration of the company's position over a period of time and not a particular instance.[15]

[2.1.5] ABILITY TO PAY ITS DEBTS

The test of insolvency is concerned with the company's ability to pay its own debts. It is not relevant that a director could borrow money on the collateral security of her or his own personal property because the definition of solvency places a restriction of the source of the money for paying the company's debts.[16] The requirement that the company pay its debts from its own resources is similar to the requirement in s 122(1) of the *Bankruptcy Act* 1966 (Cth) that the person pay his debts "from his own moneys".[17]

---

10 *Fliway Transport Pty Ltd v Soper* (1988) 7 ACLC 129.
11 *Pioneer Concrete Pty Ltd v Ellston* (1985) 10 ACLR 289 at 301.
12 *Taylor v Carroll* (1991) 9 ACLC 1592.
13 *Pioneer Concrete v Stule* (1996) 14 ACLC 534.
14 See *Re Newark Pty Ltd (in liq)* (1991) 6 ACSR 255.
15 Re *Universal Management Ltd (in liq)* (1981) NZ CLC 95-026.
16 *Geraldton Building Co Pty Ltd v Woodmore* (1992) 8 ACSR 585.
17 *See Sandell v Porter* (1966) 115 CLR 666.

The "own money" requirement was affirmed by Boon JR in *Khoury v Rosemist Holdings Pty Ltd.*[18] In that case, although the company, Rosemist, had an excess of assets over liabilities on the face of its balance sheet its director, Mr Jabbour, and his family trust had been paying the debts of Rosemist for an extended period of time. Considering a cash flow test of insolvency, Boon JR concluded that:

> Rosemist has no cash, bank accounts or assets other than a possible contingent asset in the form of a defended counter claim against Mr Khoury [the Plaintiff]. Rosemist is unable to pay its debts as they arise out of its own monies; and Mr Jabbour, his family trust and his relatives have paid Rosemist's debts for it as and when they have fallen due at least since 1 July 1998. In these circumstances, it appears to me that despite the fact that Rosemist may have an excess of assets over liabilities, it is clearly unable to pay its debts as and when they fall due. Thus, the surrounding circumstances point to Rosemist having been insolvent for a considerable period of time within the meaning of s 95A of the *Corporations Law*.

In the case of *Powell v Fryer*[19] Prior J noted that s 95A does not contain a specific reference to a requirement that the debts must be payable from the company's own money. However, his Honour looked to all of the assets available to the company to meet its debts in considering whether the company was insolvent. In doing so his Honour did not take into account the personal assets of directors of the company.

Whether or not a company is able to pay its debts is not determined solely on a balance sheet test of solvency, that is, on the basis of a surplus of assets over liabilities. Rather, the emphasis is on cash flow solvency.[20] This has allowed the Courts to distinguish between a mere temporary cash flow problem and an endemic shortfall of working capital, the latter indicating insolvency.[21] Often, for many companies, there is a coincidence of both types of insolvency. Although the cash flow test is the primary test of insolvency under s 95A, it is possible that a total preponderance of assets over liabilities might infer the solvency of a company.[22]

All cash resources available to a company, including credit resources, are to be taken into account.[23] In appropriate cases promises of financial support may also

18 Unreported, Fed Ct, Aust, Boon JR, 15 April 1999.

19 Unreported, Sup Ct, SA, Prior J, 14 April 2000.

20 See *Bank of Australasia v Hall* (1907) 4 CLR 1514; *Rees v Bank of New South Wales* (1964) 111 CLR 210; *Sandell v Porter* (1966) 115 CLR 666; *Hymix Concrete Pty Ltd v Garritty* (1977) 13 ALR 321.

21 *Hymix Concrete Pty Ltd v Garritty* (1977) 2 ACLR 559; *Re Newark Pty Ltd (in liq)* (1991) 6 ACSR 255; *Taylor v Carroll* (1991) 9 ACLC 1592.

22 *Switz Pty Ltd v Glowbind Pty Ltd* (2000) 18 ACLC 343 per Hodgson CJ.

23 See *Metropolitan Fire Services Pty Ltd v Miller* (1997) 23 ACSR 699.

be taken into account.[24] Relevant factors here will be the strength of the promise and the financial capacity of the promisor to abide by it. The cash resources available include funds that may be obtained by the sale, mortgage or pledge of assets within a short period of time.[25] Thus, unless a company is unable to raise additional cash resources from the prompt sale of readily saleable assets, a temporary lack of liquidity will not necessarily give rise to an inference of insolvency.[26] In determining credit resources one must consider the times extended to the company to pay its creditors and the times at which it will receive payments of debts owing to it.[27] In the words of Mahoney JA in *Dunn v Shapowloff*:[28]

> What will constitute ability to pay must be determined, in a realistic way, by reference to the facts of the particular case, after taking into consideration, inter alia, the company's assets and liabilities and the nature of them, and the nature and circumstances of the company's activities.

On this basis, Courts have recently been moving to consider insolvency with a sense of commercial reality.[29]

[2.2] Philosophy/rationale

The rationale for introducing a statutory definition of insolvency was to clarify the meaning of insolvency and provide guidance for directors seeking to plan the management of their company with a degree of certainty.[30] Although s 95A has been helpful in this regard, its reliance on the judicial interpretation of phrases such as "due and payable" and "ability to pay its debts" means that directors will have to keep abreast of case law on a continuing basis in order to obtain some degree of certainty. To the extent that the definition of insolvency relies on a judicial interpretation to provide practical guidelines the definition of solvency remains uncertain. Given the long history of insolvency laws and the inability to determine a specific definition of the term "insolvency", this outcome is not surprising.

24 *Dunn v Shapowloff* (1978) 3 ACLR 775.
25 See *Rees v Bank of New South Wales* (1964) 111 CLR 210.
26 *Expo International Pty Ltd (rec apptd) (in liq) v Chant* (1979) 4 ACLR 679.
27 *Heide Pty Ltd (t/as Farmhouse Smallgoods) v Lester* (1990) 9ACLC 958.
28 (1978) 3 ACLR 775.
29 *Hamilton v BHP Steel Pty Ltd* (1995) 13 ACLC 1540; *Sutherland v Sunshine Clothing (Aust) Pty Ltd* (1995) 13 ACLC 1808; *Ernwest Products Pty Ltd v Olifent* (1996) 22 ACSR 202; *Khoury v Rosemist Holdings Pty Ltd* (unreported, Fed Ct, Aust, Boon JR, 15 April 1999); *Powell v Fryer* (unreported, Sup Ct, SA, Prior J, 14 April 2000).
30 Corporate Law Reform Bill 1992 (Cth), *Draft Legislation and Explanatory Paper* (1992), para 571.

The presumption of continuing insolvency and the presumption based on the lack of adequate accounting records aim to remedy the situation where the liquidator is hindered in her or his functions by being a virtual stranger to the financial affairs of the company.[31] Directors should not be shielded from liability where they have failed to keep proper records of the company's financial affairs.

[2.3] History/former law

The statutory definition of solvency was introduced into the Law by the *Corporate Law Reform Act* 1992 (Cth). Prior to this time, there was no statutory definition of insolvency. Before the introduction of s 95A, s 589(4) specified when a company would be deemed to be unable to pay its debts. However, the Courts have long grappled with the definition of insolvency in a number of important cases considered in the context of other legal regimes.

Prior to 1982 the insolvent trading provisions looked only to the company's ability to pay the particular debt contracted in consideration of its other liabilities.

The Harmer Report dealt in detail with the need to introduce statutory presumptions of insolvency. It concluded that:

> The fact of insolvency may be proved in various ways. However a liquidator, being a stranger to the past business operations of a company, is often confronted with considerable difficulty in affirmatively establishing that a company was insolvent at a time prior to the winding up, even though there may be every indication that this was the case. In many cases the liquidator will have to cope with either inadequate or meaningless company accounting records or no accounting records at all. To meet some of these difficulties it is proposed that there should be some presumptions to assist the liquidator in certain circumstances. The Commission recommends the following presumptions:
>
> - Presumption of continuing insolvency
> - Presumption of 'balance sheet' insolvency
> - Presumption where accounting records are obscure."[32]

The Law Council of Australia and the Law Society of South Australia argued that any such presumptions would be contrary to the principle that a person is innocent until proven guilty. However, in light of the possibility for civil penalty

31 ALRC, *General Insolvency Inquiry* Report No 45, Vol 1 (1988), para 290.
32 ALRC, *General Insolvency Inquiry* Report No 45, Vol 1 (1988), para 290.

consequences of breach of the duty to prevent insolvent trading rather than criminal consequences, such arguments fail to carry significant weight.

After considering the need for a presumption of continuing insolvency, the Harmer Report recommended the introduction of statutory presumptions. Although it also recommended a presumption of "balance sheet" insolvency,[33] this recommendation was not implemented. Submissions to the ALRC indicated a number of reasons for its omission.[34] However, the notion of "balance sheet" insolvency is clearly inconsistent with the need to adopt a commercially realistic cash flow test of corporate insolvency and any presumption of this nature would conflict with the accepted approach to insolvency.

In addition, the recommendation that a presumption of insolvency exist where adequate accounting records have not been kept or produced to the liquidator was substantially altered when introduced into the Law. The Harmer Report had recommended that the inadequate accounting records presumption include a requirement as to the unlikeness of the company paying its unsecured creditors more than 50 cents in the dollar. Two members of the Commission dissented from the recommendation of the Commission on the basis that the presumption should not be contingent upon the expected dividend to unsecured creditors. This opinion was also expressed by a submission of the Victorian Bar Council which argued that the inclusion of the "expected dividend" criteria would create a number of problems.[35] This dissenting opinion was carried into the statutory presumption introduced into the Law which is not dependent on an expected dividend.

---

33 The ALRC recommended "... that there be a presumption that circumstances of insolvency exist at a particular time where it can be shown that the liabilities of the company, including its contingent and prospective liabilities, exceeded its assets at that time. The Commission further [recommended] that there be a similar presumption where current liabilities exceed current assets and there are insufficient assets reasonably capable of being realised or charged so as to enable the company to pay its current liabilities".

34 For example, The Law Council of Australia, the Law Society of South Australia, and the Victorian Bar Council suggested that many assets would not show up on a balance sheet assessment of the assets of the company, including goodwill, copyright or patents. In addition, it would be impossible to make a valuation of these intangible assets. The Law Council of Australia argued that it would be impossible to quantify contingent liabilities included within the company's liabilities.

35 ALRC, *General Insolvency Inquiry* Report No 45, Vol 1 (1988), para 290. The Council criticised the requirement that the company be unlikely to pay its unsecured creditors more than 50 cents in the dollar, and suggested that such a requirement could raise several problems:

- Whose opinion as to the likely total dividend would be relevant and at what time was the opinion to be formed?
- The statement of affairs is often wide of the mark in its estimate of the total dividend and the manner of realisation of the assets and the length and difficulty of the liquidation may significantly affect the amount of the total dividend.

The Council also objected in principle to the notion that, where admittedly no records or only inadequate records have been produced, the burden of proof might be different in the case of an estimated final dividend of 49 cents from the burden where the estimated dividend is 51 cents in the dollar.

[2.4] Notable cases

[2.4.1] *SWITZ PTY LTD V GLOWBIND PTY LTD*

Switz Pty Ltd v Glowbind Pty Ltd[36] considered s 95A of the *Corporations Law*.

In this case the Court considered both the "cash flow" and "balance sheet" approaches to insolvency and the extent to which a temporary lack of liquidity will prove determinative. Switz had served a statutory demand on Glowbind requiring Glowbind to pay $1.3m in debts within 21 days. Glowbind did not comply with the statutory demand and Switz applied for the immediate winding-up of Glowbind. Glowbind resisted this winding-up application on the basis that it was solvent.

Glowbind submitted that it had a current surplus of assets over liabilities and that its cash flow crisis could be averted by the sale of some of its assets or by external loans. The main asset which Glowbind submitted it could sell within a relatively short period of time to raise funds was a property on which a number of home units had been constructed and in respect of which many contracts had already been exchanged with purchasers. Glowbind submitted that, although the cash flow test was promulgated by s 95A, a temporary lack of liquidity should not be determinative in assessing insolvency. However, Switz submitted that s 95A does require a cash flow rather than balance sheet test of insolvency. Switz submitted that Glowbind had a number of debts which were due and owing and which had been outstanding for some time, although demand for payment had not been made until the statutory demand. Switz further submitted that the home units construction property was not a readily realisable asset as it would take between three months and one year to realise the property and that this did not represent a "temporary" lack of liquidity.

The Court agreed with Switz and ordered the winding-up of Glowbind. The court held that a number of debts had been due and owing for some time and there were no assets of Glowbind which could be readily realised to satisfy the debts. These factors suggested that, under the cash flow test of insolvency, there was more than a temporary lack of liquidity on the part of Glowbind.

Although endorsing the cash flow test of insolvency, the Court also held that, in certain circumstances, a total preponderance of assets over liabilities may infer that a company is insolvent.

Whilst this case is useful in its consideration of the various tests of insolvency, it does give rise to the question of how long a period may be required to establish a "temporary" lack of liquidity. There do not seem to be any clear guidelines as to the meaning of "temporary" and so this length of time will largely be determined on the facts and circumstances of each case.

---

36 (2000) 18 ACLC 343; Sup Ct, NSW, 27 March 2000 per Hodgson J.

[2.4.2] *KHOURY V ROSEMIST HOLDINGS PTY LTD*

Khoury v Rosemist Holdings Pty Ltd[37] considered s 95A of the *Corporations Law*.

In this case the Court supported a cash flow test of insolvency based on a commercially realistic assessment of the entirety of the financial resources available to a company. Boon JR specifically considered the ability of the company to pay its debts out of its own money, assets and resources as an indicator of its solvency or insolvency. The mere fact that the company's balance sheet depicted an excess of assets over liabilities was not determinative. As the debts of the company had been paid by the director of the company, his family trust and his relatives, rather than out of the company's assets, the company was found to be insolvent. Clearly a company can be insolvent for the purposes of s 95A of the Law despite having an excess of assets over liabilities on its balance sheet. This makes it essential for directors to have an ongoing knowledge of the full state of the company's financial affairs rather than merely reviewing its balance sheets on a periodic basis.

[2.4.3] *STARGARD SECURITY SYSTEMS PTY LTD V GOLDIE*

Stargard Security Systems Pty Ltd v Goldie[38] considered s 95A of the *Corporations Law*.

The case arose in relation to an application for summary judgment in relation to the insolvent trading provisions.

In considering the meaning of the definition in s 95A, Master Bredmeyer referred to cases decided under the *Bankruptcy Act* and other predecessor provisions.[39] His Honour looked at the definition of insolvency from a commercially realistic cash flow perspective and held that:

> In assessing solvency or insolvency, it is relevant to look not only at the company's likely income, but also at the company's likely debts.[40]

Within the ambit of "likely income", Master Bredmeyer considered the expectation of the defendant director that the company's cash flow would increase significantly, based on expected cash flow projections resulting from increased sales that were formulated for the purposes of general business plans. Such future contingencies were considered relevant to the solvency of the company based on a cash flow perspective of solvency and insolvency.

---

37 Unreported Fed Ct, Aust, 15 April 1999 per Boon J.

38 (1994) 13 ACSR 805.Sup Ct, WA, 1 July 1994 per Master Bredmeyer.

39 See *Bank of Australasia v Hall* (1907) 4 CLR 1514; *Rees v Bank of New South Wales* (1964) 111 CLR 210; *Sandell v Porter* (1966) 115 CLR 666; *Heide v Lester* (1990) 3 ACSR 159; *Dunn v Shapowloff* (1978) ACLC 40-451.

40 (1994) 13 ACSR 805 at 814.

[2.4.4] *METROPOLITAN FIRE SYSTEMS PTY LTD V MILLER*

Metropolitan Fire Systems Pty Ltd v Miller[41] considered s 95A of the *Corporations Law*.[42]

Einfeld J held that in determining insolvency it is necessary to take into account all of the resources of the company, including its credit resources. Considering insolvency from a cash flow perspective, Einfeld J decided that relevant factors include time extended to the company to pay its creditors and the time it will receive payment of its debts.

[2.4.5] *ASC V FOREM – FREEWAY ENTERPRISES PTY LIMITED*

ASC v Forem[43] considered s 588E of the *Corporations Law*.

In this case the Court considered the insolvency trading provisions and used the presumption of insolvency based on accounting records to establish that the company was insolvent at the time it incurred the relevant debts. The company was in the business of assembling and retailing computers and had the practice of obtaining 50 per cent of the invoice value from the customer up-front.

The company's financial records did not have a general ledger showing the balance of assets and liabilities, not did it have a record of money paid to the company or payments made by it. There was no less formal method of record keeping either. There were cheque butts issued by the company but these did not record the payee or what the payment was made for. There was not even a record of the money received from the company's customers or a list of outstanding obligations to customers. It appeared that the company did not even bank money received from customers into its bank account but rather disbursed such funds immediately to the benefit of suppliers or employees. It was important to determine the company's liability to any particular customer. The Court held that the company was insolvent at the time it incurred the debts using the presumption in s 588E(4). The director was disqualified for 12 years and was penalised $200,000.

[2.5] Interesting quotes

[2.5.1] WIDE RANGE OF FACTORS TO BE CONSIDERED IN ASSESSING SOLVENCY

A number of cases considering insolvency have affirmed that insolvency in Australia is to be determined by a cash flow test rather than a simple test of

41 Fed Ct, Aust, 22 May 1997 per Einfeld J.
42 (1997) 23 ACSR 699.
43 (1999) 17 ACLC 511; Fed Ct, Aust, 4 March 1999 per Madgwick J.

balance sheet insolvency. The recent cases of *Powell v Fryer* and *Khoury v Rosemist Holdings Pty Ltd* have already been discussed above.

In *Rees v Bank of New South Wales*,[44] Barwick CJ highlighted that when determining the solvency of a company a wide range of factors must be taken into account including the nature of the business and all available cash and credit resources:

> It is quite true that a trader, to remain solvent, does not need to have ready cash by him to cover his commitments as they fall due for payment, and that in determining whether he can pay his debts as they become due regard must be had to his realisable assets. The extent to which their existence will prevent a conclusion of insolvency will depend on a number of surrounding circumstances, one of which must be the nature of the assets and in the case of a trader, the nature of his business.[45]

This perspective received further judicial support in *Sandell v Porter*:[46]

> Insolvency is expressed ... as an inability to pay debts as they fall due out of the debtor's own money. But the debtor's own moneys are not limited to his cash resources immediately available. They extend to moneys which he can procure by realisation by sale or by mortgage or pledge of his assets within a relatively short time – relative to the nature and amount of the debts and to the circumstances, including the nature of the business of the debtor. The conclusion of insolvency ought to be clear from a consideration of the debtor's financial position in its entirety and generally speaking ought not to be drawn simply from evidence of a temporary lack of liquidity. It is the debtor's inability, utilising such cash resources as he has, or can command through the use of his assets, to meet his debts as they fall due which indicates insolvency.[47]

The case of *Dunn v Shapowloff*[48] also reaffirmed this cash flow test of insolvency:

> What will constitute ability to pay must be determined in a realistic way by reference to the facts of the particular case and after taking into consideration ... the company's assets and liabilities and the nature of them, and the nature and circumstances of the company's activities ... The cash expected to be available at the particular time will be relevant but not necessarily determinative. It will, for example, be relevant to consider whether the company could be expected to pay

44 (1964) 111 CLR 210.
45 (1964) 111 CLR 210 at 218.
46 (1966) 115 CLR 666.
47 (1966) 115 CLR 666 at 670.
48 (1978) 3 ACLR 775.

> the debt by borrowing; whether, if it must realise assets to obtain the money to pay the debt it can be expected to do this by the relevant time and at what price; and whether what it will have to do in paying and being able to pay the debt will involve the company or its officers in voidable transactions, improper preferences, or breach of obligations under the general law or relevant legislation. It would, I think, be proper, in a particular case, for account to be taken appropriately of a promise, legally binding or otherwise, to provide money or financial assistance, by loan, subscription for share capital, or by the provision of a guarantee.

Support for this proposition was also provided by the case of *Heide v Lester*:[49]

> In determining whether the company would be able to pay the debt as and when it became due all the cash resources to the company, including credit resources, are to be looked at in determining those credit resources there are to be taken into account the times extended to the company to pay its creditors, on the one hand, and the times within which it will receive payment of debts owing to it on the other hand.[50]

[2.6] Checklists

Due to the nature of insolvency as a cash flow test indicated by an endemic shortfall of working capital, rather than a temporary lack of liquidity, it may often be difficult for directors to recognise the insolvency of their company. However, there are some early warning signs directors should always be aware of in order to recognise the possibility of corporate insolvency. These can also be used by insolvency practitioners in assessing the state of solvency of the relevant company at the time the relevant debt was incurred for the purposes of bringing an action under the insolvent trading provisions.

[2.6.1] GENERAL SIGNS OF INSOLVENCY

There are a number of factors which may be indicators of insolvency:[51]

- lack of, or poorly organised, internal accounting methods and plans;
- lack of budgets or budget forecasts;
- sustained loss-making activity ;
- poor cash flow;
- financial records which are either incomplete or poorly organised and maintained;

49 (1990) 3 ACSR 159.
50 (1990) 3 ACSR 159 at 165.
51 See N Coburn, *Insolvent Trading: A Practical Guide* (John Libbey & Co, Sydney, 1998), pp 141-143.

- increasing levels of debt;
- consistent delay in payments to creditors;
- unpaid liabilities such as PAYE deductions, superannuation and other tax payments;
- increasing involvement of financiers in company management;
- lack of sustainable profit from key business area;
- over-reliance on future projected income;
- need to refinance or restructure debt;
- substantial investment in uneconomic commitments;
- reliance on future projected income or over reliance on one project to solve all financial problems;
- losses from major long-term contracts;
- management focus on a limited number of projects;
- main supplier ceases to supply, or general sustained shortage of supplies;
- loss of a primary market or licence.
- maturation of fixed-term borrowings without prospect of repayment;
- loss of employees, sustained industrial problems, lack of cohesion amongst Board members;
- lack of corporate plan and vision for company.

[2.6.2] A DIRECTOR'S CHECKLIST TO AVOID INSOLVENCY

Directors and others involved in the management of the company can take a number of steps to minimise the risk of their company becoming insolvent:[52]

- Ensure that adequate systems of financial monitoring are set up within the company.
- Ensure periodic valuations of the company's assets and liabilities are made and that valuations are accurate and conducted by a suitably qualified professional.
- Ensure that those responsible for the financial oversight of the company are appropriately qualified and possess the necessary expertise.
- Meet regularly with relevant professionals, such as accountants and lawyers, to assess the financial position of the company.
- Set and adhere to corporate budgets.
- Set and adhere to an overall long-term corporate plan.
- Question any continuing loss-making activity with a view to rectifying the situation through ending the project or reassessing its funding.
- Immediately investigate any complaints made from suppliers or creditors.
- Ensure risk is diversified to an appropriate extent and avoid a concentrated investment in a limited number of high-risk projects.

52 See N Coburn, *Insolvent Trading: A Practical Guide* (John Libbey & Co, Sydney, 1998), pp 141-143.

- Ensure adequate management and information systems are established within the company.
- Ensure clear communication and cohesion between Board members and others involved in the management of the company.
- Discourage loans to directors if they involve and unacceptable credit risk and if loans are taken insist on repayment within reasonable time.
- Ensure assets are valued at a realistic level by competent and professional valuers.

To Whom Do the Duties Apply?

3

"... *a corporation is an abstraction. It has not a mind of its own any more than it has a body of its own; its active and directing will must consequently be sought in the person of somebody who for some purposes may be called an agent, but who really is the directing mind and will of the corporation, the very ego and centre of the personality of the corporation.*"[1]

1 *Lennard's Carrying Co Ltd v Asiatic Petroleum Co Ltd* [1915] AC 705 at 713 per Viscount Haldane LC.

OBJECTIVES

This Chapter will:

- introduce the statutory definitions of "director" and "officer" in order to determine the scope of persons bound by duties to a company in or nearing insolvency;
- thoroughly analyse the nature of "de facto" and "shadow" directors and the extent to which banks, insolvency practitioners and others may be caught by the duties;
- discuss the exemption for professional advisers and the way in which this will provide a safe harbour for those persons who might otherwise be caught by the duties;
- discuss the concept of a holding company operating as a "shadow" director of its subsidiaries.

[3.1] General overview

[3.1.1] ELEMENTS OF LIABILITY

The Law imposes a wide range of duties and responsibilities on directors and other officers. However, the law on who can be considered a director or officer is far from settled.

The definition of"director" within the law has a wide ambit. Included within the definition are people:

- who act in the position of a director, by whatever name called and whether or not validly appointed ("de facto director"); and
- whose instructions or wishes the directors of the corporation are accustomed to act in accordance with ("shadow director").

Persons acting in a professional capacity or business relationship are exempted from the operation of these provisions provided they are merely giving advice to the directors.

Whilst both directors and officers are subject to most of the duties within the Law (including the duty of care and diligence, proper use of position and information, and the duty of good faith) only directors are subject to the duty to prevent insolvent trading.

It is important for officers of companies to be aware of obligations imposed on them. A definition of "officer" was introduced into the Law in 2000. An officer is defined as:

(a) a director or secretary of the corporation; or
(b) a person:
  (i) who makes, or participates in making, decisions that affect the whole, or a substantial part, of the business of the corporation; or
  (ii) who has the capacity to affect significantly the corporation's financial standing; or
  (iii) in accordance with whose instructions or wishes the directors or the corporation are accustomed to act (excluding advice given by the person in the proper performance of functions attaching to the person's professional capacity or their business relationship with the directors or the corporation); or
(c) a receiver, or receiver and manager, of the property of the corporation; or
(d) an administrator of the corporation; or
(e) an administrator of a deed of company arrangement executed by the corporation; or
(f) a liquidator of the corporation; or
(g) a trustee or other person administering a compromise or arrangement made between the corporation and someone else.

This definition of "officer" applies to the statutory duties imposed on directors and officers under Ch 2D of the Law.

Importantly receivers, liquidators and administrators are subject to these statutory duties. This is consistent with the rationale behind the provisions to ensure that those with effective control of a company should act in its best interests.

Interestingly, the s 9 definition of "officer" creates the concept of a "shadow officer". The concept of a "shadow director" is outlined below. However, it is not clear what is intended by this definition of a "shadow officer", especially as no mention was made to it in the *Explanatory Memorandum to the Corporate Law Economic Reform Program Act* 1999. The concept of a "shadow officer" seems to substantially overlap with a "shadow director" with mirror provisions regarding instructions or wishes the directors of the company are accustomed to act in accordance with. The usefulness of the inclusion of a "shadow officer" is also placed in doubt when one considers that it is only shadow directors whom are subject to the duty to prevent insolvent trading and all those persons who fall within the definition of a "shadow officer" also fall within the definition of a "shadow director". Bearing this in mind, it is important to mark the boundaries of whom is a director.

[3.1.2] ALTERNATE DIRECTORS

An alternate, or substitute, director may be appointed to a Board to act in the place of an alternate director. They have the same authority as the director for whom they are acting. An alternate director is subject to the same legal duties and liabilities as other directors.[2] Alternate directors have no legal status when they are not acting in their capacity as an alternate director.

[3.1.3] DE FACTO DIRECTORS

Section 9 includes within the definition of a "director" a person appointed to the position of a director regardless of the name that has been given to their position ("de facto director"). A person may be a de facto director even if they are generally engaged in the affairs of the company, rather than performing specific functions.[3] De facto directors are subject to the same duties and liabilities as directors properly appointed, including the duty of care and diligence and the duty to prevent insolvent trading.[4]

---

2 *Markwell Bros Pty Ltd v CPN Diesels (QLD) Pty Ltd* (1982) 7 ACLR 425; *Strathmore Group Ltd v Fraser* (1991) 9 ACLC 3140; *Androvin v Figliomeni* (1996) 14 ACLC 1461.

3 *Mistmorn Pty Ltd (in liq) v Yasseen* (1996) 14 ACLC 1387 per Davies J at 1395.

4 See *Corporate Affairs Commission v Drysdale* (1978) 141 CLR 236 at 242-243 per Mason J.

[3.1.4] SHADOW DIRECTORS

Section 9 includes within the definition of "director" a person who is not validly appointed to the position of director but whose instructions or wishes the directors of the company are accustomed to act in accordance with ("shadow directors"). This is intended to situate the true source of decision-making within the company and to hold such people responsible for the consequences of their decisions.[5] Shadow directors are also subject to the same duties and liabilities as directors properly appointed, including the duty of care and diligence and the duty to prevent insolvent trading.

Each element of the definition of a "shadow director" must be examined in order to determine the extent of those included within the definition.

Most of the leading cases on shadow directors do not involve a consideration of the current legislative provisions but were decided under the common law. Whilst the results are largely the same whether decided under the s 9 definition or the current law, there are some differences.

(a) "Person"

The definition of "person" within the Law includes a "body politic or corporate" as well as an individual.[6] Only an individual can be a validly appointed as a director.[7] However, the extended definition of "director" in s 9 means that a corporation can be a "director" even though it cannot be "appointed" as such. At common law in a number of cases liability has been imposed on a holding company for effectively being a director of its subsidiary.[8]

(b) Instructions or wishes

"Instructions and wishes" can be distinguished from "advice". Whereas a person is required or compelled to follow "instructions", "advice" is merely an opinion and is merely suggested, but not ordered, as a course of action.

In this sense, "instructions" involve no element of choice on the part of those being instructed and suggests the absence of available alternatives. Most of the cases decided under the common law have considered whether or not the shadow director proffered "instructions or directions" and, for this reason, have focused on whether or not a person was compelled to follow a particular course of action. The inclusion of the term "wishes" within the statutory definition indicates a legislative attempt to overcome this. Although "wishes" and "advice" may often be difficult to distinguish in practice, it is arguable that the inclusion of the term "wishes" is intended to catch those who may not issue identifiable

5 See *Australian Securities Commission v AS Nominees Ltd* (1995) 13 ACLC 1822 at 1838.
6 *Corporations Law*, ss 9 and 85.
7 *Corporations Law*, s 221(3).
8 See *Standard Chartered Bank of Australia v Antico* (1995) 131 ALR 1; and *Kuwait Asia Bank EC v National Mutual Life Nominees Ltd* [1991] 1 AC 187.

instructions or directions but who generally make their desires, intentions and wishes known.

A single instruction or wish is unlikely to satisfy s 9 as the plural "directions or wishes" suggests a number of acts. In addition, a single act is unlikely to result in the directors becoming "accustomed to act" upon it. However, it may be possible that a single instruction or wish of fundamental importance which results in an action repeatedly being taken by the company will fulfill this requirement.[9] In the absence of case law on the point it is unclear whether the instructions or wishes must be given to the Board as a whole or merely to a particular director. This may be a crucial issue in determining whether the directors are accustomed to act in accordance with the directions or wishes. Arguably, s 9 implicitly requires the instructions or wishes to be given to the Board as a whole. However, it is also arguable that if a person gives instructions or wishes to a dominant managing director or nominee director, and the Board is accustomed to act in accordance with their instructions, then from a policy perspective the person is effectively contributing a vital element of decision-making in the company's affairs.

(c) "Directors of the body"

It is not settled whether or not all of the Board members, or merely a majority of Board members, must be accustomed to act in accordance with a person's instructions or wishes. There has been some support for the argument that all directors must be accustomed to act in accordance with the instructions or wishes.[10]

The decision in *Kuwait Asia Bank EC v National Mutual Life Nominees Ltd*[11] indicates that a minority of directors accustomed to act in accordance with a person's instructions or wishes will be insufficient to form a shadow directorship at common law.

Since decisions made by the Board are often made by a simple majority of directors, requiring a simple majority of directors to be accustomed to act in accordance with the person's instructions or wishes would be a preferable position. The position may be somewhat different if decisions are made by a different majority of the Board. To require *all* Board members to be so accustomed would be an unnecessary restriction on the scope of the section.

(d) "Accustomed to act"

This element is intended to cover those persons with effective control of a company, making decisions that the directors of the company simply follow without

9 See M Markovic, "The Law of Shadow Directorship" (1996) 6 AJCL 323.
10 *Re Lo-Line Electric Motors Ltd* (1988) 4 BCR 415.
11 *Kuwait Asia Bank EC v National Mutual Life Nominees Ltd* [1991] 1 AC 187.

independent thought, analysis or discretion. It suggests some sort of ongoing control or interference in internal affairs. As stated by Millet J in *Re Hydrodam (Corby) Ltd*:[12]

> What is needed is ... a pattern of behaviour in which the board did not exercise any discretion or judgment of its own, but acted in accordance with the direction of others ...

The phrase "accustomed to act" implies that a single instruction or wish will be insufficient to produce an ongoing relationship of control by a third party. Unless the particular instruction or wish is of fundamental importance and results in repeated action being taken, a large degree of interference resulting from continual directions and instructions will be required to satisfy the requirements of the section. As stated in *Dairy Containers Ltd v NZI Bank Ltd*:

> After all, by definition, the company's affairs are being effectively run by that person.[13]

Hodgson J reiterated this notion of continual control and interference with little or no independent discretion by the company's directors in *Standard Chartered Bank v Antico*:

> In my view, the conditions imposed following the decision to fund Giant [the subsidiary] in March 1989 [by the holding company Pioneer] show *a willingness and ability to exercise control, and an actuality of control*, over the management and financial affairs of Giant. In my view also, the decision as to how Giant was to be funded by Pioneer, and as to the taking of security, was *never the subject of careful consideration by the Giant board*, but was accepted by the Giant board as something necessary or as a fait accompli.[14]

For directors to be "accustomed" to act in accordance with another's instructions or wishes, it is not necessary for the director to follow *every* instruction received. The term "accustomed" suggests that the director must generally accept the instructions of the person. In others words, the director must customarily accept and act upon the person's instructions or wishes.

It is worth noting the position of the appointors of nominee directors in this regard. In *Kuwait Asia Bank EC v National Mutual Life Nominees Ltd*[15] the Privy Council held that a majority shareholder which appointed two of the five

12 [1994] 2 BCLC 180.
13 (1995) 7 NZ CLC 96-669.
14 131 ALR 1 at 70 (emphasis added).
15 *Kuwait Asia Bank EC v National Mutual Life Nominees Ltd* [1991] 1 AC 187.

directors of a company was not a shadow director as it was unlikely that the nominee directors were "accustomed to act" in accordance with its instructions or wishes. This suggests that the extent to which nominee directors take third party interests into account will be an important determinant in deciding whether or not that third party is in fact a shadow director. Appointors of nominee directors, or other third parties the nominee director receives instructions from, must keep this provision firmly in mind.

[3.1.5] PROFESSIONAL CAPACITY OR BUSINESS RELATIONSHIP EXEMPTION

Section 9 is designed to encompass all those who have a decision-making role within the company. It is not intended to cover those who merely offer advice or suggestions on particular issues. For this reason, s 9 provides that a person will not fall within the definition of "director" merely because the directors or members of the board are accustomed to act on *advice* given by that person in their professional capacity or as a result of a business relationship with the directors, members of the Board, or the company as a whole. Accordingly, an exemption is provided to *advisers*.

It is conceivable that advice given in a professional capacity or business relationship may in fact lead to instructions or wishes. The danger in this possible overlap between professional or business advice on the one hand and instructions and wishes on the other is of particular relevance to financial institutions with insolvent corporate clients, holding companies with insolvent subsidiaries, and "company doctors" or accountants or lawyers with insolvency expertise.

[3.1.6] RISKS FOR COMPANY DOCTORS, BANKS AND OTHER FINANCIAL INSTITUTIONS PARTICIPATING IN INFORMAL WORK-OUTS

There have been no cases to date where a financial institution has been held to be a shadow director. However, in times of economic difficulty, financial institutions will be keen to become actively involved in the internal affairs of their corporate clients facing insolvency. If the degree of this involvement is to the extent that the financial institution is making decisions for the corporate client, the risk is that the financial institution will be considered a shadow director.[16] In such cases banks and other financial institutions exercising management discretion in important strategic issues may be caught by the definition of "director".

"Company doctors" or accountants or lawyers with insolvency expertise often undertake a review of a company's financial affairs and operations to aid the recovery of failing businesses. Major creditors of the company often appoint

16 For an excellent discussion of the risk for banks and other financial institutions see M Markovic, "Banks and Shadow Directorships: Not an 'Almost Entirely Imaginary' Risk on Australia" (1998) 9(4) JBFLP 284.

them. Company doctors also run the risk of becoming shadow directors if they assume effective decision-making power and control of the company's affairs when assisting the financial recovery. An example of this overlap between advice on the one hand and directions and instructions on the other was provided by *Re Tasbian (No 3)*.[17] This will be analysed in more detail below. Briefly, in this case a chartered accountant named Nixon was appointed to an ailing retail business (Tasbian) by a finance company (Castle). As Tasbian had never traded at a profit, Nixon was appointed to get the company "on track" and producing a profit, which he was ultimately unable to achieve. However, during his appointment, Nixon had taken over effective control of Tasbian as he had required all Tasbian cheques to be countersigned by himself, had bargained with external entities on Tasbian's behalf, negotiated an informal moratorium with Tasbian's trade creditors and so on. In this way, he was not merely providing advice but was exercising decision-making powers and control on behalf of Tasbian and was thus found to be a de facto director of Tasbian. In addition, Nixon had acted beyond his professional expertise by engaging in a tax avoidance scheme designed for Tasbian. This unprofessional conduct indicated that he was not covered by the "professional" advice exemption. As a result, Nixon was held to be a "director" of Tasbian and was subjected to disqualification and other sanctions.

Clearly, the distinction between advice on the one hand and instructions and wishes on the other is important to maintain to receive protection under s 9. The wide definition of "director" will threaten those involved in "work-outs" or other forms of financial management.

[3.1.7] HOLDING COMPANIES AS SHADOW DIRECTORS

In addition to the insolvent trading provisions which impose liability on holding companies for the debts of their insolvent subsidiaries,[18] holding companies with subsidiaries face the possibility of being shadow directors. This possibility will be of particular concern to holding companies with subsidiaries in financial difficulty. Again, in times of economic difficulty a holding company is likely to exercise management discretion and general decision-making powers in relation to the affairs of its subsidiary. If the Board of the subsidiary simply accepts these decisions without independent analysis, the holding company may possibly be acting as a shadow director.

Particularly relevant in this regard is the decision in *Standard Chartered Bank v Antico*,[19] which will be analysed in detail below. Although the facts of the case are quite complex, it is sufficient to note that the holding company (Pioneer) owned 42 per cent of its subsidiary (Giant) and had three nominee directors appointed to its Board. Giant had entered into a number of financial agreements

17 [1992] BCC 358.
18 See Ch 7.
19 (1995) 131 ALR 1.

with Standard Chartered, particularly the provision of a discount and bill acceptance facility of A$30m, the payment of which was extended on a number of occasions. When Giant was wound up, Standard Chartered commenced proceedings against Pioneer under the insolvent trading provisions, claiming that Pioneer was a director of Giant and was liable for its insolvent trading. After reviewing numerous circumstances such as the financial reporting requirement imposed on Giant by Pioneer, the making of strategic decisions by Pioneer, and other financial and management control issues, Hodgson J concluded that Pioneer was a shadow director of Giant and was liable for the debts of Giant under the insolvent trading provisions. In the words of Hodgson J, these circumstances showed a "... willingness and ability [of Pioneer] to exercise control, and an actuality of control, over the management and financial affairs of Giant".[20]

Clearly, these circumstances indicated that Pioneer was not merely providing advice, but was giving instructions to Giant that were being implemented by Giant without any independent consideration. The effective source of decision-making within Giant was found in Pioneer. Whilst it is possible for a holding company to be a shadow director of its subsidiary, the way in which advice is communicated to the subsidiary will be determinative in deciding whether or not it amounts to instructions.

[3.2] Philosophy/rationale

Duties and liabilities are imposed on directors and officers as a consequence of the organic view of corporate personality. Under this perspective of what constitutes a company, a company is regarded as a natural entity constituted of natural persons rather than an artificial construct. Organic theory perceives companies in an anthropomorphic way, likening a corporation to a human body. This personification views directors and officers as the "mind and will" of the corporation.

The first reference to this "directing mind and will" concept was in 1915 by Viscount Haldane LC in *Lennard's Carrying Co Ltd v Asiatic Petroleum Co Ltd*:

> ... a corporation is an abstraction. It has not a mind of its own any more than it has a body of its own; its active and directing will must consequently be sought in the person of somebody who for some purposes may be called an agent, but who really is the *directing mind and will* of the corporation, the very ego and centre of the personality of the corporation.[21]

20 (1995) 131 ALR 1 at 70.
21 [1915] AC 705 at 713 (emphasis added).

The most resonant statement of organic theory can be found in Lord Denning's judgment in *Bolton (Engineering) v Graham & Sons*:

> A company may in many ways be likened to a human body. It has a brain and nerve centre which controls what it does. It also has hands which hold the tools and act in accordance with directions from the centre. Some of the people in the company are mere servants and agents who are nothing more than hands to do the work and cannot be said to represent the mind or will. *Others are directors … who represent the directing mind and will of the company, and control what it does.*[22]

The notion of directors and officers as the "directing mind and will" of a corporation was firmly implanted into law with the landmark case of *Tesco Supermarkets v Nattrass*:

> A living person has a mind which can have knowledge or intention or be negligent and he has hands to carry out his intentions. A corporation has none of these: it must act through living persons … then the person who acts is not speaking or acting for the company. He is acting as the company and his mind which directs his acts is the mind of the company. There is no question of the company being vicariously liable. He is not acting as a servant, representative, agent or delegate. He is an embodiment of the company … his mind is the mind of the company.[23]

In this sense, the definition of "director" and "officer" must extend to all those who constitute the "directing mind and will" of a company. The justification of the extension of the definition of "director" to include de facto and shadow directors is that these persons constitute a significant point of decision-making and control within the company, and are thus part of its "directing mind and will".

The formalisation of the position of de facto and shadow directors is commensurate with the increased social expectations of directors. After the Australian corporate collapses of the 1980s, social concern over the roles and power of directors significantly increased. In the words of Rogers J in *AWA Ltd v Daniels*:

> One of the most striking features of the law concerning directors' duties is the insistence that directors accept more and more responsibility for oversight of a company's affairs at the same time as the affairs of companies become more and more complex and diverse.[24]

22 [1957] 1 QB 159 (emphasis added).
23 [1972] AC 513 at 570.
24 *AWA Ltd v Daniels* (1992) 10 ACLC 933 at 1013.

The recognition of this complexity and diversity suggests that the ambit of those involved in the corporate decision-making process may be more diverse than traditionally thought, thus legitimising the extension of the definition of "director" to include de facto and shadow directors.

In 1989 the Cooney Committee stated the acceptance of the extensive power of directors to control the decision-making process:

> Directors are the mind and soul of the corporate sector. They are crucial to how it operates and to how its great power is exercised. They determine the character of corporate culture. Their actions can have a profound effect on the lives of a great number of people, be they shareholders, employees, creditors, or the public generally. They can weaken and even suppress market forces. They can disturb and destroy the environment.[25]

In this sense, given the pervasive extent of corporate decision-making power and the diffuse location of this power, the definition of "director" is extended to include all those involved in the decision-making process. Accordingly it encompasses all those who can truly be termed the "directing mind and will" of the corporation.

[3.3] History/former law

Aickin J in *Corporate Affairs Commission v Drysdale* discussed the history of the definition of the term "director". His Honour said:

> The history of the definition is somewhat curious and perhaps worth noting. Its origin appears to be in the *Companies Clauses Consolidation Act* 1845 (Imp) s 3 of which contains the following provision:
>
> > '"Directors", – the expression "the directors" shall mean the directors of the company, and shall include all persons having the direction of the undertaking whether under the name of directors, managers, committee of management, or under any other name.'

In the *Joint Stock Companies Act* 1856 and 1857 (Imp) and in the *Companies Act* 1862 (Imp) there was no definition of the word "director" but, by the *Companies Act* 1900 (Imp) s 30, a definition was introduced which has survived in subsequent consolidations without change. It was as follows: "The expression

25 Senate Standing Committee on Legal and Constitutional Affairs, *Company Directors' Duties* (1989), para. 2.3.

'director' includes any person occupying the position of director by whatever name called."[26]

It was clearly intended to encompass all those who exercised true decision-making power within the company.

With the instigation of each State's *Companies Act*, the definition of "director" stated:

> 'Director' includes any person occupying the position of director of a corporation by whatever name called and includes a person in accordance with whose directions or instructions the directors of a corporations are accustomed to act." This extended the ambit of the definition to include shadow directors as well as de facto directors. These two concepts were divided into para (a) and (b) for conceptual clarity with the introduction of the *Companies Code* in 1982. This Code also extended the definition to include persons "acting in the position of director ... whether or not validly appointed to occupy or, duly authorised to act in, the position.

Prior to the introduction of the *Corporate Law Economic Reform Program Act* 1999 (Cth), the definition of "officer" contained the problematic terms "executive officer" and "employee". The meaning given to "executive officer" generally included those who took part in the management of the company at a senior level. However, the meaning of "management" was equally unclear. In *Commissioner for Corporate Affairs v Bracht*, Ormiston J stated:

> It may be difficult to draw the line in particular cases, but in my opinion the concept of 'management' for present purposes comprehends activities which involve policy and decision making, related to the business affairs of a corporation, affecting the corporation as a whole or a substantial part of that corporation to the extent that the consequences of the formation of those policies or the making of those decisions may have some significant bearing on the financial standing of the corporation of the conduct of its affairs.[27]

Similarly, the meaning of "employee" was problematic. It was held that in order to be considered an "officer", employees of a company must exercise substantial responsibilities.

In order to overcome these deficiencies in definitional certainty, the definition of "officer" in s 9 was amended by the *Corporate Law Economic Reform Program Act* 1999 (Cth).

---

26 (1978) 142 CLR 236 at 248.
27 (1989) 7 ACLC 40 at 48.

[3.4] Notable cases

[3.4.1] *SECRETARY OF STATE FOR TRADE & INDUSTRY V DEVERELL*

Secretary of State for Trade & Industry v Deverell[28] considered the *Company Directors' Disqualification Act* 1986 (UK). This case[29] was decided by the Court of Appeal of England and Wales and indicates factors which Australian Courts are likely to consider when claims of a shadow directorship are pleaded.

EuroExpress was a tour operator which was eventually placed into voluntary liquidation with debts of £4.46m. The relevant persons against whom a shadow directorship was claimed, Mr Deverell and Mr Hopkins, were not an appointed director of EuroExpress but were generally involved in the affairs of EuroExpress. The UK Secretary of State of Trade & Industry sought disqualification orders against Mr Deverell and Mr Hopkins.

The Court of Appeal considered that there are three main considerations to which regard should be made when deciding whether or not a person is a shadow director. These are:

- The purpose of the shadow directorship provisions is to identify those persons who are not professional advisers but who have a real influence over the affairs of the company.
- It is not necessary that the relevant person have an influence over the conduct of all of the affairs of the company.
- The directors need not be entirely subservient or surrender their independent judgment completely, but rather it must be shown that the relevant person had a material influence over the conduct of the company's affairs.

Applying this test, the Court of Appeal held that both Mr Deverell and Mr Hopkins were shadow directors of EuroExress.

[3.4.2] *DEPUTY COMMISSIONER OF TAXATION V AUSTIN*

Deputy Commissioner of Taxation v Austin[30] considered s 60 of the *Corporations Law*. It involved a cross claim by the Deputy Commissioner of Taxation (DCT) against Mr Austin, an alleged de facto director of Talljade Pty Ltd (Talljade). The liquidator of the company had previously brought a successful action under the unfair preference provisions against the DCT for the recovery of the group tax and penalties Talljade had paid to the DCT.

Mr Austin and his wife had been friends with another couple. The two wives operated a restaurant business together. Talljade was a $2 company incorporated

28 CA, England and Wales, 21 December 1999 per Morritt and Potter LJJ and Morison J.
29 [2000] 2 WLR 907.
30 Fed Ct, Aust, 27 August 1998 per Madgwick J.

to incur debts for the supply of goods and services for the restaurant and for the payment of wages for the employees.

Mr Austin was appointed a director of Talljade for three months to assist during a period when both families were experiencing personal difficulties. After this time Mr Austin sought to resign his directorship and asked his accountant to prepare documents to this effect. Despite the documents having been prepared, they were never lodged with ASIC.

Following his purported resignation, Mr Austin undertook numerous negotiations with the DCT for the payment of outstanding group tax and penalties, countersigned Talljade company cheques in favour of the DCT, issued stop notices to Talljade's bank and commenced negotiations with trade creditors and with prospective purchasers in an attempt to sell the restaurant.

The Court considered the nature of de facto directorships within small family companies. Madgwick J also considered that an important factor in deciding what constitutes a de facto directorship is whether the person exercises top level management functions. In small family companies with a narrow range of activities and functions persons acting as Mr Austin did are more likely to be exercising top management functions.

Although he had only intended to assist the company in times of difficulty, and despite his purported resignation, Mr Austin had practical direction and control over Talljade and had exercised top management functions. The Court had little difficulty in holding that Mr Austin was a de facto director of Tallijade and he was ordered to pay over $50,000 to the DCT.

[3.4.3] *STANDARD CHARTERED BANK OF AUSTRALIA V ANTICO*

Standard Chartered Bank of Australia v Antico[31] considered s 556b of the *Companies (Qld) Code* and s 5 of the *Companies (NSW) Code*. This case highlights the dilemma holding companies are faced with when their subsidiary, or another controlled entity, becomes insolvent or faces general financial difficulty. This case was decided under the predecessor provision of s 556 of the *Companies (Qld) Code* because the insolvent trading provisions and the national scheme legislation was not in effect at the time of the relevant events (during 1988 and 1989).

Pioneer International Ltd (Pioneer) owned 42 per cent of Giant Resources Ltd (Giant). Pioneer had three nominee directors on the board of Giant, out of a total of nine directors. Standard Chartered Bank had entered into a number of financial arrangements with Giant, including a discount and bill acceptance facility of A$30m in 1988, which was extended to 30 June 1989. Giant failed to repay the A$30m by 30 June 1989, and Standard Chartered Bank agreed to an overdraft facility which extended the payment date of the A$30m to 31

31 (1995) 131 ALR 1; Sup Ct, NSW, 9 August 1995 per Hodgson J.

December 1989 at the latest. Giant was wound up in 1990, having failed to repay the $30m. Standard Chartered Bank commenced proceedings against Pioneer pursuant to the insolvent trading provisions of the Law. Pivotal to its claim was the assertion that Pioneer was a director of Giant and thus bound by the insolvent trading provisions.

In a detailed and lengthy judgment, Hodgson J considered whether or not Pioneer could be considered a de facto or shadow director of Giant:

> On the question of whether Pioneer was a director of Giant, it is clear that it was never appointed a director; so the questions is whether it was, in terms of the definition of director ..., a person occupying or acting in the position of director, or a person in accordance with whose directions or instructions the directors of Giant were accustomed to act.[32]

Concerned with whether or not Pioneer had a decision-making role within Giant, Hodgson J accepted that the mere fact that Pioneer was the holding company of Giant was not sufficient to render it a director:

> It is clear that the mere fact that Pioneer owned indirectly 42% of the shares of Giant, and had three nominees on its board, is insufficient to make Pioneer either a director or a person who took part in the management of Giant.[33]

Similarly, his Honour stated:

> I accept that a holding company is not a director of its subsidiaries, merely because it has control of how the boards of its subsidiaries are constituted ...[34]

In addition, his Honour decided that none of the three nominee directors took action as agents or officers of their appointor Pioneer, but rather took action as directors of Giant.

However, a number of additional circumstances amounted to proof that Pioneer had effective control and substantial decision-making power within Giant. In particular, Pioneer imposed financial reporting requirements on Giant, made strategic decisions on important issues which were implemented by the directors of Giant without independent consideration, and had effective managerial and financial control of Giant's affairs. The general lack of independent analysis by the directors of Giant of these strategic issues suggested that Giant's directors merely accepted as a fait accompli the decisions made by Pioneer. To this extent, the directors of Giant received directions and instructions from

32 (1995) 131 ALR 1 at 65–66.
33 (1995) 131 ALR 1 at 66.
34 (1995) 131 ALR 1 at 70.

Pioneer and were accustomed to act in accordance with these directions and instructions. Hence, Pioneer was a shadow director of Giant:

> In my view, the conditions imposed following the decision to fund Giant in March 1989 show a willingness and ability to exercise control, and an actuality of control, over the management and financial affairs of Giant ... In my view, the directors of Giant, including [the nominee directors appointed by Pioneer], simply accepted the decisions which had effectively been made by Pioneer.[35]

Whilst Hodgson J did not explicitly refer to the term "shadow director", his Honour's conclusions regarding the willingness and ability to exercise substantial control and decision-making power support this conclusion.

Importantly, the approach of Hodgson J indicates that Courts will not be concerned to identify narrow or specific instructions from holding companies to their subsidiaries or controlled entities in order to establish a shadow directorship. Such a narrow technical approach is likely to be rejected in favour of a general examination of the role played by the holding company in the decision-making process of the subsidiary. This is entirely consistent with the rationale of s 9 to cover those with effective control of a corporation through involvement in the decision-making process.

Holding companies must be careful in their dealings with their subsidiaries. They should ensure that the directors of their subsidiaries have a policy of independently considering any information proffered by the holding company. Holding companies will need to allow the Board of the subsidiary to act independently and make decisions in the sole interest of the subsidiary or risk being held liable for the debts of the subsidiary if it sinks into insolvency.

[3.4.4] *DAIRY CONTAINERS LTD V NZI BANK LTD*

The New Zealand case of *Dairy Containers Ltd v NZI Bank Ltd*[36] considered s 2 of the *Companies Act* (NZ). This case also dealt with the law of shadow directorships relating to holding companies and their subsidiaries. It juxtaposes the wide definition of "instructions and wishes" in *Standard Chartered Bank v Antico* with a strict, narrow definition.

Dairy Containers (Dairy) was a wholly-owned subsidiary of the New Zealand Dairy Board (NZDB). All of Dairy's directors were nominee directors appointed by NZDB and were senior executives within NZDB. After Dairy made substantial financial losses, particularly due to the fraudulent activities of Dairy's managers, Dairy sued its auditors for failing to detect these frauds. The auditors counterclaimed for contributory negligence, asserting that NZDB was a shadow director of Dairy.

35 (1995) 131 ALR 1 at 70.
36 (1995) 7 NZ CLC 96-669; HC, NZ, 28 November 1994 per Thomas J.

In his judgment, Thomas J recognised the close working relationship between Dairy and NZDB:

> In truth, [Dairy's] operation was an integral part of NZDB's overall operation of making, processing and selling dairy products.[37]

His Honour acknowledged the almost total control of Dairy's operations by NZDB, arguing that their operating relationship was "symbiotic".

However, Thomas J did not find that the directors of Dairy were accustomed to act in accordance with directions or instructions from NZDB. Although as employees of NZDB the directors of Dairy were accustomed to act in accordance with instructions from NZDB, his Honour failed to identify as a matter of fact any such instructions:

> ... as directors of [Dairy] they did not as a matter of fact receive directions or instructions from [NZDB]. They were, as directors of [Dairy], standing (or sitting) in the shoes of NZDB at the board table, but they had not and did not receive directions or instructions from their employer [NZDB] ... NZDB delegated the responsibility of running the company in its interest to them. But *it did not give them identifiable directions or instructions as such.*[38]

Because no directions or instructions from NZDB to Dairy could be identified, NZDB could not be held to be a shadow director of Dairy.

This decision must be treated cautiously in an examination of the position of holding companies and their subsidiaries in relation to shadow directorships. It is particularly important to note that this case adopts a strict and narrow approach as to what can be considered an instruction. The search for identifiable instructions effectively limits the extent to which holding companies will be included within the definition of "director" as such specific instances will be difficult, if not impossible, to locate. Contrast the narrow approach adopted here with the wide perspective adopted by Hodgson J in *Standard Chartered Bank v Antico* in which his Honour found a willingness and ability to exercise control sufficient evidence to hold Pioneer a director of Giant.

[3.4.5] *RE TASBIAN (NO 3)*

Re Tasbian (No 3)[39] identifies the overlap between "advice" on the one hand and "instructions" on the other in relation to the professional advisers and business relationship exemption under s 9.

37 (1995) 7 NZ CLC 96-669 at 96-966.
38 (1995) 7 NZ CLC 96-669 at 268, 811 (emphasis added).
39 [1992] BCC 358.

Nixon, a chartered accountant, was appointed to Tasbian, an ailing finance company, by a finance company (Castle). Tasbian had never traded at a profit, and Nixon was appointed as an insolvency specialist to "turn the company around" and start it producing a profit. Nixon failed to do this, and when Tasbian went into liquidation it had debts of almost £1.5m. The issue in the case was whether Nixon was a mere professional adviser, or had become a shadow or de facto director and thus able to be disqualified as a "director". The UK definition of "director" is similar to the Australian definition in its recognition of persons being directors even if they are not appointed as such.

A number of factors suggested that Nixon had become more than a mere professional advisor or consultant and had taken over full control of Tasbian:[40]

- he required all of Tasbian's cheques to be countersigned by him as a result of amending Tasbian's bank mandate;
- he initiated and instituted a tax avoidance scheme to minimise Tasbian's income tax liability;
- he reviewed Tasbian's trading fortnightly;
- he dealt with external organisations, such as the UK Department of Trade and Industry, on Tasbian's behalf;
- he conducted negotiations with another company for the possible takeover of Tasbian;
- he negotiated an informal trade moratorium with Tasbian's trade creditors; and
- he was paid for these services by Tasbian itself.

In reply, Nixon claimed that he remained a mere professional advisor because he did not order goods or services for Tasbian and was not involved in the "hiring and firing" of employees.

The Court of Appeal decided that Tasbian had assumed an executive and managerial role within Tasbian and had effective control of its affairs, rendering him a director of Tasbian. Instrumental in this regard was his requirement that he sign all of Tasbian's cheques:

> This meant that he [Nixon] was concerned with which of [Tasbian's] creditors got paid and in which order, and to that extent it would appear ... that he was able to control the company's affairs. This seems to me to raise at least an arguable case that he was either a shadow or de facto director.[41]

40 For a more detailed assessment of the facts, see G Syrota, "Insolvent Trading: Hidden Risks for Accountants and Banks Participating in 'Work Outs'" [1993] WALR 329.

41 [1992] BCC 358 at 364 per Balcombe LJ, Lord Donaldson MR and Stuart-Smith LJ concurring.

Quite clearly, Nixon did not merely offer advice to the Board but took over all its functions. For this reason, he was a de facto director of Tasbian.

Professional advisers and "company doctors" should be particularly careful when investigating a company's affairs to avoid being held a director. If found a director, a number of heavy penalties could be imposed, including personal liability for insolvent trading. For this reason, an "arm's length" relationship should be sought.

[3.4.6] *PLAYCORP PTY LTD V SHAW*

Playcorp Pty Ltd v Shaw[42] clarifies that an alternate director will only be subject to directors' duties and liabilities, particularly insolvent trading, when acting in their position as alternate director.

In this case the plaintiff commenced proceedings against a number of directors, including an alternate director, for insolvent trading. The alternate director had not attended Board meetings or received Board papers. Under the company's constituent documents, the alternate director only acted as a director in the absence of his appointor and did not have any duties under other circumstances. Accordingly, he could not be held liable for insolvent trading for acts done when he was not entitled to exercise his powers of a director and did not in fact do so. Alternate directors must make sure that the constituent documents of their respective corporation specifies that they are only bound by the duties, responsibilities and liabilities of a director when they are acting in their capacity as such.

[3.5] Checklist

A number of factors should be considered by an insolvency practitioner in determining whether or not a person is acting as a de facto or shadow director:

- whether the information provided to a member of the Board of directors, or the Board as a whole, is in the form of a command and does not indicate that any further discretion can be exercised;
- whether at least a simple majority of the Board of directors often implements the advice directions given to them without any real independent analysis or consideration;
- whether these first two points have occurred on more than one occasion, or the occasion on which they have occurred was in relation to an issue of fundamental importance that resulted in repeated action;
- whether the person has some other sort of control over the decision-making process of the company;

42 (1993) 11 ACLC 641.

- whether the person is an appointer of a nominee director to the Board of a company who often acts with the appointer's best interests in mind, rather than weighing the appointer's interests against the interests of the company.

A number of precautions can be taken to avoid being a de facto or shadow director:

- Alternate directors should make sure that the Articles of Association of their company specifies that they are only bound by the duties and responsibilities of a director when they are called upon to act as such and are in fact acting as such. To avoid liability, these should clearly state that they are only bound by directors' duties and obligations when acting in their capacity as an alternate director.
- The appointor of a nominee director must ensure that the nominee director independently assesses and presents to the board for assessment any advice given by the appointor.
- Whilst nominee directors are able to consider third-party interests, such as those of their appointor, they should avoid merely complying with these interests without careful consideration. This is because a shadow directorship may accrue as a result of general control rather than identifiable directions or instructions.
- Professional advisers and consultants must word their terms of appointment very carefully to state that they are merely providing advice to the corporation and are not issuing commands.
- Professional advisers, consultants, and financial institutions must ensure that the appointed, or de jure, directors of the corporation they are advising independently assess and consider all of their recommendations before implementation. A requirement to this effect should be put in writing.
- Holding companies must present their advice and ideas to the boards of their subsidiaries and other controlled entities particularly in times of financial difficulty and avoid taking over the board's role or the entity's affairs. Although in many cases the Boards of their subsidiaries are likely to reach the same decision as the holding company, it is important for the Board of the subsidiary to reach this result of its own accord after advice from the holding company.

[3.6] Loopholes/deficiencies

[3.6.1] ALL OF THE DIRECTORS OR A MAJORITY OF DIRECTORS ACCUSTOMED TO ACT?

Section 9 does not state whether or not "the directors of the body" refers *all* of the directors or a *majority* of directors being accustomed to act in accordance with directions or instructions. To require all directors to be so accustomed to act would provide a serious restriction in the Law, as there arguably would be few occasions on which all directors would be so accustomed to act. As decisions of the Board are usually made by a *majority* of directors, a preferable position is to require a *majority* of directors to be so accustomed.

[3.6.2] INSTRUCTIONS OR WISHES GIVEN TO THE BOARD AS A WHOLE?

Section 9 does not state whether it requires "instructions or wishes" to be given to the Board as a whole, or whether it is sufficient if they are given to a dominant Board member. A preferable policy position is to recognise that if a person gives instructions or wishes to a dominant managing director or nominee director then that person is effectively having a say in the decision-making of the company. In this sense, they possess a degree of control of the company's affairs and they should be subject to the same duties, responsibilities and liabilities imposed on other directors.

[3.6.3] MEANING OF "ADVICE" AND "INSTRUCTIONS OR WISHES"

The Law does not provide a definition of the terms "advice" and "instructions or wishes". Although it has been assumed that advice refers to matters in which the directors retain some discretion, and instructions and wishes refer to a command, the wording of the section does not make this clear. It is possible that "instructions and wishes" in fact encompass "advice".

[3.6.4] DEFINITION OF "OFFICER"

With the introduction of the s 9 definition of officer outlined above, and the continued operation of the s 2A definition of director, the Law now contains two definitions of officer. Some confusion results from this. No mention was made of this within the *Explanatory Memorandum to the Corporate Law Economic Reform Program Act* 1999. It would appear that the s 82A definition has a broader ambit as it applies to officers of a "body corporate" or "entity" whereas s 9 applies to officers of a corporation only. However, the operation of s 82A is questionable given that a "body corporate" includes a corporation. Whereas receivers who are not also managers, receivers and managers appointed by the Court and Court appointed liquidators are included within the s 9 definition they are specifically excluded from the operation of s 82A. Conversely employees are included within s 82A but excluded from s 9. It is arguable that the s 82A definition is intended to apply where the Law refers specifically to a "body corporate" or "entity" and the s 9 definition to apply where the Law refers to a "corporation". However, this is dubious given that a "body corporate" includes a corporation.

[3.7] Proposals for law reform

[3.7.1] DIRECTORS' DUTIES AS AN APPROPRIATE METHOD OF CORPORATE REGULATION?

Arguably the insistence on directors' duties and liabilities as an appropriate method of corporate regulation is questionable. Shown to stem from a certain perspective of what constitutes a company, this method of regulating corporate behaviour is arguably ill suited to deal with many modern corporate phenomena. In recent times, renewed calls have been made for individual director liability to be replaced with corporate liability per se. Although it is difficult to see how this could work in the context of insolvent trading, it represents an interesting and challenging policy consideration.

Strong proponents of this view are Fisse and Braithwaite, who argue for a system of "enforced accountability" to be instituted in which companies themselves will be held directly liable for offences but simultaneously required to impose internal disciplinary measures on the individuals responsible for the offence.[43]

Fisse and Braithwaite argue that directors' duties and liabilities is a cumbersome and costly method of corporate regulation. They argue that the imposition of duties, responsibilities and liabilities on directors fails to reflect the diffuse managerial structure within companies and that the extended definition of "director" does not seem to embrace the ability of those on the Board of Directors to delegate their functions to middle and lower level management, thus escaping liability themselves. They argue that, in addition, it results in resource-intensive investigations of individual action and fails to confront the ability of corporations to obscure internal accountability and other "cover-up" procedures, such as transferring suspected personnel out of the jurisdiction. Through its resource-intensive nature, agency costs are necessarily increased for regulators and companies themselves, increasing the costs of doing business. The imposition of liability on companies themselves may avoid many of these deficiencies. In the words of Fisse:

> In a society moving increasingly toward group action it may become impractical, in terms of allocation of resources, to deal with systems through their components. In many cases it would appear more sensible to transfer to the corporation the responsibility of policing itself, forcing it to take steps to ensure that the harm done does not materialise through the conduct of people within the organisation. Rather than having the state monitor the activities of each

43 See B Fisse, "The Social Policy of Corporate Criminal Responsibility" (1978) 6(3) *Adelaide Law Review* 361; B Fisse and J Braithwaite, "The Allocation of Responsibility for Corporate Crime: Individualism, Collectivism and Accountability" (1988) 11 *Sydney Law Review* 468.

person within the corporation, which is costly and raises practical enforcement difficulties, it may be more efficient to force the corporation to do this, especially if sanctions imposed on the corporation can be translated into effective action at the individual level.[44]

This approach has been adopted in the *Criminal Code Act* 1995 (Cth).[45] Under this Act, a body corporate may be found guilty of any criminal offence, including one punishable by imprisonment. The fact that the corporation could not physically commit the offence is irrelevant. A "physical element" of an offence can be committed by an employee or agent of the corporation regardless of their seniority and is directly attributable to the corporation. Most significantly, the "fault element" of an offence can be attributed to the Board of Directors, a "high managerial agent", or a corporate culture within the organisation that directed, tolerated or encouraged non-compliance. This imposition of criminal liability on corporate entities is a significant move away from traditional director liability in the realm of criminal law. Directors should be aware of the provisions of the Act, particularly the emphasis on "corporate culture" as a basis for liability. The need to ensure that adequate compliance policies are established and communicated throughout the corporation is likely to form part of the duty of care and diligence, although it is possible that a decision not to institute such measures may be protected under the business judgment rule: see Ch 16 at [16.1.6]. In any event, it suggests that in the future directors may no longer be the targets of corporate regulatory policy. If the aim of corporate law is to challenge, and ultimately change, corporate behaviour and activities, such a trend is to be welcomed.

44 B Fisse, "Recent Developments in Corporate Criminal Law and Corporate Liability to onetary Penalties" (1990) 13(1) UNSWLJ 1 at 31.

45 See T Woolf, "The Criminal Code Act 1995 (Cth) – Towards a Realist Vision of Corporate Criminal Liability" (1997) 21(5) *Criminal Law Journal* 257.

What Is a Debt?

"*A company incurs a debt when by its choice, it does or omits something which, as a matter of substance and commercial reality, renders it liable for a debt for which it otherwise would not have been liable.*"[1]

"*The words 'incurs' and 'debts' are not words of precise and inflexible denotation. Where they appear ... they are to be applied in a practical and commonsense fashion, consistent with the context and with the statutory purposes.*"[2]

1 *Standard Chartered Bank of Australia v Antico* (1995) 131 ALR 1.
2 *Hawkins v Bank of China* (1992) 10 ACLC 588.

OBJECTIVES

This Chapter will:

- consider the various fundamental elements of a debt both at common law and under the Law;
- set out various categories of "debt" for the purposes of the Law and consider when a debt may be incurred under each category;
- set out the circumstances in which the law deems a debt to have been incurred.

[4.1] General overview

To bring an action for insolvent trading, it must be shown that a company has in fact incurred a debt. It is also necessary to determine the exact time when this debt was incurred.

The time of incurring the debt is important because it is at this time that the state of mind of the director must be assessed. The director's belief about the company's ability to pay its debts as and when they fall due is determined at the time of incurring the particular debt. If at the time the debt was incurred there were reasonable grounds to suspect that the company would not be able to pay its debts as and when they fell due, the director would be liable under the insolvent trading provisions.

There is no definition of "debt" within the Law. Numerous judicial interpretations must be examined in order to determine what "debt" means in different contexts. There is no "quick and fast" rule of what constitutes a debt as its meaning varies according to the type of transaction in question.[3] However, there are a number of fundamental guiding principles that have been established to aid in the interpretation of "debt".

"Debt" has been interpreted to bear its ordinary technical meaning as something recoverable by an action for debt and thus must be ascertained or capable of being ascertained.[4] Therefore, a "debt" signifies an obligation for the payment of money or money's worth. Many authorities suggest that the obligation must be for an ascertained liquidated sum.[5]

The terms "incurs" and "debt" are words of flexible meaning. Their meaning changes in accordance with the context in which they are used. This was emphasised by Gleeson CJ in *Hawkins v Bank of China*:

> The words 'incurs' and 'debts' are not words of precise and inflexible denotation. Where they appear ... they are to be applied in a practical and commonsense fashion, consistent with the context and with the statutory purposes.[6]

The statutory purpose of the definition of "debt" is to encourage directors to focus on the overall management of their company's financial affairs. In this sense, the central focus of the definition is to achieve an appropriate level of vigilance by directors for the overall financial affairs of their company. For this reason, what constitutes a "debt" has broad economic and social policy implications. Clearly,

3 *Rema Industries and Services Pty Ltd v Coa; Re Taspac Thermoforming Pty Ltd* (1992) 10 ACLC 530.
4 *Ogden's Ltd v Weinberg* (1906) 95 LT 567 per Lord Davey, *Hussein v Good* (1990) 8 ACLC 390.
5 *3M Australia Pty Ltd v Watt* (1984) 9 ACLR 203, *Jelin v Johnson* (1987) 5 ACLC 463.
6 *Hawkins v Bank of China* (1992) 10 ACLC 588 at 595.

the meaning of "debt" in any situation requires a flexible consideration from the point of view of commercial reality.[7]

At a fundamental level, the company must commit a positive act to bring a debt into existence. In this sense a debt can only be incurred by a positive, voluntary act that signifies the company's willingness and intention to be bound. Its ordinary use implies that it is an obligation actually incurred.[8] Hodgson J stated in *Standard Chartered Bank v Antico*:

> In my opinion, a company incurs a debt when, by its choice, it does or omits something which, as a matter of substance and commercial reality, renders it liable for a debt for which it otherwise would not have been liable.[9]

For this reason a contractual agreement for the supply of goods can be considered a debt,[10] but the imposition of a judgment debt cannot because there is no positive act on the part of the company to bring the judgment debt into existence.[11]

This approach was criticised by Bryson J in *Shepherd v ANZ.*[12] In his Honour's opinion, obligations imposed by law, such as revenue law, can be debts for the purpose of the insolvent trading provisions "whether or not the acts or omissions which the company chose to be involved in brought them into existence". The difference in approach between Hodgson J and Bryson J is that whereas Hodgson J considered the act of the company to be determinative, Bryson J focused on the act of the creditor in electing to be treated as a creditor by crystallising a debt due by demanding payment. These two approaches are not entirely inconsistent. In essence they both consider the substance of the transaction as instrumental, rather than the form of the transaction, in the light of a commercially realistic interpretation of a transaction between two parties.

Section 588G(1A) deems that debts are incurred for the purposes of s 588G if a company takes certain action at certain times. There are seven such instances set out in s 588G(1A):

(1) When a company is paying a dividend, a debt is incurred for the purposes of s 588G when the dividend is paid, or if the company has a constitution that provides for the declaration of dividends, when the dividend is declared.
(2) When a company makes a reduction of share capital to which Div 1 of Pt 2J.1 applies (other than a reduction that consists only of the cancellation of a share or shares for no consideration), when the reduction takes effect.

---

7 *Standard Chartered Bank of Australia v Antico* (1995) 131 ALR 1; *Hawkins v Bank of China* (1990) 10 ACLC 588.
8 *Hawkins v Bank of China* (1992) 10 ACLC 588.
9 (1995) 131 ALR 1 at 57.
10 *Hussein v Good* (1990) 8 ACLC 390.
11 *Jelin v Johnson* (1987) 5 ACLC 463.
12 (1996) 14 ACLC 987.

(3) When a company is buying back shares (even if the consideration is not a sum certain in money), when the buy-back agreement is entered into.
(4) If a company is redeeming redeemable preference shares that are redeemable at its option, when the company exercises the option.
(5) When a company issues redeemable preference shares that are redeemable otherwise than at its option, when the shares are issued.
(6) When a company financially assists a person to acquire shares (or units of shares) in itself or a holding company, when the agreement to provide assistance is entered into or, if there is no agreement, when the assistance is provided.
(7) When a company enters into an uncommercial transaction (within the meaning of s 588FB), other than one that a Court orders, or a prescribed agency directs, the company to enter into, when the uncommercial transaction is entered into.

This final category was introduced by the recent *Corporations Law Amendment (Employee Entitlements) Act* 2000. This Act amended the s 588G(1A) to deem that a company incurs a debt for the purposes of the insolvent trading provisions when it enters into an "uncommercial transaction" (as defined under the voidable transaction provisions). If the effect of an uncommercial transaction is that the company is unable to pay its debts as and when they fall due the company will be deemed to have "incurred a debt" for the purposes of the insolvent trading provisions by entering into that uncommercial transaction. Accordingly, for this new category to apply the relevant uncommercial transaction will have to impact on the solvency of the company.

Broadly speaking, an uncommercial transaction is one that a reasonable person in the company's circumstances would not have entered into having regard to the benefits and detriments to the company of entering into the transaction and respective benefits to other parties to the transaction.

This amendment means that directors will be liable for insolvent trading in circumstances where the company has not actually incurred a "debt" at the relevant time but rather entered into an "uncommercial transaction".

This provision will mean that directors must bear in mind the solvency of the company when engaging in related party transactions. However, the uncertainty and extremely wide latitude which plagues the uncommercial transactions provisions generally will undoubtedly create many problems within the context of the insolvent trading provisions. As the name of the amending Act suggests, the amendments were introduced in the context of the new Pt 5.8A which is introduced to protect employee entitlements, particularly in the context of corporate insolvency. Despite this noble cause, the legislators have not considered how this already broad category which is beset by definitional laxity will create confusion within the insolvent trading provisions. In the absence of case law, more guidance will be required by the legislators to determine the boundaries of this new category.

For the purposes of determining the meaning of "debt" in different contexts, the ongoing business expenses of companies have been divided into three categories. A few examples have been provided below by way of illustration. The approach is not entirely logically consistent in all cases.

[4.1.1] OBLIGATIONS UNDER CONTINUING CONTRACTUAL ARRANGEMENTS

(a) Leases

The pivotal case dealing with this issue was decided under s 556 of the Companies Code, a predecessor to s 588G. In *Russell Halpern Nominees Pty Ltd v Martin*[13] the Full Court of the Supreme Court of Western Australia emphasised that a positive act must be committed in order to bring a debt into existence. Burt CJ was of the opinion that a debt is a positive act that exposes a director or a person who takes part in the management of the company when the debt was incurred to criminal liability:

> Whatever the expression 'incurs and debt' might mean, it is clearly descriptive of an act when done by the company in the stated circumstances exposes a director of the company ... when the debt was incurred, when the act was done, to criminal liability.[14]

A lease represents a continuing or serial obligation. The only act that satisfies the "positive act" requirement in the context of a lease is the initial entering into of the contract of lease. Therefore, a company incurs a debt when it first enters into a contract of lease. The company does not incur a debt each and every time rent becomes payable under the lease because there is no positive act on the part of the company on these occasions. It would be unacceptable to decide otherwise because this would be to say that:

> ... if a company when in all respects financially sound were to enter into a lease for a term of years and at some time thereafter and for reasons which could not be anticipated it were to fall on bad times and be unable to pay its debts, the directors would thereafter and on every rent day within the remainder of the term be guilty of an offence for the reason that on the rent day the company 'incurs a debt'.[15]

13 (1986) 4 ACLC 393.
14 (1986) 4 ACLC 393 at 396.
15 (1986) 4 ACLC 393 at 397.

This decision restricted the ambit of the insolvent trading provisions to a limited number of situations. It would be a rare event where at the time of entering into a lease a company is unable to pay its debts as and when they fell due.

Where there is a periodic tenancy or a holding over after expiry of a term, it is arguable that it is the failure of the tenant company to take steps to terminate the lease at the end of each period which would incur the debt for rent. In the words of Hodgson J in *Standard Chartered Bank v Antico*:

> ... where there is a periodic tenancy, or a holding over after expiry of a term, the company can put a stop to the accrual of rent liability by giving notice to quit and/or giving up possession; so in those cases, in my opinion, it would be the failure from time to time to take those steps which, as a matter of substance, would make the company liable for each rent instalment accruing from a time when such a step would have stopped the rent accruing. On each occasion when the company could terminate the lease but does not do so, it would incur the rent for the period to which this omission committed the company.[16]

(b) Workers compensation insurance and other features of contracts of employment

Russell Halpern Nominees Pty Ltd v Martin has had ramifications for the judicial interpretation of "debt" in other contexts. Two areas heavily influenced have been workers compensation insurance and other features of contracts of employment, such as the payment of salaries.

The company usually pays workers compensation insurance at the time of entering into the contract of employment with an employee. This initial contract of employment could be seen as a positive act by the company. In *State Government Insurance Corporation v Pollock*[17] Seaman J held that a premium for workers compensation insurance is a debt, incurred at the time the insurance contract is entered into:

> ... the liability for the premium did not arise by the operation of a statute but by the voluntary act of [the company] in employing workmen and in obtaining a policy to cover its workers" compensation liabilities in respect of them.[18]

Following this line of reasoning, it is likely that salaries, wages and other incidents of the employment contract are debts incurred by the company at the time of entering into the initial contract of employment rather than on each and every

16 (1995) 131 ALR 1 at 57.
17 (1993) 11 ACLC 839.
18 (1993) 11 ACLC 839 at 842.

pay day. Other incidents of the contract of employment may include liability for redundancy or retrenchment payment and obligations in relation to long service leave and holiday pay.

(c) Interest and financing

The only case to decide whether or not an agreement to pay interest constitutes a debt is *John Graham Reprographics Pty Ltd v Steffens.*[19] In this case, Connolly J regarded the situation before him as resembling that in *Russell Halpern Nominees Pty Ltd v Martin* and followed the reasoning in that case. Thus, interest incurred under an agreement to pay interest is a debt incurred at the time of entering into the initial contract. In this way, failure to pay interest does not, of itself, constitute the incurrence of an independent debt. This approach was criticised by Zelling AJ in *BL Lange v Bird*[20] where his Honour argued that:

> Interest is not 'incurred' when the debt is incurred; the interest flows from non-payment later, and it is difficult to fit the concept of interest into the statutory debt which flows from the application of the section.[21]

The position is somewhat different in relation to bill financing. In contrast to the decision in *John Graham Reprographics Pty Ltd v Steffins, Standard Chartered Bank v Antico*[22] decided that interest on a principal debt may be considered an independent "debt" in relation to bill financing. According to Hodgson J, where a loan is for a fixed term the borrower incurs interest for the term of the loan as a debt:

(a) when the loan agreement was entered into, when early repayment of the principal is not a realistic option for the borrower; or
(b) from day to day, when early repayment is a realistic option for the borrower.

However, where the loan is not for a fixed term, or the fixed term has expired, the borrower incurs interest as a debt:

(a) when the loan was entered into, when repayment is not a real option for the borrower; or
(b) from day to day, when repayment is a real option for the borrower.

Where refinancing occurs, and the borrower enters into a new agreement to pay interest on a loan that is due or overdue for repayment, the borrower incurs interest as a debt:

(a) when the new loan agreement is entered into; or

19 (1987) 5 ACLC 904.
20 (1991) 9 ACLC 1015.
21 (1991) 9 ACLC 1015 at 1018.
22 (1995) 131 ALR 1.

(b) when the original loan agreement was entered into, when the borrower is unable to repay the existing loan and the new loan agreement is in substance merely an extension of time for repayment of the principal.

This clearly establishes that refinancing does amount to the incurring of a debt under the insolvent trading provisions where there is an entry into a new agreement that is not a mere extension of the existing finance facility. In order for a new independent debt to be created as a result of refinancing, the new loan agreement must be different in substance from the existing loan agreement. In the words of Hodgson J:

> In general terms, the more of an option repayment is, the stronger is the case for saying that the debt for interest is incurred by entering into the new agreement; and similarly, the more different the new agreement is from the original agreement, the stronger is the case for saying that the liability for interest under the new agreement is not the same liability as it would otherwise (in any event) have had.[23]

It is not clear when repayment will be a "real option" for the borrower, but the Court is likely to look at the financial affairs of the company and the assets and funds available to it to repay the loan. What is clear is that at the time of refinancing, directors must turn their mind to the financial position of the company and examine its ability to repay the interest in the principal.

The decision in *Standard Chartered Bank v Antico* builds on the decision in *John Graham Reprographics Pty Ltd v Steffins* but also incorporates the critique made in *BL Lange v Bird*. It represents a commercially realistic response to the problems raised by interest and bill financing within the context of insolvent trading.

(d) Guarantees and other contingent liabilities

Guarantees and other contingent liabilities are considered "debts" for the purposes of the insolvent trading provisions. In the case of a guarantee, whilst the liability of a guarantor arises at the time of entry into the contract, the primary debt does not arise until the primary debtor defaults. In *Hawkins v Bank of China*[24] the Court held that directors are liable at the time of entry into the guarantee, despite the fact that the primary indebtedness may not arise for some years later. Thus, a guarantee and other contingent liabilities are "debts" incurred at the date of agreement.

23 (1995) 131 ALR 1 at 60.
24 (1992) 10 ACLC 588.

[4.1.2] OBLIGATIONS IMPOSED BY STATUTE OR OTHERWISE INCURRED BY OPERATION OF LAW

(a) Payroll tax

When a company employs an employee, the employer becomes liable to pay payroll tax under the *Payroll Tax Assessment Act* 1971 (Cth). Payroll tax becomes owing when it is ascertainable, and this is usually at the end of each month. In *Commissioner of State Taxation (WA) v Pollock*[25] the Full Court of the Supreme Court of Western Australia held that payroll tax constitutes a debt for the purposes of insolvent trading. Ipp J decided that payroll tax only becomes a "debt" owing upon the expiry of the month in which the payroll tax has been incurred, because it is only at this time that the amount of payroll tax to be paid can be ascertained. However, a company incurs a contingent liability for payroll tax upon employing an employee in any given month. Ipp J concluded that it would be contrary to the purpose of the insolvent trading provisions to confine their application to simple contract cases.

Thus, payroll tax is a "debt". It becomes a debt owing when it is ascertainable, but in the interim it is a contingent liability.

It should also be noted that a company's liability to remit PAYE deductions deducted from employee's salaries is a debt and is incurred when the deduction was made: s 588F.

(b) Sales tax

It is currently uncertain whether or not sales tax is a "debt". Again the approach of the Courts does not appear to be logically consistent.

In *Castrisios v McManus*[26] Cox J decided that sales tax is not a debt because there is no act on the part of the company that can be identified as one that brings the debt into existence. Cox J defined tax as "a compulsory contribution to the support of government, levied on persons, property, income, commodities, transactions etc".[27] The reliance placed on the compulsory nature of tax resulted in Cox J concluding that a company does not voluntarily contract or enter into an obligation to pay an amount of money when it must pay sales tax. In the words of the magistrate at first instance:

> The liability to pay the tax is a consequence of the contractual agreement between the wholesale merchant and the person to whom he sells, but it does not have the essential elements of an agreement which is necessary to give rise to a debtor-creditor relationship.[28]

---

25 (1993) 11 ACLC 16.
26 *Castrisios v McManus* (1991) 9 ACLC 287.
27 (1991) 9 ACLC 287 at 296.
28 (1991) 9 ACLC 287 at 296.

This decision is placed in doubt by the reasoning and decision in *Commissioner of State Taxation (WA) v Pollock*. According to Noble, had Cox J focused on the definition of "debt" as "that which is owed or due; anything which one person is under an obligation to pay or render to another", it is likely that his Honour would have found sales tax to be a debt for the purposes of insolvent trading.[29]

The recent case of *Powell v Fryer*[30] held that sales tax is a "debt" for the purposes of the insolvent trading provisions. Prior J held that a penalty imposed by the Commissioner of Taxation for failure to pay sales tax was a further debt incurred at the time that the penalty is assessed.

(c) Judgment debt

A debt requires an ascertained or liquidated sum. In *Jelin Pty Ltd v Johnson*[31] a claim for damages for misleading and deceptive conduct was held not be a debt because there was no ascertained sum at the time the action arose. In addition, there is no act on the part of a company that can be considered a requisite positive act. Neither the action on which the claim for damages is based nor the resulting judgment is a positive act by a company. This decision has been supported in a number of subsequent cases.[32]

(d) Penalties

It is not clear whether a penalty is a debt for the purpose of the insolvent trading provisions. Under the approach of Hodgson J in *Standard Chartered Bank v Antico* a penalty would not be a debt as there is no positive act to bring it into existence. However, the approach of Prior J in *Powell v Fryer*[33] suggests that the Court may consider penalties for the failure to pay taxes or other obligations imposed by law as a "debt". Prior J found that penalties are "debt". Prior J found that penalties are "debts" incurred at the time when the late payment penalty is assessed. The approach of Prior J can be reconciled with late payment penalties imposed as a result of a failure to comply with an obligation imposed by law, such as payment of taxes, but it is difficult to see how a penalty could be considered a "debt" when it does not stem from such a source.

[4.1.3] OBLIGATIONS INCURRED IN CONSEQUENCE OF THE ACQUISITION OF GOODS AND SERVICES

(a) Supply of goods

Whilst incurring a debt for the supply of goods is a "debt" for the purposes of the insolvent trading provisions, an issue arises as to when the debt is incurred.

29 T Noble, "When Does a Company Incur a Debt Under the Insolvent Trading Provisions of the Corporations Law?" (1994) 12(5) CSLJ 297 at 300.
30 Unreported, Sup Ct, SA, Prior J, 14 April 2000.
31 (1987) 5 ACLC 483.

Although earlier cases suggest that this will be upon delivery of the goods, recent cases indicate that there is no "hard and fast" rule to this effect.

In *Hussein v Good*[34] it was held that a debt is incurred when goods are supplied. As a result, a director who allowed a company to order goods at a time when the company was solvent but which subsequently became insolvent prior to delivery of the goods would not be liable under the provisions. This provided a large loophole through which companies could avoid liability for goods ordered. It placed creditors at a serious risk where they incurred expense in relation to the goods prior to delivery.[35]

This deficiency was recognised in the recent case of *Leigh-Mardon Pty Ltd v Wawn*.[36] In this case, Hodgson J decided that there is:

> ... no hard and fast rule that a company incurs the debt for gods sold and delivered at the time when the goods are delivered to the company, and not at any earlier time.[37]

In this way, the terms of trade, the nature of the goods, and their marketability must also be considered. Hodgson J stated that a company incurs a debt:

> ... when it chooses to do or omit to do something which, as a matter of substance and commercial reality, renders it liable for a debt for which it otherwise would not have been liable.[38]

Thus, the act or omission may be the order itself or the acceptance of delivery of the goods, depending on the facts of the case. If the goods are readily saleable by the vendor, it is more likely that the debt is incurred by the acceptance of delivery. On the other hand, if the goods are not readily saleable to another purchaser, it is more likely that the debt is incurred at the time of placing the order for the goods.[39]

(b) Failure to supply goods

In *Reed International Books Australia Pty Ltd (t/a Butterworths) v King & Prior Pty Ltd*[40] the central issue was the failure to supply goods. Reed had ordered paper

33 Unreported, Sup Ct, SA, Prior J, 14 April 2000.
34 (1990) 8 ACLC 390.
35 See also *Rema Industries and Services Pty Ltd v Coad* (1992) 7 ACSR 766; and *Taylor v Powell* (1993) 10 ACSR 174.
36 (1995) 17 ACSR 741.
37 (1995) 17 ACSR 741 at 749.
38 (1995) 17 ACSR 741 at 749.
39 (1995) 17 ACSR 741 at 750. See also J O'Donovan, "Corporate Insolvency" (1996) 14 CSLJ 2 at 120–121. For example, if goods are manufactured specially for a particular company and contain certain indicia, such as the company's artwork, it is unlikely to be of commercial value to anyone else.
40 (1993) 11 ACLC 935.

from a wholesaler who subsequently invoiced Reed upon receiving the paper from a supplier. However, receivers were appointed to the wholesaler. Although Reed was notified of this, they proceeded to pay the wholesalers for the invoiced paper. However, before delivery of the paper could be made, the supplier repossessed the paper. Reed sued the directors of the wholesaler under s 592 of the Law claiming that accepting money for the delivery of the goods constituted a debt and this debt was incurred whilst insolvent.

The Court held that no debt was incurred but rather Reed could sue for breach of contract. Thus, accepting payment for the delivery of goods does not constitute a debt.

This decision seems inconsistent with the rationale for the insolvent trading provisions. If the philosophy behind the term "debt" is to deal with the situation where a company obtains a benefit or something for value for which it cannot pay it is difficult to reason why the acceptance of payment for goods and subsequent failure to deliver is not a "debt". In the future, Courts may be prepared to find that accepting payment for the delivery of goods does constitute a debt.

[4.2] Philosophy/rationale

The duty to prevent insolvent trading aims to direct the attention of directors and managers to the overall financial management of the company.

As a result, the rationale behind the phrase "incurs a debt" is to deal with the situation where a company obtains a benefit or something for value for which it cannot pay.[41] The need to focus on the overall financial management of the company prompts an interpretation that is flexible and accords with commercial reality. In the words of Mosley:

> The ultimate question of what constitutes a debt can be viewed as coming down to the degree of vigilance which should be demanded from company directors. A high degree of vigilance might act as a disincentive to business whereas if the standard is too low, creditors, including the government, may suffer. Such questions relate to broad economic and social considerations ... It may be that these questions are ... beyond the scope of the courts which have limited resources and deal only with specific cases.[42]

41 *Commissioner of State Taxation (WA) v Pollock* (1993) 11 ACLC 16 per Hawkins J.

42 J Mosley, "Insolvent Trading: What is a Debt and When is One Incurred?" (1996) 4(4) ILJ 155 at 157.

[4.3] History/former law

The first statutory provision to deal with incurring a debt was s 303 of the *Companies Act* 1962 (Cth), the initial insolvent trading provision. This provided for the "contracting of a debt", in contrast to the present formulation "incurs a debt". These two concepts differ, as pointed out by Foster J in *Law v Coburn*:

> The words 'a debt contracted' are, in my judgment, very different from the words 'incur a debt'.[43]

The explicit reference to "contracting " in s 303 suggests a distinct legislative intention to include only debts voluntarily contracted by a company within the ambit of the early insolvent trading provisions.

The narrow approach of s 303 of the *Companies Act* was carried over to its successor, s 556(1) of the *Companies Code*, despite the seemingly different legislative interpretation envisaged by the drafters indicated by the change from "contracting a debt" to "incurs a debt". The impact of s 303 to the interpretation of s 556 was best seen in the case of *Shapowloff v Dunn*,[44] where the High Court determined that a liability under a "debt" arose when the debt was "contracted". This reference to "contract" rather than "incur" is indicative of the continued narrow approach. A large number of cases were decided under s 556(1) and this narrow approach impacted heavily on these decisions. For example, the decision in *Halpern Nominees Pty Ltd v Martin* restricted the operation of the section to those rare circumstances where at the time of entering into an agreement the company was unable to pay its debts as they fell due.

Greater flexibility was given to the term "debt" with the decision in *Hawkins v Bank of China*. Applying the phrase "incurs a debt" in a practical and common sense manner consistent with their statutory purpose, the Court departed from earlier authority and included a contingent liability as a debt within the insolvent trading provisions. Particularly important was the statement by Kirby that "... it was clearly the intention of those presenting the [*Companies*] *Code* to Parliament that s 556 would increase, and not reduce or limit, the obligations imposed on officers of the corporation."[45] This emphasis on flexibility, common sense and statutory intention now pervades the judicial interpretation of the phrase "incurs a debt".

The need for a commercially realistic construction of the phrase has dominated judicial decisions under the successors to s 556(1), s 592(1) of the Law and the current s 588G. This trend can be seen in the decisions of *Leigh-Mardon Pty*

43 *Law v Coburn* [1972] 1 WLR 1238 at 1243 per Foster J. Cited in *Castrisios v McManus* (1991) 9 ACLC 287 at 296 per Cox J.

44 (1981) 148 CLR 72.

45 *Hawkins v Bank of China* (1992) 10 ACLC 588 at 599.

Ltd v Wawn[46] and *Standard Chartered Bank of Australia v Antico*.[47] In the former case, the Court held that there is no definitive rule that a company "incurs a debt" at the time at the time the goods are delivered. Hodgson J indicated that particular circumstances, commercial reality and common sense may deem the ordering of goods as the time of "incurring" the debt.

In the latter case, a wide interpretation of the phrase "incurs a debt" was taken to find interest incurred as a result of refinancing a debt.

The positive act requirement, coupled with common sense, commercial reality and a flexible approach are likely to dominate the way in which "incurs a debt" is interpreted under the section.

[4.4] Notable cases

[4.4.1] *HAWKINS V BANK OF CHINA*

Hawkins v Bank of China[48] considered s 592(1)(a) of the *Corporations Law* and s 556 of the *Companies (NSW) Code* and specifically dealt with the position of guarantees as debts under the insolvent trading provisions. The Bank of China (the Bank) brought an action for A$5m under the insolvent trading provisions at the time (s 556) against two directors and one manager of Equiticorp International (Equiticorp). This amount represented the amount of a guarantee that Equiticorp had entered into with the Bank in respect of two other companies in the same group as Equiticorp. The Bank brought proceedings when the other companies went into provisional liquidation. The first issue was whether a contingent liability in the form of a guarantee was a debt for the purposes of the insolvent trading provisions. The second issue revolved around whether such a debt would be incurred at the time of entering into the agreement or upon default by the primary debtor.

Gleeson CJ defined "guarantee" to mean the undertaking of a contingent liability which may mature into a presently payable debt if subsequent events occur.[49] His Honour decided that unacceptable results would follow from the conclusion that a liability under a guarantee would only become a debt when a demand was made after default by the primary debtor. His Honour provided the example of the harsh consequences that would follow if civil or criminal penalties were imposed on directors of a company who entered into a contract of guarantee at a time when their company was financially sound but which subsequently faced financial difficulties at the time the guarantee was called

46 (1995) 17 ACSR 741.
47 (1995) 131 ALR 1.
48 (1992) 10 ACLC 588 CA, NSW, 1 May 1992 per Gleeson CJ, Kirby P and Sheller JA.
49 (1992) 10 ACLC 588 at 592.

upon. Clearly, at the time the guarantee was made, the directors would not have known that their company would be unable to meet its commitment when demand was made. Gleeson CJ felt that the unfair consequences following from such a result ruled against the finding that a guarantee is a debt incurred when a valid demand for payment is made. His Honour concluded that his finding is consistent with the statutory objectives of the insolvent trading provisions, particularly because guarantees are such an obvious and common means by which companies come to owe debts.

Kirby P discussed the expression "incurs a debt" and found that it is:

> ... entirely apt to describe an act on the part of a corporation whereby it renders itself liable to pay a sum of money in the future as a debt. The act of 'incurring' happens when the corporation so acts as to expose itself contractually to an obligation to make a future payment of a sum of money as a debt. The mere fact that such a sum of money will only be paid upon a future contingency does not make the assumption of the obligation any less 'incurring' a 'debt'.[50]

In this way his Honour agreed with Gleeson CJ that the debt under a guarantee is "incurred" when the contract of guarantee is entered into. His Honour also found that it is consistent with the statutory objectives of the insolvent trading provisions to include contingent liabilities, such as guarantees, within their ambit:

> It would be absurd if an officer of an insolvent corporation could, with impunity, cause the corporation to enter into a guarantee of a liability which could immediately thereafter mature into an absolute obligation as a debt. The whole purpose or object of s 556 of the [Companies] Code was to discourage officers of corporations from improvidently committing the corporation to obligations to pay money as a debt when they have reasonable grounds for supposing that their corporation is (or will, upon incurring the debt in question) become insolvent.[51]

Noble highlights a number of problems resulting from the decision in *Hawkins v Bank of China*. She argues that the words "incur a debt" do not adequately provide for the variety of fact situations that can arise under the insolvent trading provisions. As a result:

> ... unsatisfactory results can flow from either interpretation where date of contract and date of delivery are separated by an interval of time.[52]

---

50 *Hawkins v Bank of China* (1992) 10 ACLC 588 at 598.
51 (1992) 10 ACLC 588 at 599.
52 T Noble, "When Does a Company Incur a Debt Under the Insolvent Trading Provisions of the Corporations Law?" (1994) 12(5) CSLJ 297 at 302.

In her view, the inclusion of contingent liabilities under the section means that creditors will suffer if there were no grounds to expect inability to pay at the time of ordering the goods but there are such grounds at the time of delivery. Conversely, she points out that if contingent liabilities are excluded from the section creditors will also suffer where a company orders goods when in financial difficulty, is placed in liquidation before payment is made, and the creditor has incurred expense.[53] Brown argues that when a guarantee is provided, the debt should be regarded as incurred at the time of default by the primary debtor.[54]

[4.4.2] *LEIGH MARDON V WAWN*

Leigh Mardon v Wawn[55] considered s 556 of the *Companies (NSW) Code.*

The judgment established a new principle for determining the time when a debt is incurred in the case of delivery of goods. The emphasis on flexibility and commercial reality evident in this case is representative of the new judicial sentiment.

Braha Corporation Pty Ltd (Braha) was a manufacturer of potato chips. At a directors' meeting in July 1989 it was decided to restrict payment to creditors by paying them only a little amount at any one time in order to satisfy them. Orders for packaging were placed by Braha with the plaintiff in September and November 1989. This packaging contained Braha's artwork and company logo. A receiver was appointed to Braha in February 1990. The plaintiff brought a claim under the insolvent trading provisions.

The main issue in dispute was the time when the debt for the packaging order was incurred. The plaintiff claimed that it was incurred at the time of ordering the goods, whereas the defendant, one of the directors of Braha, argued that it was upon delivery of the goods.

To that point, the Courts had been adamant that a debt for goods was incurred upon delivery of the goods.[56] However, Hodgson J held that:

> ... there is no hard and fast rule that a company incurs the debt for goods sold and delivered at the time when the goods are delivered to the company, and not at any earlier time.[57]

According to Hodgson J, a debt is incurred when a company chooses to do or omits something "... which, as a matter of substance and commercial reality,

53 T Noble, "When Does a Company Incur a Debt Under the Insolvent Trading Provisions of the Corporations Law?" (1994) 12(5) CSLJ 297 at 302.

54 A D Brown, "Does Section 592 Apply to Guarantees? The Risks Increase After the Hawkins Case" (1993) 11(1) CSLJ 34 at 40.

55 (1995) ACSR 741; Sup Ct, NSW, 8 June 1995 per Hodgson J.

56 See for example *Hussein v Good* (1990) 8 ACLC 390.

57 *Leigh-Mardon Pty Ltd v Wawn* (1990) 17 ACSR 741.

renders it liable for a debt for which it otherwise would not have been liable".[58] This point in time will vary between different circumstances, and it will always be important to examine the terms of trade between the company and suppliers.[59] The saleability of the goods will always be a central factor in this examination. If the supplier can easily sell the goods elsewhere, it is more likely that the debt is incurred upon delivery of the goods. However, if the goods cannot readily be sold elsewhere, it is more likely that the debt is incurred upon placing the order for the goods.

As the packaging supplied contained Braha's artwork it was not readily saleable elsewhere. For this reason, the debt was incurred at the time the goods were ordered. Because at the time of ordering the packaging there were reasonable grounds to suspect that Braha would be unable to pay its debts as and when they fell due the plaintiff was successful.

[4.4.3] *STANDARD CHARTERED BANK V ANTICO*

Standard Chartered Bank v Antico[60] considered s 5 of the *Companies (NSW) Code* and s 556 of the *Companies (Qld) Code.*

Although this case dealt explicitly with the position of bill financing and interest under the insolvent trading provisions, the attempts of Hodgson J to formulate a unifying principle within the term "debt" warrants analysis.

In his article, Mosley comments that up until this decision "... various informal 'categories' of cases had developed and judges had tended to reason by analogy from one category to another".[61] With the categorisation of legal principles and definition of "debt" according to the type of transaction in question, numerous logical inconsistencies arose between cases. A prominent example of such inconsistency is the discrepancy between the cases dealing with contingent liabilities, particularly between *Hussein v Good* and *Hawkins v Bank of China*. The judicial approach has hindered the ability of business to achieve certainty in their business dealings.

To counter these deficiencies, Hodgson J attempted to formulate a unifying legal principle consistent with the existing thematic categories. This principle is:

> [A] company incurs a debt when by its choice, it does or omits something which, as a matter of substance and commercial reality, renders it liable for a debt for which it otherwise would not have been liable.[62]

58 (1990) 17 ACSR 741 at 749.

59 See J O'Donovan, "When Do Companies Incur Debt? Sooner Than You Think!" (1996) 14(2) CSLJ 120.

60 (1995) 131 ALR 1; Sup Ct, NSW, 9 August 1995 per Hodgson J.

61 J Mosley, "Insolvent Trading: What is a Debt and When is One Incurred?" (1996) 4(4) ILJ 155 at 167.

62 *Standard Chartered Bank v Antico* (1995) 131 ALR 1 at 57.

Hodgson saw this formulation as having three aspects that could cause difficulty in particular cases:[63]

(a) whether the company has a choice to do (or omit) the act or not;
(b) whether it is the act or omission, or something else, that renders the company liable for the debt; and
(c) whether the company would otherwise (in any event) have been liable for the debt.

It is this central principle and its three aspects that should be considered in determining whether or not a particular transaction constitutes a debt.

Hodgson J applied this principle to existing categories of legal principle, including leases, payroll tax and guarantees, and found that it is entirely consistent with existing principles.

[4.5] Interesting quotes

[4.5.1] CENTRAL DEFINITIONAL PRINCIPLE

Hodgson J espoused the central unifying principle for the definition of the term "debt" in *Standard Chartered Bank v Antico*:

> [A] company incurs a debt when, by its choice, it does or omits something which, as a matter of substance and commercial reality, renders it liable for a debt which it otherwise would not have been liable.[64]

This also highlights that at a fundamental level the company must commit a positive act to bring a debt into existence.

[4.5.2] "DEBT" TO BE INTERPRETED IN A FLEXIBLE AND COMMONSENSE FASHION CONSISTENT WITH COMMERCIAL REALITY

The need for "debt" to be interpreted in a flexible and commonsense manner consistent with commercial reality was emphasised by Gleeson CJ in *Hawkins v Bank of China*:

> The words 'incurs' and 'debts' are not words of precise and inflexible denotation. Where they appear … they are to be applied in a practical and commonsense fashion, consistent with the context and with the statutory purposes.[65]

63 (1995) 131 ALR 1 at 57.
64 *Standard Chartered Bank v Antico* (1995) 131 ALR 1 at 57.
65 *Hawkins v Bank of China* (1992) 10 ACLC 588 at 595.

[4.6] Loopholes/deficiencies

[4.6.1] POTENTIAL FOR LIMITED APPLICATION

Despite the enunciation of a unifying principle by Hodgson J in *Standard Chartered Bank v Antico*, a number of discrepancies exist between decisions which may result in a narrow definition of "debt" and a subsequent limited application of the insolvent trading provisions. Particularly problematic are the areas of contingent liabilities, including orders for the supply of goods, guarantees and leases.

[4.6.2] PROBLEMS WITH INCLUDING AND EXCLUDING CONTINGENT LIABILITIES

The Court in *Hawkins v Bank of China* decided that contingent liabilities are debts within the insolvent trading provisions and are incurred when the initial contract is entered into. This reversed the decision in *Hussein v Good* in relation to guarantees, but reiterated the decision in *Russell Halpern Nominees Pty Ltd v Martin* regarding leases.

A number of problems can arise whenever there is an interval of time between the initial entering into a contract and a stipulated event. As Noble has argued, these problems stem from the inability of the term "incurs a debt" to account for the wide range of fact situations that can arise under the insolvent trading provisions.[66] The inclusion of contingent liabilities means that creditors will suffer if the company orders goods when it is solvent but subsequently becomes unable to pay its debts. Conversely, creditors will also suffer if contingent liabilities are excluded for the provisions if a company orders goods whilst insolvent and is placed into liquidation before payment is made, and the creditor has incurred expense.[67]

The unifying principle of Hodgson J in *Standard Chartered Bank v Antico* provides little guidance as to the resolution of this deficiency. The application of this principle is consistent with the decision in *Hawkins v Bank of China* to include contingent liabilities as a debt incurred upon the initial contract of guarantee. It does not discuss of consider the unjust effects of such an inclusion.

[4.7] Checklist

[4.7.1] GENERAL CHECKLIST

Due to the judicial trend of categorising "debts" into the type of transaction involved and the almost infinite number of possible categories, the following is a

66 T Noble, "When Does a Company Incur a Debt Under the Insolvent Trading Provisions of the Corporations Law?" (1994) 12(5) CSLJ 297 at 302.

67 T Noble, "When Does a Company Incur a Debt Under the Insolvent Trading Provisions of the Corporations Law?" (1994) 12(5) CSLJ 297 at 302.

general checklist to assist in determining whether or not a debt has been incurred:

- Is the transaction for an ascertained sum of money?
- Has the company committed a positive act to bring the "debt" into existence?
- Does this positive act indicate the company's intention to be bound by the act or transaction?
- Does the company have a choice to do (or omit to do) the act?
- Is it the act (or omission) that renders the company liable for the debt?
- Would the company have been liable for the debt in any event?

[4.8] Proposals for law reform

It is submitted that there are a number of problems created by the term "incurs a debt". Most of these problems stem from the inability of this simple phrase to cover the wide variety of fact situations that can arise under the insolvent trading provisions. The judicial approach has traditionally been to categorise cases into the type of transaction in question. However, this has created inconsistencies within and between these categories and has failed to provide any definition certainty. It was for this reason that Hodgson J in *Standard Chartered Bank v Antico* attempted to formulate a unifying principle applicable to all types of transactions and consistent with the rationale and philosophy behind the decisions to date. Whilst this has provided a large degree of definitional certainty and guidance, it does not resolve some of the more specific inconsistencies in particular categories.

A fundamental hindrance to definitional certainty is the inability of Courts to make the policy judgments required by the section. Their lack of resources and ability only to deal with a few specific cases makes the development of a coherent policy almost impossible.

Although the wide term "incurs a debt" has been problematic, a precise and specific legislative definition may also be problematic because it will also fail to cover the wide variety of fact situations that can arise under the provisions. Arguably for this reason, statutory reform focusing on a precise definition of "debt" should not be encouraged. Any move in this direction may be inconsistent with the underlying need for flexibility and a commonsense application of the provisions.

The intervention of Parliament may be warranted in the resolution of specific definitional problem areas and inconsistencies. High on this list are the discrepancies between payroll tax and sales tax, and the difference in position between guarantees and leases.

PART B

The Duty to Prevent Insolvent Trading

PART B, *continued*

What Are Reasonable Grounds to Suspect Insolvency?

5

"... *[to suspect means] more than a mere idle wondering whether [something] exists or not; it is a positive feeling of actual apprehension or mistrust, amounting to a slight opinion, but without sufficient evidence.*"[1]

1 *Queensland Bacon Pty Ltd v Rees* (1966) 115 CLR 266 at 303 per Kitto J.

OBJECTIVES

This Chapter will:

- consider when a director may have "reasonable grounds" to suspect the insolvency of the company to which she or he is appointed;
- thoroughly analyse what could be considered as "reasonable grounds";
- discuss the difference between a suspicion and an expectation and the effect this has on the exposure of directors for the insolvent trading of his or her company.

[5.1] General overview

Subsections 588G(2) and (3) impose a duty on directors to prevent insolvent trading. A key element in establishing a breach of this duty is to prove that there were reasonable grounds for suspecting that the company was insolvent or would become insolvent by incurring the debt.

When it is proved that there was an awareness of reasonable grounds to suspect insolvency, the onus shifts to the director to prove that a contravention did not occur.

This element of liability has a number of elements.

[5.1.1] REASONABLE GROUNDS

The determination of what are "reasonable grounds" to suspect insolvency is central to the operation of the provisions. Reasonable grounds are assessed by the objective standard of a director of ordinary competence:

> ... [the test is] one of objectively reasonable grounds which must be judged by the standard appropriate to a director of ordinary competence ... Questions of knowledge of and participation in the incurring of the relevant debt are now relegated to the status of factual matters which may arise should the director seek to establish one of the statutory defences afforded by the legislation. The establishment of liability is therefore not contingent on elements personal to the respondents.[2]

The Court will determine what a reasonable director of ordinary competence would have done in the circumstances and then determine whether the actions or omissions of the particular director were reasonable in the circumstances. In this sense the test is an objective one.

However, it is not entirely clear whether the Courts will in practice take subjective factors into account in determining an objective standard. Arguably subjective factors such as the size and type of company will be relevant to the degree of competence which can be expected of a director of ordinary competence of that company. Although there are some professional company directors, there is no concrete objective standard to which ordinary company directors can aspire. In fact, the diversity of company structures, size, type and nature do not lend to a uniform standard. Arguably the standard of a director of ordinary competence varies according to the size, type and nature of each particular company as well as the particular experience which the director held herself or himself out as having upon appointment to that office.

2 *Metropolitan Fire Systems Pty Ltd v Miller* (1997) 23 ACSR 699 at 703 per Einfeld J.

[5.1.2] SUSPICION

The requirement of reasonable grounds to "suspect" differs from the requirements under the earlier insolvent trading provisions that required reasonable grounds to "expect". There is a great difference in meaning between the terms "suspect" and "expect".[3] To "suspect" has been described as:

> … more than a mere idle wondering whether [something] exists or not; it is a positive feeling of actual apprehension or mistrust, amounting to a 'slight opinion, but without sufficient evidence'.[4]

A suspicion of a fact creates a reason to look into or consider the possibility of the existence of the fact.

In contrast, to "expect" has been held to mean:

> … to anticipate the occurrence or the coming of an event which is more than a mere hope or possibility.[5]

In this sense, it implies a measure of confidence that something is expected to happen.[6]

[5.2] Philosophy/rationale

The lowering of the threshold for liability to a mere awareness of reasonable grounds to suspect insolvency is intended to increase the ambit of the insolvent trading provisions. The rationale behind the inclusion of "suspicion" is to increase the responsibility of directors for the overall financial management of the company. This change also brings the insolvent trading provisions in line with other duties imposed on directors, particularly the duty of care and diligence.

The ALRC set out the rationale for this change in emphasis as requiring a higher standard of care from directors.[7] This was clearly stated as follows:

> … the Commission intends that a rigorous standard be applied to directors. It is one thing to trade with shareholders' money. It is another thing to trade relying on the credit provided by third parties. Directors should be responsible for ensuring that the solvency of their company be monitored on a continuing basis. If they even suspect that the company may be trading while insolvent, they should

3 *3M Australia Pty Ltd v Kemish* (1986) 4 ACLC 185 at 192 per Foster J.

4 *Queensland Bacon Pty Ltd v Rees* (1966) 115 CLR 266 at 303 per Kitto J.

5 *3M Australia Pty Ltd v Kemish* (1986) 4 ACLC 185 at 192 per Foster J.

6 *Commonwealth Bank of Australia v Friedrich* (1991) 9 ACLC 946; *Dunn v Shapowloff* (1978) 3 ACLR 775.

7 ALRC, *General Insolvency Inquiry* Vol 1 (1988), para 287.

examine its affairs closely to ensure that there are reasonable grounds to expect that it will be able to pay its debts.[8]

[5.3] History/former law

Elements of suspicion have been central to the insolvent trading provisions developed over the last few decades. The element of suspicion is of recent import, with incorporation into the test for contravention only with the introduction of s 588G. Prior to this, the test was based on grounds of expectation, rather than suspicion.

[5.3.1] EARLY CASES – OBJECTIVE

The first provision to include these mental elements in the test for contravention was s 303(3) of the *Companies Act* 1961–1971 (Cth), which was later repealed and replaced by s 374(c). Section 303(3) based contravention on "no reasonable or probable grounds of expectation". The construction of this section was considered in *Dunn v Shapowloff*.[9] Mahoney JA stated:

> For the offence to be proved, it must appear that the officer had no reasonable or probable ground of expectation, after taking into consideration the other liabilities, if any, of the company at the time, of the company being able to pay the debt. The subsection refers not merely to expectation, but to a ground of expectation … If subjectively, he had an expectation that the company would be able to pay the debt, he would still be open to conviction if there were no such grounds in existence objectively. Correspondingly, if he had subjective expectation that the company would not be able to pay the debt, I am inclined to think that the effect of the word 'had' is that the fact that, unknown to him, there was a reasonable or probable ground of expectation, would not prevent his being convicted. If the proper conclusion be that what Mr Shapowloff did was to be concerned in the company contracting the debt not caring whether it would be able to pay it or not, he would, in my opinion, still be open to conviction if it appeared the objectively there was no such ground of expectation.

In this way, the early cases held that liability was to be assessed by determining whether there were objectively reasonable grounds to expect solvency, looking at all the facts known to the director at the time of contracting the debt. These circumstances were then examined to see if they suggested a reasonable or probable ability of the company to pay its debts.[10]

8 ALRC, *General Insolvency Inquiry* Vol 1 (1988), para 304.
9 (1978) 3 ACLR 775.
10 *Shapowloff v Dunn* (1981) 148 CLR 72 at 87.

This formulation of liability was carried over into the new provisions under s 556(1) of the *Companies Code*, as recognised in *3M Australia Pty Ltd v Kemish*.[11] Foster J recognised that there were some differences between s 303(3) and s 556(1), particularly the new blend of civil and criminal liability under s 556(1). Foster J established that reasonable grounds to expect solvency are reasonable grounds according to the standards of a director or manager of ordinary competence. His Honour held that the term "expect" is very different to "suspect", and that to expect "goes beyond a mere hope or possibility".[12] In addition, Foster J decided that the relevant time to assess awareness is immediately before the incurring of the relevant debt in order to eliminate any sense of hindsight.[13]

[5.3.2] LATER CASES – INTERPRETED IN LIGHT OF OTHER DUTIES

This test of reasonable grounds for expectation increasingly became more onerous as more cases were decided under s 556(1). In *Statewide Tobacco Services Ltd v Morley*,[14] Ormiston J decided that s 556(1) could not be considered in isolation but had to be looked at in the context of the whole range of directors duties, particularly the duty of care and diligence.[15] His Honour concluded that directors must stay well informed of company affairs in order to avoid breaching the insolvent trading provisions.

The heavy burden placed on directors as a result of this interpretation well acknowledged by Ormiston J:

> It is thus apparent that in enacting the present section, the legislation has deliberately sought to impose a heavier burden on directors and other officers of companies that happen to become insolvent. In my opinion, it is part of a consistent legislative pattern over recent years, whereby the duties and obligations of directors and company officers have been increased and made more onerous.[16]

This increasingly onerous statutory interpretation prevailed with the introduction of s 592(1) of the Law. Subsection 592(1) affirmed that the test for contravention was whether there were "reasonable grounds to expect that the company [would] be able to pay all its debts as and when they become due".[17] In *Commonwealth Bank of Australia v Friedrich*,[18] Tadgell J accepted that the duty

11 (1986) 4 ACLC 185.
12 (1986) 4 ACLC 185 at 192.
13 (1986) 4 ACLC 185 at 192.
14 (1990) 2 ACSR 405.
15 (1990) 2 ACSR 405 at 412.
16 (1990) 2 ACSR 405 at 413.
17 Section 592(1)(b)(i).
18 (1991) 9 ACLC 946.

to prevent insolvent trading must be interpreted in the context of all of the duties and obligations imposed on company directors:

> To speak of a director of ordinary, reasonable or average competence or prudence, or indeed of an ordinary reasonable or average director, is to give no very useful description, whereas a person seeking properly to perform the duties of a director of a particular company can be identified by reference to more specific criteria of which ordinariness, reasonableness and averageness are, or may be, merely ingredients ... I reject the view that the duties imposed by law upon a director are not relevant as a whole for the purpose of considering whether there are reasonable grounds ...[19]

Accordingly, the Court was directed to look at the insolvent trading provisions as a whole.

[5.3.3] SUSPICION

Despite the intention of Parliament, creditors bore a heavy onus in proving a case under s 592(1). As a result of the heavy onus on the plaintiff, few cases were brought under the insolvent trading provisions. This heavy onus and the high cost of litigation were criticised by many commentators.[20] As a result of this pressure, the ALRC concluded that the test for contravention should be changed to a mere "suspicion" of insolvency:

> If they even suspect that the company may be trading while insolvent, they should examine its affairs closely to ensure that there are reasonable grounds to expect that it will be able to pay its debts.[21]

This recommendation was put into effect with the introduction of s 588G. The change from "expectation" to "suspicion" was clearly intended to increase the responsibility of directors for the financial affairs of their company and to make it easier for creditors to sue on the basis of insolvent trading.

[5.4] Notable cases

[5.4.1] *METROPOLITAN FIRE SYSTEMS PTY LTD V MILLER*

Metropolitan Fire Systems Pty Ltd v Miller[22] was the first authoritative case to deal with s 588G. It is particularly important for its comments on the operation of the term "reasonable grounds to suspect" insolvency.

19 (1991) 9 ACLC 946 at 955.

20 A Herzberg, "Insolvent Trading" (1991) 9 CSLJ 285; A Herzberg, "The Metal Manufacturers Case and the Australian Law Reform Commission's Insolvent Trading Recommendations" (1989) 7(3)

The facts of the case are simple. Raydar was an electrical contractor. In December 1993 it agreed to do work for another company called Reed. A director of Raydar, Miller, organised for Metropolitan to do some of the work for Reed as a subcontractor. In 1994 Miller gave assurances to Metropolitan that it would be paid for the work because Raydar was shortly expecting payment from Reed. This assurance was given despite the fact that by December 1993 Raydar was in debt to another company who had applied to the Supreme Court in late 1993 for Raydar to be wound up. Metropolitan commenced proceedings against Miller under s 588G.

The Court decided that at the time Raydar incurred the debt to Metropolitan it was insolvent. It also decided that at that time there were reasonable grounds to suspect that Raydar was insolvent. Einfeld J held that the test for deciding whether reasonable grounds existed was:

> ... one of objectively reasonable grounds which must be judged by the standard appropriate to a director of ordinary competence.[23]

In this way, reasonable grounds are to be assessed according to the standard expected of a director of reasonable competence. A director of reasonable competence is likely to have some knowledge and understanding of financial reports and audit reports and general skills in financial management and strategic decision-making.

[5.5] Checklists

[5.5.1] CHECKLIST – REASONABLE GROUNDS

It has already been shown that what are considered "reasonable grounds" to suspect insolvency are judged by the standards appropriate to a director of ordinary competence. Although special skills and qualifications held by an individual director are not relevant in this determination, a director must ensure that he or she possess the necessary skills and information of an ordinary director. Without these, a director may trigger the insolvent trading provisions.

When seeking to establish liability under the insolvent trading provisions, an insolvency practitioner should assess whether the relevant director:

- is informed of the general affairs of the company;

CSLJ 177; J Dabner, "Trading Whilst Insolvent – A Case for Individual Creditors Rights Against Directors" (1994) 17 UNSWLJ 547; R Baxt, "Limited Liability for Directors Who Do Not Authorise the Incurring of Debts" (1988) 16 ABLR 390.

21 ALRC, *General Insolvency Inquiry* (1988), para 304. See also para 287.

22 *Metropolitan Fire Systems v Miller* (1997) 23 ACSR 699. FCA, 22 May 1997 per Einfeld J.

23 *Metropolitan Fire Systems v Miller* (1997) 23 ACSR 699 at 703 per Einfeld J.

- is informed about the financial affairs of the company;
- regularly monitors the general affairs of the company and its financial affairs;
- seeks up-to-date information as to the affairs of the company on a continuing basis;
- keeps an up-to-date valuation of the company's assets and main debtors and creditors;
- has general competence in reading and understanding financial and audit reports;
- meets or corresponds with the company accountants and auditors on a regular basis.

[5.5.2] CHECKLIST – SUSPICION

Directors are required to have foresight of their company's possible insolvency on the basis of suspicion. A suspicion amounts to a "positive feeling of apprehension or mistrust".

An insolvency practitioner seeking to establish liability under the insolvent trading provisions should assess whether the director:[24]

- is regularly informed of the general affairs of the company;
- is regularly informed of the financial affairs of the company;
- keeps an up-to-date valuation of the company's assets and its main debtors and creditors;
- closely monitors debts that are incurred by the company;
- personally assesses the ability of the company to pay its debts as and when they fall due whenever a debt is incurred;
- seeks professional advice regarding the ability of the company to pay its debts as and when they fall due whenever their personal assessment indicates a potential problem or inability to pay;
- if insolvency is suspected, prevents the debt from being incurred;
- if insolvency is suspected, notifies the board of their suspicion;
- if this suspicion is made clear to the board, ensures accurate minutes are taken of the board meeting.

[5.6] Loopholes/deficiencies

A number of deficiencies have been identified in the "reasonable grounds to suspect" test.

A number of commentators have questioned the utility of the formulation as a whole. Dabner asserts that this test for liability promotes a risk adverse

24 See N Coburn, *Insolvent Trading: A Practical Guide* (John Libbey & Co, Sydney, 1998), p 131.

corporate culture that is ultimately detrimental to the entrepreneurial spirit.[25] The Victorian Bar Council argued that the term "suspect" is not a commercial term and that directors should not be required to make important business decisions on the basis of mere suspicion.[26] For this reason Pollard claims that this formulation is one element of the insolvent trading provisions that may not increase certainty for directors.[27]

Austin has argued that the test introduces particular problems for directors of holding companies as the test effectively places directors of holding companies in the same position as the subsidiaries, requiring vigilant monitoring of the subsidiary by the holding company particularly where the principal operating company is the subsidiary.[28] This argument is effectively quashed by the introduction of s 187 that allows directors of wholly-owned subsidiaries to take the interests of the holding company into account without breaching the rule against conflict of interests.

Although it cannot be said that this formulation may not present difficulties, it is acknowledged as a great improvement on the formulation under s 592 as it increases the ambit of the insolvent trading provisions. The assertion that the formulation dampens entrepreneurial spirit is questionable.

25 J Dabner, "Trading Whilst Insolvent – A Case for Individual Creditor Rights Against Directors" (1993) 17(2) UNSWLJ 562.

26 Submission 195, ALRC, *General Insolvency Inquiry* Vol 1 (1988), para 287.

27 S M Pollard, "Fear and Loathing in the Boardroom: Directors Confront the New Insolvent Trading Provisions" (1994) 22(6) ABLR 392 at 399.

28 R P Austin, "The Corporate Law Reform Bill – Its Effect on Liability of Holding Companies for Debts of Insolvent Subsidiaries" March 1996 (5) *Butterworths Corporation Law Bulletin* 65 at 68.

What Constitutes a Failure to Prevent the Company Incurring a Debt?

6

"*The law recognises companies as separate legal entities. Companies necessarily conduct their affairs through their directors, who assume no liability for the transaction which they conduct as agents for their companies. However, where the actions of a company's directors contribute significantly to its insolvency, creditors who face the prospect of receiving no payment or part payment of their debts on insolvency may have a legitimate grievance, particularly when the directors have taken risks relying on credit given by others. This has been recognised by the legislature, which has enacted provisions in an attempt to make company directors liable for the debts of the company where the business of the company has been conducted fraudulently or without due regard to the ability of the company to pay its debts.*"[1]

1 ALRC, *General Insolvency Inquiry* Report No 45, Vol 1 (1988), para 322.

OBJECTIVES

This Chapter will:

- consider the general circumstances in which a director may be held to have failed to prevent the company incurring a debt;
- analyse the level of awareness required of a director who may be the subject of an insolvent trading action.

[6.1] General overview

The Law imposes a positive duty on directors to prevent insolvent trading. The centre of this duty lies in s 588G(2) and (3). Under these sections, failure to prevent the company incurring a debt whilst it is insolvent is specified to have both civil and criminal consequences.

Under s 588G(2) where a director fails to prevent the company incurring the debt and he or she was aware that there were reasonable grounds for suspecting insolvency, or a reasonable person in their position in the company's circumstances would have been so aware, a civil penalty may be imposed.

Section 588G(3) outlines when a breach of the insolvent trading provisions will constitute a criminal offence. A person will commit an offence under the insolvent trading provisions where:

- the person is a director of the company when it incurs a debt; and
- the company is insolvent at that time, or becomes insolvent by incurring that debt, or by incurring at that time debts including that debt; and
- the person suspected at the time when the company incurred the debt that the company was insolvent or would become insolvent as a result of incurring that debt or other debts; and
- the person's failure to prevent the company incurring the debt was dishonest.

Breach of these sections also gives rise to the ability for the liquidator or creditors to seek compensation directly from the director: see Div 4, Pt 5.7B.

A number of elements of these subsections must be examined including the required level of awareness and the meaning of dishonesty.

[6.1.1] AWARENESS

Section 588G(2) states that there are two distinct tests for determining the level of awareness of possible insolvency required by a director before that section is contravened. The two tests are divided into a subjective (s 588G(2)(a)) and an objective limb: s 588G(2)(b). Accordingly, a director contravenes s 588G(2) if at the relevant time the director was aware, or should have been aware, that there were reasonable grounds to suspect that the company was insolvent.

Under s 588G(3) actual subjective awareness must be established. This is due to the additional requirement of a dishonest intent under s 588G(3)(d). A dishonest intent can only be formed where there is an actual awareness of reasonable grounds for suspecting insolvency.

(a) Section 588G(2)(a) – subjective awareness

Although s 588G(2)(a) states that a director contravenes the insolvent trading provisions if they were aware of grounds for suspecting insolvency, this does not mean that a director must in actual fact know of the company's possible or impending insolvency. All that is required is to show that the director was actually aware that reasonable grounds existed for suspecting insolvency.

The subjective component will require the Court to look at the actual state of mind of the director at the relevant time. It has been asserted that the inclusion of this element of awareness helps to ensure that a realistic standard is imposed on directors.[2]

(b) Section 588G(2)(b) – objective awareness

If it cannot be established that the director had actual awareness of reasonable grounds for suspecting insolvency, contravention of the insolvent trading provisions can also result if the director should have been aware that there were reasonable grounds for suspecting insolvency. Accordingly, the Court will determine whether a reasonable person in a like position in a company in the company's circumstances would have been so aware.

On a general level, the model reasonable person would be able to read and understand in general terms the company's accounts and auditor's report.[3] However, the inclusion of the term "in a like position in a company in the company's circumstances" allows the Court to have regard to a wide range of factors, including:[4]

- the size of the company;
- the type of business conducted by the company;
- the composition of the board;
- whether the director was an executive or non-executive director;
- the delegation of functions and responsibilities between directors;
- the distribution of work between board members and management;
- professional qualifications and special expertise held by the director.

The discretion and latitude available to the Court is obvious and allows the Court to alter the objective test in light of subjective factors.[5]

This objective component clearly recognises the differences between executive and non-executive directors through the inclusion of the term "in a like position". A higher onus is placed on executive directors to remain informed of the state of solvency and the general financial affairs of the company than non-executive directors.

---

2 R Langford, "The New Statutory Business Judgment Rule: Should it Apply to the Duty to Prevent Insolvent Trading?" (1998) 16(7) CSLJ 533 at 550.

3 *Commonwealth Bank of Australia v Friedrich* (1991) 9 ACLC 946.

4 See *Commonwealth Bank of Australia v Friedrich* (1991) 9 ACLC 946.

5 See S Worthington, "Liability for Insolvent Trading: Routes and Rules in Reform" (1992) 10(3) CSLJ 214.

This objective component is directly related to the duty of care and diligence imposed on directors, because directors will need to exercise due care and diligence.

[6.1.2] TIME TO ASSESS AWARENESS

The time that the awareness of the director is assessed is immediately before the particular debt was incurred.[6] This eliminates all sense of hindsight.

[6.1.3] DISHONESTY

Liability under s 588G(3), the criminal offence provision, can only be established if the director's failure to prevent the company incurring the debt was dishonest. Dishonesty is not defined within the Law. Generally, an act is done dishonestly where it is done with the knowledge that it will produce adverse consequences.[7] "Dishonesty" is likely to mean an intentional, willed, or deliberate act.[8] It is likely to involve an element of deceit or fraud. In this way, a reasonable but mistaken director would not be at risk under s 588G(3).

[6.2] Philosophy/rationale

The rationale for imposing a duty on directors to prevent insolvent trading is that it is assumed that this is the best method to protect unsecured creditors and avoid insolvent trading. This was summarised in the Harmer Report:

> The law recognises companies as separate legal entities. Companies necessarily conduct their affairs through their directors, who assume no liability for the transaction which they conduct as agents for their companies. However, where the actions of a company's directors contribute significantly to its insolvency, creditors who face the prospect of receiving no payment or part payment of their debts on insolvency may have a legitimate grievance, particularly when the directors have taken risks relying on credit given by others. This has been recognised by the legislature, which has enacted provisions in an attempt to make company directors liable for the debts of the company where the business of the company has been conducted fraudulently or without due regard to the ability of the company to pay its debts. In addition, there are several provisions under which a director may be disqualified. It has not been suggested to the Commission that directors should not be accountable for irresponsible behaviour, particularly where it affects creditors of the company.[9]

6 *Metropolitan Fire Systems Pty Ltd v Miller* (1997) 23 ACSR 699.
7 *R v Bonollo* [1981] VR 633.
8 See *Chew v R* (1991) 173 CLR 626.
9 ALRC, *General Insolvency Inquiry* Report No 45, Vol 1 (1988), para 272.

[6.3] History/former law

The duty to prevent insolvent trading has been a feature of statutory regulation since the 1960s.

Prior to the duty in its current form within the Law, various statutes imposed a duty to prevent insolvent trading, including s 303 of the *Companies Act* 1961 (Cth) and s 592 of the Law. These initial duties were built on the recognition of the large detrimental effect insolvent trading was having on the Australian economy.

Section 592 differs from the current s 588G in a number of ways. Briefly, the threshold for liability was changed from an expectation of solvency to a mere suspicion of insolvency and the defences were clarified.[10]

Prior to the introduction of s 588G, a breach of the duty to prevent insolvent trading under s 592(1) could give rise to both civil and criminal sanctions. This was criticised in the Harmer Report who recommended that only civil sanctions apply. They argued that criminal sanctions were deemed unnecessary because:[11]

- criminal sanctions are not appropriate for something that can occur as a result of mere negligence;
- civil liability provided a sufficient sanction and incentive for directors to avoid insolvent trading; and
- civil liability consequences are more directly capable of benefiting unsecured creditors of a company.

This recommendation was implemented and, until recently, breach of the duty of insolvent trading under s 588G directly gave rise to civil sanctions. However, under the old s 1317FA, where a contravention was done knowingly, intentionally, or recklessly and either dishonestly or fraudulently, a criminal sanction could be imposed.

The retention of criminal liability only where an act was done with the requisite criminal intent was designed to penalise the most serious breaches of the insolvent trading provisions. However, the mental elements in s 1317FA were confusing. In order to clarify when a breach of the insolvent trading provisions would constitute a criminal offence, the current s 588G(3) was introduced by the *Corporate Law Economic Reform Act* 1999 (Cth). This clearly stipulates that a criminal offence will be committed where the failure to prevent the company incurring the debt was done dishonestly.

10 See The Parliament of the Commonwealth of Australia, *Corporate Law Reform Act 1992: Explanatory Memorandum*, paras 1084–1087.

11 See The Parliament of the Commonwealth of Australia, *Corporate Law Reform Act 1992: Explanatory Memorandum*, para 1087. See ALRC, *General Insolvency Inquiry* Report No 45, Vol 1 (1988), para 322.

[6.4] Notable cases

Two cases provide an interesting judicial analysis of the existence of reasonable grounds to suspect insolvency.

[6.4.1] *QUICK V STOLAND PTY LTD*

Quick v Stoland Pty Ltd[12] considered s 588G of the *Corporations Law*.

In this case the Court considered the circumstances in which directors ought to be aware that their company may be trading while insolvent.

A creditor sued a previous director of the relevant company under the insolvent trading provisions to recover debts which had been incurred by the company to the creditor.

In examining whether there were reasonable grounds for the director to suspect that the company may be insolvent at the time the relevant debts were incurred, Finkelstein J considered company correspondence as indicators of such reasonable grounds and to determine whether the company would be able to pay its debts as and when they fell due. Three pieces of company correspondence were instrumental in this regard. The first was a letter written to a trade creditor stating that the company would not be able to pay the debt it owed other than to provide the creditor with an item of equipment as a partial discharge of the debt. The second was a letter to a creditor which stated "we regret to advise you that we are unable to pay this debt at this time due to unforeseen circumstances that have put pressure on our ability to meet our liabilities. If there should be a change in our position, we will advise you accordingly, however the immediate future appears extremely clouded". The third was a letter to the ANZ Bank which stated that the company was only able to continue trading with the assistance of the Bank's overdraft facility.

Finkelstein J held that such correspondence was particularly important in an assessment of the solvency of the company. His Honour said that in this regard it was more valuable than financial records. On the basis of this company correspondence, he had no difficulty in finding that there were reasonable grounds for the director to suspect that the company was insolvent when it incurred the debts to the creditor or may become insolvent by incurring the debts.

[6.4.2] *CREDIT CORP PTY LTD V ATKINS*

Credit Corp Pty Ltd v Atkins[13] considered s 592 of the *Corporations Law*.

In this case the Court considered circumstances in which a passive director may have reasonable grounds to suspect the insolvency of the company. Mr and Mrs Atkins were the only two directors of the company. The couple divorced and

12 (1998) 29 ACSR 130; Fed Ct, Aust, 25 September 1998 per Branson, Emmett and Finkelstein JJ.
13 (1999) 17 ACLC 756; Fed Ct, Aust, 31 March 1999 per O'Loughlin J.

lived in different towns in South Australia. In order to fulfil a contract Mr Atkins purchased expensive equipment. This was conveyed to Mrs Atkins who said that this was not a concern to her. There were a number of factors which suggested that at the time this debt was incurred the company was insolvent. These included the severe lack of income derived by the company between contracts, the need for a regular preparation of a list of outstanding creditors, the company's inability to pay its small income tax payment for one financial year, and the admission by Mr Atkins that the company did not have the funds to pay a number of creditors.

Mrs Atkins submitted that she did not have reasonable grounds to suspect the insolvency of the company. She argued that she knew very little of the company's operations and believed at all relevant times that the company was, and would remain, solvent. She pointed to the distance between herself and her estranged husband as support for her argument that she was not aware of the financial circumstances of the company, as well as the fact that she had put her house at risk in support of the company's purchase of the equipment.

The Court held that Mrs Atkins was never actively involved in the incurring of a debt by the company. However, she did have reasonable grounds to suspect that the company was insolvent or would become so by purchasing the equipment. In particular, at the time the relevant debts were incurred she met with the company's accountant and was presented with a list of the outstanding creditors of the company. Accordingly, she could not deny that she was aware of the possible insolvency of the company at the time it incurred the debts. Although she was not actively involved in the day-to-day management of the company, she had reasonable grounds to suspect that it was insolvent at the time it purchased the equipment.

[6.5] Interesting quotes

[6.5.1] TIME FOR ASSESSING AWARENESS

Foster J in *3M Australia Pty Ltd v Kemish* confirmed that the time for assessing suspicion and awareness is immediately before the relevant debt was incurred in order to eliminate any sense of hindsight:[14]

> Clearly, if some event occurred after the incurring of the subject debt, which produced the situation of the company's inability to pay all its debts, but which was, at the relevant time, beyond the limits of reasonable foreseeability, then such an event could not form part of the 'reasonable grounds' envisaged by this

14 *3M Australia Pty Ltd v Kemish* (1986) 4 ACLC 185.

> section. Conversely, if the happening of such a future event were reasonably foreseeable at the relevant time, by a director or manager of reasonable competence, it would form part of the 'reasonable grounds'. Equally, the fact that a person can look back to the financial situation of the company at the time when the subject debt was incurred, and express the view that the relevant 'reasonable grounds' to expect then existed, does not mean that some impermissible operation of 'hindsight' is taking place, provided that in expressing that view, the person is doing no more than evaluating facts which were or should have been known to the defendant at the time of the incurring of the debt. Consequently, the evidence of an appropriate expert, reviewing the situation as it obtained at the time when the relevant debt was incurred, is both admissible and helpful in determining whether objectively 'reasonable grounds' did or did not exist at that time.[15]

[6.6] Checklist

Awareness of reasonable grounds to suspect insolvency is assessed both subjectively and objectively. The legislature has provided written guidelines for directors and the Courts to consider whether directors have acted reasonably in assessing grounds of possible insolvency.[16] These should be of benefit to insolvency practitioners in assessing the reasonableness of a director's assessment of solvency:

- Directors of a large company should ensure that among their number there should be one or more who are talented in the field of corporate financial management.
- Directors of a large company should read, be able to understand and seek any necessary clarification of the key financial information put before the Board, such as a balance sheet and a profit and loss statement.
- The Board should ensure that appropriately skilled people are engaged to carry out the company's accounting functions.
- The Board should require relevant accounting information to be supplied ahead of regular Board meetings at which key financial decisions are to be made, and that, where a significant borrowing is to be undertaken, the management should supply the Board with a statement of the company's current financial position as well as the particulars of the way in which the principle, interest and other charges are to be serviced over the anticipated term of the loan.

15 *3M Australia Pty Ltd v Kemish* (1986) 4 ACLC 185 at 192 per Foster J.
16 Corporate Law Reform Bill 1992, *Public Exposure Draft and Explanatory Paper* (1992), para 1229.

- The Board should make arrangements for monitoring the use of any authorisation granted in relation to the use of the company seal, the entering into contracts with financiers or the signing of cheques and bills of exchange.
- Where the nature of the business may expose the company to a high risk of sudden liquidity restriction, or the company is known by the director to be in a delicate financial position, extra care and more rigorous safeguards may need to be adopted.

Quite clearly, directors of all companies must keep informed of the general and financial affairs of the company.

[6.7] Loopholes/deficiencies/tricks/hints

A number of weaknesses in the wording of the duty to prevent insolvent trading have been advanced.

Pollard has questioned the efficacy of the phrase "By failing to prevent" in s 588G(2), arguing that it has no connection to the following phrase "the person contravenes this section if ...".[17] He argues that this phrase may need to be removed as it contradicts the defence under s 588H(5) where protection is available where the director took all reasonable steps to prevent the company from incurring the debt.

Coburn has questioned the need for s 588G(2)(a) to be included within the formulation for contravention, arguing that its subjective component is virtually superfluous in light of the ability of the court to consider subjective factors under the objective component contained in s 588G(2)(b).[18] However, Pollard argues that the subjective limb is essential as it makes clear to directors the need to be capable of understanding the significance of financial accounts.[19]

[6.8] Proposals for law reform

In order to clarify the availability and utility of the defence under s 588H(5), where a director took all reasonable steps to prevent the incurring of the relevant debt, it may be useful to delete the phrase "By failing to prevent" from s 588G(2). This phrase does indeed seem superfluous as liability is clearly imposed by the phrase "the person contravenes this section if". For the purposes of

17 S M Pollard, "Fear and Loathing in the Boardroom: Directors Confront New Insolvent Trading Provisions" (1994) 22(6) ABLR 399 at 399–400.

18 N Coburn, *Insolvent Trading: A Practical Guide* (John Libbey & Co, Sydney, 1998), p 48.

19 S M Pollard, "Fear and Loathing in the Boardroom: Directors Confront New Insolvent Trading Provisions" (1994) 22(6) ABLR 399 at 400.

clarity, the reference to "By failing to prevent" should be removed from s 588G(2). It has already been excluded from the ambit of s 588G(3).

Coburn has argued that the subjective awareness test contained in s 588G(2)(a) is made redundant by the Court's ability to take subjective factors into account under the objective awareness test in s 588G(2)(b). However, his suggestion that the subjective test in s 588G(2)(a) should be removed must be rejected. Pollard argues that the inclusion of the subjective limb makes the compliance requirements clear and thus minimises the risk of contravention for directors.[20] In this way, he argues that its inclusion is of benefit to those directors who do ensure that adequate compliance systems are in place and who delegate tasks and responsibilities, thus enhancing the reliability of the "reasonable reliance" defence under s 588H(3). The inclusion of s 588G(2)(a) is important in clarifying the need for directors to ensure that they are suitably qualified for the tasks and responsibilities they must fulfil and to reassert the need for adequate delegation, communication and compliance systems to this end.

20 S M Pollard, "Fear and Loathing in the Boardroom: Directors Confront New Insolvent Trading Provisions" (1994) 22(6) ABLR 399 at 400.

Making a Holding Company Liable

"*One of the recurring features of recent company failures in Australia and overseas has been the use of complex group structures to conceal the flow of funds within the group and to subvert directors' duties. These structures have been used to disguise asset stripping and to prolong insolvent trading.*"[1]

"*... [the separate entity principle] operated unfairly where the business activity of a company had been directed or controlled by a related company. It is as though the related company was acting as a 'director' of the other company and causing it to incur debts and liabilities.*"[2]

1 J O'Donovan, "Group Therapies for Group Insolvencies", in M Gillooly, *The Law Relating to Corporate Groups* (Federation Press, Sydney, 1993), p 46.
2 ALRC, *General Insolvency Inquiry* Vol 1 (1988), para 334.

OBJECTIVES

This Chapter will:

- consider the definition of a holding company and the utility and appropriateness of this definition;
- outline the elements of liability for a holding company to be held liable for the insolvency trading of it's subsidiary;
- discuss the defences available to a holding company;
- compare and contrast the elements of liability and defences available to a holding company for insolvent trading and those for other types of directors;
- consider recent proposals to introduce pooling of group assets and contribution orders.

[7.1] General overview

[7.1.1] ELEMENTS OF LIABILITY

Holding companies are exposed to liability for the insolvent trading of their subsidiaries. As a result the ability of a holding company to completely guarantee liability in a subsidiary has been curtailed.

The elements of liability establishing contravention by a holding company under s 588V parallels those for directors contained in s 588G.

Section 588V provides that a holding company contravenes the Law if:

- it was the holding company of a subsidiary at the time when the subsidiary incurred a debt; and
- that debt caused, or was incurred during, the insolvency of the subsidiary; and
- there were reasonable grounds to suspect that the subsidiary was insolvent or would become insolvent by incurring that debt, or any other debt at that time; and either
- the holding company or any of its directors was aware of reasonable grounds for suspecting the subsidiary's insolvency; or
- having regard to the nature of the holding company's control over the subsidiary, it was reasonable to expect that a holding company in the circumstances of the holding company, or any of its directors, ought to have been aware of those grounds for suspicion.

A holding company that contravenes this section is not guilty of an offence (s 588V(2)) but may be liable for compensation equal to the amount of loss or damage.

It is significant that the section refers to "corporations" and not just "companies". A government parent corporation may be found liable under the provisions unless it is an "exempt public authority" and outside the definition of a "corporation" under s 9 of the Law.

(a) Definition of holding company

Under s 46, the holding company – subsidiary relationship is formed when where a body corporate:

(a) controls the board composition of another body corporate;
(b) controls at least 51 per cent of the voting power of another body corporate;
(c) holds at least 51 per cent of the share capital of another body corporate; or
(d) is a subsidiary of a subsidiary of another body corporate.

In this way, it is a test of majority power. In brief, a holding company/subsidiary relationship is formed where one entity holds at least 51 per cent of the issued share capital in another entity, or "controls" it.

(b) Insolvency

The meaning of insolvency under s 95A of the Law has already been analysed in Ch 2.

(c) Reasonable grounds to suspect

As discussed earlier, case law indicates that to "suspect" requires:

> ...more than a mere idle wondering whether [something] exists or not; it is a positive feeling of actual apprehension or mistrust, amounting to a slight opinion, but without sufficient evidence.[3]

In this sense "suspecting" is synonymous with predictability[4] and is a good reason to consider or look into the possibility of the existence of the fact. Accordingly, the meaning of "suspect" within s 588V(1)(c) implies the need for a holding company, or any relevant director, to form the impression that the subsidiary in question may be insolvent within the meaning of s 95A of the Law.

Case law on s 592 suggest a number of factors that the Court will consider when assessing reasonable grounds to suspect including.[5]

- factors or commercial considerations supporting the belief of solvency;[6]
- the holding company's expectation of potential revenue of the subsidiary that might have been available to it;[7]
- the subsidiary's ability to service debt;[8] and
- a prediction of the ability of the subsidiary to pay its debts.[9]

The ALRC hoped that the inclusion of the term "reasonable grounds to suspect" would lead directors of holding companies to act on their suspicions rather than expectations and that consequently they would be more rigorous in their monitoring of the company's financial affairs.[10]

(d) Awareness of reasonable grounds for suspicion

An element of liability is that there must have been reasonable ground for either the holding company, or at least one director of the holding company, to suspect

---

3 *Queensland Bacon Pty Ltd v Rees* (1966) 115 CLR 266 at 303 in relation to s 122(1) of the *Bankruptcy Act* 1966 (Cth).

4 *3M Australia Pty Ltd v Kemish* (1986) 4 ACLC 185.

5 See N Coburn, *Insolvent Trading: A Practical Guide* (John Libbey, Sydney, 1998), p 112.

6 *Standard Chartered Bank v Antico* (1995) 18 ACSR 1; *Commonwealth Bank of Australia v Friedrich* (1991) 9 ACLC 946; *State Tobacco Services Pty Ltd v Morley* (1990) 2 ACSR 405; *Carrier Air Conditioning Pty Ltd v Kurda* (1993) 11 ACSR 115.

7 *TNT Channel Nine v Scotney* (1995) 17 ACSR 116.

8 *International Business Strategies Pty Ltd v Lucas* (1995) 17 ACSR 269.

9 *Australian Securities Commission v MR Lawless & SL Lawless* (unreported, Magistrates Ct, Tasmania, 19 December 1995).

10 ALRC, *General Insolvency Inquiry* Vol 1 (1988), para 287 and 288.

that the holding company was, or may become, insolvent. This can be established by one of two means.

Subsection 588V(1)(d)(i) is subjective and requires the Court to consider whether the holding company, or at least one director of the holding company, was in actual fact aware of reasonable grounds for suspecting insolvency.

In contrast, s 588V(1)(d)(ii) is objective and requires the Court to consider whether a holding company in the holding company's circumstances and having regard to the nature and extent of the holding company's control over the subsidiary's affairs, or at least one director of such a holding company, would have been so aware.

The requirement that only one director of the holding company is aware, or should be aware, of the subsidiary's insolvency in order to attract liability is quite a harsh and stringent threshold. The elements of reasonable grounds for suspecting insolvency by an individual director were outlined in Ch 5 at para [5.1].

However, the elements of proving awareness of actual suspected insolvency, or reasonable grounds for so suspecting, by a holding company itself are quite different to those involved for proving an individual director, or natural person. A company is an abstraction and cannot do anything of its own accord. Rather, it is dependant upon the actions and activities of its directors. Accordingly, directors have traditionally been regarded as the "directing mind and will" of a company.

In this way corporate knowledge, including actual knowledge of awareness of grounds for suspecting the insolvency or possible insolvency of its subsidiary, is often imputed to its directors. Accordingly, in fulfilling this element of liability the knowledge of the individual directors of the holding company will often be relevant. There will often be a substantial overlap between the knowledge of a director of the holding company and the holding company itself.

However, there is a growing body of literature regarding corporate knowledge irrespective of the knowledge of a company's constituent directors. Most of this literature is focused on the general "corporate culture" within a company and is intended to take cognisance of the complex nature of corporate decision-making, the sometimes diffuse nature of delegation and responsibility within companies and the entire corporate structure.

For example, the *Corporate Criminal Act* 1995 (Cth) under which a body corporate may be found guilty of any criminal offence, including one punishable by imprisonment. The fact that the company could not physically commit the offence is irrelevant. A physical element of an offence can be committed by any employee or agent of the company regardless of seniority and is directly attributable to the company. Most significantly, the fault element of an offence can be attributed to the Board, a high managerial agent, or a corporate culture within the company which directed, tolerated or encouraged non-compliance.[11]

In the context of s 588V(1)(d), this notion of corporate knowledge suggests that a Court may take the overall corporate culture of a holding company into account in determining liability for the insolvent trading of its subsidiary. This "corporate culture" may include elements such as the nature and extent of reporting requirements between the subsidiary and the holding company, the nature of the relationship between the subsidiary and holding company and the general control of the subsidiary's affairs by the holding company. As noted below in, the acknowledgment by the legislature that such factors can be taken into account in determining liability under s 588V(1)(d) suggests that the corporate culture of a holding company may assist in proving subjective or objective knowledge of the insolvency, or possible insolvency, of it's subsidiary.

[7.1.2] FACTORS THE COURT WILL CONSIDER WHEN DETERMINING IF THE ELEMENTS OF LIABILITY HAVE BEEN ESTABLISHED

When determining whether the elements of liability have been established, the Court is likely to have regard to the following factors:[12]

- the nature of the relationship between the holding company and subsidiary;
- reporting arrangements;
- the nature of the enterprise carried on by the subsidiary;
- the extent to which the day-to-day activities are controlled by the subsidiary;
- the relevant skill of the holding company's directors to perform their functions; and
- the behaviour of the board in establishing mechanisms for the monitoring and control of both the holding company and of the subsidiary.

[7.1.3] RECOVERY PROCEEDINGS

If a holding company has contravened s 588V, under s 588W the liquidator of the subsidiary may recover from the holding company, as a debt due to the subsidiary, an amount equal to the amount of loss or damage suffered if:

- the holding company has contravened s 588V in relation to the incurring of a debt by the subsidiary;
- the person to whom the debt is owed has suffered loss or damage in relation to the debt because of the subsidiary's insolvency;
- the debt was wholly or partially unsecured when the loss or damage was suffered; and
- the subsidiary is being wound up.

Proceedings by the liquidator must be commenced within six years of the commencement of the winding-up of the subsidiary: s 588W(2).

11 For commentary on this Act, see T Woolf, "The Criminal Code Act 1995 (Cth) – Towards a Realistic Vision of Corporate Criminal Liability" (1997) 21(5) *Criminal Law Journal* 257; and D Andrew, "The New Commonwealth Criminal Code" (1995) 69(9) *Law Institute Journal* 908.

12 Australian Commonwealth Government, *Corporate Law Reform Bill 1992: Draft Legislation and Explanatory Paper* (1992), para 1274.

[7.1.4] APPLICATION OF COMPENSATION

Section 588Y restricts the application of recovery compensation. It provides that the amount paid to a subsidiary is not available to pay a secured debt of the subsidiary unless its unsecured debts have been paid in full. This gives priority to unsecured debts in the application of compensation recovered from the holding company.

This is based on the recommendation by the ALRC that compensation be disposed in this way, as unsecured creditors are most likely to feel the impact of insolvency.[13] This is commensurate with Ramsey's assertion that secured creditors are more efficient bearers of risk than unsecured creditors because of their ability to avoid the risk at a lower cost.[14]

[7.1.5] DEFENCES

The legislation provides statutory defences to a holding company to escape liability. These defences are contained in s 588X and are essentially identical to those contained in s 588H.

Section 588X protects the holding company and the relevant director in the following circumstances:

- when the debt was incurred by the subsidiary, the holding company and each relevant director of the holding company (if any) had reasonable grounds to expect, and did expect, that the subsidiary was solvent at that time and would remain solvent even if it incurred that debt and any other debts that it incurred at that time (s 588X(2));
- at the relevant time that the debt was incurred by the subsidiary, the holding company and each relevant director of the holding company (if any) had reasonable grounds to believe, and did believe, that a competent and reliable person was providing adequate information to the holding company about whether the subsidiary was solvent, and that the person was fulfilling that responsibility (s 588X(3);
- the relevant director of the holding company did not take part in the management of the company at the time the debt was incurred due to illness or for some other good reason, and thus the fact that they were aware under s 588V(1)(a)(i) is disregarded (s 588X(4);
- if the holding company took all reasonable steps to prevent the subsidiary incurring the debt: s 588X(5).

Although the equivalent defences under s 588H are relevant to a consideration of the defences under s 588X, a number of distinguishing features in relation to holding companies must be considered.

13 ALRC, *General Insolvency Inquiry* (1988), para 320.

14 I M Ramsey, "Holding Company Liability for the Debts of an Insolvent Subsidiary: A Law and Economics Perspective" (1994) 17(2) UNSWLR 521 at 541.

In relation to the first defence under s 588X(2), the company and any relevant director must prove that they expected on reasonable grounds that the subsidiary was solvent and would remain solvent even if it incurred that debt or any other debt at that time. However, the burden placed on holding companies is greater than that placed on subsidiaries or other corporations. This is because it will be more difficult for a director of a holding company to obtain the necessary information and to initiate appropriate actions to prevent the subsidiary from incurring the debt. This will be particularly true where there are a number of subsidiaries within the corporate group.

The directors of the holding company must make relevant inquiries and they cannot be content to rely on a mere periodic monitoring of the subsidiary. They must put themselves in a position where they have a sound understanding of the financial affairs of the subsidiary. To this end, they may wish to seek independent financial advice in relation to transactions undertaken by the subsidiary that may cause it to become insolvent.[15]

The s 588X(2) defence is also stringent because it requires *each director* of the holding company to have reasonable grounds to expect and to prove that they did in fact expect, that the subsidiary was and would remain solvent. Liability can be established under s 588V if only *one director* had reasonable grounds to suspect that the subsidiary would not remain solvent. This is an extremely high standard.

The second defence is based on reasonable "delegation and reliance". This defence under s 588X(3) has two limbs, each of which must be satisfied.

The first limb of the "delegation and reliance" defence requires the company or relevant director to establish their belief in the existence of a proper and adequate system for managing and monitoring the financial status and solvency of the subsidiary. It also requires a belief that the delegate responsible for these matters was continuing to fulfil that responsibility. These beliefs must be based on reasonable grounds.

The focus of this limb is not on ascertaining whether the delegate is in fact competent and reliable, but that the director actually believed on reasonable grounds that this was the case. It is not clear what inquiries should be made of a delegate's competence or reliability.

In this way, the section encourages the holding company and its directors to establish a proper system of financial monitoring of the subsidiary.

The second limb under the "delegation and reliance" defence requires the corporation and any relevant director to prove that they expected that the subsidiary was solvent at the time the debt was incurred. This expectation must be a result of relying on information regarding the solvency of the subsidiary provided by the delegate.

15 *Standard Chartered Bank v Antico* (1995) 18 ACSR 1 at 17.

The third defence under s 588X(4) has already been shown in relation to s 588H(4) to be very wide. Apart from the fact that a causal connection must be made between the good reason and non-participation, few parameters of the defence have been explored.[16]

Finally, s 588X(5) provides a defence where reasonable steps have been taken to prevent insolvency. This clearly includes action taken by the holding company to appoint an administrator to the subsidiary, when that action was taken, and the results of that action: s 588H(6).

[7.1.6] WHEN IS A HOLDING COMPANY A "DIRECTOR" OF A SUBSIDIARY?

A holding company can, in certain circumstances, be considered the director of one or more of its subsidiaries and thus be held directly liable under s 588G.[17] This is a result of the extended definition of a director contained in s 9 to include any person in accordance with whose directions or instructions the directors of the subsidiary are accustomed to act. This reflects commercial practice in which a holding company may have significant control over the internal affairs of its subsidiaries. To avoid liability under s 588G, holding companies should ensure that their affairs are not too closely connected with the affairs of their subsidiaries. However, this advice may be difficult, if not impossible, to apply in practice.

There are differences between the causes of action under s 588G and s 588V. In particular, to bring a successful action under s 588G it must be proved that the subsidiary acted on the instructions or wishes of the holding company, which may be difficult to prove in practice particularly in the absence of clearly identifiable instructions. However, if bringing proceedings under s 588V a litigant would only need to prove that at least one director of the holding company was aware, or had reasonable grounds for suspecting, that the subsidiary was insolvent or may become insolvent. In order to qualify for the defence under s 588X(2) the holding company would need to prove that every director of the holding company had reasonable grounds to expect, and did expect, that the company was and would remain solvent. This imposes a high standard on holding companies and as only the knowledge of one relevant director is required may provide a good basis for brining an action for insolvent trading. In contrast, s 588G requires proof that "a director" had reasonable grounds for suspecting the insolvency, or possible insolvency, of the subsidiary. The use of the phrase "a director" in relation to a holding company indicates that it is likely that the knowledge of more than one director will be required, and may in fact require corporate knowledge of the holding company per se.

16 S M Pollard, "Fear and Loathing in the Boardroom: Directors Confront New Insolvent Trading Provisions" (1994) 22(6) ABLR 399 at 408.

17 *Standard Chartered Bank v Antico* (1995) 18 ACSR 1.

For these reasons it may often be easier to bring an action for insolvent trading against the holding company of a subsidiary under s 588V rather than s 588G. However, in most cases it may be appropriate to plead s 588V and s 588G in the alternative.

[7.2] Philosophy/rationale

[7.2.1] *SEPARATE ENTITY V ENTERPRISE THEORY*

The imposition of liability on a holding company for the insolvent trading of its subsidiary indicates a shift away from separate entity theory in Australian corporate jurisprudence.

Separate entity theory views a corporation as a juridical person with rights and duties "... separate from those of the persons who may from time to time be its shareholders".[18] Within a corporate group context this means that each corporation is regarded as a separate legal entity and consequently "... the group's debts are allocated separately to each corporation in the group, on the basis that each debt is incurred by a separate entity".[19]

Separate entity law has been the historical foundation for company law in Australia. The traditional reluctance of the Courts to disregard separate entity theory is reflected in landmark decisions. In *Industrial Equity Ltd v Blackburn*[20] the High Court held that the profits of subsidiaries are not the profits of the holding company because of their control of general meetings that determine the distribution of these profits. Similarly, Mason J in *Walker v Wimborne*[21] emphasised that the law relating to directors' duties has historically been based on the separate entity theory:

> ... the emphasis given by the primary judge to the circumstances that the group derived a benefit from the transaction tended to obscure the fundamental principles that each of the companies was a separate and independent legal entity, and that it was the duty of the directors of Asiatic to consult its interests and its interests alone in deciding whether payment should be made to other companies.[22]

In *Re Austcorp Tiles Pty Ltd*[23] the Court refused to depart from the separate entity theory to allow a liquidator to distribute funds held by them to creditors of three

18 R P Austin, "Problems for Directors Within Corporate Groups" in M Gillooly (ed), *The Law Relating to Corporate Groups* (Federation Press, Sydney, 1993), p 133.
19 R P Austin, "Problems for Directors Within Corporate Groups" in M Gillooly (ed), *The Law Relating to Corporate Groups* (Federation Press, Sydney, 1993), p 133.
20 (1977) 137 CLR 567.
21 *Walker v Wimborne* (1976) 137 CLR 1.
22 *Walker v Wimborne* (1976) 137 CLR 1 at 7.
23 (1992) 10 ACLC 62.

companies when it was unclear what proportions of these funds were the actual assets of which companies. Such a situation resulted from the fact that the group consisted of four companies but held only one bank account to which all income was deposited and all debts paid out of, leading to uncertainty about which company owned the group's assets.

However, the separate entity theory is falling into disrepute in many sectors of the legal, business and judicial community with the enterprise theory of corporate groups often being preferred. In contrast to separate entity theory, enterprise theory acknowledges the economic unity of a corporate group. It treats group debts as belonging to the group rather than being allocated to a part of that group.

Strong calls have been made within Australia for the jurisprudential adoption of enterprise theory.

However, the Companies and Securities Advisory Committee (CASAC) has warned that the Courts must be careful in applying single enterprise theory and to accommodate the organisational complexities in such an application.[24] In their words:

> If applied inflexibly, they may expose a parent company to full liability for all the groups' debts, even where group governance is decentralised and particular group companies exercise considerable autonomy. They may also encourage managers to structure the group in a highly hierarchical and centralised manner, even where this is inefficient, to reduce the parent's financial exposure. Also, the recovery rights of unsecured creditors of parent companies would be exposed to the financial risks of all the group's activities. At the same time, creditors of controlled group companies could gain a windfall from the parent company providing, in effect, a form of liability insurance against any defaults by its group companies.

With such concerns in mind, the need for the law to reflect the realities of corporate groups,[25] as recognised by enterprise theory, has been embraced in Australia through the introduction of s 588V. By imposing liability on a holding company for the insolvent trading of its subsidiary where the holding company, or a relevant director of the holding company, knew that the subsidiary was insolvent, the law reflects the realities of corporate groups where holding companies often exercise substantial control and influence over the decisions and actions of its subsidiaries. Similarly, the ability of wholly owned subsidiaries to take the interests of its holding company into account in acting in its own best interests

24 CASAC, *Corporate Groups: Final Report* (May 2000), para 1.64.

25 See J Scott, "Corporate Groups and Network Structure" in J McCahery, S Picciotto and C Scott, *Corporate Control and Accountability: Changing Structures and the Dynamics of Regulation* (Oxford University Press, Oxford, 1993), p 291: "Our theories of how businesses operate must recognise the reality of corporate groups and a whole range of inter-corporate relations".

is a recognition of the enterprise nature of many corporate groups. In addition to these legislative developments, the Courts appear to be moving more towards a recognition of the enterprise nature of corporate groups. This was most recently emphasised in *Re Switch Telecommunications Pty Ltd (in liq)*[26] which is discussed below at para [7.4.1].

In this way, s 588V and other provisions within the Law are embracing the shift from separate entity to enterprise theory within Australian corporate jurisprudence.

[7.3] History/former law

The separate entity principle has traditionally shielded a holding company from liability for the debts of its insolvent subsidiary. This principle has upheld the separate legal personality of each company within a corporate group and has prevented access to the assets of the holding company to cover debts incurred by an insolvent subsidiary.

The injustices caused by the entity theory of corporate law began to be embraced by the judiciary in the late 1970s[27] and by the mid-1980s Australian Courts were expressing dissatisfaction with the conflict between commercial reality and the strict application of corporate law.[28] In relation to the previous position at common law, Rogers AJA highlighted the unsatisfactory position as follows:

> ... as the law presently stands, in my view the proposition advanced by the plaintiff that the corporate veil may be pierced where one company exercises complete dominion and control over another is entirely too simplistic. The law pays scant regard to the commercial reality that every holding company has the potential and, more often than not, does, exercise complete control over a subsidiary.[29]

The ability of subsidiaries to shield their holding companies from liability for their insolvency became a recurring problem on the Australian corporate landscape in the 1980s. This loophole in corporate law was exposed in a number of high profile cases including the collapse of the Qintex, Adelaide Steamship and Bond groups of companies. This led to substantial injustice where creditors had to sue undercapitalised subsidiaries or were not sure who to sue when they had

26 (2000) 35 ACSR 172 per Santow J.

27 *Walker v Wimborne* (1975) 137 CLR 1 per Mason J; and *Re Southard and Co Ltd* [1979] 1 WLR 1198 at 1208 per Templeman LJ.

28 See *Qintex Australia Finance Ltd v Schroders Australia Ltd* (1990) 3 ASCR 267; and *Briggs v James Hardie & Co Pty Ltd* (1989) 7 ACLC 841.

29 *Briggs v James Hardie & Co Pty Ltd* (1989) 7 ACLC 841 at 862 per Rogers AJA.

been dealing with the company as a whole.[30] Once the Australian legislature realised that the entity theory of corporate law had little relevance to commercial reality they looked for a different approach to corporate groups. The enterprise theory of corporate law is one such approach.

By the mid-1980s, the Australian legislature had commenced a wide-scale study of insolvency laws in Australia. The ALRC reiterated judicial sentiment towards the injustices caused by the separate entity principle:

> ... [the separate entity principle] operated unfairly where the business activity of a company had been directed or controlled by a related company. It is as though the related company was acting as a 'director' of the other company and causing it to incur debts and liabilities.[31]

The ALRC recommended changes to the separate entity principle, calling for liability for the insolvent trading of a subsidiary to be imposed not just on a holding company but on any "related company". This was expressed in para 335 of the Harmer Report which set down three criteria to which the Court could have regard when determining whether or not it would be just to impose such liability. Paragraph 335 states:

> [It is proposed] to give the court a wide discretion to order that a company is or has been a related company pay the liquidator all or part of an amount which is an admissible claim in the winding up 'if it is satisfied that it is just'. Three specific criteria to which it [is] proposed the court may have regard [are]:
>
> - the extent to which the related company took part in the management of the company;
> - the conduct of the related company towards the creditors of the company; and
> - the extent to which the circumstances that gave rise to the winding up of the company are attributable to the actions of the related company.

Clearly, the rationale behind the recommendations of the Harmer Report was that in many corporate groups the holding company effectively controls the subsidiary and is like a de facto director and should be held liable in the same way as a director for debts incurred whilst the company is insolvent.[32]

The recommendations were supported by a number of submissions including the Queensland Law Society and the Commonwealth Department of Public

30 See *Qintex Australia Finance Ltd v Schroders Australia Ltd* (1990) 3 ASCR 267; and *Re Lonhro (No 3)* [1989] BCLC 480.

31 ALRC, *General Insolvency Inquiry* (1988), para 334.

32 See J Rogers, unpublished commentary, *Corporate Groups Conference*, 12 June 1992, Murdoch University, Western Australia.

Prosecutions. However, the Law Council of Australia opposed the recommendations on a number of grounds.[33] The first of these was the significance of the separate entity principle as a cornerstone of Australian corporate jurisprudence. The Law Council of Australia also argued that it would not be possible for a parent company to satisfy itself that it would not be liable for the debts of subsidiary where projects are financed on a limited recourse basis. Added to these concerns were fears of general commercial uncertainty and problems for auditors and company directors in producing accounts representing a true and fair view of a parent company. These arguments were rejected by the ALRC which asserted that these claims were unjustified as liability would only arise where the subsidiary was or became insolvent, and that accounting difficulties and general uncertainty were not sufficiently serious to deter the imposition of liability on a parent company.[34]

Clearly, whilst the thrust of the ALRC's recommendations were adopted by the legislature and incorporated into the Law, the resultant legislative amendments were significantly narrower than the ALRC's recommendations through its focus on holding company liability rather than related company liability. Section 588V, effective from 23 June 1993, has no effect on related companies which are not holding companies of an insolvent subsidiary as defined in s 46 of the Law.

More recently, CASAC has published its Final Report on corporate groups. This Final Report considered, amongst other things, a number of issues including the nature of corporate groups, appropriate definitions of corporate groups, alternative methods of regulation of corporate groups and a number of issues relating to directors of group companies. The recommendations of CASAC are discussed below, where relevant.

[7.4] Recent cases

[7.4.1] *RE SWITCH TELECOMMUNICATIONS PTY LIMITED (IN LIQ)*

Re Switch Telecommunications Pty Ltd (in liq)[35] considered ss 447, 449, 510 and 1322 of the *Corporations Law*.

In this case the Supreme Court of New South Wales considered the possibility of pooling assets of two related companies in liquidation. Although not strictly relevant to liability imposed on a holding company for the insolvent trading of it's subsidiary, the case is relevant to an assessment of the increasing

33 ALRC, *General Insolvency Inquiry* (1988), para 336.
34 ALRC, *General Insolvency Inquiry* (1988), para 336.
35 (2000) 35 ACSR 172; Sup Ct, NSW, 10 August 2000 per Santow J.

propensity of Courts towards the enterprise theory of corporate groups and the possible consequences this may have for future regulation of corporate groups.

Two related companies, Switch Telecommunications Pty Limited and Switch Operators Pty Limited, were both in voluntary liquidation after a period of external administration. The creditors of both companies had approved a deed for the pooling of the assets of both companies and the liquidator of each company approached the court for orders to facilitate the deed under s 511 of the Law. The orders were uncontested and sought all necessary for the combination of the assets of the two companies for realisation and distribution to the creditors of each of the two companies.

The liquidators submitted that the affairs of the two companies were so intermingled as to render it impractical to keep the affairs of each company separate during liquidation. Two alternative options were presented to the court as the basis on which the orders sought could be made. The first was approaching the Court under the s 479(3) ability of the liquidator to apply to the court for directions during a winding-up and seeking the Court to make a pooling order under s 447A of the Law. Such an order would provide a basis on which the liquidators could seek a Court-approved compromise or arrangement with creditors under s 477(1)(c) and s 477(2A) of the Law. The second was for the Court to issue orders under s 510 of the Law which would facilitate an arrangement between the company and the creditors, which would be sanctioned by a special resolution of the company and a resolution of the creditors.

Santow J refused to utilise the s 447A approach, preferring the leave such a possibility to cases where there are no other possible alternatives available.

However, Santow J held that poling orders could be made under s 510 of the Law. This option was, in the opinion of Santow J, an attractive alternative as it had the advantage of being binding on non-voting creditors, minority dissident creditors and contributories if the appropriate resolutions are passed. In his Honour's review of Australian case law regarding s 510 of the Law, Santow J noted a number of principles including the need for non-voting or dissident creditors to either consent to the arrangement or be pari passu with the voting creditors in order for the arrangement to be binding on them. Santow J also noted that the term "arrangement" is quite broad and is likely to include many bona fide proposals including compromises. Santow J also stated that s 510 of the Law applies only to voluntary liquidations.

However, Santow J considered that s 510 may be problematic where it is impossible to clearly determine the creditors of each company, despite the fact that it may be obvious that the creditor was a creditor of one company or the other. In any event, this problem could be overcome by a remedial order under s 1322(4) of the Law allowing the combined meeting of creditors of both companies to be treated as a meeting of each company and thus satisfying the requirements of s 510(10(b) of the Law. However Santow J also stated that it remains to be seen whether, in the case of a minor dissenting creditor, s 1322(4) of the Law could be used to permit such voting in combination.

The pooling arrangement was approved by the Court as it had been properly considered and sanctioned by the creditors and contributories of each company. According to Santow J, the use of s 510 and remedial orders under s 1322(4) of the Law provided the safest course for those seeking pooling orders.

[7.5] Checklist

[7.5.1] A HOLDING COMPANY'S CHECKLIST – PREVENTING LIABILITY

In order to minimise the risk of liability being imposed on a holding company under s 588V, holding companies and their directors should ensure that their subsidiaries act appropriately and do not engage in insolvent trading. To achieve this goal holding companies and their directors could adopt steps such as the following:

- Ensure the holding company has adequate systems for financial monitoring of the other group companies.
- Ensure that competent and reliable delegates are responsible for the oversight of this financial monitoring.
- Ensure all delegates are suitably qualified.
- Ensure all delegates have an appropriate amount of work to complete. Workloads should not be too onerous.
- Ensure all delegates have reasonable and appropriate time limits placed on them for the completion of work.
- Ensure that there is an excellent communication network established between the delegates and the board of directors, the Chairman and other relevant directors.
- Consider allocating an executive director to formally liaise with the delegates responsible for financial oversight on a weekly or fortnightly basis.
- Ensure that the directors of all related companies, especially subsidiaries, independently evaluate any directions or advice provided by the holding company before implementation.
- If a subsidiary may be facing financial difficulties, ensure that prompt investigation of the financial affairs is conducted by the holding company.
- If a subsidiary may be insolvent, ensure that it does not incur any substantial debts without the prior approval of the board of directors of the holding company.
- If insolvency may be impending, promptly appoint a suitably qualified independent professional adviser to investigate the financial situation and provide advice.

- If a related company, especially a subsidiary, appears to be insolvent promptly consider the appointment of an administrator.
- Since the knowledge or suspicion of one director is all that is needed to establish liability, make sure that directors know this and keep the Board fully informed about what is going on within the company.

[7.5.2] A HOLDING COMPANY CHECKLIST – WHEN PROCEEDINGS HAVE BEEN COMMENCED UNDER SECTION 588V

When an insolvency practitioner is seeking to establish liability on a holding company for the insolvent trading of its subsidiary, he or she should consult the following:

- Does the holding company control the board composition of the subsidiary? Does the holding company have a legally enforceable right in this regard?
- Does the holding company control at least 51 per cent of the voting power of the subsidiary?
- Does the holding company hold at least 51 per cent of the share capital of the subsidiary?
- Is the subsidiary insolvent within the meaning of s 95A of the Law?
- At the time the debt was incurred by the subsidiary, were there reasonable grounds to suspect that it was insolvent?
- What is the nature of the relationship between the holding company and the subsidiary?
- Are there adequate financial reporting systems in place?
- Has the board implemented adequate systems for monitoring the holding company and the subsidiary?
- What is the nature of the business carried on by the holding company?
- What is the nature of the business carried on by the subsidiary?
- What sort of control does the holding company have over the day-to-day management of the subsidiary?
- Do the directors of the subsidiary always act on directions or advice from the holding company without any real independent evaluation?
- If the holding company thought that the subsidiary was solvent at the time it incurred the debt, did the holding company expect that the subsidiary would remain solvent even if it incurred this debt? Why was this opinion formed? Are there any records or documents supporting this opinion?
- Did the holding company initiate any action to prevent the subsidiary incurring the debt?
- Had the function of monitoring the financial solvency of the subsidiary been delegated?
- What sort of delegation system was in place?

- Did the holding company and its Board of directors periodically review the performance of these delegates?
- What was the required level of care the delegates were required to exercise in monitoring the financial solvency of the subsidiary?
- Were the delegates required to produce work of a high standard?
- Were the delegates suitably qualified for the tasks they were performing?
- How much work were the delegates required to complete? What time limits were imposed on the delegates for completing this workload?
- Did the holding company rely on information from the delegates in assessing the solvency of the subsidiary?
- Did the director of the holding company take part in the management of the holding company at the time the subsidiary incurred the debt?
- Was the director of the holding company absent from performing by duties in the holding company at the time the subsidiary incurred the debt? Why was the director absent? If the director was ill, do have records from a reliable source to prove this?
- Did the holding company take all reasonable steps to prevent the subsidiary from incurring the debt?
- Did the holding company take any action to appoint an administrator to the subsidiary? When was that action taken and what were the results of that action?

[7.6] Loopholes/deficiencies and proposals for law reform

[7.6.1] REPLACING THE HOLDING COMPANY/ SUBSIDIARY RELATIONSHIP DEFINITION WITH A WIDER TEST OF "CONTROL"

The Law does not specifically define corporate groups. The notion of a "corporate group" is essentially an umbrella concept which covers a wide range of relationships and forms of economic organisation. The Law does contain two, quite divergent, concepts of a corporate group. The first of these is the holding company and subsidiary concept and the second is not concept of parent companies and controlled entities.

The s 46 test of the holding company/subsidiary relationship is essentially one of majority power where the relationship will be established when one body corporate holds at least 51 per cent of the issued share capital of another body corporate, or "controls" that body corporate. Under s 50 of the Law, holding companies, their subsidiaries and related bodies corporate form a corporate group.

However, somewhat broader tests for corporate groups are applied by the Law and the Australian Accounting Standards for particular purposes. Australian Accounting Standard AASB 1024 defines control as:

> ... the capacity of an entity to dominate decision-making, directly or indirectly, in relation to the financial and operating policies of another entity so as to enable that other entity to operate with it in pursuing the objectives of the controlling entity.[36]

Under this definition, control of one body corporate by another body corporate is not determined by the legal form of the relationship between the two entities but rather by the nature and substance of the relationship. According to CASAC:

> This emphasis on substance ensures that the test [of control] applies to all entities whose financial and operating policies are being dominated by the parent company.[37]

The commentary which accompanies AASB 1024 indicates a number of factors which would usually indicate control by one body corporate over another body corporate. These include:

- the capacity to dominate the composition of the board of directors or governing board of the second entity;
- the capacity to appoint or remove all or a majority of the directors or governing members of the second entity;
- the capacity to control the casting of a majority of the votes cast at a meeting of the board of directors or the governing board of the second entity;
- the capacity to cast, or regulate the casting of, a majority of votes that are likely to be cast at a general meeting of the second entity, irrespective of whether the capacity is held through shares or options.
- the existence of a statute, agreement, trust deed or any other scheme, arrangement or device which, in substance, gives an entity the capacity to enjoy the majority of the benefits and to be exposed to the majority of the risks of the second entity, notwithstanding that control may appear to be vested in another party.

Section 50AA of the Law also sets out a definition of control. Similarly to AASB 1024, s 50AA is concerned with the practical influence which one entity may

---

36 Under AASB 1024, "capacity" is defined to mean ability or power, whether direct or indirect, and includes ability or power that is presently exercisable as a result of, by means of, in breach of, or by revocation of, or any of or any combination of trusts, relevant agreement and practices, whether or not enforceable.

37 CASAC, *Corporate Groups: Final Report* (May 2000), para 1.20.

exert over another entity and the fact that such control was not actively exercised is not determinative. In this sense, the tests encompass a degree of de facto control which is not envisaged by the holding company/subsidiary definition contained in s 46 of the Law.

CASAC has recommended that the s 46 holding company/subsidiary definition be repealed and that the s 50AA definition of control apply throughout the Law, including in relation to the potential liability of a holding company for the insolvent trading of its subsidiary by virtue of s 588V.[38] In the view of CASAC:

> A control test focuses on real power and influence, rather than on the sometimes more formal criteria in the holding/subsidiary tests.[39]

If a control test is applied throughout the Law, such a test should be the same throughout the Law. If this were otherwise, a collection of companies could be treated as a corporate group for some purposes but not others and would be likely to cause significant uncertainty for companies. However, is it really necessary to effect this change?

The existing s 46 holding company/subsidiary definition may have contributed to a number of complex corporate group restructurings and the frustration of unsecured creditors who are prevented from using measures, such as the insolvent trading provisions, to recover some of the debt due to them. Through the mechanism of complex group structures, many corporate groups have been able to organise their business structures to avoid establishing a holding company/subsidiary relationship. Sometimes complex networks of cross-shareholdings of shares marginally below the requisite 50 per cent level may led to effective but non-legal "control" of the group by a small number of directors or one body corporate within the group. In light of the language employed by s 588V, none of the companies in such groups would be in a legal holding company/subsidiary relationship and thus would not be held accountable under the insolvent trading provisions unless sufficient "control" was exercised.

Consequently, if a holding company owns under 51 per cent of the issued share capital in a subsidiary, and effective "control" cannot be identified, in itself a concept marred by an incomplete definition and difficult to prove, liability under s 588V will not be incurred despite the fact that the group in question may in fact carry on business as a group rather than as a collection of constituent individual companies. This may produce substantial injustice for many creditors dealing with corporate groups.

However, there are some arguments against the inclusion of a pervasive definition of "control" throughout the Law. In situations where unsecured creditors

38 CASAC, *Corporate Groups: Final Report* (May 2000), p 15 [Recommendation 1].

39 CASAC, *Corporate Groups: Final Report* (May 2000), para 1.41.

are frustrated as a result of complex cross-shareholdings amongst group companies, it is arguable that disgruntled creditors could bring an action against a holding company as a shadow director of the subsidiary, using the s 9 definition of "director" and the s 588G insolvent trading provisions. As outlined above in para [7.1.1], creditors can bring alternative actions against a holding company for the insolvent trading of its subsidiary under the insolvent trading provisions of either s 588V or s 588G. However, as discussed in para [7.1.6], it may often be easier for creditors to bring an action under s 588V rather than under s 588G. As discussed in para [7.1.6], although s 588G encompasses the s 9 definition of a director, the use of the term "a director" in s 588G in relation to a holding company suggests that either corporate knowledge generally must be proved or the knowledge of more than one director be so proved. This is likely to prove difficult in practice. However, it is possible to argue that the availability of proceedings against a holding company as a shadow director of its insolvent subsidiary precludes the need to import a wider definition of "control" within the Law.

A further problem which could result from applying the s 50AA test of "control" in the context of holding company liability for the insolvent trading of its subsidiary is that it could create uncertainty for companies as they might find themselves liable for the insolvent trading of another group company which they did not consider themselves liable for, given the subjective nature of the control test. This is because there may be in practice a degree of uncertainty about when "control" exists.

It is also possible that, in the context of insolvent trading, the inclusion of a "control" test similar to that contained in s 50AA of the Law may result in more than one group company becoming liable for the insolvent trading of another group company because it is theoretically possible for more than one group company to control another group company.[40] However, in the words of CASAC:

> Presumably, if a control test were adopted for insolvent trading, all the controlling group companies could be held to be jointly and severally liable in the insolvency of a controlled group company, subject to one or more of the controlling group companies establishing a defence, as provided by [s 588X of the] *Corporations Law*.[41]

Despite these possible shortcomings, the intention of the legislature in enacting the insolvent trading provisions was clearly to protect the interests of unsecured creditors. In particular, the rationale of providing protection against insolvent trading to creditors dealing with corporate groups, was stated by the ALRC to be prevent an unfair operation of the separate entity principle.[42] The current s 46

40 See CASAC, *Corporate Groups: Final Report* (May 2000), para 1.29.
41 CASAC, *Corporate Groups: Final Report* (May 2000), para 1.29.
42 ALRC, *General Insolvency Inquiry* Vol 1 (1988), para 334.

holding company/subsidiary definition as it applies to s 588V may be frustrating the legislature's intention. CASAC's recommendation has yet to be considered by the legislature, however this general legislative intention may result in moves towards a general control test throughout the Law, or at least in relation to s 588V, in the future.

[7.6.2] CONTRIBUTION ORDERS AND POOLING OF GROUP ASSETS DURING LIQUIDATION

Two other possible avenues for reform in the context of liquidation of group companies are contribution orders and the pooling of group assets.

Australia currently has no equivalent of contribution orders. Under a contribution order a group company not being wound up is required to contribute specific funds to cover some or all of the debts of another group company in liquidation. Such orders are available in New Zealand under s 271(1)(a) of the New Zealand *Companies Act* 1993 (NZ). Under the New Zealand legislation, an application for a contribution order can be made by a liquidator, creditor or shareholder of the company in liquidation. However, similarly to the Australian insolvent trading provisions, any such payment made under a contribution order is paid directly to the company to meet the company's debts as a whole rather than being paid to a particular creditor or shareholder.[43] Before it makes a contribution order, a New Zealand court must be satisfied that it is just and equitable to make such an order. The matters which are taken into account include the nature and extent of any intermingled management between the companies in question, the conduct of the related company to the creditors of the company in liquidation, whether the actions of the related body corporate gave rise to the liquidation of the company in liquidation and any other matter the court thinks fit to consider.[44] According to CASAC, the Courts of New Zealand have not often exercised their contribution order power, often as a result of the difficulty involved in reconciling the interests of the two sets of unsecured creditors who have dealt with the two companies separately.[45]

The 1988 Harmer Report by the ALRC recommended the introduction of a general contribution order power into the Law. This recommendation was ultimately not adopted, however the legislature did introduce s 588V in relation to the possible liability of a holding company in relation to the insolvent trading of its subsidiary. Submissions to the ALRC and CASAC raised a number of problems with the introduction of general contribution order provisions.[46] One of the main concerns was that such a provision would provide a broad discretion to

43 Section 271(1)(a) of the *Companies Act* 1993 (NZ).
44 Section 272(1) of the *Companies Act* 1993 (NZ).
45 CASAC, *Corporate Groups: Final Report* (May 2000), para 6.38.
46 See ALRC, *General Insolvency Inquiry* Vol 1 (1988), para 336; and CASAC, Corporate Groups: Final Report (May 2000), paras 6.42-6.44 and para 6.50.

Courts and consequently create a great uncertainty for external lenders to corporate groups. In particular, external lenders would find it impossible to determine the extent of one group company's liabilities because the Court could subsequently order it to pay any or all of one of its related company's debts if such a company is in liquidation. This concern led the legislature to reject the general contribution order proposals.[47] Similar sentiments have led CASAC to reject any suggestions of the need to include a general contribution order provision in the Law.[48] CASAC has also rejected the need for a limited contribution order provision, such as in the case of protecting the interests of employees if their employer goes into liquidation, based on the proposals, and recent amendment to the Law, with regards to employee entitlements. These reforms are discussed in Ch 19 at para [19.1.3].

Pooling orders permit the assets and liabilities of two or more group companies in liquidation to be merged. A pooling order gives the Court a broad equitable power to "... require a contribution from a company to its related company or, if both are insolvent, to wind them up as if they were one company".[49] Pooling orders are available in New Zealand[50] and the United States of America.[51]

Australia currently has no specific provision for pooling orders to be made. Pooling orders are available in limited circumstances under group cross-guarantee arrangements, schemes of arrangement, voluntary administrations, and liquidations. Voluntary pooling has been undertaken by liquidators[52] and ASIC[53] with the approval of the Courts in some circumstances, usually where all creditors have sanctioned the pooling of group assets.

As was seen in the case of *Re Switch Telecommunications Pty Ltd (in liq)*,[54] which was discussed above at para [7.4.1], and other cases,[55] Australian Courts have found methods of approving voluntary pooling by liquidators of companies with intermingled affairs. In the opinion of Santow J in *Re Switch*, s 510 of the Law provides a power to the Court to approve voluntary pooling arrangement. In *Re Switch Telecommunications Pty Ltd (in liq)* Santow J also discussed the possibility of s 447A and s 477 of the Law also being utilised by liquidators to seek Court

---

47 See the first draft of the *Explanatory Memorandum to the Corporate Law Reform Act* 1992 (Cth), para 1271.

48 CASAC, *Corporate Groups: Final Report* (May 2000), p 167 [Recommendation 21].

49 J O'Donovan, "Group Therapies for Group Insolvencies" in M Gillooly (ed), *The Law Relating to Corporate Groups* (Federation Press, Sydney, 1993), p 88.

50 Subsection 271(1)(b) of the *Companies Act* 1993 (NZ).

51 Section 105 of the United States *Bankruptcy Code.*

52 *Dean-Wilcocks v Soluble Solution Hydroponics Pty Ltd* (1997) 24 ACSR 79; and *Re Charter Travel Co Ltd* (1997) 25 ACSR 337.

53 See, for example, *Re Remy Moffatt* (unreported, Fed Ct, Aust, 6 October 1998). See CASAC, *Corporate Groups: Final Report* (May 2000), para 6.79.

54 (2000) 35 ACSR 172.

55 See, for example, *Dean-Wilcocks v Soluble Solution Hydroponics Pty Ltd* (1997) 24 ACSR 79 and *Re Charter Travel Co Ltd* (1997) 25 ACSR 337.

orders approving and facilitating voluntary pooling arrangements.[56] However, a number of Australian cases have questioned whether such provisions should be used to approve and facilitate pooling orders.[57] Accordingly, although there are avenues for achieving pooling orders under the current provisions of the Law, there is no clear and consistent legislative basis for these avenues and the Courts have not provided a clear and consistent response to the usefulness of such provisions. As a result, debate has arisen regarding the need for specific statutory provisions facilitating pooling orders.

Specific statutory provisions for pooling orders have often been discussed as a useful addition to Australian insolvency law.[58] The Harmer Report specifically recommended the introduction of pooling orders where a group's affairs have been intermingled.[59] Senate proposals in 1998 suggested that an additional criterion be "the extent to which the insolvent company has, at any time, engaged in one or more transactions that have resulted in the value of the insolvent company's assets being reduced".[60] A number of arguments opposing pooling orders by the Law Council of Australia resulted in the recommendations of the Harmer Report being rejected.[61]

CASAC has recommended that the Law be amended to permit liquidators to pool the unsecured assets and the liabilities of two or more group companies in liquidation with the prior approval of *all* unsecured creditors of those companies.[62] The basis for this recommendation is that, in certain circumstances, the ability of liquidators to pool assets and liabilities may reduce the complexities of many group insolvencies and may increase the return to creditors.[63] CASAC submits that the need to gain the approval of all unsecured creditors safeguards the interests of unsecured creditors and prevents them from being compromised.[64] This argument and recommendation is persuasive. On the basis of the same arguments, CASAC has also recommended that the Law be amended to permit the Court to make pooling orders in the liquidation of two or more companies as long as the power does not affect the rights of external secured creditors and allows individual external creditors to apply to have a pooling order adjusted to

56 See also *Dean-Wilcocks v Soluble Solution Hydroponics Pty Ltd* (1997) 24 ACSR 79.

57 See, for example, *Re Austcorp Tiles Pty Ltd* (1992) 10 ACLC 62 and *Mentha v GE Capital Ltd* (1997) 27 ACSR 696.

58 The National Companies Bill 1975 (Cth), cl 433, would have empowered a Court to order a holding company to pay the debts of its subsidiary where the circumstances made it just and equitable to do so.

59 ALRC, *General Insolvency Inquiry* Vol 1 (1988), para 335.

60 Senate, Hansard, 25 June 1998 at 3589.

61 These arguments opposing pooling orders included the separate entity principle, the difficulties such orders would create in the context of project financing and general uncertainty. Cited in CASAC, *Corporate Groups: Discussion Paper*, para 6.73.

62 CASAC, *Corporate Groups: Final Report* (May 2000), p 177 [Recommendation 22].

63 CASAC, *Corporate Groups: Final Report* (May 2000), para 6.83.

64 CASAC, *Corporate Groups: Final Report* (May 2000), para 6.83.

take their particular circumstances into account.[65] Again, this argument and recommendation is persuasive and consistent with the intention of the legislature to protect the interests of unsecured creditors without jeopardising the interests of other secured creditors.

However O'Donovan warns against the adoption of pooling orders:

> The success of these provisions will be determined to a large extent by the way they are applied by the courts. Unfortunately, some of the early cases suggest that the provisions are being applied in ways which go far beyond the legitimate interests of creditors. These interests must be balanced against the need to protect the investment of shareholders and creditors of the solvent companies in the group. An unduly robust approach might disturb the delicate relationship between debt and equity and discourage lenders from advancing money to a particular company on the security of its assets through fear that those assets might not ultimately be available to meet its debts. In Australia, where the debt to equity ratio is relatively high, this might have devastating effects on honest corporate activity.[66]

In O'Donovan's view, a more appropriate reform would be to require a compulsory contribution to an insurance scheme to protect unsecured creditors as a condition of registration.

Although pooling orders would provide an additional avenue for relief for unsecured creditors, any reform introducing such measures must be carefully framed to ensure an appropriate balance between competing interests. If they were to be introduced pooling orders should be restricted to group companies that had some degree of control over the financial and general policy affairs of the insolvent company. The recommendations of CASAC in relation to both voluntary and Court ordered pooling appear to recognise and promote these principles.

---

65 CASAC, *Corporate Groups: Final Report* (May 2000), p 181 [Recommendation 23].

66 J O'Donovan, "Group Therapies for Group Insolvencies" in M Gillooly (ed), *The Law Relating to Corporate Groups* (Federation Press, Sydney, 1993), p 88-89.

Using Reasonable Grounds as a Defence to an Action

8

"... *to anticipate the occurrence or the coming of an event which is more than a mere hope or possibility.*"[1]

1 *3M Australia Pty Ltd v Kemish* (1986) 4 ACLC 185 at 192 per Foster J.

OBJECTIVES

This Chapter will:

- set out the elements of the defence of reasonable grounds to expect solvency;
- consider the difference between an expectation and a suspicion;
- analyse what could be considered as "reasonable grounds" and debate whether a wholly objective or an objective/subjective test should be applied.

[8.1] General overview

The defence in s 588H(2) excludes from liability directors who can prove that, at the time the debt was incurred, they had reasonable grounds to expect, and did in fact expect, that the company was solvent at that time and would remain solvent even if that debt, or any other debt, was incurred. This "reasonable grounds to expect solvency" defence requires the director to establish the existence of grounds to expect solvency, the reasonableness of these grounds, and her or his actual belief in the fact of solvency.[2]

The defence in s 588H(2) is only available in proceedings under the civil penalty, s 588G(2). It is not available in proceedings for a criminal offence under s 588G(3): see s 588H(1).

[8.1.1] EXISTENCE OF GROUNDS TO EXPECT SOLVENCY

While primary liability accrues under the insolvent trading provisions where there exist grounds for "suspecting" insolvency, the defence available under s 588H(2) is expressed in terms of "expecting" insolvency.

The difference between the terms "suspect" and "expect" has already been identified.

The standard for exculpation is higher than to attract primary liability. As a result, liability is established where grounds exist for merely suspecting insolvency, but to establish the defence requires further investigation of facts and inquiry commensurate with forming an expectation of continuing solvency.

This is consistent with the philosophy and rationale of the insolvent trading provisions to increase the responsibilities of company directors for the overall financial management of the company.

[8.1.2] REASONABLENESS OF GROUNDS TO EXPECT SOLVENCY

It is unclear what the phrase "reasonable grounds" means within the context of s 588H(2). The meaning of this phrase has become the fundamental question in the interpretation of the "reasonable grounds to expect solvency" defence. Consequently, it is unclear what the required standard of reasonableness is in establishing the existence of grounds to expect solvency.

The essential issue is whether "reasonable grounds" requires an objective consideration of what the director ought to have known, or refers to a mix of objective elements and subjective facts actually known by a director.

Importantly, with the introduction of the s 588H insolvent trading provisions came a change in terminology from the predecessor provisions of s 588H(2),

2 The breakdown of the defence in this way was recommended by Foster J in *3M Australia Pty Ltd v Kemish* (1986) 4 ACLC 185 in relation to a comparable defence under s 592(2)(b).

s 556(2)(b) and s 592(2)(b). Whereas these predecessor provisions referred to a "reasonable cause to expect solvency", s 588H(2) requires "reasonable grounds" to expect solvency. This change from "reasonable cause" to "reasonable grounds" has produced the unintended effect of placing in question the meaning of the phrase "reasonable grounds" and the significance of case law developed on the meaning of "reasonable cause". On a fundamental level, the central question in the interpretation of s 588H(2) is:

> … whether the newly introduced reference to 'reasonable grounds to expect', in the light also of the other changes in formulation of relevance to its interpretation, displaces the body of case law accumulated with respect to s 592(2)(b) to impose a wholly objective standard of 'reasonable grounds to expectation' whose content is unaffected by the actual position occupied in the company by the director who invokes the defence and his or her knowledge and experience.[3]

Two opinions have been expressed on this matter. The first argues that the change in terminology from "reasonable cause" to "reasonable grounds" imports a wholly objective standard of reasonableness. In this way, whether or not a director has established reasonable grounds to expect solvency will be determined by reference to what a reasonable director of ordinary competence would have done in the circumstances. The focus of this line of argument is on what a director ought to have known if he or she was properly fulfilling her or his duties and responsibilities. In contrast, the second line of argument asserts that the phrase "reasonable grounds" does not impose a wholly objective standard of reasonableness but rather seeks to achieve an appropriate balance between objective and subjective factors, continuing the line of case law developed under the predecessor provisions. The central focus of this argument is on what a director ought to have known and what the director did actually know in consequence of her or his knowledge, experience and position within the company.

Each of these perspectives will be considered separately. Arguably the second perspective is the appropriate standard, and the phrase "reasonable grounds to expect" should be held to incorporate a mix of subjective and objective elements, with an emphasis on objective considerations. This is consistent with the philosophy of the insolvent trading provisions to increase the responsibilities placed on company directors whilst also recognising the diversity in managerial and organisational patterns. However, regardless of which perspective is ultimately adopted, the end result will be substantially identical. That is that the Courts, in interpreting the predecessor provisions to s 588H(2), have been moving towards the imposition of an increasingly onerous and objective standard and accordingly

3 *Australian Corporation Law: Principles and Practice* (looseleaf, Butterworths, Sydney, 1991), para 5.7B.0570.

the standard of reasonableness expected of directors will largely be one of objectively reasonable grounds.

As an expectation can only be assessed with reference to future circumstances, assessment of the reasonableness of this expectation will also be directed to future circumstances.[4]

(a) "Reasonable grounds" as a wholly objective standard – a new line of reasoning?

Herzberg has argued that the change in terminology from reasonable cause to reasonable grounds was intended to displace the body of case law developed in relation to the "reasonable cause to expect" defence, s 592(2)(b), thereby rejecting the blend between subjective and objective elements.[5] Accordingly, the phrase "reasonable grounds" is to be considered wholly objectively. The focus of the defence is on what a director ought to have known, and the inquiries they ought to have made, in relation to the solvency of the company. Elements personal to the director are only relevant to the extent that they discharge the second limb of the defence, namely that the director did in fact expect that the company was and would remain solvent.

This argument draws as its basis the settled interpretation of the term "reasonable grounds" as it relates to primary liability under s 588G(1)(c). Liability is triggered under the insolvent trading provisions if there were "reasonable grounds to suspect insolvency". In this context, reasonable grounds are determined by an objective test. The Court will determine what a reasonable director of ordinary competence would have done in the circumstances and then determine whether the actions or omissions of the particular director were reasonable in the circumstances.[6]

(b) "Reasonable grounds" as a balance of subjective and objective elements – a continuation of cases under section 592(2)(b)

The argument that the phrase "reasonable grounds" intends to impose a wholly objective standard of reasonableness is not entirely convincing. To suggest that the defence in s 588H(2) should be assessed by an objective standard produces logically inconsistent results. If objectively reasonable grounds exist to suspect insolvency, it is impossible for there also to exist objectively reasonable grounds to expect solvency, particularly in light of the higher standard required under the term "expect". If the case were otherwise, there would effectively be no defence provided by s 588H(2).

4 *TCN Channel Nine Pty Ltd v Scotney* (1995) 17 ACSR 116.

5 A Herzberg, "The New Insolvent Trading Legislation", paper presented at *Corporate Law Workshop*, Business Law Section, Law Council of Australia, October 1992, pp 21–22.

6 Corporate Law Reform Bill 1992, *Public Exposure Draft and Explanatory Paper* (1992), para 101.

If the notion of a wholly objective criterion for assessing the reasonableness of grounds for expecting solvency is rejected, this means that the appropriate standard of "reasonable grounds" is that of a balance between subjective and objective elements, with an emphasis on objective considerations. This has been the position developed by the Courts in relation to the predecessor provisions to s 588H(2), particularly s 592(2)(b). This standard of reasonableness means that the case law developed in relation to ss 556(2)(b) and 592(2)(b) will be relevant in determining the meaning to be given to "reasonable grounds" in the context of s 588H(2), despite some fundamental differences between s 592(2)(b) and s 588H(2).[7] The Court will not be guided by the objective standard of a reasonable director of ordinary competence. In contrast, the determination will be made according to the standard of a director in a like position in a company in the circumstances of the company. This test takes into account the knowledge, experience and position held by the director and the nature, size and complexity of the organisation.

This ability to consider subjective and objective elements, with an emphasis on objective considerations, is consistent with the philosophy of the insolvent trading provisions. It recognises that increased responsibilities must be placed on company directors whilst simultaneously addressing the need to address the diversity between managerial and organisational patterns between modern companies covered by the Law.

(c) Same end result under either test

Although the meaning of "reasonable grounds" has hindered the clarity of the defence available under s 588H(2), the interpretation given under either of the two perspectives discussed above will produce substantially the same result. If the wholly objective criteria test is adopted as the appropriate standard for exculpation under s 588H(2), what will be fundamentally required of directors is to carefully monitor the financial situation of the company and its solvency, and to stay informed of the company's affairs. If the subjective and objective test is adopted, the development of the case law under s 592(2)(b) suggests that the standard required of directors is becoming increasingly onerous and largely objective in any event. This is particularly noticeable in cases such as *Commonwealth Bank of Australia v Friedrich*.[8] Accordingly, what is fundamentally required of directors under the "subjective and objective" test will also be to stay carefully informed as to the financial situation of the company.

Therefore, despite argument to the contrary, the appropriate standard for assessing the reasonableness for grounds for expecting solvency should be a

7 Section 588H(2) excludes the double negative in s 592(2)(b), it puts the onus of proof on the defendant rather than the prosecution, and it adds a further requirement of an actual expectation of solvency. See *Australian Corporation Law: Principles and Practice* (looseleaf, Butterworths, Sydney, 1991), para 5.7B.5070.

8 (1991) 9 ACLC 946.

combination of subjective and objective factors. However, despite this seeming uncertainty and continuing academic debate as to the requisite standard, directors should remain cautious as to what is expected of them, regardless of which test is ultimately decided to be applicable.

[8.1.3] ACTUAL EXPECTATION OF SOLVENCY

In contrast to the defence under s 592(2)(b), the defence under s 588H(2) requires the director to prove that he or she believed in actual fact in the solvency of the company and its continuing solvency.

The meaning of "expect" has already been discussed above. In order to satisfy the requirements of the defence, a director must prove that he or she had a large degree of confidence in the solvency of the company, and anticipated its continuing solvency in a manner displaying more than a mere hope or possibility.

All subjective elements personal to the defendant will be considered in determining the actual belief of continuing solvency. Such factors will include the knowledge, experience and position held by the director.

[8.2] Philosophy/rationale

The "reasonable grounds to expect solvency" defence in s 588H(2) is intended to excuse from liability those directors who have sought to involve themselves in the general affairs and financial management of their company and who, as a result, had a genuine belief in the continuing solvency of their company. It exonerates directors who have taken a responsible and reasonable role in the management of their company. In keeping with the general philosophy of the insolvent trading provisions, a blending of subjective and objective elements with emphasis on the latter is the preferred standard of reasonableness under the defence.

The higher standard for exculpation, indicated by the inclusion of the term "expect" rather than "suspect", is entirely consistent with this general philosophy of the insolvent trading provisions.

This result is particularly important for non-executive directors, as it indicates the need for them to remain well informed of the company's financial affairs and the need to constantly inquire. Directors who passively rely on the information presented by executive directors and who fail to acquaint themselves with the company's affairs may not be afforded the protection of the defence.

[8.3] History/former law

Although the defence in s 588H(2) is framed in terms of "reasonable *grounds* to expect", it is useful to consider judicial interpretations of the predecessor defences, ss 556(2)(b) and 592(2)(b), which are both framed in term of "reasonable cause to expect". This analysis will highlight the meaning of the words "reasonable cause", suggesting possible inferences for an interpretation of the phrase "reasonable grounds", and reveal any similarities or differences between the two phrases. As this historical analysis shows, the phrase "reasonable cause" has traditionally represented a blending of subjective and objective elements in a consideration of reasonableness. However, the most recent decisions suggest that "reasonable cause" imposes an increasingly objective and onerous standard on directors. For this reason, there seems to be little difference between an interpretation of "reasonable grounds" based on a wholly objective criteria or one that seeks to continue the line of reasoning developed under the "reasonable cause" cases importing both subjective and objective elements because both will have substantially the same result for directors.

One of the earliest decisions to deal with the phrase "reasonable cause" was *Shapowloff v Dunn*. This clearly established that reasonableness is assessed by reference to the facts of the company's condition as the director knew them, and the knowledge and expertise he or she actually possessed. Carruthers J in *Pioneer Concrete Pty Ltd v Ellston*[9] accepted this proposition. In this case, Carruthers J held that "reasonable cause" imported a blending of subjective and objective elements. His Honour decided that in order to qualify for the defence under the predecessor provision to s 588H(2), s 556(2)(b), the defendant had to prove that at the time the debt was incurred:

> ... *he had no cause reasonable grounded in the whole of the circumstances existing as he knew them* to expect that the company would not be able to pay all its debts as and when they became due or that if the company incurred that debt it would not be able to pay all its debts as and when they fell due.[10]

This approach was accepted and applied by Connolly J in *John Graham Reprographics Pty Ltd v Steffens*[11] who decided that the appropriate standard was an objective standard applied to the facts that the director actually knew. Further acceptance of this approach was made by O'Bryan J in *Heide Pty Ltd t/a Farmhouse Smallgoods v Lester*.[12]

However, judicial opinion soon became critical of this approach. Perhaps as a result of the corporate crashes of the late 1980s and the questionable ethical activities of many company directors during that period, the Courts sought to increase the standard of reasonableness required of a director before he or she would be afforded the protection of the defence. A series of cases sought to

9 (1986) 10 ACLR 298.
10 (1986) 10 ACLR 298 at 301 (emphasis added).
11 (1987) 5 ACLC 904.
12 (1990) 8 ACLC 958.

increase the standard of reasonableness to include both subjective and objective elements, but making the standard increasingly objective and onerous. This was largely achieved by interpreting the term "reasonable cause" in light of the other duties required of directors. As the notion of "sleeping directors" was displaced, the Courts sought to ensure that directors remained constantly involved in the financial management of their company. Consequently, the standard of reasonableness under the "reasonable cause to expect solvency" was measured not merely by the actual knowledge and understanding of the particular director, but also by what the director should have known if he or she was properly fulfilling the responsibilities and duties of her or his office.

At first instance in *Metal Manufacturers Ltd v Lewis*,[13] Hodgson J considered that in determining what was reasonable cause:

> ... one can have regard to facts and circumstances actually known to the defendant, and also facts and circumstances which the defendant ought to know, having regard to the defendant's position in the company and the duties associated with that position ... one can have regard to such matters as illness and absence of a person in order to decide whether or not he has reasonable cause to expect something, but I do not think one can have regard to a person's complete ignorance of his duties as a director of a company and his complete neglect of such duties.[14]

This aspect of the decision was not challenged on appeal.

This test was adopted at first instance in *Morley v Statewide Tobacco Services*,[15] where Ormiston J put more emphasis on what a director ought to have known rather than what he or she actually knew. Clearly, Ormiston J sought to increase the responsibilities of company directors for the financial management of their company by interpreting the duty to prevent insolvent trading and its various defences in light of the other duties and responsibilities required of company directors. It is worth quoting at length the decision of Ormiston J:

> In light of the various duties now placed on company directors, it would not appear unreasonable that they should apply their minds to the overall position of the company. In other words, a defendant is not entitled to say that he or she was told a minimal number of facts about the company's financial affairs but chose to ignore the possibility of other facts, or at least failed to inquire as to other relevant facts. What is reasonable, therefore, is related in part to the extent of the inquiries that the director has made and should have made about the company's

13 (1987) ACLR 122.
14 (1987) ACLR 122 at 129.
15 (1990) 2 ACSR 405.

> solvency. A director should not in those circumstances be entitled to hide behind the ignorance the company's affairs which is of his own making or, if not entirely of his making, has been contributed to be his own failure to make further necessary inquiries. On the other hand directors are not required to have omniscience. It is not yet to be assumed that directors shall apply themselves full-time to the company's business. There is still a place for part-time and advisory directors. Directors are entitled to delegate to others the preparation of books and accounts and the carrying on of the day-to-day affairs of the company. What each director is expected to do is to take a diligent and intelligent interest in the information either available to him or which he might with fairness demand from the executive or other employees and agent of the company.

The Appeal Division agreed with this standard, and concluded that:

> … it does not seem right in this day and age that a director who takes sufficient interest in his duties to be fixed with knowledge of insolvency, may, if he neglects to act, become criminally and civilly liable, whereas a director who wholly ignores the obligations imposed upon him by the [*Corporations Law*] can escape that liability by pleading his own ignorance of the relevant facts.[16]

This standard of reasonableness, asserting that "reasonable cause" is to be assessed by reference to an increasingly objective and onerous standard whilst retaining its blend between subjective and objective considerations, has been applied in many subsequent Courts.[17] In *Commonwealth Bank of Australia v Friedrich*,[18] Tadgell J preferred a primarily objective test for assessing reasonableness when finding that an honorary non-executive who had been subjected to fraud by the Chief Executive Officer could not rely on the defence because he had failed to keep sufficiently informed of the financial affairs of the company. The director had failed to read auditors' accounts and to make general inquires regarding financial issues. Despite the fraud by the Chief Executive Officer, the director would have known that the company was in financial difficulty if he had kept himself informed as to the financial standing and solvency of the company. His failure to do this meant that he did not have "reasonable cause to expect solvency".

Clearly, the meaning of "reasonable cause to expect" has been developed by the Courts to a stage where the standard of reasonableness is increasingly objective and onerous. This development has significance for the interpretation of the phrase "reasonable grounds to expect" in s 588H(2). It is not clear that the Courts consider cases decided under the "reasonable cause" test in applying the

16 (1995) 8 ACSR 320.

17 See *Rema Industries and Services Pty Ltd v Coad* (1992) 10 ACLC 530; and *Group Four Industries Pty Ltd v Brosnan* (1992) 10 ACLC 1437.

18 (1991) 9 ACLC 946.

"reasonable grounds" test. Most reported cases under the current s 588H(2) have either not expressly considered the "reasonable cause" cases at all, or have automatically assumed an objective standard which takes into account some subjective factors without any explanation of why this is the appropriate test to be applied.

However, as discussed above, what is required of directors will be fundamentally and substantially the same whether the phrase "reasonable grounds" is intended to introduce a wholly objective standard or to apply the reasoning developed under interpretation of the predecessor provisions. Under either interpretation of the phrase "reasonable grounds" directors will be required to stay well informed of the financial affairs of the company and to fulfil their duties responsibly and effectively.

[8.4] Notable cases

[8.4.1] *STARGARD SECURITY SYSTEMS PTY LTD V GOLDIE*

Stargard Security Systems Pty Ltd v Goldie[19] considered ss 588G and 588H of the *Corporations Law*.

In dismissing an application for summary judgment, Master Bredmeyer held that a director who relied on a business plan prepared by an employee in forming his expectation of solvency was entitled to rely on the defence in s 588H(2). Master Bredmeyer held that if the sales estimate contained in the business plan was achieved, it was reasonable to expect that the company would remain solvent. Even though the sales estimate itself was unrealistic in itself, predicting that sales would rise fourfold, Master Bredmeyer decided that the director did actually believe that the estimate was realistic, particularly in light of the special relationship between the company and the creditor under which repayments were lenient. As a result, the Court found that the director had a reasonable expectation that the company would be able to pay its debts as and when they fell due if the projected sales estimate was achieved.

Clearly, the Court looked at whether the "reasonable grounds" the director sought to rely on were realistic. Even though an objective standard was the Court's primary consideration, it clearly took subjective factors into consideration, such as the favourable trading terms between the company and the creditors. This indicates that the Court considers the appropriate standard to be one of a mix of subjective and objective elements, with a primary focus and emphasis on objective factors. The Court did not make any specific reference to the "reasonable cause" cases in applying the "reasonable grounds" definition.

---

19 (1994) 13 ACSR 805; Sup Ct, WA, 1 July 1994 per Master Bredmeyer.

The case is also important because it reiterates that future contingencies, such as sales estimates, can clearly be taken into account when assessing the reasonableness of grounds for expectation.[20] This is a necessary result of the nature of an expectation.

[8.4.2] *METROPOLITAN FIRE SYSTEMS V MILLER*

Metropolitan Fire Systems v Miller[21] considered s 556 of the *Companies (NSW) Code* and ss 558G and 558H of the *Corporations Law*.

In this case, a subcontracting company (Raydar) agreed to do some work for a company (Reed) and subsequently subcontracted electrical work to another company (Metropolitan). Assurances were given by one of the directors, Miller, to Metropolitan that payment was shortly expected from Reed. However, other creditors sought to wind up Raydar prior to payment being made to Metropolitan. Miller sought to rely on the defence in s 588H(2). However, the Court rejected this claim finding that any "… optimism regarding the company's future was based on hope rather than reasonable expectations".[22] The Court did not make any express reference to the "reasonable cause" cases in applying s 588H(2) but automatically assumed an objective standard which takes some subjective factors into account without any explanation as to why this is the appropriate test to apply.

In light of the evidence received, it could not be said on reasonable grounds that the company was and would remain solvent. There was no reason to believe that Reed would pay any money to Raydar when these assurances were made and other creditors had already began disputing Raydar's accounts and were generally taking an aggressive attitude towards Raydar:

> These factors, in addition to the situation brought about by the actions of [the other creditors who were seeking to wind up Raydar], and the unlikelihood that either the company or the directors could raise significant funds, show that at the time Raydar incurred the debt to Metropolitan, there were no reasonable grounds to expect that Raydar would be able to pay this or any other debts as and when they fell due.[23]

---

20 See also *TCN Channel Nine Pty Ltd v Scotney* (1995) 17 ACSR 116, where the Court held that it was reasonable to expect solvency based on an expectation that increased expenditure on advertising would increase revenue flows.

21 (1997) 23 ACSR 699; Fed Ct, Aust, 22 May 1997 per Einfeld J.

22 (1997) 23 ACSR 699 at 711.

23 (1997) 23 ACSR 699.

[8.5] Interesting quotes/high profile matters

[8.5.1] *COMMONWEALTH BANK OF AUSTRALIA V FRIEDRICH* – FRAUD AND REASONABLE EXPECTATIONS

Although decided under a predecessor provision to s 588H(2), s 556(2)(b), the case of *Commonwealth Bank of Australia v Friedrich*[24] provides a high profile example of reasonable expectations in the context of fraud committed by a Chief Executive Officer.

Mr Eise was the part-time Honorary Chairman of the Victorian Branch of the National Safety Council (NSC). Mr Friedrich was the Chief Executive Officer. The State Bank of Victoria, which was subsequently acquired by the Commonwealth Bank, leant the NSC over $97m. As a result of fraud committed by Mr Friedrich, the accounts of the NSC showed an excess of assets over liabilities. Mr Eise failed to read the auditors reports into the solvency of the NSC, had not ensured the board considered the company's accounts in detail, and had signed off these accounts. Mr Eise subsequently sought to rely on the "reasonable cause to expect" defence in s 556(2)(b), arguing that as a result of the fraud committed by Mr Friedrich regarding the company's accounts he had reasonable cause to expect that the NSC was and would remain solvent.

However, the Court rejected this argument. Tadgell J preferred to assess the standard of reasonableness in accordance with a subjective and objective test, but giving far greater importance to what Mr Eise would have known if he had been properly fulfilling his duties and responsibilities as a director and Chairman. In the absence as to basic inquiries regarding the company's accounts, the failure to read the company's accounts or auditors reports, and the failure to ensure the board considered the company's accounts in detail, Mr Eise could not claim that he had a reasonable expectation that the company was and would remain solvent. This was in spite of the fraud committed by Mr Friedrich. If Mr Eise had been properly fulfilling his duties, checking the company accounts and all facts associated with the preparation of these accounts, he would not have been able to form an expectation as to the solvency of the NSC. It is likely that he would have discovered the fraud committed by Mr Friedrich.

Accordingly, directors should be aware that fraud committed by a director or executive involved in the preparation of the company accounts will not excuse them from liability under the defence in s 588H(2). Failure to take an active interest in the financial affairs of the company and a failure to check the facts on which company accounts and predictions as to solvency are based will mitigate against the ability to form a reasonable expectation as to solvency.

24 (1991) 9 ACLC 946.

[8.5.2] BASIC REQUIREMENTS OF DIRECTORS UNDER THE DEFENCE

In *Morley v Statewide Tobacco Services*,[25] Ormiston J outlined what is fundamentally required of directors under the "reasonable cause to expect" defence under s 556(2)(b). This is relevant to directors seeking to rely on the "reasonable grounds to expect solvency" defence in s 588H(2), as s 588H(2) is modelled on the old s 566(2)(b):

> What each director is expected to do is to take a diligent and intelligent interest in the information either available to him or which he might with fairness demand from the executive or other employees and agent of the company. However, at the least, a director cannot now assert from a state of total ignorance that he or she had no reasonable cause to expect that a company could not pay its debts as they fell due, within the meaning of [s 592(2)(b)] ... Moreover, to fail to make any inquiries whatsoever is not excusable and an opinion on the company's solvency based on that ignorance could not be characterised as reasonable. Even in a small company a director should ask for and receive figures, albeit of a basic kind, on a more or less regular basis. If that is sought and it reveals no difficulties and the director has no other reason to suspect the company may not be able to pay its debts as they fall due, then the director may be shown to have acted reasonably.[26]

[8.6] Checklist

In order to escape liability by establishing the "reasonable grounds to expect solvency" defence in s 588H(2) directors are well advised to take a number of steps. These are also factors which insolvency practitioners should consult when seeking to bring an action against a director for insolvent trading. These factors include whether a director has:

- taken an active interest in the financial management and financial affairs of the company;
- taken an active interest in the general affairs of the company;
- sought to perform her or his duties and responsibilities with care and diligence;
- taken an interest in the information provided by executive or other employees as to the solvency of the company;
- made further inquiries if the information provided suggested the need for such an inquiry;

25 (1990) 2 ACSR 405.
26 (1990) 2 ACSR 405 at 431.

- checked that all facts and assumptions used as a basis for the information as to solvency are correct;
- constantly applied herself or himself to a consideration of the solvency of the company;
- made periodic forecasts as to the solvency of the company and communicated this in board meetings.

[8.7] Loopholes/deficiencies

The largest deficiency in the defence in s 588H(2) is the uncertainty as to the meaning of "reasonable grounds". The legislation does not make clear whether the change in terminology from "reasonable cause" to "reasonable grounds" is intended to impose a wholly objective standard of reasonableness or retain the blending of objective and subjective elements.

Although it could be argued that this lack of definition creates a considerable weakness within the defence,[27] its ambiguity may be merely of academic significance. Regardless of whether the defence is seen in terms of a wholly objective standard or a mix of subjective and objective factors, and in light of the judicial propensity to increase the weight given to objective factors under a consideration of the predecessor provisions, directors will be required to take an active interest in the financial management of their company to receive the protection of the defence.

[8.8] Proposals for law reform

The uncertainty surrounding the use of the phrase "reasonable grounds" should be remedied. Although the lack of clarity may hold no practical significance for directors in the performance of their duties, a final resolution on the meaning of the phrase would provide certainty. The legislation should clarify whether the standard of reasonableness under the defence is to be assessed in wholly objective terms or by a mix of subjective and objective factors, with more weight given to objective factors.

---

27 See for example N Coburn, *Insolvent Trading: A Practical Guide* (John Libbey & Co, Sydney, 1998), pp 69-70.

Using Reasonable Reliance as a Defence

9

"*A director should not ... be entitled to hide behind ignorance of the company's affairs which is of his own making or, if not entirely of his own making, has been contributed to by his own failure to make further necessary inquiries. On the other hand, directors are not required to have omnipresence ... Directors are entitled to delegate to others ... What each director is expected to so is to take a diligent and intelligent interest in the information either available to him or which he might with fairness demand from the executives or other employees and agents of the company.*"[1]

1 *Statewide Tobacco Services Ltd v Morley* (1990) 8 ACLC 827 at 847 per Ormiston J.

OBJECTIVES

This Chapter will:

- set out the elements of the "reasonable reliance" defence.

[9.1] General overview

The defence in s 588H(3) allows a director to escape liability under the insolvent trading provisions if he or she expected that the company was solvent at the time the debt was incurred as a result of relying on information provided by a competent and reliable person who was responsible for providing information pertaining to the solvency of the company.

The defence in s 588H(3) is only available in proceedings under the civil penalty s 588G(2). It not available in proceedings for a criminal offence under s 588G(3): s 588H(1).

It is intended to encourage directors to ensure proper and adequate financial management systems are in place and thus promote legal compliance.[2]

The defence has two limbs, each of which must be satisfied. Subsection 588H(3)(a) requires the director to establish her or his belief in the existence of a proper and adequate system for managing and monitoring the financial status and solvency of the company. It also requires a belief that the delegate responsible for these matters was continuing to fulfil that responsibility. These beliefs must be based on reasonable grounds. The focus of this limb is not on ascertaining whether the delegate is in fact competent and reliable, but that the director actually believed on reasonable grounds that this was the case.

Subsection 588H(3)(b) requires the director to establish her or his expectation of continuing solvency on the basis of information provided by that delegate. An expectation based on information provided by any other person is not relevant to the defence. An expectation is the anticipation of the occurrence or the coming of an event that is more than a mere hope or possibility.[3] It implies a measure of confidence that something is going to happen.[4] It is not required that this expectation of solvency be based on reasonable grounds. This presents a problem particularly in relation to directors of small companies.

The defence implies that a director must at least take a partially active role in ensuring that proper systems are set up for financial management and monitoring, reviewing the satisfactory performance of the responsible delegate or delegates, and thus places a high standard on directors.[5]

A director does not have to establish that the delegate was in fact competent and reliable, but rather that he or she believed on reasonable grounds that this was the case. It is not clear what inquiries should be made of a delegate's competence or reliability. Where a person is competent and reliable but also dishonest, and where the director had no reason to expect the dishonesty, the director can rely on the defence in s 588H(3).[6]

2 ALRC, *General Insolvency Inquiry* Vol 1 (1988), para 307.

3 *3M Australia Pty Ltd v Kemish* (1986) 4 ACLC 185 at 192 per Foster J.

4 *Commonwealth Bank of Australia v Friedrich* (1991) 9 ACLC 946 at 956 per Tadgell J.

5 S M Pollard, "Fear and Loathing in the Boardroom" (1994) 22(6) ABLR 392 at 407.

6 N Coburn, *Insolvent Trading: A Practical Guide* (John Libbey & Co, Sydney, 1998), p 71.

By implying the need for a partially active role and reasonable inquiries to be made, the defence in s 588H(3) complements the ability to delegate and rely on others as provided under other director's duties, particularly the duties under ss 180 to 183 of the Law and their common law equivalents.

[9.2] Philosophy/rationale

The inclusion of this defence implements a recommendation of the Harmer Report that directors cannot be expected to have control over every action taken within a corporation and that a defence of this nature would encourage a proper system of financial management and hence legal compliance.[7]

Accordingly, the defence in s 588H(3) seeks to recognise the diffuse and diverse organisational structure of many corporations and that the corresponding delegation of tasks and functions means that directors will often rely on others in the performance of their duties. The defence recognises that the complex realities of modern corporate life will often require directors to delegate many important functions and to rely on advice provided by these delegates when making decisions. It provides an incentive to directors to ensure that adequate financial management systems are in place with competent and reliable persons taking care of the company's financial matters.

The defence is not intended to allow directors to remain passive. In the words of Baxt:

> The director must, however take a partially active role in the affairs of the company. The director must ensure that a proper form of delegation has been created. Secondly, the director must assess the information that is provided to him/her. And furthermore, while the section does not state this, the relevant director must ensure that the form of delegation established is periodically reviewed. This is assumed from the fact that the defence requires a competent and reliable person to be responsible and that adequate information is provided. Unless review procedures are undertaken by directors in relation to both these matters the mere setting up of a procedure etc may not be sufficient.[8]

[9.3] History/former law

The defence in s 588H(3) has no predecessor provisions, although similar arguments were accepted in relation to the defence under s 592(2)(b)(i).[9]

7 ALRC, *General Insolvency Inquiry* Vol 1 (1988), para 307.
8 R Baxt, "New Insolvent Trading Rules for Directors" (1993) *Company Director* 12.
9 *Statewide Tobacco Services Ltd v Morley* (1990) 8 ACLC 827.

[9.4] Notable cases

[9.4.1] *CAPRICORN SOCIETY LTD V LINKE*

Capricorn Society Ltd v Linke[10] considered s 592 of the *Corporations Law*.

Although decided under s 592(2)(b)(i), this decision provides guidance as to the probable approach of the court in considering s 588H(3). It suggests that despite delegation and reliance, a director must continue to make appropriate inquiries.

Linke, Hodge and Verco were directors of a company. Upon accepting their appointments as directors of the company, Hodge and Verco made it clear to Linke that they did not want to get involved in the day-to-day management of the business but would rely on Linke in this regard, due to their inexperience in such matters and Linke's extensive previous experience.

Having become directors of the company, both Hodge and Verco were active in monitoring the financial performance of the company, making inquiries of Linke regarding its financial position. Hodge and Verco repeatedly asked Linke for accounts to be presented, but these were delayed and, when presented, handwritten. The general impression conveyed by Linke was that the company was a shell company with $1m tax losses and no other assets or liabilities. However, Linke seriously misled Hodge and Verco about the financial position of the company. He provided numerous false financial reports indicating that the company was trading at a profit.

At one point, Linke presented some figures to Verco and, in recognition of his limited accounting ability, Verco passed these figures on to his son who was a chartered accountant. His son made inquiries of Linke, but received no reply. At a director's meeting in December 1991 at which the company's solicitor and accountant were also present, Linke presented handwritten figures indicating a strong financial performance and stated that proper accounts were not presented due to continuing computer problems.

To the surprise of Hodge and Verco, a receiver was appointed to the company in March 1992. A creditor brought an action for insolvent trading against the directors and Hodge and Verco sought to escape liability.

The Court held that Hodge and Verco could escape liability. They had taken a responsible attitude toward the financial management of the company and had agreed to leave financial matters to the responsibility of a third director who had experience with financial matters. They had made continuous relevant inquiries as to the financial standing of the company and were provided with a plausible excuse as to why proper accounts were not available. Verco had sought professional financial advice from a chartered accountant, his son, when he was placed in doubt as to the financial performance of the company.

10 (1995) 17 ACSR 101 (Sup Ct, SA, 5 May 1995 per Bowen Pain J).

Clearly, in order to satisfy the requirements of the defence in s 588H(3), a director must act responsibly in the delegation and reliance on functions, must inquire about the financial standing of the company on a regular basis, should seek professional advice when in doubt, and to check factual concerns.

[9.5] Interesting quotes

[9.5.1] SCOPE AND PROBABLE INTERPRETATION OF THE DEFENCE

In *Statewide Tobacco Services Ltd v Morley*[11] Ormiston J provided a good example of the attitude to be adopted by courts in the interpretation of the defence in s 588H(3):

> A director should not … be entitled to hide behind ignorance of the company's affairs which is of his own making or, if not entirely of his own making, has been contributed to by his own failure to make further necessary inquiries. On the other hand, directors are not required to have omnipresence. It is not yet assumed that directors shall apply themselves full-time to the company's business. There is still place for part-time and advisory directors. Directors are entitled to delegate to others the preparation of books and accounts and the carrying on of the day-to-day affairs of the company. What each director is expected to so is to take a diligent and intelligent interest in the information either available to him or which he might with fairness demand from the executives or other employees and agents of the company.[12]

[9.6] Checklist

[9.6.1] CHECKLIST – GENERAL

The defence in s 588H(3) contains, and implies, a number of key requirements for directors. Insolvency practitioners should consult these when bringing an action for insolvent trading. In other words, has the director:

- taken, at the least, a partially active role in ensuring proper management systems are established for financial management;
- acted in a generally responsible manner and with due consideration of all the circumstances when delegating the responsibility for the financial oversight of the company;
- made regular inquires of those delegates providing information;

11 (1990) 8 ACLC 827.
12 (1990) 8 ACLC 827 at 847.

- checked factual matters on which the information and advice as to the solvency of the company is based;
- taken professional advice when information as to solvency is not forthcoming, repeatedly delayed, or generally presented in an unprofessional manner.

[9.6.2] CHECKLIST – BELIEF IN DELEGATE'S COMPETENCE AND RELIABILITY

In order to qualify for the defence in s 588H(3), a director does not need to establish that the delegate was in fact competent and reliable but only their belief on reasonable grounds that this was the case. To satisfy themselves that they believe a delegate responsible for overseeing the company's financial affairs to be competent and reliable on reasonable grounds, directors should ensure the following, both upon the initial delegation and thereafter. In addition, insolvency practitioners should consider these when bringing an action for insolvent trading. Has the director:

- made sure that the level of work required by each delegate is appropriate and not onerous, in light of the nature of the business and complexity of the organization;
- considered the number of duties and tasks required to be performed by each delegate and their ability to satisfactorily perform the financial oversight function;[13]
- considered whether time limits imposed on staff are reasonable;
- ensured all relevant staff are adequately qualified – professional qualifications and attendance of seminars and conferences are paramount in this regard;
- considered the ability of management to be flexible and aware of competing priorities in their delegation of work;
- ensured that the accounting system for monitoring and analysing the solvency of the company is up-to-date, accurate, and generally maintained to a high standard;
- regularly reviewed the performance of those delegates responsible for monitoring the solvency of the company.

[9.7] Loopholes/deficiencies

[9.7.1] EXPECTATION OF SOLVENCY DOES NOT HAVE TO BE BASED ON REASONABLE GROUNDS

The defence in s 588H(3) only requires a director to believe in the solvency of the company on the basis of information provided by a delegate responsible for

13 See *Australian Securities Commission v Fairlie* (1993) 11 ACLC 669, where the Court considered that despite the general competence of a delegate, her or his involvement in other duties may compromise their ability to effectively perform the particular function in question. Cited in N Coburn, *Insolvent Trading: A Practical Guide* (John Libbey & Co, Sydney, 1998), p 135.

the oversight of the company's financial position. Interestingly, it does not appear to require the belief of this solvency to be based on reasonable grounds. On this interpretation, a director who believed in the solvency of the company based on information provided by a competent and reliable delegate could avoid liability even if a reasonable person would not have had this expectation of solvency.

This seems to depart from the general requirement of reasonableness pervasive throughout the insolvent trading provisions. However, of course, a director might face evidentiary difficulties in proving that he or she believed in the solvency of a company based on information provided where a reasonable person would not have had that expectation.

[9.7.2] DELEGATION AND RELIANCE DOES NOT HAVE TO BE REASONABLE IN THE CIRCUMSTANCES

Subsection 588H(3) does not require the delegation or reliance to be reasonable, warranted, or justified in the circumstances. However, circumstances in which a Court would not find that delegation was reasonable in the circumstances may be few and far between.

Directors might decide to delegate duties of financial oversight and restrict their active role in the financial affairs of the company to no more than periodically asking questions of those responsible to ensure that they are fulfilling their responsibilities. Some might consider this to be an inadequate performance by directors of their very role in running a company. It could be argued that such a delegation should only be encouraged on proof that the delegation was reasonable and warranted in the circumstances.

In this technical sense, the delegation and reliance provisions under insolvent trading differ from the delegation and reliance provisions under other directors' duties, particularly under ss 189, 190 and 198D of the Law, which require the delegation and reliance to be made in good faith and after making proper inquiry if the circumstances indicated the need for inquiry. However, when one looks at the defence as a whole and considers that in order to establish the defence a director must believe that there exists a proper system for monitoring the financial affairs of the company and must still periodically review the company's financial performance, it would seem that the practical effect of this defence is to reinforce the need for proper inquiry.

[9.8] Proposals for law reform

[9.8.1] SHOULD THERE BE AN EXPLICIT "REASONABLE GROUNDS" REQUIREMENT?

The requirement of reasonableness is generally present throughout the insolvent trading provisions. Liability only arises under the insolvent trading provisions if there were "reasonable grounds to suspect solvency", the defence in s 588H(2) requires "reasonable grounds" to expect solvency, and the defence in s 588H(5) of taking steps to prevent the incurring of the debt must be "reasonable".

However, this reasonable grounds requirement appears to be lacking from the face of the defence in s 588H(3). It is possible that a director may be able to escape liability if he or she relied upon information provided by a competent and reliable person despite the fact that no other reasonable person would have had such an expectation of solvency. Such a result is unlikely though as the director still needs to convince the Court that he or she had an actual belief in the solvency of the company. If the circumstances indicate that a reasonable person would not have held such a belief, it will be difficult, if not impossible, for the director to raise enough evidence to convince the Court otherwise.

Although not explicitly stated, the defence in s 588H(3) seems to include a reasonableness requirement and requires a fair degree of diligence on the part of directors. In order to make out the defence the director needs to believe that the delegate was competent and reliable, needs to believe what the delegate says and may still need to make further inquiries if the circumstances indicate a need for them.

In any event, the Courts are likely to interpret s 588H(3) consistently with the other delegation and reliance provisions of the Law as this interpretation of statutory rights and obligations consistent with other duties and responsibilities has been applied in a number of leading cases within the last decade.[14]

14 See *Commonwealth Bank of Australia v Friedrich* (1991) 9 ACLC 946; *Group Four Industries v Brosnan* (1992) 8 ACSR 463; and *Leigh-Mardon Pty Ltd v Wawn* (1995) 17 ACSR 741.

Using Non-participation as a Defence

10

"*Mr Bott clearly did not show a proper degree of commitment to involvement on the financial management of the company, for he was never involved in financial management at all. He ought to have realised that by not having any such involvement, he was not properly discharging his responsibilities as a director ... He ought, in short, to have confronted Mr Moore and insisted upon proper involvement in the company's affairs. He cannot now treat Mr Moore's deceptive conduct as a good reason for not taking part in management when he did not assert his rights as a director from the outset and with vigour.*"[1]

1 Austin J in *Tourprint v Bott* (1999) 32 ACST201 and 217.

OBJECTIVES

This Chapter will:

- set out the elements of the "non-participation" defence;
- consider what could be considered as an "other good reason";
- outline a need for a causal connection between the illness or other good reason and the non-participation.

[10.1] General overview

The defence in s 588H(4) excludes those directors from liability whom through illness or other good reason did not take part in the management of the company at the time the relevant debt was incurred. It is based on the idea that it is not appropriate to hold a director liable if he or she was not in a position to influence the management of the company.

The "illness or other good reason" defence is only available in proceedings under the civil penalty s 588G(2). It is not available in proceedings for a criminal offence under s 588G(3): s 588H(4).

In the absence of any Court decisions on the defence, the ambit of "illness" and "other good reason" are unclear. It is likely that "illness" will include nervous or psychological problems, such as nervous breakdowns or general stress. "Other good reasons" may include absence due to a personal material interest in the matter, being an alternate director, the appointment of a receiver or liquidator, or an extended stay overseas with the permission of the Board.[2]

The defence should only apply to directors who have acted with care and diligence, who have been responsible in the performance of their duties, and who have actively participated in management. This is consistent with the *Explanatory Memorandum to the Corporate Law Reform Act* 1992 (Cth). In this way the defence would arguably only operate where events develop within a short period of time and the director in question has no opportunity to appoint an alternative director.

This *may* mean that a director who has been ill prior to the incurring of the debt and who continued to occupy her or his position in bad health might not have acted responsibly and diligently. The failure to appoint an alternate director combined with continued absence and non-participation in management due to illness may not represent responsible behaviour. This is more possible in smaller companies, such as those controlled by only two directors. In such circumstances it might not be appropriate to extended protection under s 588H(4).

A direct causal connection must be established between the illness or other good reason and the non-participation in management. A director who habitually fails to take part in the management of the company but who happens to be ill at the time that the relevant debt is incurred might not receive the protection offered by the defence. Accordingly, a passive director who was ill when the particular debt was incurred might not be able to rely on s 588H(4).

---

2 See P Grawehr, "A Comparison Between Australian and European Insolvent Trading Laws" (1996) 14(1) CSLJ 16 at 21.

[10.2] Philosophy/rationale

The Harmer Report clearly highlighted that the rationale behind the defence in s 588H(4) is to exclude from liability those who were not in a position to take part in the management of the company at the time the debt was incurred.[3] It is based on the idea that it is not appropriate to hold a director liable if he or she was not in a position to influence the management of the financial affairs of the company at the relevant time.

[10.3] History/former law

Subsection 588H(4) replaces the "lack of authority/consent" defence available under s 592(2) which was deficient in its protection of directors who had failed to take a sufficiently active role in the management of the company.[4]

This deficiency in the s 592(2) "lack of authority/consent" defence enhances the proposition that the defence under s 588H(4) is only available to directors who are diligent and who actively participate in the management and financial affairs of the company.

[10.4] Notable cases

[10.4.1] *TOURPRINT INTERNATIONAL PTY LTD V BOTT*

Tourprint International Pty Ltd v Bott[5] considered s 588G and s 588H of the *Corporations Law*.The issue in this case was whether a director could establish that he had reasonable grounds to expect, and did expect, that the company was and would continue to be solvent. It was also argued that the fact that the director was deceived and excluded from management by another director of the company was "other good reason" for not taking part in the management pursuant to s 588H(4).

Austin J considered that the case was a "cautionary tale for directors, especially in the small business sector". The defendant director, Mr Bott, was the director of a company in respect of which he received no financial information. He nonetheless became aware that the company was in financial difficulty and was experiencing more than a temporary cash flow, despite it incurring debts in excess of $500,000 during this time.

3 Australian Law Reform Commission, *General Insolvency Inquiry* Report No 45,Vol 1 (1988), para 312.

4 See *Corporate Law Reform Act 1992: Explanatory Memorandum* (1992), paras 1081 and 1086.

5 (1999) 32 ACSR 201 (Sup Ct, NSW, 15 June 1999 per Austin J).

The Court found that during the relevant period there were reasonable grounds for suspecting that the company was insolvent. The grounds arose out of the state of the company's financial records, the growing deficiency of creditors over debtors and the absence of any significant assets other than trade debtors and cash. Austin J noted:

> Anyone aware of facts disclosed by that information would have realised that the company was hopelessly insolvent throughout the relevant period.

Austin J found that Mr Bott was not entitled to rely upon the defence in s 588H(2). His Honour held that had proper inquiries been made, Mr Bott would have come to realise the serious operational problems which had arisen in the company. Mr Bott's state of knowledge was such that he was aware that there were reasonable grounds for suspecting that the company was insolvent at the time that it incurred the debts and his awareness of such grounds continued for the whole of the relevant period. Mr Bott's own evidence was that he was aware that "there was a problem" and had heard his fellow director complaining about cash flow. Given this, Mr Bott did not have reasonable grounds for expecting that the company was, and would remain solvent, and if he did have any such expectation it was not based on reasonable grounds.

Even if Mr Bott was not so aware, the Court found that a reasonable person in a like position in a company in the company's circumstances would have been aware that there were reasonable grounds to suspect insolvency.

Mr Bott also attempted to rely on s 588(4) arguing that the "good reason" that he did not take part in the management of the company was because he was excluded from the management as a result of deceptive conduct on the part of the other directors. The Court rejected Mr Bott's contention that he had been deceived by his accountant but accepted that he had been misled by the other director, Mr Moore. However, the Court found that Mr Bott's failure to have a more active role in management was not referrable to any reason which was a "good reason" for the purposes of s 588H(4). Austin J noted that there were no reported decisions which interpreted the words "other good reason" in the context of the present section but pointed to cases under the previous s 592 in which the following circumstances arose:

- an alternate director, who acts only when a regular director cannot do so is not acting as a director when the debt is incurred;
- a director goes overseas and requests another director to be appointed in his place.

The Court found that Mr Bott clearly did not show a proper degree of commitment to involvement in the financial management of the company for he was never involved in the financial management at all. Mr Bott ought to have realised that by not having any such involvement, he was not properly discharging his responsibilities as a director.

[10.5] High profile matters

Although not directly relevant to the elements of the defence in s 588H(4), the events surrounding the attempted extradition of Christopher Skase from Majorca are an important indication of the need for Courts to thoroughly investigate claims of illness by company directors.[6] The failed extradition attempt by the Australian Securities Commission suggests to Courts applying s 588H(4) that when a director is claiming protection due to illness, the Court must satisfy itself of the reliability of this claim through an inspection of sound medical reports and other strong evidence.

[10.6] Checklist

If a director is seeking to rely on the defence in s 588H(4), an insolvency practitioner seeking to prosecute the director for insolvent trading should consider the following:

- If non-participation due to illness is being claimed, is the illness substantial or trivial? Is it likely that the illness has affected the capacity of the director to make informed business decisions?
- If non-participation due to illness is being claimed, have accurate medical reports been promptly obtained? Are these medical reports from a reliable source?
- If a conflict of interest has prevented participation and is the ground for "some other good reason" claim, has the Board been notified of the conflict of interest? Has the Board given approval for the director to participate despite the conflict? Has any other resolution of the problem been reached?
- If geographical factors (such as an overseas holiday) are preventing participation and are sought to be established as "some other good reason", has the approval of the Board been sought or has the director received approval for the absence?
- Is it likely that the illness or other reason materially or substantially affected the ability of the director to participate in the management of the company?
- Was an alternate director appointed?

6 See N Coburn, *Insolvent Trading: A Practical Guide* (John, Libbey, Sydney, 1998), p 73. See also G Monsterrat, "Commonwealth v Christopher Skase: A Matter of Life or Death or a Nomination for an Oscar?" (1995) Vol 18(2) UNSWLR 502.

- Is illness or some other reason preventing the director from participating in the management of the company on a habitual or extended/protracted basis?

[10.7] Loopholes/deficiencies/tricks/ hints

[10.7.1] INHERENT VAGUENESS AND UNCERTAINTY

In the absence of judicial consideration of the terms "illness" and "other good reason", it is unclear what will be included within the ambit of these terms. For this reason, the defence in s 588H(4) is inherently vague and uncertain. The term "other good reason" is particularly problematic in this regard. Early consideration was made by the Harmer Report of what should be included within the scope of s 588H(4). Mention was made in the Harmer Report of the need to avoid the inclusion of a phrase that is unnecessarily unclear or onerous:

> ... two submissions regarded the phrase 'other unavoidable cause' as unclear and unduly onerous. [One submission] suggested 'other reasonable cause' but that wording may permit a director to be absent in circumstances that are reasonable, but not consistent with the necessary commitment to an involvement with the management if a company in financial difficulties (for example if the director takes an overseas holiday). Accordingly, the Commission recommends that a director have a defence where, by reason of illness or other sufficient cause, he or she did not participate in the management of the company at the relevant time.

The phrase "other sufficient cause", recommended by the Harmer Report, was replaced in the legislation by the term "other good reason". However, this has not had the effect of producing greater certainty.

[10.7.2] STRUCTURAL DEFICIENCIES

The phrase "if the person was a director of the company at the time when the debt was incurred" is largely redundant. It is not contained in any of the other three defences in s 588H. The phrase merely repeats a condition for liability under s 588G(1)(a).

[10.8] Proposals for law reform

The legislature should reformulate the defence under s 588H(4) to specify that it will only be available to directors who have acted with care and diligence. The inclusion of the term "good reason" in the defence does not clarify what is expected of directors when they are sick or absent for some other reason.

Directors should be required to give appropriate notice of their absence and appoint an alternate director if required. If ill or absent for some other reason for an extended period of time or on repeated occasions, the director should be required to appoint an alternate director or resign. In such circumstances, the director should not be able to rely on the defence in s 588H(4) if they have failed to appoint an alternate director or resigned because diligence would require this of a director. A director who habitually fails to take part in the management of the company, even if through illness or some other good reason, should not be entitled to rely upon the defence in s 588H(4).

Using an Assertion that Reasonable Steps Were Taken to Prevent the Incurring of a Debt as a Defence

"*If the circumstances are that a director knows or should know that the company is incurring debts which it will not be able to pay as they fall due, and does not try to prevent this by persuasion, calling a meeting etc., then authority or consent may well be implied, even if the debts are being incurred by a managing director, and the defendant has not the power, according to the constitution of the company, to override the managing director's decisions.*"[1]

1 *Standard Chartered Bank of Australia v Antico* (1995) 131 ALR 1 at 113 per Hodgson J.

OBJECTIVES

This Chapter will:

- set out the elements of the "reasonable steps taken to prevent insolvency" defence;
- analyse what could be considered as "reasonable" steps;
- discuss the need for genuine effort to be exerted, for unequivocal action to be taken and for all reasonable steps to be taken.

[11.1] General overview

Subsection 588H(5) provides a defence to proceedings against a director under the insolvent trading provisions. It is available to directors who took all reasonable steps to prevent the company incurring the relevant debt. It interacts with Pt 5.3A of the *Corporations Law* where s 436A(1)(a) allows the directors of a company to appoint an administrator if they believe that the company is insolvent or is likely to become insolvent at some future time. It also interacts with s 1317JA(3) which makes clear what the court can take into consideration when excusing a director for contravention of s 588G.

The defence under s 588H(5) is only available in proceedings under the civil penalty s 588H(2). It is not available in proceedings for a criminal offence under s 588G(3): s 588H(1).

Relief is only provided under s 588H(5) if all reasonable steps are taken to prevent the incurring of the debt. What is considered reasonable steps has been a point of ongoing debate.

[11.1.1] WHAT ARE REASONABLE STEPS?

The Harmer Report recommended that the term "reasonable" be included within the defence.[2] Although the aim of the defence was to "... minimise a possible loss to the creditors of the company by [encouraging a director to take] action to prevent the company from engaging in insolvent trading",[3] the inclusion of the term "reasonable" suggests that the interests of directors are still considered important. This balance to be achieved between the often competing rights and interests of creditors and directors has been the defining point of tension within the interpretation of this subsection, and indeed the insolvent trading provisions as a whole.

What is reasonable will depend upon the circumstances of each case. In determining whether the steps the director took were reasonable, s 588H(6) provides that the Court may have regard to a number of factors including:

- any action the person took with a view to appointing an administrator of the company;
- when that action was taken; and
- the results of that action.

Although s 588H(6) looks at any action the director took to appoint an administrator, this appointment must be reasonable and timely in the circumstances. The mere appointment of an administrator will not be satisfactory where this action was left to the last minute.

2 ALRC, *General Insolvency Inquiry* Vol 1 (1988), paras 310–311.
3 ALRC, *General Insolvency Inquiry* Vol 1 (1988), para 310.

Other factors will also be relevant in determining whether the steps taken were reasonable, including the size and nature of the company, the size of the relevant debt, and the grounds that gave rise to the suspicion of insolvency.[4] Clearly, the Court will consider whether adequate steps were taken to minimise the risk to creditors, consistent with the policy behind the insolvent trading provisions.

[11.1.2] GENUINE EFFORT AND UNEQUIVOCAL ACTION

It is clear that in order to qualify for the defence a director must have made a genuine effort to prevent the incurring of the debt. Once a director suspects insolvent trading, he or she must take clear, positive and unequivocal action to do all they can within their powers to either prevent the debt being incurred or, if they do not have the necessary power to prevent the debt being incurred, to draw the problem to the attention of a person who does have the necessary power.

As soon as the company's solvency is in doubt, a director must call a board meeting, ensure accurate minutes are taken of this meeting, advise staff about the issue, and seek professional advice.

If a director does not have authority in the particular area in which the debt is being incurred, he or she must notify the person in charge of that area of the suspected insolvency. The fact that a director does not have authority in a particular area will not prevent liability being imposed under s 588G(2).[5] If the person in charge of the area does not take action to prevent the debt being incurred, the director must take clear, positive and unequivocal action to prevent the debt being incurred.

[11.1.3] BUSINESS JUDGMENT RULE DOES NOT APPLY

The business judgment rule does not apply to decisions made in relation to insolvent trading. This is because the business judgment rule aims to encourage entrepreneurial risk taking by directors and thus conflicts with the creditor-protection rationale of the insolvent trading provisions. The business judgment rule will not be relevant in determining the reasonableness of any steps taken by a director. Whether or not this is appropriate will be dealt with below.

[11.1.4] ALL REASONABLE STEPS MUST BE TAKEN

It is important to note that all reasonable steps must be taken by a director in order to qualify for this defence. This means that the requirements of the defence are potentially onerous and may require resignation in some circumstances. It may not be necessary for a director to resign if he or she cannot prevent the incurring of the debt if he or she has argued vigorously in favour of entering voluntary administration. There is some authority that such a failure to prevent the

4 *Corporate Law Reform Act* 1992, Public Exposure Draft and Explanatory Paper (1992), para 1240.
5 *Byron v Southern Star Group Pty Ltd* (1997) 15 ACLC 191.

incurring of a debt may be due to an overbearing director or board of directors, in which case a particular director may escape liability.[6] However, mere protesting by a director that he or she has reservations about the course of action will not be enough to escape liability.[7] It may not be sufficient to merely clearly and consistently express reservations to the actions of the company. Clear, positive and unequivocal action must be taken.

[11.2] Philosophy/rationale

The defence in s 588H(5) furthers the objectives of the insolvent trading provisions by encouraging directors to take positive steps to protect the interests of creditors, to be active in the financial management and monitoring of their company, and to take early action over its financial problems.

This defence seeks to achieve an appropriate balance between the interests of creditors and directors. By advancing the need to minimise risk and loss to creditors through incentives to place a suspected insolvent company into early administration, and simultaneously recognising that what is required of directors must be reasonable in the circumstances, it has sought to achieve this balance. It protects the efforts of honest and diligent directors and coincides with the duty of care and diligence and the general emphasis on promoting active involvement in the affairs of the company.

[11.3] History/former law

The defence in s 588H(5) is modelled on s 214(3) of the United Kingdom's *Insolvency Act* (1986),[8] which absolves a director from liability if he or she has taken every step to minimise potential loss to the company's creditors. It is also modelled on s 592(2)(a) of the Law which applies to debts incurred before 23 June 1993.

[11.4] Notable cases

[11.4.1] *BYRON V SOUTHERN STAR GROUP PTY LTD*

Byron v Southern Star Group Pty Ltd[9] considered s 556 of the *Companies (NSW) Code.*

---

6 *Dempster v Mallina Holdings Ltd* (1994) 15 ACSR 1.

7 *Byron v Southern Star Group Pty Ltd* (1997) 15 ACLC 191.

8 Subsection 214(3) of the *Insolvency Act* (1986) states:

Although *Byron v Southern Star Group Pty Ltd*[10] was decided under s 556 of the *Companies (NSW) Code*, the principles enunciated in this case are relevant to the interpretation of the defence in the context of s 588G(2). The defence under which this case was decided was that the relevant debt was incurred without the director's express or implied authority or consent.

The facts of the case are straightforward and are reproduced from the ACLC Report. Mr Byron was an executive director of a company. He knew, or had reason to suspect, that the company would be unable to pay its debts. Mr Byron also knew that the company needed a supply of goods in order to enable it to continue to trade, and knew that there was a real probability that the company would deal with Southern Star Group Pty Ltd for this reason. However, he had no authority to order goods for the company or to decide whether the company should deal with Southern Star.

Orders giving rise to a debt to Southern Star were placed without Mr Byron's knowledge. After he became aware of the orders, Mr Byron told the company's managing director that he objected to the company trading with Southern Star. He took no other action to prevent further purchases from Southern Star.

A winding-up order was made against the company. Southern Star brought proceedings against Mr Byron under s 556 of the *Companies Code* to recover debts incurred by the company when it had ordered goods from Southern Star. Mr Byron sought to rely on the defence in s 556(2) of the *Companies Code*, arguing that the debts had been incurred without his authority or consent.

The Court rejected this argument. Simon AJA clearly stated that more was required of Mr Byron to prevent the incurring of the debt. It was not sufficient for him to merely state his opinion that the company should not incur the debts. Even though he had no authority to deal with Southern Star, he was required to take positive and unequivocal action to prevent the company incurring the debt. Simon AJA decided that although Mr Byron had expressed reservations about the relevant debt, it was clear that:

> ... at all material times, both before and after [Byron had gone on holidays he knew] that the company needed the supply of video tapes in order to enable it to keep trading in its duplication business ... He knew before he went on holidays ... that there was a very real probability that the company would purchase

"The court shall not make a declaration under this section with respect to any person if it is satisfied ... that [the] person took every step with a view to minimising the potential loss to the company's creditors (assuming [the director] to have known that there was no reasonable prospect that the company would avoid going into insolvent liquidation) that [the director] ought to have taken."

9 CA, NSW, 20 December 1996 per Sheller JA, Simos AJA and Aberdee AJA.

10 *Byron v Southern Star Group Pty Ltd* (1996) 15 ACLC 191.

> tapes from [Southern Star] despite his reservations. On his return from holidays he became aware … that the company had actually commenced purchasing tapes from [Southern Star]. He expressed lack of agreement to those purchases but … must have known that there was, at the very least, a real probability that such purchases would continue despite his expressed lack of agreement.[11]

Simon AJA held that something more positive and unequivocal had to be done by Mr Byron. It would not have been unreasonable to expect Mr Byron to have taken:

> … steps to prevent those purchases, beyond simply saying that he had reservations and did not agree with them, more especially having regard to the fact that he would know that such purchases would result in the incurring by the company of debts which the company would not be able to pay.[12]

His Honour accepted the decision of Hodgson J in *Standard Chartered Bank v Antico*[13] in relation to what a director should do to prevent their company incurring the relevant debt. The statement by Hodgson J in that case is reproduced below in para [11.5.1].

Due to his failure to take positive and unequivocal action, Mr Byron could not claim that the debt had been incurred without his authority or consent.

[11.5] Interesting quotes

[11.5.1] WHAT IS REQUIRED OF A DIRECTOR TO ESTABLISH THE DEFENCE

In *Standard Chartered Bank v Antico*[14] Hodgson J stated the basic requirements for a director to establish the "lack of authority/consent" defence under s 592(2)(a). As s 588H(5) is modelled on the defence in s 592(2)(a), these are applicable to the "all reasonable steps taken to prevent the incurring of the debt" defence in s 588H(5). A director should be aware that there:

> … may be circumstances in which the failure of a single director to seek to persuade a managing director not to incur a debt, or to call a directors' meeting with a view to stopping the incurring of debts, or to resign, or to seek to have the company wound up, could amount to giving authority or consent to the incurring of a debt [or the failure to take all reasonable steps to prevent the

11 (1996) 15 ACLC 191 at 199–200.
12 (1996) 15 ACLC 191 at 200.
13 (1995) 131 ALR 1.
14 (1995) 131 ALR 1.

> incurring of the debt] ... If the circumstances are that a director knows or should know that the company is incurring debts which it will not be able to pay as they fall due, and does not try to prevent that by persuasion, calling a meeting etc, then authority or consent [or a failure to take all reasonable steps to prevent the incurring of the debt] may well be implied, even if the debts are being incurred by a managing director, and the defendant has not the power, according to the constitution of the company, to override the managing director's decisions.[15]

[11.6] Checklist

[11.6.1] WHAT WILL BE CONSIDERED REASONABLE

In order to determine what are reasonable steps to take to prevent the incurring of the debt, a director should consider a number of factors. These factors can also be used by an insolvency practitioner when bringing an action for insolvent trading:

- the size and nature of the company;
- the size and nature of the debt;
- the delegation of functions between directors and management;
- what gave rise to the suspicion of insolvency.

[11.6.2] WHAT ARE REASONABLE STEPS TO TAKE

To qualify for the defence in s 588H(5) a director is well advised to take a number of steps. These factors can also be used by insolvency practitioners when bringing an action for insolvent trading. In other words, has the director:

- taken an active interest in the financial affairs of the company to ensure that any action taken to prevent the incurring of the debt is done promptly;
- upon suspecting insolvency, notified the board, senior management and other relevant staff of the suspected insolvency;
- informed the managing director of the suspected insolvency and the director's objection to the incurring of the debt;
- called a Board Meeting to state the director's objection to the company incurring the debt;
- ensured accurate minutes are taken of the Board Meeting;
- if the debt is being incurred in an area in which the director has no authority to operate, sought to persuade the person in charge of the relevant area to avoid incurring the debt;
- taken all appropriate steps to appoint an administrator as soon as possible after suspecting insolvency;

15 (1995) 131 ALR 1 at 113 per Hodgson J.

- taken clear, positive and unequivocal action to prevent the incurring of the debt;
- if the above steps are unsuccessful, has the director clearly and consistently stated her or his objection to the incurring of the debt; if the debt is substantial in nature, and yet the company refuses to accede to the director's wishes and indicates that it will incur the debt, has the director considered resigning.

[11.7] Deficiencies

The requirements of the section may be particularly onerous for directors where liability has only been established under the objective limb of s 588G(2)(b). Where liability has been established in this way, a director would not have been personally aware of suspected insolvency and thus would not have taken any reasonable steps to prevent the incurring of the debt.

[11.8] Proposals for law reform

The statutory business judgment rule introduced by the *Corporate Law Economic Reform Program Act* 1999 (Cth) does not apply in the context of insolvent trading.[16] Various groups have lobbied for the business judgment rule to apply to decisions made in relation to insolvent trading. This question of application may well become a significant point of debate in future law reform proposals.

The reason for the exclusion of the business judgment rule to insolvent trading is that insolvent trading is regarded as a discrete area of law in which, so it is said, it would not be appropriate for the presumptions of the business judgment rule to operate.[17] Additionally, the philosophy behind the business judgment rule is remarkably different to that of the insolvent trading provisions. Whereas the business judgment rule aims to encourage entrepreneurial risk taking and facilitate innovation, the insolvent trading provisions are concerned with the protection of creditors and encouraging directors to place insolvent companies into administration as early as possible. Clearly, the exclusion of the application of the business judgment rule from the duty to prevent insolvent trading is consistent with the philosophy and rationale of the insolvent trading provisions.[18]

---

16 See Corporate Law Economic Reform Program, Directors' Duties and Corporate Governance, para 5.2.3.

17 See Corporate Law Economic Reform Program, Directors' Duties and Corporate Governance, para 5.2.3.

18 See generally R Langford, "The New Statutory Business Judgment Rule: Should it Apply to the Duty to Prevent Insolvent Trading" (1998) 16(7) CSLJ 533.

In any event the elements of the business judgment rule are to a large extent already used in determining liability under the insolvent trading provisions and it is arguably unnecessary to extend the business judgment rule to the insolvent trading duty. These elements include the requirements of good faith and proper purpose such as considering the interests of creditors, the duty to inform oneself, and the need to make decisions in the best interests of the company. If a director is found to have breached the insolvent trading provisions and is unable to rely on the defence in s 588H(5), or indeed any of the defences in s 588H, he or she would almost certainly not be able to seek refuge in the business judgment rule either.

Against this background, it would be inappropriate and against the policy of the insolvent trading provisions to allow the business judgment rule to have application to the duty to prevent insolvent trading.

Other Grounds for Relief: Sections 1318 and 1317S

12

"*... one purpose sought to be achieved...is to avoid persons of appropriate experience and ability being deterred from taking up positions with [a company], particularly as a director, by reason of any resultant exposure to liability in circumstances when they have acted in good faith.*"[1]

1 *State Bank of South Australia v Marcus Clarke* (1996) 19 ACSR 606 at 643.

OBJECTIVES

This Chapter will:

- set out the basis of the grounds for exculpation under s 1318 and s 1317S of the Law;
- consider the extent to which s 1318 represents a similar ground of relief as the statutory business judgment rule.

[12.1] General overview

Sections 1318 and 1317S both provide a possible basis for directors to escape liability under the insolvent trading provisions. Section 1317S also provides a possible avenue for relief for directors facing proceedings for breach of the statutory duties under s 180 to s 183, including the duty of care and diligence.

Section 1318 generally provides a basis for relief in civil proceedings resulting from negligence, default, or breach of duty or trust whereas s 1317S provides relief from civil liability arising out of a contravention of a civil penalty provision.

[12.1.1] SECTION 1318

Section 1318 allows a Court to relieve certain persons from liability in civil proceedings for negligence, default, breach of duty or breach of trust, if the person establishes that he or she acted honestly, and that he or she ought fairly to be excused for the negligence, default, breach of duty or trust having regard to all of the circumstances of the case including those connected with their appointment. There is some authority to suggest that it also applies in the case on contributory negligence and other actions for damages under a breach of contract.[2]

Section 1318 applies to an officer of a corporation (which includes a director), an auditor of a corporation, an expert, and a receiver, receiver and manager, liquidator or other person appointed or directed by the Court to carry out any duty under the Law in relation to a corporation, including executive officers and company secretaries: s 1318(4).

Section 1318 can provide relief in proceedings brought by a party other than the company.[3] A person who merely apprehends that proceedings may be brought against them can apply for relief under the section: s 1318(2).

Although s 1318 is unlikely to apply to proceedings brought under the predecessor provisions to s 588G, especially under s 592,[4] the fact that the duty to prevent insolvent trading under s 588G imposes a positive duty on directors means that s 1318 is likely to apply to s 588G.[5]

There is no express equivalent in s 1318 that the person must have acted "reasonably" in order to be excused. However, the degree of care and diligence that the person exercised will be relevant in determining whether the person ought fairly to be excused in the circumstances.[6] The Courts seem reluctant to exercise their discretion under the section where a person has breached their duty of care and diligence.[7] Similarly, the Courts are reluctant to exercise their

2 *AWA Ltd v Daniels* (1992) 10 ACLC 933 at 1006 per Rogers CJ Comm D.

3 See *Daniels v AWA Ltd* (1995) 13 ACLC 614.

4 See *Commonwealth Bank of Australia v Friedrich* (1991) 9 ACLC 946.

5 See M Hyland, "Insolvent Trading: Does Section 1318 Apply?" (1996) 34(4) *Law Society Journal* 44.

6 See *Commonwealth Bank of Australia v Friedrich* (1991) 9 ACLC 946.

7 See *AWA Ltd v Daniels* (1992) 10 ACLC 933.

discretion where a director has benefited from their breach of duty[8] or remains in wrongful possession of company property.[9] For these reasons, it is arguable that where the person seeking relief has not acted reasonably in the circumstances and with care and diligence it is unlikely that s 1318 relief will be granted. Consequently, s 1318 has similar effects to the newly introduced statutory business judgment rule: see Ch 16 at [16.1.6]. In this way, where a claim for breach of s 180 is brought simultaneously with a claim for breach of s 588G(2) and the person is unable to rely on the statutory business judgment rule it is unlikely that the Court will exercise its discretion under s 1318 in their favour.

[12.1.2] SECTION 1317S

Section 1317S provides a basis for relief from liability under a civil penalty provision where the person has acted honestly and the person ought fairly to be excused in the circumstances of the case. It applies to the duty to prevent insolvent trading and the statutory duties contained in s 180 to s 183. When deciding whether or not to excuse a person for a breach of s 588G, the Court can have regard to any action the person took to appoint an administrator to the company, when the action was taken, and the results of the action: s 13175(3). A person can apply for relief in advance if their apprehends that proceedings may be brought against them under a civil penalty provision: s 13175(4).

[12.2] Philosophy/rationale

Perry J succinctly stated the rationale behind s 1318 in *State of South Australia v Marcus Clark*:

> ... one purpose sought to be achieved ... is to avoid persons of appropriate experience and ability being deterred from taking up positions with [a company], particularly as a director, by reason of any resultant exposure to liability in circumstances when they have acted in good faith.[10]

Arguably, the same rationale underlies s 1317S.

However, it is interesting to note that similar rationales have been advanced for the newly introduced statutory business judgment rule.[11] The defence in

7 See *AWA Ltd v Daniels* (1992) 10 ACLC 933.
8 *Re Lasscock's Nurseries Ltd (in liq)* [1940] SASR 251. See also *Permakraft (NZ) Ltd (in liq) v Nicholson* (1982) 1 ACLC 488.
9 *Guinness plc v Saunders* (No 2) (1987) 3 BCC 520.
10 (1996) 19 ACSR 606. Note that the comments of Perry J are made in relation to s 29 of the *State Bank of South Australia Act* 1983 (SA).
11 See Corporate Law Economic Reform Program Proposals for Reform, *Directors' Duties and Corporate Governance: Facilitating innovation and Protecting Investors*, Paper No 3 (1997), paras 5.2.1–5.2.2.

s 1318 has similar effects to that of the business judgment rule. It has already been argued that it is inappropriate to extend the reach of the business judgment rule to the insolvent trading provisions due to this difference in philosophy between the two provisions. Whereas the business judgment rule aims to encourage entrepreneurial risk taking and facilitate innovation,[12] the insolvent trading provisions are concerned with the protection of creditors and encouraging directors to place insolvent companies into administration as early as possible. If director protection is generally not a point of emphasis within the philosophy of the insolvent trading provisions, it seems difficult to justify the avenues for relief from liability under s 1318 and s 1317S. Although no cases have dealt with s 1318 or s 1317S, it is hoped that the Courts will find an appropriate balance between promotion of entrepreneurial appointments and creditor protection.

[12.3] History/former law

Section 1318 is based on United Kingdom legislation that was intended to prevent penal provisions in the Companies Acts from operating unfairly. In contrast to the position in the United Kingdom, the Victorian Full Court decided that such provisions should only afford protection to those exposed to civil liability. On the basis of this decision, the National Companies Bill 1976 (Cth), s 535 of the *Companies Act* 1981 (Cth), and s 1318 of the Law were all expressly limited to civil liability.

The application of s 1318 to the insolvent trading provisions is questionable. It was held not to apply to the predecessor provision to s 588G, s 592. In *Commonwealth Bank of Australia v Friedrich*[13] Tadgell J held that s 592 did not impose a positive duty on directors and therefore directors subject to proceedings under s 592 could not rely on s 1318 as a basis for relief. Hodgson J followed this interpretation in *Standard Chartered Bank of Australia v Antico*.[14] His Honour agreed that s 592 does not impose a positive duty on directors, and was concerned that the inclusion of "those who took part in the management of the company" within s 592 but their exclusion from the definition of "officer" in s 1318 would mean that the application of s 1318 would be capricious. However, with the new insolvent trading provisions imposing a positive duty on directors such historical problems seem to have been overcome.

---

12 See Corporate Law Economic Reform Program Proposals for Reform, *Directors' Duties and Corporate Governance: Facilitating innovation and Protecting Investors*, Paper No 3 (1997), para 5.2.2.

13 (1991) 9 ACLC 946.

14 (1995) 131 ALR 1. For opinions questioning these conclusions see *Byron v Southern Star Group Pty Ltd t/a KGC Magnetic Tapes* (1995) 13 ACLC 301; and *Bans Pty Ltd v Ling* (1995) 13 ACLC 524.

Section 1317S is modelled on its predecessor provision, s 1317JA. Section 1317S forms part of an overall restructuring of the Law intended to clarify the Law in relation to directors' duties.

[12.4] Notable cases

[12.4.1] *KENNA AND BROWN PTY LTD (IN LIQ) V KENNA*

Kenna and Brown Pty Ltd (in liq) v Kenna[15] considered ss 588G, 588H and 1318 of the *Corporations Law.*

The liquidators made several claims against the directors of a building company including a claim for recovery of funds allegedly caused by breach of duties to the plaintiff company including breaches by the first and third defendants of the insolvent trading provisions. The claim was brought under s 588M which deals with directors' liability to compensate the company.

The first and third defendants were each directors. The first defendant, Mr Kenna, conducted the administration of the business and the third defendant, Mr Brown, supervised the building works. The Court found that the company had been insolvent at the time that the relevant debts were incurred and that in view of the company's financial position and failure to secure further funding, together with the expansion of its activities, there were reasonable grounds to suspect that the company was insolvent or would become insolvent.

In relation to Mr Kenna, the Court found that he was aware of the financial position of the company and that he had breached s 588G.

As for Mr Brown, the Court found that he had not been aware of the financial position of the company such as to satisfy s 588(2)(a) but found that a reasonable person in a like position in a company would have been so aware.

Mr Brown relied on a number of defences. First, his defence under s 588H(2) was that he had reasonable grounds to expect that the company was solvent and would remain solvent. Mr Brown's counsel emphasised that it was Mr Kenna alone who attended to the financial affairs of the partnership. The Court accepted that but considered the fact that Mr Brown's practice of consulting the company's accountant for approval and explanation of the accounts had ceased a year before the time in question. Mr Brown was also aware that two new supervisors had been employed and that there had been no new funding. The Court found that even if Mr Brown had expected that the company was solvent or would remain solvent that there were no reasonable grounds for that expectation.

Mr Brown also relied on a defence under s 588H(3) claiming that he had relied on the company's accountant. The Court considered the fact that Mr

15 (1999) 32 AC SR 430; Sup Ct, NSW, 2 June 1999 per Bergin J.

Brown had not been told about three new large building projects until after they had been taken on. In those circumstances, it should have been clear to Mr Brown that he was not being informed about what was going on. The Court rejected the s 588H(3) defence, finding that Mr Brown did not have reasonable grounds to believe that he was being adequately informed.

The most interesting aspect of the case concerns Mr Brown's reliance on s 1318 of the Law. He sought an order of the Court that he acted honestly and fairly and ought fairly to be excused under s 1318 of the Law. The first question was whether a breach of s 588G was something that could be excused under s 1318. Previously in dealing with a predecessor provision, s 556, Tadgell J in *Commonwealth Bank v Friedrich*[16] found that liability under s 556 arose not in account of the performance of a forbidden act, or omission. The only prerequisite for liability under s 556 was taking part in the management of the company, therefore it was not a default or breach of duty which could be excused under s 1318. Hodgson J in *Standard Chartered Bank of Australia v Antico*[17] approved of what Tadgell J had said and also pointed out that s 556 imposed liability on those people who were not officers of the company but who were merely taking part in the management of the company. His Honour was concerned that the predecessor to s 1318 might act capriciously in those circumstances. Hodgson J also pointed to the wording of the defences in s 556(2) which gave the appearance of being a full elaboration of the circumstances in which the legislature considered that persons falling within s 556(1) ought to escape liability.

There is no longer any doubt that a breach of the insolvent trading provisions can be excused under s 1318.

In deciding whether to exercise her discretion, Bergin J considered the following factors that had been put forward by Counsel for the liquidator that should count against the granting of relief:

- Mr Brown had not been able to make out any of the s 558H defences.
- Mr Brown had shown a disregard of his obligations as a director.
- Mr Brown's failures had allowed the company's business to be ruined.
- Mr Brown had failed to intelligently inquire about the affairs of the company.
- The armoury of legal powers that were open to Mr Brown to ensure that the loss suffered by the company was not so suffered could be contrasted with the limited rights of the creditors.

Bergin J found that the fact that Mr Brown had not been able to make out the defences should not influence her decision as to whether or not to exercise her discretion. Ultimately, it was the fact that Mr Brown had made no inquiries about

16 [(1991) 9 ACLC 946.
17 (1995) 131 ALR 1.

the company's financial situation which led her Honour to decide not to exercise her discretion under s 1318 in favour of Mr Brown.

[12.5] Checklist

If a director is considering claiming relief under s 1318 or 1317S they should consider the following:

- If they suspect that proceedings may be commenced against them, consider the availability of claiming relief under s 1318 or 1317S. If relief is possible, consideration should be given to making such an application to the Court for relief. Whether or not an application should be made will be determined on a case-by-case basis.
- If claiming relief under s 1318, gather evidence supporting the argument that they have acted responsibly in the fulfilment of their duties and have not breached their duty of care and diligence.
- If claiming relief under s 1317S, review any action they have taken to appoint an administrator.
- If claiming relief under either section, gather evidence supporting the argument that they have generally acted honestly and responsibly in the fulfilment of their duties. It is not clear what factors the Court will have regard to when considering a claim for relief, but if they have acted in good faith they are more likely to be granted relief.

[12.6] Hints

[12.6.1] CLAIM RELIEF IF PROCEEDINGS APPREHENDED

Under s 1318(2) and 1317S(4) a person can apply for relief under their provisions if proceedings to which the sections apply are apprehended. This is in contrast to the defences under s 588H, which can only be utilised after proceedings have commenced. If a director or officer suspects that proceedings may be commenced against them, and relief under either of the sections is possible, they should consider making an application for such relief.

PART C
Other General Duties

PART C, *continued*

General Fiduciary Duties and Their Utility

13

"*Equity has a long-standing tradition of intervention in the activities of company directors, agents, trustees, solicitors and the like in the cause of exacting high standards of business and professional conduct.*"[1]

1 P D Finn, *Fiduciary Obligations* (Law Book Co, Sydney, 1977), p 1.

OBJECTIVES

This Chapter will:

- consider the general nature of fiduciary duties;
- discuss the elements of number of fiduciary duties at common law;
- indicate the ways in which insolvency practitioners may bring an action for breach of fiduciary duty.

[13.1] General overview

A director's relationship with the company is fiduciary in nature.

A fiduciary relationship is formed when a fiduciary undertakes or agrees to act for or on behalf of, or in the interests of, another person in the exercise of a power or discretion which will affect the interests of that other person.[2] A fiduciary refers to the person undertaking to act on behalf of another. Equity imposes special duties and obligations on fiduciaries.

There are many recognised forms of fiduciary relationships, which include agent and principal, trustee and beneficiary, and company and director.[3] The duties of a fiduciary vary in accordance with the circumstances that give rise to the relationship.[4]

Due to the special nature of the fiduciary relationship between a company and a director, the director's position of temptation and the vulnerability of shareholders, a number of duties and obligations are placed on directors to promote a high standard of loyalty. There are positive and negative aspects of this overall duty of loyalty. The positive aspects include the duty to act in good faith for the benefit of the company as a whole, the duty to avoid fettering discretions, and the duty to exercise powers only for a proper purpose. The negative aspect is primarily constituted by the duty to avoid conflicts of interest. In addition to these a common duty of care and diligence is also imposed on directors as a result of the relationship of close proximity between directors and the company.

These fiduciary duties are imposed on directors and senior executive officers. Senior executive officers are those people who take part in the management of the company and who have an active policy-making role.[5] It should be noted that the duty to avoid a conflict of interest applies to directors, partners, and even employees.[6]

A breach of these fiduciary duties may give rise to liability to account for improper profits made as a result of the breach and a liability to pay equitable compensation for loss of company assets.[7] For damages to be awarded there must be a causal link between the breach of duty and the damage suffered by the company. However, the Courts are taking an increasingly wide and strict interpretation of the causation requirement in order to fulfil the philosophy of fiduciary duties and avoid harm to the company.[8]

---

2 P Nygh and P Butt, *Butterworths Concise Australian Legal Dictionary* (Butterworths, Sydney, 1997), p 157.

3 *Aberdeen Railway Co v Blaikie Bros* [1843–60] All ER 249.

4 *Hospital Products Ltd v United States Surgical Corp* (1984) 156 CLR 41 at 69.

5 *CCA (Vic) v Bracht* (1988) 7 ACLC 40 per Ormiston J.

6 See *Hivac Ltd v Park Royal Scientific Instruments Ltd* [1946] Ch 169.

7 Corporate Law Economic Reform Program, *Directors' Duties and Corporate Governance: Facilitating Innovation and Protecting Investors*, Paper No 3, AGPS, Canberra, 1998, para 4.3.2.

8 See *O'Halloran v RT Thomas and Family Pty Ltd* (1998) 16 ACLC 1705. For a discussion of this case see R Baxt, "Does There Have to be a Causal Link between a Breach of a Director's Fiduciary

The fiduciary duties imposed on directors will be analysed separately. Many have been embodied in statutory form within the Law. Mention will be made where this has been done.

[13.1.1] DUTY TO ACT IN GOOD FAITH FOR THE BENEFIT OF THE COMPANY AS A WHOLE

Honesty is the cornerstone of fiduciary duties. However, in most situations more than honesty will be required of directors. There are two requirements of the duty to act in good faith in the interests of the company as a whole. A subjective duty of good faith is imposed on directors as fiduciaries under which they must act "bona fide in what they consider – not what the court may consider – is in the interests of the company".[9] Directors must also give proper consideration to the interests of the company. Knowledge that they are not acting in the best interests of the company or in disregard of these interests will result in a breach of the duty.

This fiduciary duty is often an issue in small proprietary companies.

This common law fiduciary duty has been encapsulated in statutory form in s 181 and s 184(1) of the Law, although there remain some differences between the two and the common law still exists.

[13.1.2] DUTY TO AVOID FETTERING DISCRETIONS

Directors have many discretions and functions conferred by the constitution of the company. Because these duties must be exercised for the benefit of the company as a whole, directors generally cannot fetter discretions conferred on them although they could agree to fetter particular discretions provided that in doing so they believe that it is in the best interests of the company.[10] Directors must give adequate consideration when they are exercising discretions and must not delegate their discretions without authority.

Authority may be given to directors to delegate their discretions in the constitution of the company. Authority is given in statutory form in s 198D of the Law, which provides for directors to delegate any of their powers unless the constitution of the company provides otherwise.

[13.1.3] DUTY TO EXERCISE POWERS FOR A PROPER PURPOSE

Directors have a number of discretions and powers conferred upon them. These will often be conferred by the company's constitution. These discretions and powers cannot be used arbitrarily for any purpose. The fiduciary relationship

Duty and the Damage Suffered by a Company?" 1999 17(1) CSLJ 54; and R Baxt, "Linking a Director's Breach of Duty and Damages" (1999) 27(1) ABLR 74.

9 *Re Smith & Fawcett Ltd* [1942] Ch 304 at 306 per Lord Greene MR.

10 *Throsby v Goldberg* (1964) 112 CLR 597.

between the corporation and the director implies that the discretions and powers must be used in the interests of the company rather than the personal interests of the director. Directors must exercise these discretions and powers for a "proper purpose".

Ipp J outlined a number of principles central in determining whether or not a director has acted for an "improper purpose" in *Permanent Building Society (in liq) v Wheeler*.[11] These principles are:

- Fiduciary powers granted to directors are to be exercised for the purpose for which they were given, not collateral purposes.
- It must be shown that the substantial purpose of directors was improper or collateral to their duties as a director. The issue is not whether business decisions were good or bad; it is whether directors have acted in breach of their fiduciary duties.
- Honest or altruistic behaviour does not prevent a finding of improper conduct. Whether acts were performed for the benefit of the company is to be objectively determined. However evidence as to the subjective intentions or beliefs is nevertheless relevant.
- The Court must determine whether, but for the improper or collateral purpose, the directors would have performed the act in dispute.

A director or officer can breach their duty of good faith if the law objectively considers that what they are doing is improper, even if they subjectively believe that what they are doing is in the best interests of the company.[12] The personal views of the director of officer as to whether or not their actions are for a proper purpose are not relevant. This is in contrast to the statutory position under s 184(1) of the Law.

Two steps are involved in the reasoning process to determine whether a director has acted for a proper purpose. First, the Court must determine the purposes for which the power may or may not be exercised. This will usually be evident from the company's constitution, which will often specify the purposes for which the discretions and powers can be exercised.[13] In the absence of any provision or guidance in the corporation's constitution, the Court will look to the nature of the company and its particular activities.[14] Secondly, the Court must then decide whether the purpose for which the power was in fact exercised is within the category of permissible purposes.[15] The subjective belief of the director as to whether or not the act is for a proper purpose is not relevant. In

11 (1994) 14 ACSR 109 at 137.

12 *Australian Growth Resources Corp Pty Ltd v van Reesema* (1988) 6 ACLC 529 at 539.

13 *Howard Smith Ltd v Ampol Petroleum Ltd* [1974] AC 821.

14 See *Whitehouse v Carlton Hotel Pty Ltd* (1987) 5 ACLC 421; and *Australian Metropolitan Life Assurance Co Ltd v Ure* (1923) 33 CLR 199.

15 *Howard Smith Ltd v Ampol Petroleum Ltd* [1974] AC 821 at 835.

determining whether the actual exercise of power was within the range of permissible purposes, the Court will have regard to all circumstances surrounding the decision.[16] Where there are mixed purposes, in order to contravene the provisions the improper purpose must be substantial, or a significantly contributing cause.[17] An improper purpose that was subordinate to a proper purpose but which triggered action would arguably not be a breach of the fiduciary duty.

The onus of proving that a director has exercised a discretion or power for an improper purpose rests with the person claiming the improper purpose.[18]

This fiduciary duty has been incorporated into statutory form under s 181 and s 184(1) of the Law. It should be noted that the statutory duty of good faith differs from the common law fiduciary duty of good faith as the statutory duty is concerned with the subjective and personal beliefs of the director or officer as to whether they acted in the best interests of the corporation.

[13.1.4] DUTY TO AVOID CONFLICTS OF INTERESTS

Directors and officers are granted discretions and powers that must be exercised in the best interests of the company. When a director has a personal interest that may conflict with the best interests of the company, it is possible that the director will not exercise her or his discretions and powers to advance the company's best interests but will rather seek to advance their own personal interest. Directors have a fiduciary duty to avoid conflict of interests.[19] In the words of Lord Herschell:

> ... a fiduciary is not, unless otherwise expressly provided, entitled to make a profit; he is not allowed to put himself in a position where his interest and duty conflict.[20]

Not all "interests" are significant enough to attach the fiduciary duty of avoidance. For the fiduciary duty to apply, the interest must be a "real sensible possibility", not theoretical, interest.[21] It must be sufficient enough to force the director, in deciding how to act, to consider both her or his concern and her or his duty to the company.[22] In this sense, it must be a substantial interest that has the potential to affect the interests of the company.

16 *Hindle v John Cotton Ltd* (1919) 56 Sc LR 625 at 630.

17 See *Darvall v North Sydney Brick and Tile Co Ltd* (1989) 7 ACLC 659.

18 *Australian Metropolitan Life Assurance Co Ltd v Ure* (1923) 33 CLR 199; *Ascot Investments Pty Ltd v Harper* (1981) 5 ACLR 328.

19 *Keech v Sandford* (1726) 25 ER 223. This decision has been confirmed in *Phipps v Boardman* [1967] 2 AC 46 at 123; *New Zealand Netherlands Society "Oranje" Inc v Kuys* [1973] 1 WLR 1126 at 1129; and *Guinness plc v Saunders* [1990] 2 AC 663.

20 *Bray v Ford* [1896] AC 44 at 51.

21 See *Industrial Development Consultants Ltd v Cooley* [1972] 1 All ER 162; *Queensland Mines Ltd v Hudson* (1978) 18 ALR 1 at 3; and *Hospital Products Ltd v United States Surgical Corp Ltd* (1975) 156 CLR 1.

22 *ANZ Banking Group Ltd v Nangadilly Pastoral Co Pty Ltd* (1978) 139 CLR 195.

In Australia, the fiduciary duty to avoid a conflict of interest has traditionally followed a strict formulation. Under this formulation, a director must not be placed in a situation where their interest and their duty to the company may conflict.[23] This means that the director would be precluded from being influenced by any conflicting interest when exercising their duty to the company, and the Court does not have to prove causation. Accordingly, good faith is irrelevant.

This strict view has been confirmed by recent cases,[24] despite the attempts of some Courts to soften the duty to merely require that a director should not take personal advantage of any conflict if one should arise.[25]

There are a number of situations in which a conflict of interest is likely:[26]

- where a director has an interest in a contract with the corporation;
- where a director uses information of the corporation;
- where director uses property of the corporation;
- where a director uses her or his office otherwise than for its proper purpose;
- where a director competes with or takes advantage of an opportunity that may be open to the corporation;
- where a director holds an office or property giving duties or interests which conflict with the duties to the corporation.

Whenever a director thinks he or she may have an interest that may conflict with the best interests of the corporation, he or she should immediately disclose this interest to the board of directors who can then consider the action to be taken.

The Law provides for disclosure of a "material personal interest". Section 191(1) provides that a director must give the other directors notice of their interest, unless the interest falls within a class of exemptions. In a proprietary company, if this disclosure is made, the director will usually be able to vote on issues to which the interest relates: s 194. However, in a public company, unless the other directors give approval (s 195(2)), the director with the conflicting interest will not be able to vote on the matter to which the interest relates nor be present while the matter is being considered: s 195(1).

These statutory duties of disclosure operate in addition to the common law fiduciary rules regarding conflicts of interests: s 193.

The severity with which the Court treats a breach of the duty to avoid a conflict of interest was displayed in recent times when the Supreme Court of South Australia found a chief executive officer liable for over $81m for failing to disclose a conflict of interest.[27]

---

23 *Phipps v Boardman* [1967] 2 AC 46.

24 *Gemstone Corp of Aust Ltd v Grasso* (1994) 13 ACSR 695.

25 *Hospital Products Ltd v United Surgical Corp* (1984) 156 CLR 41.

26 H A J Ford and R P Austin, *Ford's Australian Corporation Law: Principles and Practice* (Butterworths, 8th ed, Sydney, 1997), pp 13,187–13,188.

27 *State Bank of South Australia v Marcus Clark* (1996) 19 ACSR 606.

[13.1.5] DUTY OF CARE, SKILL AND DILIGENCE

In addition to the statutory duty of care and diligence contained in s 180 of the Law, directors owe a common law duty of care, skill and diligence to the performance of their duties and functions.[28] This common law duty stems from the law of negligence and the relationship of proximity between the director and the corporation.[29] This common law duty applies to both executive and non-executive company,[30] although the standard expected of executive directors will usually be higher than that expected of non-executive directors.

The appropriate standard of care is measured objectively. A director must exercise the degree of care that a reasonable person would exercise.[31] The standard of skill required of directors is measured objectively. Although directors are not expected to bring any particular qualifications to their office, they should have at least a minimal understanding of financial affairs,[32] and if any special qualifications are possessed these must be used.[33] In regards to the standard of diligence required, although directors are not bound to give continuous attention to the affairs of the company[34] they are expected to place themselves in a position to guide and monitor the management of the company.[35] The business judgment rule applies to this common law duty of care, skill and diligence: s 180(2).

A breach of the common law duty of care, skill and diligence may give rise to an obligation to pay damages.[36]

[13.2] Philosophy/rationale

The rationale for imposing fiduciary duties on directors stems from the fact that directors are essentially agents of the company.

Due to their position as the centre of the personality of the company, and the vast powers and discretions they possess, many opportunities for mismanagement are possible. The directors are placed in a position of temptation whilst the shareholders are vulnerable to the actions of the directors. In order to ensure that directors do not mismanage the affairs of the company, fiduciary duties are imposed on them. In other words, the imposition of fiduciary duties on directors and senior executives is supported in policy terms.

28 *Daniels t/as Deloitte Haskins & Sells v AWA Ltd* (1995) 13 ACLC 614; and *Permanent Building Society (in liq) v Wheeler* (1994) 14 ACSR 109.
29 *Daniels v AWA Ltd* (1995) 13 ACLC 614.
30 *Permanent Building Society (in liq) v Wheeler* (1994) 14 ACSR 109.
31 *Daniels t/as Deloitte Haskins & Sells v AWA Ltd* (1995) 13 ACLC 614.
32 *Commonwealth Bank of Australia v Friedrich* (1991) 9 ACLC 946 per Tadgell J.
33 *Re Brazillian Rubber Plantations and Estates Ltd* [1911] 1 Ch 425.
34 *Re City Equitable Fire Insurance* [1925] Ch 407.
35 *Daniels t/as Deloitte Haskins & Sells v AWA Ltd* (1995) 13 ACLC 614 at 664,
36 See *Re Dawson (dec'd)* [1966] 2 NSWLR 211.

[13.3] History/former law

That directors and senior executive officers owe fiduciary duties to the corporation of which they are directors is no surprise. The proposition is derived from that fact that in early English law joint stock companies were constituted by deeds of settlement of which the directors were trustees of the corporate assets.[37] It was not a large step for the Courts to apply these principles to incorporated corporations.

[13.4] Notable cases

[13.4.1] *STATE BANK OF SOUTH AUSTRALIA V MARCUS CLARK*

A high profile case dealing with a breach of the fiduciary duty to avoid a conflict of interest is *State Bank of South Australia v Marcus Clark*.[38]

Mr Clark was the Chief Executive Officer of the State Bank of South Australia (State Bank). He was also a director of a New Zealand company, Equiticorp Holdings (Equiticorp), as well as some of Equiticorp's subsidiaries. Mr Clark possessed many of the shares in Equiticorp.

Equiticorp lent $27m to APA. Shares held by APA in a third company, Oceanic, were given by APA as security for the loan.

Due to his position as director of Equiticorp, Mr Clark was aware that Equiticorp was reliant upon the funds expected to be repaid by APA. He was also aware that APA was having liquidity problems of its own. Because of this, he was aware that the sale by APA of its shares in Oceanic was likely to impact heavily on the ability of APA to repay its loan to Equiticorp.

The State Bank subsequently entered negotiations with APA to acquire its shares in Oceanic. Mr Clark did not disclose his position of conflict to the board of the State Bank. The board did not otherwise become aware of Mr Clark's position of conflict as the negotiations were carried out in a hurried manner and there was not sufficient time for the State Bank to conduct a thorough investigation of the value or Oceanic itself.

Following the purchase of the shares by the State Bank, it was discovered that the value of the shares in Oceanic was significantly less than what the State Bank had paid for them. The State Bank therefore suffered a great financial loss. The State Bank brought an action against Mr Clark for breach of his fiduciary duty to avoid a conflict of interest.

37 R Tomasic, J Jackson and R Woellner, *Corporations Law: Principles, Policy and Process* (Butterworths, Sydney, 1996), p 337.

38 (1996) 19 ACSR 606. Sup Ct, SA, 29 March 1996 per Perry J.

The Supreme Court of South Australia held that Mr Clark had breached his duty to avoid a conflict of interest. According to Perry J:

> ... Mr Clark, as a director of Equiticorp Holdings and as a director of the bank, owed duties to two companies (or, more accurately, a company and a statutory corporation) whose interests did not necessarily coincide. Equiticorp Holdings had an interest in securing the timely repayment by APA of the $27m loan by Equiticorp Australia to APA. The bank, on the other hand, had an interest in acquiring the Oceanic shares owned by APA at a price that was not excessive after a proper valuation could be made and considered. Mr Marcus Clark owed a duty to ensure that no more was paid by the bank to APA, if a transaction for the acquisition of the shares was to proceed, than they were worth. However, as a director of Equiticorp Holdings, he had an interest in securing a position where the bank paid to APA before 31 March 1988 the highest amount which it could be persuaded to pay for the Oceanic shares. The larger the payment to APA, the more effective would be the enhancement of APA's ability to discharge the loan due to it by Equiticorp Australia. The potential conflict in the discharge of the fiduciary duties owed to each company was magnified by reason of the holding by Mr Marcus Clark's family of 500,000 shares in Equiticorp Holdings, which gave rise to an indirect pecuniary benefit in circumstances where substantial cash payment was to be made to one of Equiticorp Holding's subsidiaries. The combination of circumstances obliged Mr Marcus Clark, if he was to discharge his fiduciary obligations to the bank, at the very least, both to disclose to the board the position in which he was placed and the fact that Equiticorp stood to gain from any payment to APA. Furthermore, it obliged him to refrain from voting at the meetings of the board of directors at which the matter was considered.[39]

However, Mr Clark had not disclosed his conflict of interest to the board of directors. He also took part in discussions by the State Bank regarding the purchase of the shares and voted on the matter. The Court had no difficulty in finding that Mr Clark had breached his fiduciary duty to avoid a conflict of interest. They also found that his failure to obtain an independent valuation of the value of APA's shares in Oceanic amounted to negligence.

The Court ordered Mr Clark to pay over $81m compensation to the State Bank.

[13.5] Checklist

In assessing whether a director has breached a fiduciary duty, insolvency practitioners should consult the following:

39 (1996) 19 ACSR 606 at 632.

- What did the director believe were the general interests of the corporation?
- What did the director believe were the specific interests of the corporation in the particular matter at hand?
- Had the director given adequate consideration to these interests when making the decision?
- Was there authority in the corporation's constitution for the director to delegate her or his powers or discretions?
- If the director sought to delegate a power or discretion by virtue of s 198D of the Law, was this delegation in the best interests of the corporation?
- For what purposes were the director's powers and discretions conferred? Was there any reference to this within the constitution of the corporation?
- Was the particular purpose which the director sought to make of this power or discretion within the purposes he or she had identified?
- Did the director have a real and substantial and significant interest in something which could conflict with her or his duties and obligations to the particular corporation?
- Had the director disclosed this interest to the board of directors?
- Had the board of directors given the director approval to participate in meetings where a matter that related to her or his conflict of interest was being discussed?
- Had the board of directors given the director permission to vote on a matter in which he or she may have had a conflict of interest?
- Does the subject matter of the decision the director was making relate to the business operations of the corporation?
- Had the director made the decision in good faith, without a material personal interest in the subject matter, informed to an appropriate extent and with a rational belief that this decision was in the best interests of the corporation?
- Was the director in a position to fully monitor and guide the management of the corporation?
- Was the director appropriately qualified and experienced for the office he or she held at the time?

Duty of Good Faith

14

"A breach of the obligation to act bona fide in the interests of the company involves a consciousness that what is being done is not in the interests of the company, and deliberate conduct in disregard of that knowledge."[1]

1 *Marchesi v Barnes* [1870] VR 434 at 438 per Gowans J.

OBJECTIVES

This Chapter will:

- discuss the elements of the statutory duty of good faith;
- consider the meaning of "the best interests of the company";
- consider the requirement of "proper purpose".

[14.1] General overview

The statutory duty of good faith encapsulates the fiduciary duty to act honestly and for proper purposes.

By virtue of s 181 of the Law, a director or other officer of a company must exercise their powers and discharge their duties in what they believe to be the best interests of the company and for a proper purpose. Failure to do so could lead to the imposition of a civil penalty. Under s 184(1), if the director or officer is dishonest in failing to fulfil this requirement, and does do intentionally or recklessly, then a criminal offence may have been committed.

Directors are obliged to act in good faith for what they personally consider to be the best interests of the company. Directors or other officers who have acted for an improper purpose will not contravene the provisions if they subjectively and honestly believed that their purpose was in the best interests of the company.[2] They may, however, still breach their fiduciary duty of loyalty if their purpose was that the Court would consider as objectively dishonest. If a director or officer knows that they are exercising their powers and discharging their duties for an improper purpose that is not in the best interests of the company, they will be guilty of a criminal offence: s 184(1).

Directors and officers must act in the best interests of the company. No duty is owed to individual shareholders or groups of shareholders of the company. However, where a company is insolvent, regard must be had to the interests of creditors.[3] Directors of wholly owned subsidiaries will act in good faith for the best interests of the subsidiary if its constitution authorises it to act in the best interests of the holding company, the director does act in good faith in the best interests of the holding company, and the subsidiary is not insolvent at this time or become insolvent as a result of the director's act: s 187.

It is submitted that there is no difference between the "interest" of the company and the "best interest" of the company. The Courts tend to use these terms interchangeably suggesting that in practical terms there is no difference between the terms.[4]

The proper purpose requirement is built on the fiduciary duty to act for proper purposes. As a fiduciary, directors must act in the best interests of the corporation and not for their own personal benefit. The Court must first determine the purposes for which the power may or may not be exercised and then decide whether the purpose for which the power was in fact exercised is within the category or permissible purposes.[5] In relation to the former, the Court will look

2 *Marchesi v Barnes* [1970] VR 434 per Gowans J.
3 *Kinsela v Russell Kinsela Pty Ltd (in liq)* (1986) 4 ACLC 215. See also *Winkworth v Edward Baron Development Co Ltd* [1987] 1 All ER 114.
4 See *Whitehouse v Carlton Hotel Pty Ltd* (1987) 162 CLR 285.
5 *Howard Smith Ltd v Ampol Petroleum Ltd* [1974] AC 821 at 835.

at the corporate constitution or, in the absence of a corporate constitution, the nature of the company and its activities.[6] In determining whether the actual exercise of power was within the range of permissible purposes, the Court will have regard to all circumstances surrounding the decision.[7] Where there are mixed purposes, in order to contravene the provisions the improper purpose must be substantial, or a significantly contributing cause.[8] An improper purpose that was subordinate to a proper purpose but which triggered action would be excluded.

[14.2] Philosophy/rationale

The statutory duty of good faith seeks to encapsulate the fiduciary duty of good faith. In this sense, the rationale behind the statutory provision is to provide incentives for directors and officers to exercise their powers and discharge their duties in the best interests of the company, through the potential imposition of harsh civil and criminal penalties. This requirement is based on the need for directors and officers to be loyal to their company and to serve its best interests and not seek to gain an improper advantage for themselves.

[14.3] History/former law

Statutory duties of good faith are based on the fiduciary duty to act in good faith for a proper purpose. The earliest Australian statutory provision to deal with this duty was s 124(1) of the *Uniform Companies Act* 1961. This stated that a director must act honestly and use reasonable diligence in the discharge of her or his duties. The duty of honesty and the duty of care and diligence were separated in 1982. Section 229(1) of the *Companies Code* continued to impose a duty of honesty on company directors. This was retained in s 232(2) of the Law.

Section 232(2) stated:

> An officer of a corporation shall at all times act honestly in the exercise of his or her powers and the discharge of the duties of his or her office.

Section 232(2) was subject to both civil and criminal sanctions. However, it was difficult to reconcile the use of the word "honesty" with the inclusion of the word "dishonesty" in the criminal penalty provision, s 1317FA.[9] The

6 See *Whitehouse v Carlton Hotel Pty Ltd* (1987) 5 ACLC 421 and *Australian Metropolitan Life Assurance Co Ltd v Ure* (1923) 33 CLR 199.
7 *Hindle v John Cotton Ltd* (1919) 56 Sc LR 625 at 630 per Viscount Finlay.
8 See *Darvall v North Sydney Brick and Tile Co Ltd* (1989) 7 ACLC 659.
9 See Corporate Law Economic Reform Program, *Directors' Duties and Corporate Governance*, para 6.5.1.

Corporations Law Simplification Task Force emphasised that the use of the term "honesty" was not consistent throughout the Law. Following its recommendation, s 232(2) was rewritten to reflect the fiduciary concept of good faith. This is now contained in s 181 of the Law, in which the word "honesty" has been omitted.

The duty contained in the current s 181 is modelled on provisions of the companies legislation in both New Zealand and Canada.

[14.4] Notable cases

[14.4.1] *MARCHESI V BARNES*

Marchesi v Barnes[10] considered ss 124 and 381 of the *Companies Act* 1961 (Vic). The approach of Gowans J in *Marchesi v Barnes*[11] is reflected in the current s 181 of the Law. In this case, Gowans J stated that to act "honestly", or in good faith:

> ... refers to acting bona fide in the interests of the company in the performance of the functions attaching to the office of director. A breach of the obligation to act bona fide in the interests of the company involves a consciousness that what is being done is not in the interests of the company, and deliberate conduct in disregard of that knowledge. This constitutes the element of mens rea in the criminal offence created by the statute.[12]

Accordingly, a director or officer will only breach their duty of good faith when they act in what they know is not in the best interests of the company. Although this test has been adopted as an appropriate test for the statutory duty of good faith, a contrary position is found in regard to the common law fiduciary duty of good faith.

[14.4.2] *AUSTRALIAN GROWTH RESOURCES CORP PTY LTD V VAN REESEMA*

Australian Growth Resources Corp Pty Ltd v van Reesema[13] considered s 229 of the *Companies (SA) Code*. A contrary view to that stated by Gowans J in *Marchesi v Barnes* was articulated by King CJ in *Australian Growth Resources Corp Pty Ltd v van Reesema.*[14] Under this perspective, a director or officer can breach their duty of good faith if the law objectively considers that what they are doing is

10 Sup Ct, Vic, 29 September 1969 per Gowans J.
11 [1970] VR 434.
12 [1970] VR 434 at 438.
13 Sup Ct, SA, 24 March 1988 per King CJ, Cox and Johnston JJ.
14 (1988) 6 ACLC 529.

improper, even if they subjectively believe that what they are doing is in the best interests of the company. In the words of King CJ:

> The section therefore embodies a concept analogous to constructive fraud, a species of dishonesty which does not involve moral turpitude. I have no doubt that a director who exercises his powers for a purpose which the law deems to be improper, infringes this provision notwithstanding that according to his own lights he may be acting honestly.[15]

Although this view has not been adopted into the statutory duty of good faith embodied in s 181 of the Law, it reflects the position at common law where a director can breach her or his fiduciary duty of good faith regardless of the intent of the particular director.

[14.5] Interesting quotes

[14.5.1] SUBJECTIVE INTENT OF DIRECTOR OR OFFICER

Under s 181, a director or officer cannot breach their statutory duty of good faith unless they personally know and believe that what they are doing is not in the best interests of the company. In addition, under s 184(1), a criminal offence will be committed where the director or officer actually knows that what they are doing is not for a proper purpose or in the best interests of the company, or are reckless to this consideration. This approach is modelled on the decision of Gowans J in *Marchesi v Barnes*:[16]

> A breach of the obligation to act bona fide in the interests of the company involves a consciousness that what is being done is not in the interests of the company, and deliberate conduct in disregard of that knowledge.[17]

[14.6] Checklist

When considering whether a director or officer has breached her or his duty of good faith, insolvency practitioners should consult the following:

- What is the nature of the decision that the director or officer is making?
- What are the best interests of the corporation in relation to this decision?
- Does the director or officer believe that the decision he or she is about to make is in the best interests of the corporation?

15 (1988) 6 ACLC 529 at 539.
16 [1970] VR 434.
17 [1970] VR 434 at 438.

- For what range of purposes has the power the director or officer is about to exercise been conferred?
- Does the director or officer believe that the nature of the decision he or she is about to make within this range of purposes?
- What are possible consequences could her or his decision have for the corporation?
- Do these possible consequences serve the best interests of the corporation?

[14.7] Deficiencies

[14.7.1] INTERACTION OF MENTAL ELEMENTS IN SECTION 184(1)

The interaction of the mental elements in the criminal offence under s 184(1) is problematic. Under s 184(1), an offence will be committed where an act is done intentionally and dishonestly, or recklessly and dishonestly. An act is done dishonestly where it is done with the knowledge that it will produce adverse consequences and in this sense implies an improper dishonest intent.[18] It is a tautology to insist that for a criminal offence an act must be done intentionally *and* dishonestly as dishonesty necessarily involves a dishonest intent. In addition, recklessness implies "*something less than intent* but more than mere negligence".[19] As dishonesty involves intent, it is difficult to see how an act can be done be recklessly and with a dishonest intent.

[14.8] Proposals for law reform

[14.8.1] REMOVAL OF "DISHONESTY" FROM SECTION 184(1)

The interaction of the mental elements in s 184(1) is problematic. This stems from the inclusion of the term "dishonestly". The rationale of the provision would be best served if the phrase "and they do so dishonestly" was removed from s 184(1). With the omission of this phrase, the criminal offence provision would still include those who know that they are acting improperly and not in the best interests of the company. Alternately, s 184(1) could be rephrased to state that:

> A director or other officer commits an offence if they recklessly or with a dishonest intent fail to exercise their powers and discharge their duties:
> (a) in good faith in the best interests of the corporation; or
> (b) for a proper purpose.

18 *R v Bonollo* [1981] VR 633.

19 P Nygh and P Butt, *Butterworths Concise Australian Legal Dictionary* (Butterworths, Sydney, 1997), p 338 (emphasis added).

Use of Position and Information

15

"... *what is 'improper' for the purposes of [the sections] cannot be determined by reference to some common, uniform, or inflexible standard which applies equally to every person who is an officer, but rather must be determined by reference to the particular duties and responsibilities of the particular officer whose conduct is impugned.*"[1]

1 *Grove v Flavel* (1986) 43 SASR 410 at 416 per Jacobs J.

OBJECTIVES

This Chapter will:

- consider the elements of the statutory duties of proper use of position and information;
- analyse the meaning of the term "improper";
- analyse the meaning of the term "information";
- discuss the irrelevance of the intention of the director or other officer and the actual accrual of a benefit.

[15.1] General overview

Directors and officers of companies have a duty to make proper use of their position and the information they acquire through their position.

These duties stem from the basic proposition that directors and officers cannot take advantage of an opportunity or information that belongs to the company without the prior approval of the company.[2] They are both closely related to the insider trading provisions that were introduced into the Law in 1991.

[15.1.1] USE OF POSITION

Section 182 prohibits a director, secretary, or other officer or employee of a company from making "improper use of position" to gain an advantage for themselves or someone else, or to cause detriment to the company. A civil penalty can be imposed under s 1317E for a breach of this duty. Section 184(2) states that where this breach is done dishonestly and either with the intention to gain an advantage or cause detriment, or recklessly, a criminal offence will have been committed. The person found guilty of committing a criminal offence under s 184(2) could be subjected to a $20,000 fine or five years imprisonment or both: see Sch 3 to the Law.

[15.1.2] USE OF INFORMATION

Section 183 prohibits a person who is, or has been, a director or other officer or employee of a company from using information gained as a result of that position to gain an advantage for themselves or someone else, or to cause detriment to the company. A civil penalty can be imposed under s 1317E for a breach of this duty. Section 184(3) states that where information is obtained and a person uses the information dishonestly either with the intention of gaining an advantage for themselves or someone else, or recklessly, a criminal offence will have been committed. A person found guilty of committing a criminal offence under s 184(3) could be subjected to a $20,000 fine or five years imprisonment or both: see Sch 3 of the Law.

Under s 183 and s 184(3), whether or not the information has been "acquired as a result of the position" will often be a question of fact in each particular case.

[15.1.3] MEANING OF "IMPROPER"

What is considered "improper" will be determined by the facts of each case. Particular regard will be had to the position of the person within the company, their role in the management of the company, and their particular functions. This was strongly supported in *Grove v Flavel*:[3]

2 *Cook v Deeks* [1916–17] All ER Rep 285.
3 (1986) 43 SASR 410.

> ... what is 'improper' for the purposes of [the sections] cannot be determined by reference to some common, uniform, or inflexible standard which applies equally to every person who is an officer, but rather must be determined by reference to the particular duties and responsibilities of the particular officer whose conduct is impugned. In this case the appellant is, and is charged as, a director ... and it is by reference to his duties as a director of that company that his use of information acquired by virtue of that office must be judged ... the word 'improper' is not a term of art. It is to be understood in its commercial context to refer to conduct that is inconsistent with the 'proper' discharge of the duties, obligations and responsibilities of the officer concerned.[4]

[15.1.4] MEANING OF "INFORMATION"

"Information" is not defined in relation to the improper use of information provisions under s 183 and s 184(3); however, it is clear that it relates to "inside" information. There is no need for any information obtained to be confidential in order for a contravention to occur.[5] The fact that a director or officer has freely discussed information before making improper use of it will not be relevant in determining whether a contravention has occurred. In relation to the insider trading provisions, "information" has been defined to include suppositions and matters relating to the intentions, or likely intentions, of a person: s 1002A(1). If this definition applied to s 183 and s 184(3), "information" would include information pertaining to the possible insolvency of a company, even if discussed openly at Board meetings and informally between Board members and other officers. However, it is unlikely that such a broad definition would be applied in the context of the improper use of information provisions. This is because the s 1002A(1) definition is much broader than the ordinary and usual meaning of the word "information" and, arguably, the drafter of the legislation would have made it clear if such an unbelievably broad and wide-ranging definition were to apply.

[15.1.5] INTENTION NOT RELEVANT

Section 182 and 183 are civil penalty provisions. This has consequences for the interpretation of the provisions. The use of the word "to" is likely to be interpreted in accordance with a wide causative interpretation, rather than a strict purposive interpretation.[6] This is in contrast to a predecessor provision, s 229(4) of the *Companies Code*, which was read with a purposive interpretation due to its nature as a criminal provision. The significance of a causative interpretation is that the intention of the director or officer is not relevant in determining whether the

4 (1986) 43 SASR 410 at 416–420 per Jacobs J.
5 *McNamara v Flavel* (1988) 13 ACLR 619 per Millhouse J.
6 *Chew v R* (1992) 7 ACSR 481.

provision has been contravened. The *purpose* of the contravention does not need to be to gain an advantage or to cause detriment, but rather the improper use of position or information must merely *cause* an advantage or detriment. In this way, there must be a clear causal link between the improper use and the advantage or detriment.[7] However, the dishonest intention of the director or officer will be relevant in determining if a criminal offence has been committed under s 184(2) or (3). A reasonable but mistaken director ought not be convicted of a criminal offence.

[15.1.6] ACTUAL ACCRUAL OF BENEFIT OR DETRIMENT NOT RELEVANT

It is important to note that the actual accrual of the advantage or detriment is not relevant. Although there must be a causal link between the contravention and the advantage or detriment, a factor precluding the advantage or detriment will not prevent a contravention of the provisions:

> Thus, an officer who makes improper use of his or her office in order to gain an advantage [contravenes the provisions], even if his or her purpose be thwarted as, for example, by the grant of an injunction preventing execution of an instrument or implementation of a transaction.[8]

[15.1.7] DIRECT OR INDIRECT FOR THEMSELVES OR SOMEONE ELSE

The advantage or detriment caused can be either direct or indirect. The advantage can be intended for themselves or "someone else". The term "any other person" under the duties in the old s 232(5) and (6) has been replaced by the term "someone else". This change in terminology was not explained in the Explanatory Memorandum nor is the term "someone else" defined within the Law. Whereas s 85A clearly defines "person" to include a body corporate as well as natural persons, it is unclear whether the term "someone else" similarly includes body corporates within their ambit, although it is possible that it does. The change in terminology suggests that a benefit derived for a body corporate may not trigger liability under the provisions. Such a result would be unsatisfactory.

[15.1.8] USE OF CRIMINAL SANCTIONS

Despite the availability of criminal sanctions under s 184(2) and (3), full use of the sanctions has rarely been made. In *Castrisios v McManus*[9] where a director was

7 *Waldron v Green* (1977–78) 3 ACLR 289.
8 *Chew v R* (1992) 7 ACSR 481 per Mason CJ, Brennan, Gaudron and McHugh JJ.
9 (1990) 4 ACSR 1.

found guilty of nine offences under a predecessor provision to s 183, a fine of $300 was imposed for each of the offences.

[15.2] Philosophy/rationale

The general rationale of the provisions is to ensure that directors and officers act for a proper purpose for the benefit of the company as a whole. This is manifest within the general fiduciary duties on which these statutory provisions are based, and the insider trading provisions in which context they are often utilised.

[15.3] History/former law

The duty imposed on directors and other officers to use their position and information acquired through this position properly is based on general fiduciary duties. The rule against conflict of interest and the corporate opportunity doctrine, whereby directors cannot take advantage of an opportunity or information that belongs to the company without the prior approval of the company,[10] are the main general law predecessors for this statutory duty.

These general fiduciary duties have been in statutory form for quite some time. Many cases dealing with the provisions discuss the predecessor provisions to s 182 and 183, s 232(5) and (6) of the Law. These provisions were modelled on the earlier provisions contained in s 229(3) and (4) of the *Companies Code.*

[15.4] Notable cases

[15.4.1] *MCNAMARA V FLAVEL*

McNamara v Flavel[11] considered s 229 of the *Companies (South Australia) Code.*

This case was decided under a predecessor provision of s 183, s 232(5). It is particularly important as it highlights the interaction between the "improper use" of information provisions and corporate insolvency.

The company "Duna World Pty Ltd" was incorporated in 1979. The defendant was a director of Duna World at the time of its change of name. In January 1985 the defendant acquired information by virtue of his position as a director that the company was experiencing serious financial difficulties. As a result of gaining this information, the defendant applied to reserve the name "Dunquil Pty Ltd", to which Duna World proposed to change its name. The defendant then

10 *Cook v Deeks* [1916–17] All ER Rep 285.
11 (1988) 13 ACLR 619. Sup Ct, SA, 1 July 1988 per King CJ, Mohr and Millhouse JJ.

made an application for the registration of the business name "Duna World", which the public had come to know as a specialised retail business carried on by the company to date. The company ceased to carry on business under the name "Duna World" and commenced trading under the name "Dunquil Pty Ltd" shortly thereafter and, on the same day, another company, Shengli Pty Ltd, was incorporated. The defendant was a director and shareholder of Shengli. A few days later Shengli commenced to carry on business under the name "Duna World". The facts of this case constituted a typical phoenix company situation.

The Court decided that the director had made an improper use of information. He had acquired the information as to the financial problems of Dunquil as a result of his position as a director of Dunquil. It was not relevant that this information as to the solvency of the company was not confidential and had been discussed freely between Board members.

The director had procured the purchase of the business name Duna World from Dunquil. This business name had value as a result of the widespread advertising and the community generally associated the business name with the products of Dunquil.

Prior to the liquidation of Dunquil, the defendant director, on behalf of his company Shengli, not only procured the business name of Duna World but also purchased all of Dunquil's stock. Following the liquidation of Dunquil, Shengli commenced to trade under the business name Duna World, on the same premises as that previously occupied by Duna World, with some of the former staff of Duna World.

The use of this information and the subsequent purchase of the business Duna World was improper. The use of the information resulted in an advantage for himself and the company Shengli. It also caused detriment to Dunquil as it depleted the assets of that company, causing detriment to the creditors of that company. The director was held to have breached s 232(5).

[15.5] Quotes

[15.5.1] USE OF INFORMATION ACQUIRED BY VIRTUE OF THE POSITION

In *McNamara v Flavel*,[12] Millhouse J considered whether or not an appellant had breached a predecessor provision to s 183, s 232(5). His Honour considered whether what the appellant did was "improper" and whether the "information" was "acquired by virtue of his position". Holding that the appellant had breached the provision, Millhouse J explained:

12 (1988) 13 ACLR 619 per Millhouse J.

> The appellant took the action he did because he saw the financial crash coming. To borrow the phrase used by Cox J in *Grove v Flavel* (138 LSJS 78 at 87) he knew of the 'financial predicament' ... As in that case, so in this ... 'there is no reason to suppose that the material upon which that could be appraised did not come to the appellant's knowledge by virtue of his position as a director'. The appellant was privy to the financial position of the company. He discussed that position with others and received advice on it. I have no doubt that he made use of 'information acquired by virtue of his' being a director. That others also may have had the information is not to the point: the test is not that the information is confidential ... it is how the information is acquired: it was acquired because of the appellant's position as a director.[13]

[15.6] Checklist

To avoid contravening s 182 or 183, or s 184(2) or (3), directors should keep a number of issues in mind. These should also be borne in mind by an insolvency practitioner when bringing an action against a director:

- A director should bear in mind her or his position within the company and the nature of the duties he or she is bound by.
- Directors should consider the use to which information they acquire through their position within the company should be put.
- When using this information, directors should consider if it is "inside" information and whether what they are doing with it is a use for which it ought to be used.
- If asked by persons outside the company for "inside" information, a director should not supply it without the prior approval of the Board.
- A director should not use her or his office to obtain benefits for herself or himself or someone else or to cause harm to the company.
- When making decisions, directors should consider whether it is in the best interests of the company.

[15.7] Deficiencies

[15.7.1] INTERACTION OF MENTAL ELEMENTS IN CRIMINAL OFFENCE

The criminal offences in s 184(2) and (3) are triggered where a director or other officer or employee of a company acts dishonestly and intentionally, or dishonestly and recklessly. The interaction of these mental elements is problematic.

13 (1988) 13 ACLR 619 at 624.

Dishonesty necessarily involves an element of dishonest intent. It seems impossible for dishonest intent to coincide with recklessness, as recklessness does not entail any specific intention but rather heedless or careless conduct where some foreseeable problems can be seen an action is still taken with an indifference to, or disregard of, those consequences.[14]

[15.7.2] "SOMEONE ELSE"

The use of the term "someone else" within the provisions is problematic. Whereas under the old subs 232(5) and (6) it was clear that the benefit could be obtained for a body corporate as well as for the individual, no such guidance is given to the meaning of "someone else". It is unclear whether it includes a body corporate within its ambit. Body corporates should be included within the provisions, particularly in light of the fact that in many small proprietary companies there may be a significant intermingling of the director's assets and affairs and the corporation's assets and affairs.

[15.8] Proposals for law reform

[15.8.1] MENTAL ELEMENTS IN CRIMINAL OFFENCE

A serious deficiency in the proper use of position and information provisions is that the interaction of the mental elements in the criminal offence provisions is logically inconsistent. It seems impossible to do an act in a reckless manner with dishonest intent. In addition, it is a tautology to imply the need to do an act intentionally and with a dishonest intent.

Subsections 184(2) and (3) may be clarified by deleting the word "dishonestly" from its current location and inserting it in paragraph (a) of both subsections. This would clarify the criminal offence provisions by specifying that the actions or omissions of the person concerned must be done with either dishonest intent or recklessly in order for a contravention to occur.

[15.8.2] CLARIFY MEANING OF "SOMEONE ELSE"

The meaning of "someone else" is unclear within the provisions. An advantage acquired for the benefit of another body corporate should trigger liability under the provisions. The term "someone else" should be defined to include a body corporate as well as natural persons, or the term "someone else" should be replaced with the term "any other person" which is clearly defined to include a body corporate.

---

14 *R v Nuri* [1990] VR 641.

Duty of Care and Diligence

16

"*On the brink of a new millennium, we should be thinking creatively about the ways in which the law can facilitate economic development and not simply coerce, regulate and control its occasional errors and ugly manifestations … Law does not develop in a vacuum. It responds to the perceived needs of the society which it serves.*"[1]

1 The Hon Justice Michael Kirby AC CMG, Justice of the High Court of Australia, Speech on *The Company Director: Past, Present and Future*, 31 March 1998, speech presented to the Australian Institute of Company Directors.

OBJECTIVES

This Chapter will:

- outline the elements of the statutory duty of care and diligence;
- discuss the ways in which this statutory duty differs from the common law duty;
- analyse the recently introduced statutory business judgment rule and the extent to which this may provide a safe harbour for directors;
- thoroughly consider the subjective factors which are relevant in determining whether or not a breach of this statutory duty has occurred.

[16.1] General overview

[16.1.1] ELEMENTS OF LIABILITY

Directors have increasingly become the focus of corporate regulators within Australia. In the last two decades drastic changes regarding the perceived role of directors within companies have been followed simultaneously by attempts by regulators to make them accountable for their decisions and actions. Recognising the need to balance the facilitation of economic development through commercial activity with accountability and responsibility, Australian corporate law has recognised the need to command respect of both principles. This recognition has prompted a recent fundamental change in directors' duty of care and diligence.

Directors are subject to common law and statutory duties of care and diligence. Whilst liability at common law has a long history, it is only within the last two decades that directors have been subject to statutory regulation of this kind. Section 180 of the Law provides that directors and officers of a corporation must exercise their powers and discharge their duties with the degree of care and diligence that a reasonable person would exercise if they:

- were a director or officer of a corporation in the circumstances of the corporation;
- occupied the office held by, and had the same responsibilities within the corporation, the director or officer; and
- had the same experience as the director or officer.

In relation to decisions regarding the business operations of the company, this degree of care and diligence will be satisfied if the director or officer makes the relevant decision:

- in good faith for a proper purpose;
- without any personal interest in the subject matter of the decision;
- informed about the subject matter of the decision to the extent they reasonably believed to be appropriate; and
- with a rational belief that the decision is in the best interests of the corporation.

The statutory duty of care and diligence is defined by an objective standard, measured by the "reasonable person", with allowances for subjective factors.

This statutory duty applies in addition to, and not in derogation of, equivalent directors' duties at common law: s 185 of the Law.

[16.1.2] TO WHOM DOES THE DUTY APPLY?

The statutory duty of care and diligence applies to directors and officers of companies.

Clearly, the statutory duty of care and diligence is imposed on a wide range of people. The expanded class is designed to include anyone who is concerned in, or takes part in, management of the company. It is not necessary for the person to be aware that their acts amount to taking part in the management of the company.[2] The expanded reference to "officers" recognises the ability of management personnel to direct or influence the company or the conduct of its activities. This is commensurate with the dominance of management within companies.[3]

[16.1.3] THE CIRCUMSTANCES OF THE CORPORATION

Section 180(1)(a) states that the circumstances of the corporation are relevant to the degree of care and diligence required to be exercised by a director or officer. Relevant circumstances may include:

- the size of the corporation;
- the nature of the business conducted by the corporation;
- the composition of the Board of directors;
- the frequency of Board meetings and other channels of communication;
- the distribution of work between directors and officers;
- the financial standing of the corporation, particularly whether it is facing insolvency; and
- policies adopted and implemented by the Board of directors (arguably including compliance programs).

[16.1.4] THE SIGNIFICANCE OF THE OFFICE HELD BY, AND THE RESPONSIBILITIES OF, THE DIRECTOR OR OFFICER

Subsection 180(1)(b) requires a consideration of the office held by, and the responsibilities of, the relevant director or officer within the company. This is a clear statutory recognition of the differences between executive and non-executive directors.

Executive and non-executive directors are both subject to the duty of care and diligence. However, due to their greater knowledge of the affairs of the relevant company and their contract of employment with the company, executive directors are generally subject to a higher burden of care and diligence than non-executive directors.[4] They must devote their full-time efforts to the affairs of the

2 *Poyser v CCA* (Vic) (1985) 3 ACLC 584.

3 See H Bosch, *The Director at Risk: Accountability in the Boardroom* (Pitman Publishing, Melbourne, 1995), pp 1–18.

4 See *Lister v Romford Ice and Cold Storage* [1957] AC 555; and *AWA Ltd v Daniels* (1992) 10 ACLC 933 at 1014-1015.

company and attend all Board meetings except when they have a proper reason for being unable to do so. They must fully acquaint themselves with the affairs of the company, formulate appropriate policies, and ensure their implementation.

Non-executive directors must take reasonable steps to acquaint themselves with the affairs of the company, but are not bound to give continuous attention to its affairs.[5] Their duties are of an intermittent nature to be performed at periodical Board meetings, and although they are not bound to attend all such meetings, they ought to attend whenever they are reasonably able to do so.[6] Despite this more limited role, non-executive directors must possess enough knowledge to be aware of the affairs of the company. In this sense, they have a duty to inquire of executive directors into the internal affairs of the company to the extent to which they are capable of fully understanding its affairs and forming an informed opinion of its financial capacity.

It is clear that a non-executive director can be held liable for a breach of the duty of care and diligence.[7] The report of the Auditor General into the collapse of the State Bank of South Australia in 1991 was resounding in this regard:

> I have some sympathy for the bank's non-executive directors. They lacked both banking experience and, in most cases, hard-headed business acumen. They were manipulated, and not properly informed of what was going on … [However] it was not beyond the capabilities of the non-executive directors to take common-sense measures and to stand no nonsense. *To be blunt, there is nothing esoteric about asking questions, seeking information, demanding explanations and extracting further details.* There is nothing unduly burdensome in expecting each director, to the best of his or her ability, to insist on understanding what was laid before them, even at the risk of becoming unpopular.[8]

The advice provided by Rogers J in the AWA case is also helpful.[9] His Honour found that the non-executive directors were not liable for any part of the losses sustained by the company as a result of foreign exchange contracts. This was because they had formulated a policy for the company's foreign exchange activities, had inquired as to whether the policy was being implemented, and had called for a report into the success of the policy. In this way, they had done all that could reasonably be expected of them in the circumstances.

---

5 *Re Australasian Venezolana Pty Ltd* (1962) 4 FLR 60.

6 *Re City Equitable Fire Insurance Co Ltd* (1925) 1 Ch 407; *AWA Ltd v Daniels* (1992) 10 ACLC 933.

7 *Re Australasian Venezolana Pty Ltd* (1962) 4 FLR 60; *Dorchester Finance Co Ltd v Stebbing* [1989] BCLC 498; *South Australia v Marcus Clark* (1996) 14 ACLC 1019.

8 K McPherson, Auditor General (SA), *Report into the State Bank of South Australia* (Vol 1), 1.5–3.6 (emphasis added).

9 *AWA Ltd v Daniels* (1992) 10 ACLC 933.

Clearly, in order to comply with their duty of care and diligence, non-executive directors must take all necessary steps to keep informed of the affairs of the company.

[16.1.5] SKILL NOT RELEVANT

A notable omission within the statutory duty of care and diligence is a general requirement of "skill". The reason for this omission is that arguably directors may bring different skills to their position, ranging from common sense and honesty to financial astuteness, and this diversity within boards of directors should be valued and encouraged. Accordingly, it is considered inappropriate to insert an objective "skill" requirement as it would imply that there was some particular skill that every director ought to possess.

It is arguably inappropriate to require directors of companies of varying sizes, business, structure and complexity to exhibit the same skills, knowledge and levels of competence. It is also inappropriate for all companies to be under the sole direction of persons with general financial and managerial skills without any diversity in skill.

However, the Senate Standing Committee on Legal and Constitutional Affairs has argued that directors must exhibit skills equivalent to those that a reasonably skilled and competent director would possess.[10] However, the omission of this "skill" requirement clearly embraces the recognition of the need for a diversity of skills for optimal corporate management.

[16.1.6] THE BUSINESS JUDGMENT RULE

The introduction of a statutory objective duty of care and diligence has been coupled with the introduction of a statutory business judgment rule in s 180(2).[11] The business judgment rule operates in relation to both the duty of care and diligence under the Law and under common law. It provides a "safe harbour" for directors and officers, shielding them from liability for claims made as a result of errors of judgment or business decisions that have adversely affected the company.[12] Provided the relevant business decisions are made in accordance with a number of factors, listed below, directors and officers will have fulfilled their duty of care and diligence in relation to that particular decision both at statute and common law.

The business judgment rule does not apply to the duty to prevent insolvent trading.

---

10 Senate Standing Committee on Legal and Constitutional Affairs, *Company Directors' Duties: Report on the Social and Fiduciary Obligations of Company Directors* (1989), paras 3.25-3.26.

11 For a recent analysis of the business judgment rule see V Priskich, "A Statutory Business Judgment Rule in Australia: Proposals and Policy" (1999) 27(1) ABLR 38.

12 See A S Sievers, "Farewell to the Sleeping Director: The Modern Judicial and Legislative Approach to Directors' Duties of Care, Skill and Diligence" (1993) 21 ABLR 111.

(a) The relationship between the duty of care and diligence and the business judgment rule

The business judgment rule acts as a rebuttable presumption that operates in favour of the propriety of directors and officers.

If a director or officer has complied with the requirements of the business judgment rule then they will not be found liable for a breach of the duty of care and diligence. However, if an opposing party can prove that a director was not acting in good faith for a proper purpose, had a material interest in the subject matter, was not adequately informed, or did not rationally believe that the decision was in the best interests of the corporation, then the director or officer will be judged according to the standard of care and diligence under s 180(1).

(b) What decisions are covered by the business judgment rule?

The business judgment rule protects business decisions. Subsection 180(3) defines "business decision" to mean any decision to take or not take action in respect of a matter relevant to the business operations of the corporation.

The business judgment rule only applies to the duty of care and diligence and its common law equivalent. It does not apply to the duty to prevent insolvent trading.

The reference to "business operations" clearly excludes any decisions made on constitutional or administrative matters. It is intended to cover most of the judgments made by directors and officers in the day-to-day running of the company. Section 180(3) does not limit the application of the business judgment rule to "risky" or purely economic decisions. It covers a wide range of decisions ranging from the selection and removal of personnel, setting policy goals, and the apportionment of responsibilities between the Board and senior executives.[13] Langford has indicated the types of decisions that will fall under the heading of "ordinary business operations of a company".[14] These include those decisions relating to:

- the company's goals;
- plans and budgeting;
- promotion of the company's business;
- acquiring assets and disposing of assets;
- raising or altering capital;
- obtaining or giving credit;
- deploying the company's personnel;
- trading.

13 See American Law Institute, *Principles of Corporate Governance: Analysis and Recommendations* (American Law Institute Publishers, St Paul, 1994), pp 172–173.

14 R Langford, "The New Statutory Business Judgment Rule", *Corporate Law Economic Reform Program, Fundraising – Capital Raising Initiative to Build Enterprise and Employment*: Paper No 2, AGPS, Canberra, 1997, p 29 (Appendix C).

However, it will not extend to decisions regarding:

- matters relating principally to the constitution of the company or the conduct of meetings within the company;
- appointment of executive officers;
- the company's solvency.

Various "preparatory decisions" to the making of a business decision are also covered. For example, a decision not to seek outside technical advice in evaluating a new product or project, if made in accordance with the requirements of the business judgment rule, would be protected.

The business judgment rule only affords protection to a business "judgment". This means that to be provided protection, a decision must have been made consciously and judgment in fact exercised. It will not operate where directors simply fail to act.

In other words, the business judgment rule does not operate where a director has not made a decision. Whether or not conscious judgment has been exercised or inattentiveness merely prevailed may be a borderline issue in some cases and will require a consideration of the relevant facts in each case. For example, what may clearly seem to be an omission on the part of a director may in truth be the result of carefully gathered information, considered by the director who appraised the risks, and decided not to install a particular policy or program. In this situation, the business judgment rule would operate to protect the director from liability. In contrast, if a director received but did not read important financial information over a period of time and allowed his company to slip into insolvency, the director would not receive such protection.

Many major business decisions will involve a number of subsidiary issues and decisions. For example, a decision to establish a new product line may require consideration of plant location, the availability of skilled employees, intellectual property, and the existence of competitive products. The exercise of judgment does not require the director or officer to direct her or his mind to all of these subsidiary issues. Rather, the director or officer need only reach a decision about the major business decision. It is this overall business decision that is the subject of the business judgment rule.

(c) Good faith for a proper purpose

In order to receive protection under the business judgment rule a director or officer must make a business decision for what they believe to be in the best interests of the company.[15] It is primarily a subjective duty.

15 *Re Smith & Fawcett Ltd* [1942] Ch 304.

Protection under the business judgment rule requires the director or officer to exercise their powers of decision making for the purpose for which they were conferred and not for any collateral purpose.

(d) Material personal interest in the subject matter of the decision

Protection under the business judgment rule requires disinterested decision-making. The business judgment rule is inapplicable in situations where a conflict of interest exists.[16]

(e) Informed about the subject matter to the extent they reasonably believe to be appropriate

An informed decision is a prerequisite for exclusion from liability under the business judgment rule. This requirement emphasises the preparation of the director or officer, rather than the quality of the decision actually made. A fundamental concern is that the extent of information required is that which the director or officer "reasonably believes to be appropriate".

According to the American Law Institute:

> In evaluating what is a reasonable belief in a particular situation, the 'informed' requirement ... should be interpreted realistically and with an appreciation of the factual context in which the business judgment was made.[17]

Clearly, the term "reasonably believes" incorporates both objective and subjective elements.

A number of elements should be examined to ascertain whether this requirement has been fulfilled, including the:

- importance of the business decision to be made;
- time available for obtaining information;
- costs related to obtaining information;
- director or officer's confidence in those who researched the matter;
- state of the company's business at the time;
- nature of competing demands for the Board's attention;
- background of the relevant director or officer; and
- role the director or officer plays within the company.[18]

---

16 See *Treadway Companies Inc v Care Corp* (1980) 638 F.2d 357.

17 American Law Institute, *Principles of Corporate Governance: Analysis and Recommendations* (American Law Institute Publishers, St Paul, 1994), p 178.

18 American Law Institute, *Principles of Corporate Governance: Analysis and Recommendations* (American Law Institute Publishers, St Paul, 1994), p 178.

Executive directors and officers will generally be required to be more informed of the company's affairs. In practice the standard required of these people will be higher than in the case of non-executive directors.

(f) A rational belief that the decision is in the best interests of the corporation

The phrase "rationally believes" is intended to permit a significantly wider range of discretion in decision making than the term "reasonable" would allow. It provides protection for business decisions which are not "reasonable" but which are no so far removed from the province of reason that liability should be imposed. Courts have used words such as "reckless disregard" or "recklessness" to convey a sense of the latitude directors and officers should be afforded when making business decisions.[19] In this sense, a belief will be rational unless it displays gross negligence, reckless indifference or deliberate disregard. However, if a business decision were to be repeated under altered circumstances and in the new context it lacked a rational basis, the business judgment rule could not provide protection to the repetition of the decision.

The belief that the business decision is in the best interests of the corporation is rational unless no reasonable person in their position would so believe.

The reference to "the best interests of the corporation" refers to the primary allegiance of the director or officer. These interests include both short and long term interests.

[16.1.7] RELIANCE ON INFORMATION OR ADVICE PROVIDED BY OTHERS

A fundamental component of the duty of care and diligence is the ability of directors and officers to delegate tasks and to rely on the information provided by these delegates.

Directors now have the statutory ability to rely on information provided by others in the performance of their functions and in carrying out their duty of care and diligence: s 198D.

Although delegation is permissible, the director is still responsible for the extent and form of the delegation. The decision whether or not to delegate functions and tasks will be protected by the business judgment rule if it accords with its requirements.

This provision will not always provide a complete defence to directors. If an opposing party can disprove any of the elements, then the reliance may be deemed unreasonable and the director may be held to have breached their duty of care and diligence. Generally a director must actually read and understand information provided to them by a delegate in order to be able to rely on it.

19 *Cramer v General Electric Telecommunications and Electronics Corp* (1979) 59 L.Ed.2d 90.

Merely requiring another person to fulfil certain functions or tasks without ensuring adequate oversight systems is not enough to ensure reasonable reliance.

[16.1.8] REMEDIES

Breach of the duty of care and diligence under s 180 only gives rise to civil sanctions. It does not provide the basis for a criminal offence.

[16.2] Philosophy/rationale

[16.2.1] WHY IMPOSE A DUTY OF CARE AND DILIGENCE?

Companies form an integral part of society through their immense capacity to facilitate wealth creation and economic development. Appropriate levels of accountability and responsibility must be balanced against the vast impact of corporate activity on the economic viability of the general community. An increase in the number of companies and shareholders within Australia has been commensurate with an increasing legislative and judicial recognition of the need to ensure adequate corporate culpability.

The issue of care and diligence reached the forefront of legislative and judicial concern following the corporate losses of the 1980s. The collapses of Rothwells, the Skase media empire, Tricontinental, the Trustees, Executors and Agency Co Ltd (TEA), the State Bank of South Australia, the Bond Corporation, Adelaide Steamship, Pyramid, the Spedley merchant banking group and many other major financial players highlighted a litany of accountability and responsibility problems within companies.[20] According to Sykes:

> Never before in Australian history had so much money been channeled by so many people incompetent to lend it into the hands of so many people incompetent to manage it.[21]

Whilst some people suggested that the explanation for such collapses lay in the personal failings of a few individuals, the more likely explanation is a complete failure of management, communication, accountability, ethics and policy. In the absence of a duty of care and diligence, modern corporate history reveals a failure of directors and officers to place sufficient weight on their accountability to their companies, shareholders, and society at large.

20 For a detailed analysis of the corporate collapses of the 1980's see R Tomasic and S Bottomley, *Directing the Top 500: Corporate Governance and Accountability in Australian Companies* (Allen and Unwin, Sydney, 1993). See also H Bosch, *The Director at Risk: Accountability in the Boardroom* (Pitman Publishing, Melbourne, 1995), pp 19–55.

21 T Sykes, *The Bold Riders* (Allen and Unwin, Sydney, 1994), p 2.

[16.2.2] RECOGNITION OF THE REALITY OF MODERN COMPANIES

An objective duty of care and diligence, placing due consideration on subjective factors, recognises the reality of modern companies. Companies are an essential element in economic advancement through attracting increased investment. However, a balance must be achieved between innovation and accountability. According to Senator Brian Gibson:

> For our economy to grow the Government must encourage those with enterprise and the willingness to take risks. On the other hand, Government will never accept that any person or organisation has the right to cheat, defraud or deceive in the name of economic advancement. Having an effective and efficient system of corporate supervision does not mean removing or downgrading the overall level of investor protection. The credibility of our corporate system, both here and overseas, will be an essential factor in attracting increased levels of investment in this country.[22]

The inclusion of an objective duty of care and diligence recognises the need to ensure director and officer compliance with appropriate standards required of them in the modern context.

The duty of care and diligence within the Law recognises that not all directors are managers. By allowing a consideration of subjective factors, the statutory duty of care and diligence addresses concerns expressed by non-executive directors that their special circumstances should be considered when determining the level of care and diligence required of them.[23] This recognition of the different roles played by executive directors, non-executive directors and officers within companies is crucial. Whilst the standard of care may not be lower for any of these three classes, the statutory duty embraces the need for executive directors and officers to retain managerial oversight and full knowledge of the company's affairs, whilst non-executive directors must ask difficult questions and contribute independent insight into corporate affairs.

[16.2.3] THE "SAFE HARBOUR" – THE BUSINESS JUDGMENT RULE

The business judgment rule is perceived as a key tool in facilitating risk taking by directors for the purpose of stimulating wealth creation and economic development.

22 Speech by the Senator the Hon Brian Gibson AM Parliamentary Secretary to the Treasurer, *The Government's View on the Corporations Law*, presented in Sydney on the 14 May 1996.

23 See Commonwealth of Australia, "Directors' Duties and Corporate Governance: Facilitating Innovation and Protecting Investors", *Corporate Law Economic Reform Program: Proposals for Reform* Paper No 3, AGPS, Canberra, 1998, p 45.

The development of the duty of care and diligence has left directors and officers feeling uncertain of their obligations and potential liability. Case law on this duty has been in a constant state of flux with Courts constantly changing policy direction.[24] This lack of certainty leads to risk-averse behaviour that will ultimately affect shareholder dividends.

The rationale behind the business judgment rule is to provide special protection to directors for informed business decisions in contrast to continual inattention to obligations. According to the American Law Institute:

> The basic policy underpinning of the business judgment rule is that corporate law should encourage, and afford broad protection to, informed business judgments (whether subsequent events prove the judgment right of wrong) in order to stimulate risk taking, innovation, and other creative entrepreneurial activities.[25]

The business judgment rule provides an incentive for directors and officers to adopt sound corporate governance practices promoting accountability, transparency, and hence investor confidence.

[16.2.4] DELEGATION AS AN ESSENTIAL TOOL

The complexity and scale of many companies compels directors and officers to delegate to and rely heavily on other directors, officers, employees and committees. Efficiency and time constraints further necessitate such delegation and reliance.

As stated in the Corporate Law Economic Reform Program:

> Uncertainty about the circumstances in which it is appropriate for a director to delegate to, or place reliance on the advice of, others could lead to an overly conservative approach to management and could impede the decision-making processes within a company.[26]

Whilst delegation of functions or reliance on information provided by others does not alone constitute compliance by a director with the duty of care and diligence, such delegation and reliance is permissible in fulfilling the duty of care and diligence obligations.

[16.2.5] ADEQUACY OF REMEDIES

Following amendment of the Law, breach of the duty of care and diligence gives rise to civil sanctions only. Criminal liability is inconsistent with the rationale of

25 American Law Institute, *Principles of Corporate Governance: Analysis and Recommendations* (American Law Institute Publishers, St Paul, 1994), p 135.

26 Commonwealth of Australia, "Directors' Duties and Corporate Governance: Facilitating Innovation and Protecting Investors", *Corporate Law Economic Reform Program: Proposals for Reform* Paper No 3, AGPS, Canberra, 1998, p 46.

the duty of care and diligence. Dishonesty and criminal intent suggest active awareness of wrongdoing rather than a failure to exercise sufficient care and diligence.

[16.3] History or former law

The duty of care and diligence has been the subject of a long evolution. Initial case law indicated that an extremely low standard was required of directors.[27] In *Re Denham and Co*[28] a director who had no accountancy background and few professional skills had not attended Board meetings or checked the company accounts. He was held not to have breached his duty of care and diligence because the Court did not expect him to realize the significance of information contained within the accounts.

As the number of companies rose, Courts began to perceive the impact corporate behaviour could have on society in general. Accordingly, judges moved towards setting standards of conduct for directors to adhere to. In the landmark case of *Re City Equitable Fire Insurance*[29] Romer LJ recognised the difficulty of imposing a purely objective standard on directors and asserted that a director:

> … need not exhibit in the performance of his duties a greater degree of skill than may reasonably be expected from a person of his knowledge and experience.[30]

This imposed a fairly low subjective, rather than objective, degree of care and diligence. Romer LJ also asserted that directors need not give continuous attention to company affairs and are able to delegate and rely on others. The position at common law remained largely unchanged for many years, however courts were increasingly reluctant to interfere with business decisions. Imprudence and errors of a degree less than gross negligence rarely resulted in liability.

By the end of the 1950s, sentiment increasingly favoured imposing a higher standard on directors. Speaking extrajudicially at a conference in 1959, Sir Douglas Menzies stated:

> It is not to be thought, however, that honest and diligent muddling will not give rise to liability. Directors of public companies are not now appointed on the premise that a directorship is a sinecure in which reasonable competence is a

27 See *Lagunas Nitrate Co v Lagunas Syndicate* [1899] 2 Ch 392; *Overend & Gurney Co v Gibb* (1872) LR 5 HL 480; *Re Brazilian Rubber Plantations & Estates Ltd* [1911] 1 Ch 425; *Re National Bank of Wales Ltd* [1899] 2 Ch 629; *Re Faure Electric Accumulator Co* (1888) 40 Ch D 141.

28 (1883) 25 Ch D 752.

29 [1925] Ch 407.

30 [1925] Ch 407 at 428.

> desirable but not a necessary qualification ... *what is in general expected of directors will tend to become the measure of what is required of them.*[31]

Legislative attempts were made to introduce such a duty of care and diligence as early as 1976 in the hope of creating greater director certainty as to the extent of obligations imposed on them.[32] Section 229 of the *Companies Act* 1981 (Cth) was the first statutory duty of care and diligence imposed on directors on the federal level.[33] Whilst on the face of it, s 229 imposed an objective standard, Courts applied a subjective reading to it,[34] rendering it as weak as the equivalent common law duty at the time.

Against this setting of weak subjective standards both at common law and under statute, the Cooney Committee recommended that the Commonwealth legislation be amended to insert an objective duty of care for directors. In their words:

> The courts have been concerned to allow for flexibility and not to hamper entrepreneurs unduly.The standards laid down, however, barely meet the requirements of contemporary business and fall far short of the standards required of other professions. There is no objective [statutory or] common law standard of the reasonably competent company director as there are objective standards for other professions ... if the modern company director wants professional status, then professional standards of care ought to apply.[35]

The Committee also recommended that directors attend Board meetings unless there is a reasonable excuse for absence, and that the Law specifically limit the extent to which directors can rely on others. Such recommendations were embraced by judiciary who made statements in a number of cases in the late 1980s that directors should be required to comply with a more realistic standard of care.[36] This was clearly expressed by Rogers CJ in *AWA v Daniels*.[37] In this landmark decision, Rogers CJ required directors to place themselves in a *reasonable* position, judged *objectively*, to monitor the management of the company, to

31 D Menzies, "Company Directors" (1959) 22 ALJ 156 at 163-164.

32 The National Companies Bill 1976 (Cth) sought to impose a stringent duty of care and diligence on directors. If enacted, cl 95(1)(b(b) would have required directors to exercise the degree of care, diligence and skill that is not less than the degree of care, diligence and skill that a reasonably prudent person would exercise in relation to his own business affairs in comparable circumstances.

33 The precursor of s 229 was introduced into Victoria in 1958 and Tasmania in 1959.

34 *Byrne v Baker* [1964] VR 443. This case was decided in relation to the equivalent section under Victorian law.

35 Senate Standing Committee on Legal and Constitutional Affairs, *Company Directors' Duties: Report on the Social and Fiduciary Obligations of Company Directors* (1989), p 28.

36 See *Metal Manufacturers Ltd v Lewis* (1988) 13 NSWLR 315; *Darvall v North Sydney Brick & Tile Co Ltd* (1989) 16 NSWLR 260; *Statewide Tobacco Services Ltd v Morley* (1992) 10 ACLC 1233; *Commonwealth Bank v Friedrich* (1991) 9 ACLC 946.

37 (1992) 10 ACLC 933.

obtain an understanding of the business affairs of the company, and to seek and rely upon specialist advice in appropriate circumstances. However, his Honour recognised that the size and complexity of modern companies often meant that directors were no longer able to make policy decisions whilst simultaneously managing the day-to-day affairs of the company. As a result, Rogers CJ made a clear distinction between the role of executive directors, managing directors and the chief executive officer and non-executive directors, with a different standard of care to be applied to the latter.[38] This approach was a clear recognition of the realities of modern companies and the increased social expectation that directors be held socially and legally responsible for their decisions and actions.

Consequently, s 232(4) was inserted into the Law in 1992. This stated that:

> In the exercise of his or her powers and the discharge of his or her duties, an officer of a corporation must exercise the degree of care and diligence that a reasonable person in a like position in a corporation would exercise in the corporation's circumstances.

The aim of this section was to impose an objective standard of care taking into account an appropriate degree of subjective factors. However, Courts tended to give the section an overly subjective gloss. This was achieved through a broad interpretation of the phrase "in a like position" which was designed to recognise that the content of directors' duties will be dependent on the company's size, complexity, financial situation and the division of responsibilities between executive and non-executive directors.[39] The lack of clarity regarding the interplay between objective and subjective factors contributed to director uncertainty, highlighted by the case of *Daniels v AWA*.[40] The majority in this case sought a more vigorous approach to directors' duties that would require directors to comply with increased, but still commercially realistic, standards. Clarke and Sheller JJ concluded that a purely objective test was required and that directors should place themselves in a reasonably adequate position to guide and monitor the

38 Rogers stated:

"... the failure to recognise and to admit that many companies today are too big to be supervised and administered by a Board of Directors except in relation to matters of high policy. The true oversight of the activities of such companies resides with the corporate bureaucracy. Senior management and, in the case of mammoth corporations, even persons lower down the corporate ladder exercise substantial control over the activities of such corporations involving important decisions and much money. It is something of an anachronism to expect non-executive directors, meeting once a month, to contribute anything much more than decisions on questions of policy and, in the case of really large corporations, only major policy. This necessarily means that, in the execution of policy, senior management is in the true sense of the word exercising the powers of decision and of management which in less complex days used to be reserved for the Board of Directors."

See *AWA v Daniels* (1992) 10 ACLC 933 at 988.

39 Commonwealth of Australia, *Explanatory Memorandum to the Corporate Law Reform Act 1992*, AGPS, Canberra, 1992, p 25, para 86.

40 *Daniels v AWA* (1995) 13 ACLC 613.

management of the corporation. The conceptual uncertainty regarding the balance between objective and subjective standards was not resolved, with the simple assertion that the law of negligence was sufficiently flexible to adapt to a variety of corporate situations.[41] Subsequent case law confirmed this uncertainty.[42]

The focus on a purely objective test in *Daniels v AWA* renewed concern regarding a business judgment rule in Australia. Courts had traditionally been reluctant to interfere with business decisions made by directors.[43] In *Harlowe's Nominees Pty Ltd v Woodside (Lakes Entrance) Oil Co NL*[44] the High Court stated:

> ... directors in whom are vested the right and duty of deciding where the company's interests lie and how they are to be served may be concerned with a wide range of practical considerations, and their judgment, if exercised in good faith and not for irrelevant purposes, is not open to review in the courts.[45]

By the late 1980s a number of government committees had recognised the need to provide statutory certainty to this traditional reluctance. In April 1989 the CSLRC recommended the enactment of a statutory business judgment rule on the ground that it would encourage business endeavour. In their view the:

> ... enactment of a business judgment rule would provide legislative recognition of the commercial reality that a limited company is a vehicle for taking commercial risks.[46]

This approach was adopted in November 1989 by the Cooney Committee which, after reviewing United States law and the recommendations of the CSLRC, recommended the introduction of a statutory business judgment rule.[47] Despite this, the introduction of a statutory business judgment rule into the Law was clearly rejected by the government in 1992. The Explanatory Memorandum

---

41 *Daniels v AWA* (1995) 13 ACLC 613 at 665. See also M Whincop, "A Theoretical and Policy Critique of the Modern Reformulation of Directors' Duties of Care" (1996) 6(1) *Australian Journal of Corporate Law* 72.

42 See *Re Property Force Consultants Pty Ltd* (1995) 13 ACLC 1051; *McFadyen v Australian Securities Commission* (1995) 17 ACSR 415; *Standard Chartered Bank of Australia Ltd v Antico* (1995) 13 ACLC 1381.

43 See *Howard Smith Ltd v Ampol Petroleum Ltd* [1974] AC 821 at 832 where Lord Wilberforce said: "It would be wrong for the court to substitute its opinion for that of the management, or indeed to question the correctness of the management's decision ... if bona fide arrived at. There is no appeal to act as a kind of supervisory board over decisions within the powers of management honestly arrived at."

44 (1968) 121 CLR 483.

45 (1968) 121 CLR 483 at 492.

46 CSLRC, *Company Directors and Officers: Indemnification, Relief and Insurance* Discussion Paper No 9, April 1989, para 74.

47 Senate Standing Committee on Legal and Constitutional Affairs, *Company Directors' Duties: Report on the Social and Fiduciary Obligations of Company Directors* (1989), pp 29–31, para 3.35.

to the Corporate Law Reform Bill 1992 stated that such a development was better left to the Courts.[48]

By 1997 the combined result of these forces was significant commercial uncertainty. An imprecise balance between a subjective and objective standard of care and diligence coupled with a precarious judicial sentiment toward a business judgment rule meant that Australian corporate law was increasingly ambiguous:

> … anyone who does business in this country knows that our present *Corporations Law* is highly prescriptive, highly complicated for directors and difficult to comply with.[49]

In order to remedy this situation, the current s 180 was introduced into the Law in order to clarify the meaning of the duty of care and diligence.

[16.4] High profile matters

The corporate collapses of the 1980s brought the duty of care and diligence to the forefront of corporate law. A number of high profile personalities were the subject of legal action sought to remedy breach of this duty. As a result, a number of high profile cases from the 1980s and early 1990s illustrate a number of interesting facts and quotes relating to the duty of care and diligence.

[16.4.1] STATE BANK OF SOUTH AUSTRALIA

The spectacular collapse of the State Bank of South Australia in 1991 led to a great deal of political acrimony and the appointment of a Royal Commission and a full investigation by the South Australian Auditor General to analyse the internal workings of the bank as well as general financial matters.[50] The Royal Commission highlighted the misleading and fraudulent actions of the Managing Director, Mr Clark, whose "management strategy sowed the natural seeds of disaster". However, the Board was criticised for failing to exercise sufficient control over the Managing Director:

---

48 House of Representatives, *Explanatory Memorandum to the Corporate Law Reform Bill* 1992, AGPS, Canberra, 1992, para 89.

49 The Hon Peter Costello MP, Commonwealth Treasurer, *Address on the Launch of the New Corporate and Financial Regulatory Framework*, Australian Securities and Investments Commission, 1 July 1998.

50 For a detailed study of the collapse of the State Bank of South Australia, See Bosch, "How Much Diligence", paper presented to the *Business Law Education Centre Conference*, March 1996; and H Bosch, *The Director at Risk: Accountability in the Boardroom* (Pitman Publishing, Melbourne, 1995), pp 109-110.

> … too often the board's response to management was passive and acquiescent and it allowed its own misgivings to be overborne … too often it simply accepted the bland and confident assurances of the managing Director.[51]

Consequently, the failure of the Board to inquire into the affairs of the bank allowed the bank to engage in a number of operations that resulted in material losses for the bank. The failure of the non-executive directors to maintain control over the executive management, stemming from their failure to inquire, was described in damning terms by the Royal Commission:

> I have some sympathy for the bank's non-executive directors. They lacked both banking experience and, in most cases, hard-headed business acumen. They were manipulated, and not properly informed of what was going on … [However] it was not beyond the capabilities of the non-executive directors to take common-sense measures and to stand no nonsense. *To be blunt, there is nothing esoteric about asking questions, seeking information, demanding explanations and extracting further details.* There is nothing unduly burdensome in expecting each director, to the best of his or her ability, to insist on understanding what was laid before them, even at the risk of becoming unpopular.[52]

This example clearly highlighted the need for non-executive directors to be sufficiently informed of the affairs of the company and to inquire for further details where necessary.

[16.4.2] *COMMONWEALTH BANK OF AUSTRALIA V FRIEDRICH*

Another case that had a remarkable impact on the awareness of directors of their duty of care and diligence was that of Mr Eise, the non-executive chairman of the National Safety Council in the case of *Commonwealth Bank of Australia v Friedrich*.[53] Mr Eise joined the Board of the National Safety Council out of community service, and had held a number of offices in a wide range of charitable organisations. Following its collapse in March 1989 the National Safety Council owed its bank, the Commonwealth Bank of Australia (CBA), A$258m. In 1991 the CBA instituted legal action against Mr Eise for failing to satisfy his duty of care and diligence.[54] The CBA claimed that Mr Eise had failed to read balance sheets, failed to concern himself with financial detail, failed to understand the

51 Cited in H Bosch, *The Director at Risk: Accountability in the Boardroom* (Pitman Publishing, Melbourne, 1995), p 109.

52 K McPherson, Auditor General (SA), *Report into the State Bank of South Australia* Vol 1, 1.5–3.6. Cited in H Bosch, *The Director at Risk: Accountability in the Boardroom* (Pitman Publishing, Melbourne, 1995), pp 109–110 (emphasis added).

53 (1991) 9 ACLC 946; Sup Ct, Vic, 3 July 1991 per Tadgell J.

54 The action was instituted against all directors; however, all but Mr Eise settled out of court.

audit reports, and uncritically accepted assurances from the Managing Director, Mr Friedrich. In his defence, Mr Eise argued that the Managing Director had been manipulative and deceitful and was an accomplished liar. Despite this, the Court held Mr Eise liable and ordered him to pay $97m to the CBA. The Court highlighted the importance of the responsibilities and obligations associated with a directorship and illustrated the way in which directors' duties must be commensurate with what society expects of them:

> As the complexity of commerce has gradually intensified (for better of for worse) the community has of necessity come to expect more than formerly from directors whose task it is to govern the affairs of companies to which large sums of money are committed by way on equity capital or loan. In response, the parliaments and the Courts have found it necessary in legislation and litigation to refer to the demands made on directors in more exacting terms than formerly; and the standard of capability required of them has correspondingly increased. In particular, the stage has been reached when a director is expected to be capable of understanding her or his company's affairs to the extent of actually reaching a reasonably informed opinion on its financial capacity. Moreover, the director is under a statutory obligation to express such an opinion annually. It follows that the director is required by law to be capable of keeping abreast of the company's affairs, and sufficiently abreast of them to act appropriately if there are reasonable grounds to expect that the company will not be able to pay all its debts in due course and he has reasonable cause to expect it.[55]

Accordingly, although the fraud of the Managing Director had been extensive, so too was the failure of directors to monitor the management of the company. This correlation between the complexity of commerce, increased social expectation, and the standard of directors' duty of care and diligence gives an indication of the attitude Courts are likely to adopt when interpreting the new provisions.

[16.4.3] AWA

In 1986 and 1987 AWA lost almost A$50m from foreign exchange dealings. AWA subsequently sued its auditors, Deloittes, for failing to warn AWA about potential losses in this regard. In response, Deloittes claimed contributory negligence against the directors of AWA for failing to put in place adequate systems of internal control or proper books and records consistent with that policy. Deloittes claimed this breached the directors' duty of care and diligence. Apart from the Chief Executive, all the directors were non-executive directors. In the Supreme Court of New South Wales, Rogers CJ found that the Chief Executive was liable, but the non-executive directors were not. Rogers CJ made a clear distinction

55 *Commonwealth Bank of Australia v Friedrich* (1991) 9 ACLC 946 at 956.

between the role of executive directors or officers and non-executive directors. Whilst executive directors must carry out their duties in accordance with an objective standard, the same could not be realistically applied to non-executive directors. In the words of Rogers CJ:

> The degree of [care and diligence] required of an executive director is measured objectively. In contrast ... non-executive directors are not bound to give continuous attention to the affairs of the corporation. Their duties are of an intermittent nature to be performed at periodic Board meetings, and at meetings of any committee of the Board upon which the director happens to be placed. Notwithstanding a small number of professional company directors there is no objective standard of the reasonably competent company director to which they may aspire. The very diversity of companies and the variety of business endeavors do not allow of a uniform standard.[56]

However, on appeal the majority of the NSW Court of Appeal decided that non-executive directors should also be held to an objective standard of care and diligence.[57] Clarke and Sheller JJA believed that all directors should place themselves in a position to guide and monitor the management of the company, and that the law of negligence was flexible enough to adapt to the particular circumstances of the case. In their words:

> A person who accepts the office of director of a particular company undertakes the responsibility of ensuring that he or she understands the nature of the duty a director is called upon to perform. That duty will vary according to the size and business of the particular company and the experience or skills that the director held himself or herself out to have in support of appointment to the office. None of this is novel. It turns upon the natural expectations and reliance placed by shareholders on the experience and skill of a particular director. The duty is a common law duty to take reasonable care owed severally by persons who are fiduciary agents ... placed at the apex of the structure of direction and management. The duty includes that of acting collectively to manage the company. Breach of the duty will found an action for negligence at the suit of the company.[58]

Although the Court of Appeal held that the non-executive directors were not in breach of their duty of care and diligence, their judgment suggests that directors

---

56 *AWA Ltd v Daniels t/a Deloitte Haskins & Sells* (1992) 10 ACLC 933 at 1014–1015.

57 *Daniels v Anderson* (1995) 13 ACLC 614; CA, NSW, 15 May 1995 per Clarke, Sheller and Powell JJA.

58 *Daniels v Anderson* (1995) 13 ACLC 614 at 665–666.

will increasingly be judged by an objective standard taking into account an appropriate degree of subjective factors. It is this decision that provided the impetus for the new statutory provisions.

[16.5] Checklist

[16.5.1] WARNING SIGNS – A CHECKLIST

Insolvency practitioners should be aware of a number of warning signs which should have alerted directors and officers of the need for prudent inquiry in order to satisfy the duty of care and diligence. When examining whether a director or officer may have breached his or her duty of care and diligence, regard should be had to the following:

- consistent late receipt of important information, particularly financial reports;
- lack of corporate plan/objectives;
- inadequate financial reports;
- structural defects in Board management;
- no investigation of mistakes by directors or taking steps to avoid mistake happening again;
- discontent amongst staff;
- lack of internal audit procedures;
- consistent dealings by directors with company funds;
- frequent customer complaints;

[16.5.2] A DIRECTOR'S CHECKLIST

Insolvency practitioners can also ask a number of questions of the general management of the company by the Board in ascertaining whether directors or officers have satisfied their duty of care and diligence:

- Is a detailed agenda consistently set for Board meetings?
- Is the Board in control of the agenda? Who decides what will be discussed?
- Are the matters on the agenda those which are important for the company's development?
- Is sufficient information being given to directors so that they can consider the issues properly?
- Do directors have enough time to consider the issues on the agenda?
- Is the Board making clear and careful decisions?
- Are accurate Board minutes being taken?
- Are the decisions of the Board being communicated to all those required to implement the decision?
- Does the Board monitor compliance with its decisions and policies?

[16.5.3] BUSINESS JUDGMENT RULE – A CHECKLIST

When a director or officer seeks to rely on the business judgment rule to escape liability for a breach of the duty of care and diligence, insolvency practitioners should consider the following:

- Is the subject matter of the decision relevant to the business operations of the corporation, in contrast to a constitutional or administrative matter?
- Has the director made an actual conscious judgment when reaching the decision?
- Has the decision been made in accordance with the purpose for which the powers of decision making were conferred?
- Does the director have a personal interest in the subject matter of the decision? Is the director in a situation of conflict of interest?
- Does the director have enough information before her or him to make an informed business decision?
- Does the director believe that the decision is in the best interests of the corporation?

[16.6] Tricks/hints

The key to avoiding a breach of the duty of care and diligence is adequate compliance programs and open channels of communication between directors, officers and other employees. A well managed company should be able to integrate appropriate compliance systems into its management structure without interfering with its commercial goals. Directors should ensure that their company has programs directed to compliance with applicable laws and regulations, that it issues policy statements to its employees to this effect, and that it maintains procedures for monitoring compliance. This will ensure that directors place themselves in a reasonable position to monitor the management of the company. Provided directors act in accordance with its provisions, the business judgment rule will operate to protect a decision concerning this oversight function, particularly in relation to which functions to delegate and what procedures are required to ensure compliance.

The importance of such compliance programs was recognised by the Australian Stock Exchange (ASX). In 1995 the ASX introduced listing rule 4.10.3 that requires all listed companies to make an annual statement about their corporate governance practices, effective from the 30 June 1996. Additionally, adequate compliance system may facilitate good "corporate culture" and avoid subsequent corporate criminal liability.[59] Clearly, compliance programs will form

59 See the *Criminal Code Act* 1995 (Cth), cl 12.3(c) and (d).

an integral part of effective corporate governance and will avoid a breach of the duty of care and diligence.

Whilst directors are able to delegate functions, they remain responsible for the form and extent of the delegation. Whilst the business judgment rule will protect the decision to delegate in many circumstances, it is important to clearly state in writing the form and extent of delegation provided.

An effective method of ensuring that directors comply with their duty of care and diligence is for a review of individual director performance to be made on an annual basis. This could be carried out by self-evaluation followed by general discussion, written evaluation of each director by each of their colleagues, or evaluation by a committee followed by a confidential report to each director. Questions to be asked should include:[60]

- Has X attended meetings regularly?
- Does X seem to devote sufficient time and attention to her/his responsibilities?
- Has X consistently been properly briefed about the matters to be discussed?
- Does X keep herself/himself sufficiently informed by making visits to the organisation's operations and by making contact with appropriate executives?
- Does X bring relevant experience to the Board table and does he/she use it effectively?
- Are X's contributions succinct and to the point?
- Do X's contributions to Board discussions carry weight with her/his colleagues?
- Does X take her/his fair share of committee work and are her/his contributions on committee of value?
- Does X maintain good personal relations with her/his colleagues and with management? Is he/she co-operative and helpful?
- Has X an actual or potential conflict of interest that may be an embarrassment to the Board?

This process highlights inadequacies in individual director performance, indicating areas for improvement to avoid breaching the duty of care and diligence.

However, documenting such responses may create evidence which may be discoverable in later proceedings. Directors may consider having a lawyer conduct the interview of the relevant directors and write their responses in order to attract legal professional privilege. Directors should be aware that unless responses to such a questionnaire are a confidential communication between a client and a lawyer for the dominant purpose of giving or receiving legal advice

---

60 See H Bosch, *The Director at Risk: Accountability in the Boardroom* (Pitman Publishing, Melbourne, 1995), p 151.

in relation to actual or anticipated legal proceedings, it will not be protected from production in any litigation. If there is a concern in this regard, directors should seek legal advice before documenting responses to such a questionnaire. In any event, a claim of privilege is no excuse not to produce a document requested in, or relevant to a category of documents requested in, an ASIC notice to produce.

Misleading and Deceptive Conduct

17

"*Misleading or deceptive conduct generally consists of misrepresentation, whether express or by silence ... its application is [not] confined exclusively to circumstances which constitute some form of representation ... ultimately in each case it is necessary to examine the conduct, whether representational in character or not, and ask the question whether the impugned conduct of its nature constitutes misleading or deceptive conduct.*"[1]

1 *Henjo Investments Pty Ltd v Collins Marrickville Pty Ltd* (1988) 79 ALR 83 at 93 per Lockhart J.

OBJECTIVES

This Chapter will:

- outline the nature of the misleading and deceptive conduct provisions and discuss the various acts which impose this duty not to mislead or deceive;
- consider the ways in which the duty not to mislead or deceive interacts with the duty to prevent insolvent trading.

[17.1] General overview

Section 52 of the *Trade Practices Act* 1974 (Cth) provides that:

> A corporation shall not, in trade or commerce, engage in conduct that is misleading or deceptive, or is likely to mislead or deceive.

Section 75B of the *Trade Practices Act* extends liability for a breach of s 52 to persons, and hence directors, if they aided or abetted the contravention or were otherwise knowingly concerned in the contravention. Damages for loss and damage suffered by an applicant can be imposed personally on directors as well as other remedies.[2]

Section 42 of the *Fair Trading Act* 1987 (NSW) contains provisions similar to s 52 of the *Trade Practices Act*, but applies to "persons" rather than "corporations". Thus, directors can be primarily liable for misleading or deceptive conduct without the need to establish aiding and abetting or other specified conduct.

Section 51AA of the *Trade Practices Act* specifies that s 52 does not apply in relation to financial services. Instead, the new regime in Pt 2, Div 2 of the *ASIC Act* 1989 (Cth) applies. Section 12DA states that a corporation must not, in relation to financial services, engage in conduct that is misleading or deceptive, or is likely to mislead or deceive. Similar provisions apply in relation to the imposition of liability on persons other than corporations and for the award of damages and other remedies.

It is beyond the scope of this book to discuss the "misleading and deceptive conduct" provisions in great detail. However, in the context of insolvency, it is important to note that the need to avoid misleading and deceptive conduct is linked with the duty to prevent insolvent trading. First, if a director incurs a debt on behalf of the company when it is insolvent, failure to disclose the true state of the company's financial affairs to the creditor may constitute an actionable breach of the misleading and deceptive conduct provisions. The creditor would need to show that the director's conduct was misleading and deceptive. For example, the creditor might be able to show that by something the director did or said or failed to do or say the creditor was mislead into believing that the company was solvent. Secondly, false assurances given by a director to a creditor as to the financial health and commercial standing of a company may also be breaches of s 52 of the *Trade Practices Act*, s 42 of the *Fair Trading Act* and s 12DA of the *ASIC Act*.

Misleading conduct by a company has been found in relation to insolvent trading because the company failed to disclose certain default clauses in contracts

2 *Trade Practices Act* 1974 (Cth), s 82. See *Enzed Holdings Ltd v Wynthea Pty Ltd* (1984) 4 FCR 450; *Porter v Audio Visual Promotions Pty Ltd* (1985) ATPR 40–547; and *Nobile v National Australia Bank Ltd* (1987) ATPR 40–787.

made with creditors.[3] However, the relevant directors were not found to be knowingly concerned in or party to that conduct by virtue of s 75B of the *Trade Practices Act*, and thus damages were not ordered against them under s 82 of the *Trade Practices Act*. Despite this, the decision provides creditors with an alternative avenue for enforcing rights.

In some circumstances a claim for misleading and deceptive conduct may be a more appropriate source of remedy for creditors than is available under the insolvent trading provisions.

[17.2] Philosophy/rationale

The general philosophy of the "misleading and deceptive conduct" provisions is to protect consumers and those to whom false representations are made. It is a provision of wide impact:

> Section 52 is a comprehensive provision of wide impact, which does not adopt the language of any common law cause of action. It does not purport to create liability at all; rather it establishes a norm of conduct, failure to observe which has consequences provided for elsewhere in the same statute, or under general law ... The view has not been taken that "conduct" necessarily involves a continuing course of conduct, or of repeated events, or of conduct known to the public or a group of the public ... Intention is not a necessary ingredient ... The tort is more objective, but is not precisely correct to apply the concept of the hypothetical reasonable man. One looks to the audience or the relevant part of it, and, eccentricities and absurdities aside, asks whether the conduct complained of was to them misleading or deceptive ...[4]

Although the provisions are generally concerned with misrepresentations, they have the potential to include a far broader range of conduct. This is consistent with the philosophy of consumer protection:

> Misleading or deceptive conduct generally consists of misrepresentation, whether express or by silence; but it is erroneous to approach s 52 on the assumption that its application is confined exclusively to circumstances which constitute some form of representation ... ultimately in each case it is necessary to examine the conduct, whether representational in character or not, and ask the question whether the impugned conduct of its nature constitutes misleading or deceptive conduct.[5]

3 *Standard Chartered Bank of Australia v Antico* (1995) 131 ALR 1.
4 *Brown v Jam Factory Pty Ltd* (1981) 53 FLR 340 at 348 per Fox J.
5 *Henjo Investments Pty Ltd v Collins Marrickville Pty Ltd* (1988) 79 ALR 83 at 93 per Lockhart J.

As a company can only act through its directors and officers, personal liability imposed on directors for procuring the contravention is consistent with the policy of consumer protection. It is intended to act as a sufficient incentive for directors to disclose all facts known to them and be truthful in their representations to other parties. This is particularly important in the context of impending insolvency.

[17.3] History/former law

The *Trade Practices Act* 1974 (Cth) came into operation on the 1 October 1974. Prior to this time there was no coherent set of principles regarding neither misleading or deceptive conduct nor personal liability for directors involved in such conduct. Section 42 of the *Fair Trading Act* 1987 (NSW) and Pt 2 of Div 2 of the *ASIC Act* were directly modelled on s 52 of the *Trade Practices Act* 1974 (Cth).

[17.4] Notable cases

[17.4.1] *STANDARD CHARTERED BANK OF AUSTRALIA V ANTICO*

Standard Chartered Bank of Australia v Antico[6] was the first case to apply the misleading and deceptive conduct provisions of s 52 and s 75B of the *Trade Practices Act* 1974 (Cth) to the insolvent trading provisions. It highlights that failure to notify a party of information that could seriously affect a transaction amounts to misleading and deceptive conduct.[7]

Giant, in which Pioneer had a 42 per cent shareholding, entered into a bill discount and acceptance facility of $30m with Standard Chartered Bank of Australia (Standard). The only security it held was security over shares purchased by Giant in another company. However, due to financial difficulties experience by Giant, Pioneer agreed to provide funding to Giant. Pioneer took a second ranking security interests over the majority of Giant's assets in which the banks, other than Standard, had security interests. On a number of occasions the finance facility between Giant and Standard was renegotiated. During renegotiations, Standard was not informed of Pioneer's security interests and was given minimal information of Pioneer's funding of Giant. In addition, Giant did not disclose a minor security shortfall under a facility with another bank, the Bank of New Zealand (BNZ).

---

6 (1995) 131 ALR 1; Sup Ct, NSW, 9 August 1995 per Hodgson J.

7 For a useful summary see T Taylor, "The Fusion of Misleading Conduct and Suspected Insolvency" *Ferrier Hodgson Professional Update* No 3, 1995.

The Court considered the effect of this failure of Giant to disclose Pioneer's security interest and its separate default to BNZ upon the ability of Giant to have reasonable grounds to expect that it would be able to pay its debts as they became due before it incurred the debt to Standard. If misleading and deceptive conduct had been committed, Giant would not have reasonable grounds to expect that it would be able to pay its debts.

The Court held that Giant's failure to disclose these security interests to Standard during negotiations amounted to misleading and deceptive conduct. The extension of time granted by Standard by Giant was directly induced by misleading and deceptive conduct on behalf of Giant. During negotiations with Standard, Giant confirmed that it had disclosed to Standard all information that was relevant to the provision of the facility. However, it had failed to disclose the default under the BNZ facility and Pioneer's security. If this information had been disclosed by Giant, Standard would have acted differently during renegotiations. It would not have renegotiated to the extension but rather would have sought to have Pioneer pay the $30m owed, or obtained some concession from Pioneer in respect of its security over Giant. Accordingly, the misleading and deceptive conduct was calculated to induce Standard to extend the finance facility, and it achieved this objective. The inability of Giant to repay the $30m, the default to BNZ, and the misleading and deceptive conduct meant that before the debt to Standard was incurred, Giant did not have reasonable grounds to expect that it would be able to pay its debts, including the debt to Standard.

However, the relevant directors were not knowingly concerned in or party to that conduct and could not be made liable for damages under s 75B of the *Trade Practices Act* 1974 (Cth).

[17.5] Interesting high profile matters

[17.5.1] RELATION BETWEEN MISLEADING CONDUCT AND SUSPECTED INSOLVENCY

In order to contravene the insolvent trading provisions, a director must suspect that there are reasonable grounds for suspecting insolvency. A transaction entered into as a result of misleading and deceptive conduct may be suggestive of the company's inability to pay its debts as and when they fall due. For example, in the Giant case:

> On 1 June 1989, Giant relied on its facility to have [Standard] discount bills; and accordingly … Giant thereby confirmed to [Standard] that its representations and warranties remained true and correct on 1 June 1989, and thus that it had disclosed to the bank all information which was material to the provision of the facility. However, Giant had not in fact disclosed the default referred to above, or

> Pioneer's resolution to take security and its obtaining of Westpac's consent ... Furthermore, in my view, [a letter from Standard to Giant] of 11 July 1989 confirmed that information about Pioneer's security was material to the provision of the facility, as was unknown to [Standard] ... I consider that [Standard] would have acted differently if the misleading conduct had not occurred ... the negotiations which in fact occurred were induced by misleading conduct and would have been ended by disclosure of that conduct ... I find that, but for the misleading conduct, the debt of $30 million would have been due from 30 June to 25 July and beyond.[8]

[17.6] Checklist

When seeking to prosecute directors for breach of misleading and deceptive conduct provisions, insolvency practitioners should consult the following:

- What is the current state of financial affairs of the corporation?
- Has the director remained sufficiently informed regarding changes to the financial position of the company?
- Has the director been asked questions pertaining to the current state of financial affairs of the corporation?
- Has the director disclosed the true financial position of the corporation in response to these questions?
- Has the director disclosed any significant factors that may cause this financial position to alter?
- Has the director ensured that adequate and up-to-date compliance systems are working within the corporation?

[17.7] Tricks/hints

[17.7.1] COMPLIANCE PROGRAMS

The existence of adequate compliance programs will have an impact on any penalty made in relation to a breach by a company of s 52 of the *Trade Practices Act* 1974 (Cth), s 42 of the *Fair Trading Act* or s 12DA of the *ASIC Act*.[9] It is possible, although somewhat unlikely, that any compliance programs set up by directors may be a relevant consideration in assessing damages to be paid under s 82. Directors should establish compliance programs that are up-to-date and effective in ensuring compliance with the misleading and deceptive conduct provisions. Australian Standard 3806 sets out guidelines to an adequate compliance program.

8 *Standard Chartered Bank of Australia v Antico* (1995) 131 ALR 1 at 98–102.

9 See s 79 of the *Trade Practices Act* 1974 (Cth). See also *ACCC v NW Frozen Foods Pty Ltd* (1996) ATPR 41–515.

Delegation and Reliance

18

"*The business of a corporation could not go on if directors could not trust those who are put into a position of trust for the express purpose of attending to details of management.*"[1]

1 *AWA Ltd v Daniels* (1992) 10 ACLC 933 at 1015 per Rogers CJ.

OBJECTIVES

This Chapter will:

- consider the statutory provisions which allow directors to delegate her or his functions to others and rely on the performance of these functions by these delegates in fulfilment of her or his duties;
- discuss the way in which directors should act in properly delegating and relying.

[18.1] General overview

There is explicit legislative recognition that directors can delegate functions to others and rely on any information provide by others in the performance of their duties. Importantly this ability to delegate and rely applies to directors only. It does not apply to officers.

Under s 198D of the Law, directors can delegate any of their powers to a committee of directors, a director, an employee, or any other person: s 198D(1). The exercise of the power by the delegate is as effective as if the director had exercised the power: s 198D(3). However, the director will be held responsible for the exercise of the power (s 190(1)) except if the director believed on reasonable grounds, in good faith, and after making any required inquiry, that the delegate was reliable and competent in relation to the power delegated: s 190(2). The director may need to periodically review the actions of the delegate and her or his overall performance. Adequate monitoring and oversight systems should be established for this purpose.

Section 189 provides that directors can rely on information and advice provided by others if the reliance was made in good faith and after making any necessary inquiries: s 189(a) and (b). This reliance will be reasonable unless the contrary is proved: s 189. This ability to rely on others relates to the directors' duties in Pt 2D.1, such as the duty of care and diligence and good faith: s 189(c). It also applies to the common law equivalents of these duties, such as the common law duty of care and diligence. It should be noted that the standard required of executive directors is higher than that expected of non-executive directors. As the delegation and reliance will be reasonable unless circumstances indicated a need for further inquiry, the in-depth knowledge of the affairs of the company possessed by executive directors will mean that they are more likely to be put on inquiry than non-executive directors.

When relying on s 189 directors must independently assess the advice and information with which they are provided. This involves a proper, unbiased assessment by the director and although an independent expert need not be retained to assess the information this may be warranted in serious circumstances. If a director possesses special skills in a certain area, they must scrutinise information relating to such an area more carefully than would be expected by a director without such skills.[2]

Specific ability to rely on information regarding the solvency of the company provided by others is provided by s 588H(3). Under this subsection, it is a defence to a claim of insolvent trading if the director had reasonable grounds to believe and did believe that a competent and reliable person was responsible for providing the director information as to the company's solvency, that the person was

2 See *Southern Resources Ltd v Residues Treatment* (1990) 3 ACSR 207.

fulfilling that duty, and that he or she did in fact expect solvency on the basis of that information: s 588H(3); see Ch 9.

[18.2] Philosophy/rationale

The delegation and reliance provisions seek to recognise the reality of modern companies and the often diverse managerial and organisational patterns they exhibit. The complexity and scale of many large companies compels directors to delegate and rely heavily on others in the performance of their duties. Efficiency and time constraints further necessitate such delegation and reliance.

As stated in the Corporate Law Economic Reform Program:

> Uncertainty about the circumstances in which it is appropriate for a director to delegate to, or place reliance on the advice of, others could lead to an overly conservative approach to management and could impede the decision-making processes within a company.[3]

Ultimately, the provisions provide an incentive for directors to ensure that adequate financial management systems are in place with competent and reliable persons taking care of the company's financial matters.

The provisions are not intended to allow directors to remain passive. A director needs to periodically review the delegate's performance and the soundness of the delegation. In the words of Baxt:

> The director must, however take a partially active role in the affairs of the company. The director must ensure that a proper form of delegation has been created. Secondly, the director must assess the information that is provided to him/her. And furthermore ... the relevant director must ensure that the form of delegation established is periodically reviewed. This is assumed from the fact that the defence requires a competent and reliable person to be responsible and that adequate information is provided. Unless review procedures are undertaken by directors in relation to both these matters the mere setting up of a procedure etc may not be sufficient.[4]

3 The Commonwealth of Australia, *Directors' Duties and Corporate Governance: Facilitating Innovation and Protecting Investors*, AGPS, Canberra, 1998, p 46.
4 R Baxt, "New Insolvent Trading Rules for Directors" (1993) *Company Director* 12.

[18.3] History/former law

Prior to the introduction of s 189, s 190, s 198D and s 588H(3) there was no statutory recognition of the ability of directors to delegate to, and rely on, others in the performance of their duties. Directors were placed in the precarious position of having to delegate functions and powers to others and rely on information and advice provided by them due to exigencies of business, but remaining unsure of the legal position of this delegation and reliance.

Discussion about delegation and reliance was rife in relation to common law duties, particularly the common law duty of care and diligence. In an early landmark case in relation to this common law duty, Romer J recognised that business efficacy will often require directors to delegate:

> In respect of all duties that, having regard to the exigencies of business, and the articles of association, may properly be left to some other official, a director is, in the absence of grounds for suspicion, justified in trusting that official to perform such duties honestly.[5]

The first modern judicial consideration of reliance was made by Rogers CJ in *AWA Ltd v Daniels*.[6] Rogers CJ acknowledged that given the diverse nature of modern companies and the often large organisational and managerial structured embodied in each directors will often have to rely on management to perform many of the day-to-day business and financial affairs of the company. Although the relevant excerpt from the judgment of Rogers CJ is set out below, it is useful to note that Rogers CJ emphasised that reliance will only be reasonable where the delegation itself was reasonable. His Honour held that in general directors can rely without verification on the information and advice provided by those so entrusted to provide that information and advice. The reliance would not be reasonable if circumstances arose which were so plain and so simple of appreciation that no reasonable person in a similar position would have relied on the particular information or advice. In other words, reliance would fail to be reasonable where circumstances arose which put the director on alert that there was need for further inquiry.

The approach of Rogers J was criticised by Clarke and Sheller JJA in *Daniels v AWA Ltd*,[7] in the NSW Court of Appeal from which the decision of Rogers J at first instance was appealed. After considering a number of judgments from the

5 *Re City Equitable Fire Insurance Co Ltd* [1925] Ch 407 at 429 per Romer J.
6 (1992) 10 ACLC 933.
7 (1995) 13 ACLC 614.

United States,[8] they concluded that the community places a greater responsibility of company directors than the judgment of Rogers J recognises. For this reason they asserted that directors cannot merely rely on others to perform functions but rather:

> ... the responsibilities of directors require that they take reasonable steps to place themselves in a position to guide and monitor the management of the company ... directors are under a continuing obligation to keep informed about the activities of the corporation. Otherwise, they may not be able to participate in the overall management of corporate affairs.[9]

However, in the years following this decision by the Court of Appeal, various Courts questioned the practicality of such reasoning and preferred to allow some delegation and reliance by directors where reasonable.[10] In ddition, the Courts continued to assess situations where delegation and reliance would be unreasonable, including failure to monitor the situation given the gravity and importance of the matter concerned[11] and failure to consider the financial position of the company at all,[12] implying that delegation and reliance were permitted within the limits of reasonableness.

Bearing these considerations and developments in mind, the legislature sought to clarify the situation regarding delegation and reliance by the introduction of ss 189, 190 and 198D into the Law. Accordingly, these build on the decision of Rogers CJ in *AWA Ltd v Daniels*, whilst taking into consideration the warnings by Clarke and Sheller JJA of the need for directors to stay informed of the affairs of the company to a reasonable degree. For this reason, the new delegation and reliance provisions seek to place limits of reasonableness on the ability to delegate and rely.

---

8 Including *Federal Deposit Insurance Corporation v Bierman* 2 F3d 1424 (1993) where Judge Ripple stated (at 1432-1433):

"Directors are charged with keeping abreast of the [corporation's] business and exercising reasonable supervision and control over the activities of the [corporation] ... A director may not rely on the judgment of others, especially when there is notice of mismanagement. Certainly, when an investment poses an obvious risk, a director cannot blindly rely on the judgment of others."

Also considered was *Rankin v Cooper* (1907) 149 F 1010 at 1013 where the Court held:

"If nothing has come to the knowledge to awaken suspicion that something is going wrong, ordinary attention to the affairs of the institution is insufficient. If, upon the other hand, directors know, or by the exercise of ordinary care should have known, any facts which would awaken suspicion and put a prudent man on his guard, then a degree of care commensurate with the evil to be avoided is required, and a want of that care makes them responsible. Directors cannot, in justice to those who deal with [the corporation], shut their eyes to what is going on around them."

9 (1995) 13 ACLC 614 at 662–664.

10 See *Australian Securities Commission v Gallagher* (1993) 10 ACSR 43 at 58–60; *Biala Pty Ltd v Mallina Holdings Ltd* (1994) 15 ACSR 1 at 62; and *Vrisakis v Australian Securities Commission* (1993) 9 WAR 395.

11 *Permanent Building Society v Wheeler* (1994) 14 ACSR 109.

12 *Metropolitan Fire Systems Pty Ltd v Miller* (1997) 23 ACSR 699 at 712.

[18.4] Interesting quotes

[18.4.1] NEED FOR DELEGATION AND RELIANCE PROVISIONS

The need for delegation and reliance provisions was asserted by Rogers CJ in *AWA Ltd v Daniels*.[13] It is worth quoting his Honour's judgment at length:

> The directors rely on management to manage the corporation … A director is justified in trusting officers of the corporation to perform all duties that, having regard to the exigencies of business, the intelligent devolution of labour and the articles of association, may properly be left to such officers … A director is entitled without verification to rely on the judgment, information and advice of the officers so entrusted. A director is also entitled to rely on management to go carefully through relevant financial and other information of the corporation and draw to the board's attention any matter requiring the board's consideration. The business of a corporation could not go on if directors could not trust those who are put into a position of trust for the express purpose of attending to details of management … Reliance would only be unreasonable where the director was aware of circumstances of such a character, so plain, so manifest and so simple of appreciation that no person, with any degree of prudence, acting on his behalf, would have relied on the particular judgment, information and advice of the officers.[14]

[18.5] Timeline/checklist

[18.5.1] WAYS IN WHICH DIRECTORS CAN RELY ON MANAGEMENT

In *AWA Ltd v Daniels*[15] the directors of AWA Ltd relied on management in a number of ways. The list formulated by Rogers CJ indicates the sorts of ways in which many directors may use the delegation and reliance provisions:

(a) to carry out the day to day control of the corporation's business affairs;
(b) to establish proper internal controls, management information systems and accounting records;
(c) reduce to writing if appropriate and communicate policies and strategies adopted by the Board;
(d) implement the policies and strategies adopted by the Board;

13 (1992) 10 ACLC 933.
14 (1992) 10 ACLC 933 at 1014–1015 per Rogers CJ.
15 (1992) 10 ACLC 933.

(e) have a knowledge of and review detailed figures, contracts and other information about the corporation's affairs and financial position and summarise such information for the Board where appropriate;
(f) prepare proposals and submission for consideration by the Board;
(g) prepare a budget;
(h) attend to personnel matters including hiring and firing of staff and their terms of employment.

[18.5.2] CHECKLIST

An insolvency practitioner who is seeking to ascertain whether reliance by a director on a delegate under s 198D or s 189 of the Law was reasonable in fulfilling the director's duties should consider the following as a guide to the reasonableness of the delegation:

- Is the relevant director an executive or non-executive director?
- What is the function that the relevant director sought to delegate?
- Is the function capable of proper delegation?
- To what extent is the function important to the business affairs of the company?
- Did the director actually believe that the delegate was competent and reliable in relation to the function or matter?
- What experience and qualifications did the delegate possess?
- What was the relationship between the delegate and the director?
- Did the director believe that the delegate was honest?
- Is the level of work that the delegate was required to do appropriate and reasonable and not too onerous?
- What time limits were imposed on the delegate?
- Did the director regularly review the performance of the delegate?
- Did the director "blindly" rely on the information and advice provided by the delegate?
- Were there any factors that suggest to the director that he or she needed to make further inquiries and not merely accept the information and advice provided by the delegate without her or his own investigation?

[18.6] Loopholes/deficiencies

[18.6.1] NOT ALWAYS COMPLETE BASIS FOR EXCULPATION

Section 189 will not always provide a complete defence to directors. If an opposing party can disprove any of the elements, then the reliance may be deemed unreasonable and the director may be held to have breached their duty of care and diligence.

[18.6.2] OVERSIGHT SYSTEMS SHOULD BE ESTABLISHED

A twofold importance and inquiry test is established under s 189 and s 190. Accordingly, if the matter that is delegated is important and circumstances or information arise that ought to put the director on inquiry, then monitoring of the actions and functions of the delegate is required.

Directors should ensure that the delegate is adequately completing the tasks or function required. A director must at least take a partially active role in ensuring that proper systems are set up for financial management and monitoring, reviewing the satisfactory performance of the responsible delegate.

[18.6.3] DELEGATION SHOULD BE IN WRITING

The delegation under s 198D should be clearly expressed in writing with the consent of all parties concerned.

[18.7] Proposals for law reform

[18.7.1] OFFICERS TO BE INCLUDED WITHIN AMBIT

It is arguable that the delegation and reliance provisions should be extended to include "officers" as well as "directors". Currently, only directors are able to delegate and rely on others in fulfillment of their duty of care and diligence. As discussed in Chapter 3 at para [3.1.1], the definition of officer was amended in 2000 to include persons who make, or participate in making, decisions which affect the business of the company as well as those who have the capacity to significantly affect the company's financial standing. This has widened the scope of those who may be caught within the definition of "officer". Again, the size and complexity of many modern companies will necessitate delegation and reliance by officers as well as those in top management positions. Arguably, the ambit of the delegation and reliance provisions should be extended to include those officers who have such wide-ranging powers over the financial standing and business direction of a company. Where any reliance by the officer on others is unreasonable, no protection would be afforded.

However, the extension of the ability to delegate and rely by "officers" may raise problems peculiar to particular types of officers. One notable example would be the position of receivers to discharge her or his statutory functions by delegating those duties to an agent retained to advise in relation to and act on the sale of mortgaged property. The Courts have traditionally rejected the ability of receivers to delegate in this way when exercising their powers of sale under s 420A of the Law and have held that a receiver is not able to reply on experts to carry out functions incidental to the sale of mortgaged property to absolve the receiver from liability.[16]

16 See *Commercial and General Acceptance Ltd v Nixon* (1981) 152 CLR 491; and *Jeogla Pty Ltd v ANZ Banking Corporation Ltd* (1999) 150 FLR 359.

PART D

Other Specific Duties

Phoenix Companies – What Are They and What Can Be Done About Them?

19

"*The phoenix is an unpredictable economic vandal, moving quietly within the Australian corporate circle.*"[1]

"*In the end, the effort which should be put into curbing the phoenix company phenomenon depends upon as assessment of the costs of making business unprofitable and risk taking too hazardous, against the costs to creditors and confidence of an excessively laissez faire approach to the misuse of the limited liability company. The problem of the phoenix company is common and perhaps endemic. It should not be ignored.*"[2]

1 N Coburn, "The Phoenix Reexamined" (1998) 8(3) *Australian Journal of Corporate Law* 321 at 322.

2 Victorian Law Reform Commission, *Curbing the Phoenix Company: Second Report on the Law Relating to Directors and Managers of Insolvent Corporations* (1995), p xiv.

OBJECTIVES

This Chapter will:

- consider the attributes of a phoenix company;
- analyse the impact of phoenix activities on the Australian economy;
- assess the penalties which can be imposed on directors responsible for phoenix activities and consider whether these have a sufficient deterrent effect;
- critically analyse the recent amendments to the Law regarding employee entitlements and discuss the recently introduced Employee Entitlements Support Scheme.

[19.1] General overview

[19.1.1] WHAT IS A "PHOENIX COMPANY"?

A number of companies and directors abuse the corporate form and the widespread availability of limited liability for the sole purpose of avoiding debt. In many instances the avoidance of taxation and/or impending insolvency may cause resort to what is commonly known as a "phoenix company".[3]

The term "phoenix company" is widely used by lawyers and other professionals. On a basic level, a phoenix company is a limited liability company:

> ... housing individuals, whether directors by name or otherwise, who abuse the corporate form by dissolving one company and creating another to avoid the payment of debt.[4]

The Victorian Law Reform Commission (VLRC) has described a phoenix company as follows:

> A limited liability company fails, unable to pay its debts to creditors, employees and the State. At the same time, or soon afterwards, the same business rises from the ashes with the same directors, under the guise of a new limited liability company, but disclaiming any responsibility for the debts of the previous company.[5]

ASIC defines phoenix activities as those when a company:[6]

- fails and is unable to pay its debts; and/or
- acts in a manner which intentionally denies unsecured creditors equal access to the available assets in order to meet unpaid debts; and
- within 12 months of closing another business commences which may use some or all of the assets of the former business, and is controlled by parties related to either the management or directors of the previous company.

[19.1.2] WIDESPREAD ECONOMIC DAMAGE FROM PHOENIX COMPANIES

Research carried out by the Australian Securities Commission[7] indicates that:

- the highest estimate of annual losses to the Australian economy as a result of phoenix activities is $1.3m, representing 0.28 per cent of GDP;

---

3 For a discussion see R Tomasic, "Phoenix Companies and Rogue Directors: A Note on a Program of Law Reform" (1995) 5(3) *Australian Journal of Corporate Law* 474 at 476.

4 N Coburn, "The Phoenix Reexamined" (1998) 8(3) *Australian Journal of Corporate Law* 321 at 322.

5 VLRC, *Curbing the Phoenix Company: First Report on the Law Relating to Directors and Managers of Insolvent Corporations* (1994), para 1.1.

6 ASC Research Paper, *Phoenix Companies and Insolvent Trading*, No 95/01, July 1996, p 1.

7 ASC Research Paper, *Phoenix Companies and Insolvent Trading*, No 95/01, July 1996, pp 2–5.

- 18 per cent of small to medium sized entities have experienced phoenix activities;
- 80 per cent of respondents who had experienced phoenix activities did not report it to the authorities;
- 45 per cent of phoenix activities appear to be in the building/construction industries;
- only 38 per cent of phoenix company groups will have a secured creditor;
- 82 per cent of respondents were prepared to continue providing credit to companies who appeared to be in financial difficulty.

Clearly phoenix activities have a widespread effect on the Australian economy, but the failure of creditors to report them to the authorities means that they often remains undetected.

Corporate groups are sometimes established for the purpose of facilitating phoenix activities. For example, during its investigations the VLRC was told of several cases where undercapitalised companies are established for the purposes of hiring labour but where the true beneficiary, but not employer, is another stronger company in the same group.[8] This stronger company exerts considerable influence over the terms and conditions of employment and has a strong influence over the workplace. However, when employees press for better conditions, the smaller employer company is wound up. When the employer company is wound up, employees may be deprived of their legal rights, including long service leave and retrenchment or severance pay without any available resort to the other financially sound company.

[19.1.3] EMPLOYEE ENTITLEMENTS

In an attempt to avoid the unfortunate situation where employees are deprived of their entitlements when their employer company becomes insolvent, the Law has been recently amended to give liquidators, and in some circumstances employees, the ability to pursue directors for personal liability for loss and damage suffered by the employee.[9] New ss 596AA-596AI (Pt 5.8A) were introduced by the *Corporations Law Amendment (Employee Entitlements)* 2000. Section 596AA states that the object of Pt 5.8A is to protect the entitlements of a company's employees from agreements and transactions that are entered into with the intention of defeating the recovery of those entitlements. Under s 596AA(2) the

8 VLRC, *Curbing the Phoenix Company: First Report on the Law Relating to Directors and Managers of Insolvent Corporations* (1994), para 2.1.13.

9 For more commentary on recent employee entitlement amendments, see M Reynolds, "The New Employee Entitlements Legislation: Prevention or Cure" (2000) 20(11) *Proctor* 22; and R Campo, "The Protection of Employee Entitlements in the Event of Employer Insolvency: Australian Initiatives in the Light of International Models" (2000) 13(3) *Australian Journal of Labour Law* 236.

entitlements which are protected by Pt 5.8A are wages, superannuation contributions, amounts due in respect of injury compensation, amounts due under and industrial instrument in respect of leave of absence and retrenchment payments. An entitlement need not be owed to the employee directly but may be owed, for example, to an employee's dependants or a superannuation fund.

Under s 596AB(1) a person must not enter into an agreement or transaction with the intention of, or with intentions that include the intention of, preventing the recovery of employee entitlements, or significantly reducing the amount of entitlements recoverable. This rule applies even if the company itself is not a party to the agreement or transaction or the agreement or transaction is approved by the Court. The rule can apply to a series of agreements and/or transactions. The intention of the relevant person will be ascertained by examining the dealings of the company and all relevant parties before, and at the time, the relevant agreement or transaction was made.

If a person breaches this rule they can be made liable to pay compensation as a debt due to the company or prosecuted for a criminal offence, in which case they may be subjected to a fine of 1,000 penalty units, imprisonment for 10 years, or both. Under s 596AC(1) a person is liable to pay compensation is the person breached s 596AB, the company is being wound up and the employees of the company suffer loss and damage because of the breach or action taken to give effect to an agreement or transaction involved in the breached. Under s 596AC(1) the person will be so liable even if they have been convicted of an offence in relation to the breach.

Under s 596AC(3), a company's liquidator can recover from the relevant person an amount equal to the loss or damage suffered by an employee as a debt due to the company. Accordingly, funds may be recovered by the liquidator for general distribution to employees. Under s 596AF and s 596AH, an employee can commence action against a person directly if he or she has the consent of the liquidator or with the leave of the Court if the employee has given the liquidator notice that he or she has suffered loss and damage as a result of a contravention of s 596AB and the liquidator has not consented to the employee commencing proceedings within three months of receiving the notice.

If a person contravenes s 596AB by incurring a debt within the meaning of s 588G (see Chapter 4 at para [4.1]), the employees ability to undertake proceedings for breach of s 596AB may be restricted. Under s 596AI(1), an employee of a company that is being wound up cannot begin proceedings for compensation under s 596AC if the person has incurred a debt within the meaning of s 588G when entering into the agreement or transaction and the company's liquidator has either begun proceedings under s 588M for breach of the insolvent trading provisions or has intervened in an application by ASIC for a civil penalty order for breach of s 588G in relation to the incurring of a debt. Section 596AI(1) also prevents an employee commencing proceedings if the liquidator has applied under s 588FF in relation to a transaction that constituted, or was part of, the contravention or if the liquidator has already begun proceedings under s 596AC in relation to the breach.

Double recovery is not possible. Under s 596AD, any amount recovered under s 596AC for a contravention of s 596AB will be taken into account in working out the amount recoverable in any other proceedings under s 596AC for a breach of s 596AB or proceedings for compensation under s 588M in relation to the incurring of a debt that is linked to the breach.

An Employee Entitlements Support Scheme was established with effect on 1 January 2000. This was established to provide a "safety net" to employees of insolvent companies in respect of their unpaid entitlements. The Scheme provides a maximum of $20,000 towards each employee's unpaid entitlements. The calculations are based on up to 29 weeks pay at ordinary time rates as follows:

- up to four weeks unpaid wages;
- up to four weeks annual leave (accrued within the last 12 months);
- up to five weeks pay in lieu of notice;
- up to four weeks redundancy pay; and
- up to 12 weeks long service leave.

The maximum rate of pay at which benefits are calculates is $40,000. Employees who have a salary of more than $40,000 can apply for assistance under the Scheme but the rate at which their entitlements will be calculated is capped at $40,000.

Such amounts will apply where the relevant State Government participates in the Scheme. To date, Labor State Governments have refused to participate in the Scheme due to the failure of the Commonwealth Government to introduce an employer-funded insurance scheme to cover employee entitlements. Labor Governments assert that this development is appropriate as it would provide full repayment of entitlements to employees out of insurance premiums paid by their employer, thus acting as an added deterrent. Where the relevant State does not participate in the Scheme, the Commonwealth Government provides 50 per cent of the relevant "safety net" amount.

It should be noted that the Employee Entitlements Support Scheme is policy only and has no legislative basis as such. Accordingly, a change of government could mean a change in the way the Employee Entitlement Support Scheme is structured and administered.

These developments in relation to employee entitlements do not guarantee a full repayment to employees of lost entitlements and it is yet to be seen what effect, if any, they have on directors who may participate in phoenix activities. Whether or not a particular employee will be satisfied with any payment received under the Scheme will depend on whether he or she resides in a Labor or Liberal State Government and the amount of entitlements lost. The amendments to the

Law may provide some ammunition to insolvency practitioners in recovering unpaid employee entitlements.

[19.1.4] REMEDIES AGAINST ROGUE DIRECTORS

When a director is involved in phoenix activities, he or she will often be breaching one or a number of directors' duties. Particular duties which are likely to be contravened include the duty of good faith and the duties regarding proper use of information and position. The common law and statutory directors duties provisions will often provide grounds for relief against delinquent directors.

If the director organises the transfer of assets from one company to a phoenix company, the phoenix company may pay a minimal or insignificant amount for the assets, or perhaps pay nothing at all. If a director establishes a phoenix company in competition to another company of which they are also a director and the phoenix company, through the director, effectively gains the use of confidential information belonging to the first company without paying for it, the director may breach her or his duties of proper use of position and information. For example, in *Mordecai v Mordecai*[10] the Court held that a breach of fiduciary duty occurred when two brothers set up a company in order to reduce the potential claim of their dead brother's estranged widow on another company because they had actively solicited the clients of the other company. This made clear use of information and insights gained in their capacity as directors of the other company and constituted a conflict of interest and improper use of information.

There are a number of ways of dealing with directors who abuse the corporate form and limited liability through the use of phoenix activities. One such method may be to disqualify the rogue directors from managing corporations to prevent them doing it again. Another such method may be to give creditors access to the director's personal assets to preclude them benefiting from their actions.

The Law was amended in 2000 to bring many of the provisions relating to directors' duties and obligations and associated offences and penalties together. This is intended to better inform company directors of their duties, however it is unclear whether rogue directors will be affected by this reorganisation of the law as the vast body of corporations law seems to have little impact upon the activities of many directors.[11]

In addition to these disqualification provisions, the remedies available for a breach of insolvent trading will often be available to creditors against rogue directors. This is because in many cases phoenix companies will be used where a company is nearing insolvency or is insolvent and the directors are allowing it to

10 (1988) 12 ACLR 751.

11 See R Tomasic and S Bottomley, *Directing the Top 500: Corporate Governance and Accountability in Australia Companies* (Allen and Unwin, Sydney, 1993), pp 75–79.

incur debts to creditors with the intention of winding up the company before repayment is made. If a director has breached the insolvent trading provisions in this way, an individual creditor has a secondary right to bring proceedings for compensation equal to the amount of "loss or damage" caused by the breach under s 588M(3). The amount of "loss or damage" is likely to include the amount of the debt and other consequential losses.

Where directors are in the process of transferring corporate assets out of the rogue company to another associated company, such as through an intra-group loan, ASIC can obtain injunctive relief under s 1324 to stop this transfer and preserve the company's assets: see s 1323 and 1324.

[19.2] Philosophy/rationale

The rationale behind these disqualification provisions for phoenix activities is not punitive. In contrast, they are concerned to protect the community by ensuring that only suitable persons are able to manage corporations in which people invest.[12]

The remedies available for phoenix activities are a result of the balance achieved between seeking to curb phoenix activities whilst simultaneously ensuring that the benefits of being a director do not outweigh the costs. Any balance achieved should not be thought of as a final solution but a process of continual evaluation:

> In the end, the effort which should be put into curbing the phoenix company phenomenon depends upon an assessment of the costs of making business unprofitable and risk taking too hazardous, against the costs to creditors and confidence of an excessively laissez faire approach to the misuse of the limits liability company. The problem of the phoenix company is common and perhaps endemic. It should not be ignored. Attempts to find remedies and to strike the right balance between competing considerations cannot be expected to result in a once and for all solution and should be kept under review.[13]

[19.3] History/former law

Prior to the recent amendments to the director disqualification provisions, the provisions relating to directors' duties and obligations and director disqualification were scattered throughout the Law. This made compliance with the Law

12 See *Commissioner for Corporate Affairs (WA) v Ekamper* (1987) 12 ACLR 519 per Franklyn J.

13 VLRC, *Curbing the Phoenix Company: Second Report on the Law Relating to Directors and Managers of Insolvent Corporations* (1994), p xiv.

difficult as directors could not easily inform themselves of their duties and any consequences for a breach of duty.

The director disqualification provisions under the previous regime were problematic. In particular, the former s 599 allowed orders of disqualification to be made against directors who were involved in the management of insolvent corporations. However, it required proof of contravention of the law beyond reasonable doubt. As a result, this provision was rarely used. In addition, the former s 600(3) provided the ASC with the power to prohibit a person from managing a corporation where the person was a director of two or more failed companies and a liquidator's report had been filed regarding the conduct of the director or its inability to pay unsecured creditors more than 50 cents in the dollar. This section had the obvious advantage of allowing the ASC to act without Court approval. However, s 600 assumed that formal steps were taken to wind up the company and did not cover the situation where the directors simply abandoned the old company name and continued to trade under the guise of a new company, and without the issue of the liquidator's report.

These provisions were criticised by the VLRC during its analysis of phoenix activities.[14] Recommendations were made for the amendment of these disqualification provisions and an increase in the period of director disqualification. These recommendations were implemented with the new director disqualification provisions.

[19.4] Interesting facts

[19.4.1] INCIDENCE AND ACTIVITIES OF PHOENIX COMPANIES

In 1996 the ASC conducted a research report into the activities of phoenix companies within small to medium sized enterprises (SMEs) and the impact of phoenix activities on the Australian economy. As a result of the research, a number of pertinent statistics were produced:[15]

- 18 per cent of SMEs have experienced phoenix activities. Of these 18 per cent, 80 per cent had experienced phoenix activities less than three times.
- 80 per cent of respondents who had experienced phoenix activities did not report that experience to the authorities.
- The lower the respondent's formal education, the more likely they were to have experienced a phoenix activity, and the greater monetary loss they were likely to have suffered.

14 VLRC, *Curbing the Phoenix Company: First Report on the Law Relating to Directors and Managers of Insolvent Corporations* (1994), Ch 3.

15 ASC Research Paper, *Phoenix Companies and Insolvent Trading*, No 95/01, July 1996, pp 2–5, cited in N Coburn, "The Phoenix Reexamined" (1998) 8(3) *Australian Journal of Corporate Law* 321.

- 45 per cent of the phoenix activity was in the building and construction industry.
- Many of the issues inherent in phoenix activities are assisted by poor management practices of SMEs themselves.
- Most phoenix companies have two directors, suggesting that they are usually small companies.
- 88 per cent of phoenix companies have an annual return outstanding while the average time these forms have been outstanding is about 2.5 years.
- The average phoenix company has had two names and has issued capital of less than $1,400.
- Only 38 per cent of phoenix companies will have a secured creditor.
- 58 per cent of phoenix companies will have unpaid taxes.
- 77 per cent of phoenix companies will not have adequate books and records.
- 77 per cent of phoenix companies will transfer corporate assets to evade paying creditors. Not all phoenix companies will actually have assets worth transferring.
- The highest estimate of annual losses to the economy as a result of phoenix activities is $1.3m.
- About 9,000 individual businesses are affected by phoenix activities each year.

[19.4.2] TYPES OF OFFENDERS

The ASC identified three types of offenders involved in phoenix activities.[16]

Innocent offenders have their personal assets tied to the success of the business and when the threat of insolvency hits the company the directors recover as much from the business as possible. As a result, assets are often transferred which speeds up the collapse and a phoenix situation will often develop. However, as directors' assets are tied to the company, the failure of the director's first company essentially eliminates most of the director's assets and if the second company collapses directors are often forced back into paid employment as the directors personal assets have been depleted. This means that they are not often repeat offenders.

Occupational hazard offenders include tradesmen who derive their income from their occupational trade. This includes many in the building and construction industries. Following the collapse of their first business, occupational hazard offenders have little choice but to continue to trade in that occupational group because it is their only means of deriving income.

Careerists are the most serious threat because they are the professionals who are aware of the law and the illegality of their action but make a conscious decision to set up phoenix companies.

16 ASC Research Paper, *Phoenix Companies and Insolvent Trading*, No 95/01, July 1996, pp 3–4, cited in N Coburn, "The Phoenix Reexamined" (1998) 8(3) *Australian Journal of Corporate Law* 321.

[19.5] Checklist

[19.5.1] A CREDITOR'S CHECKLIST – PRECAUTIONS

A number of precautions can be taken by creditors where they suspect phoenix activities of a debtor company:[17]

- If payment is outstanding, consider a floating charge or other form of security over the debtor company's assets, particularly if an agreement for payment by instalments is breached.
- Do not let unpaid debt pass unnoticed by the debtor company. Make it company practice to contact debtor companies and inquire when they might be expected to pay the outstanding amount. Be careful not to allow for unreasonable or numerous extensions of time for payment without reasonable prospects of repayment.
- When advancing significant credit, research fully the background of the company and directors involved to see if they have a habit of phoenix activities or non-payment of debt generally (for example, search the ASIC register of disqualified directors).

[19.5.2] A CREDITOR'S CHECKLIST – REMEDIES

If a creditor has extended credit to a company that has collapsed without payment of the creditor's debt and has subsequently established itself via a phoenix company, the creditor should consider the following:

- Prior to the financial collapse of the company, obtaining a Court injunction to prevent the directors from transferring the corporate assets out of the company.
- Discuss with ASIC the availability of disqualification procedures.
- If insolvent trading has occurred, pursue the creditor's secondary right to bring compensatory proceedings under s 588M(3). The creditor can claim that amount of "loss and damage" suffered as a result of the insolvent trading, which may include consequential loss.

[19.6] Loopholes/deficiencies

[19.6.1] DIMINISHED CORPORATE ASSETS

The ability of directors to transfer corporate assets out of the corporation prior to its collapse means that its move to insolvency is sped up and the directors are provided with substantial assets in order to establish a new phoenix company with the resources of the old company.

---

17 See N Coburn, "The Phoenix Reexamined" (1998) 8(3) *Australian Journal of Corporate Law* 321.

[19.6.2] SHADOW DIRECTORS NOT INCLUDED

Although the director disqualification provisions aim to prevent the control of companies by rogue directors, in most instances this will not prevent companies from being controlled by rogue shadow directors.[18]

[19.6.3] PROFESSIONAL ASSISTANCE

Careerist offenders require professional advice. Professional lawyers and accountants are contributing to the problem by assisting directors involved in phoenix activities in establishing new enterprises.

[19.6.4] AVOIDANCE OF LIQUIDATION

Directors who suspect insolvency or know their company is insolvent can place their corporation into voluntary administration, thus avoiding liquidation, minimising the risk of an insolvent trading action against them and may stand a better chance of recovering assets from the company in order to establish a phoenix company. Administrators are limited in their powers by what they are required to do and it is also possible for rogue directors to appoint an administrator who may have a bias in their favour.

[19.6.5] REFUSAL OF LIQUIDATOR TO BRING ACTION

The cost of bringing proceedings against rogue directors can be high. Often the amount owed by companies involved in phoenix activities will be a small amount. In these situations it may not be cost effective for a liquidator to institute Court proceedings. Remedies available under the insolvent trading provisions may not be pursued or disqualification orders sought.

[19.7] Proposals for law reform

[19.7.1] MAREVA INJUNCTION

The VLRC recommended a system for the preservation of corporate assets to prevent the transfer of these assets in order to facilitate the establishment of a phoenix company.[19] It recommended the introduction into the Law of a statutory process analogous to a Mareva injunction that would enable the Courts to freeze the assets of a director which are assets on which the corporation has a just claim. This would greatly aid the prevention of phoenix companies by preventing the transfer of corporate assets to an associated company.

---

18 See R Tomasic, "Phoenix Companies and Corporate Regulatory Challenges" (1996) 6(3) *Australian Journal of Corporate Law* 461 at 465.

19 VLRC, *Curbing the Phoenix Company: First Report on the Law Relating to Directors and Managers of Insolvent Corporations* (1994), para 4.1.44.

[19.7.2] BUSINESS NAME REGISTER

The VLRC has also recommended that a Business Name Register should be maintained by ASIC so that rogue directors are not able to use a business name similar to that of a failed company they were associated with. ASIC currently maintains the National Names Index which lists all company names reserved or in use within Australia. The act of maintaining a National Business Name Register may somewhat increase the chance of preventing rogue directors from engaging in phoenix activities; however, more stringent checks by ASIC when a request to reserve a business name may be more appropriate. A National Business Names Index may assist in this regard.

Directors' Personal Liability for Unremitted Tax Deductions

20

"*This measure will ensure solvency problems are confronted earlier and the escalation of debts will be prevented. The amendments proposed will result in a company either meeting its obligations to pay the amounts deducted to the Commissioner or going into voluntary administration or liquidation. Directors will only become liable for unremitted amounts when those options are not taken by their company.*"[1]

1 Senator Bob McMullan, Second Reading Speech to the *Insolvency (Tax Priorities) Amendment Act* 1993 (Cth), Senate, 19 May 1993, p 880.

OBJECTIVES

This Chapter will:

- outline the regime which imposes personal liability on directors for unremitted tax reductions;
- discuss the ways in which directors can avoid this personal liability;
- consider the defences available to directors.

[20.1] General overview

When a company is suffering liquidity problems, it is not uncommon for the company to fail to remit PAYE tax deductions to the Commissioner of Taxation (The Commissioner).

Section 221C(1) of the *Income Tax Assessment Act* 1936 (Cth) (ITAA) obliges an employer to make PAYE tax deductions from the salaries of its employees at the prescribed rate. Section 221F(5) obliges the employer to pay the Commissioner the amount of any deduction the employer makes.

Since 1 July 1993, the Australian Taxation Office (ATO) no longer enjoys a priority claim in insolvency administrations over other unsecured creditors for unpaid group tax (income tax deducted from employees' salaries by their employer; PAYE tax).[2] The ATO merely ranks as an ordinary unsecured creditor for these unpaid taxes.

However, the ITAA has been amended by the *Insolvency (Tax Priorities) Legislation Amendment Act* 1993 (Cth) to introduce procedures for the collection of group taxes that are required to be paid to the ATO. These amendments introduce a system of issuing penalty notices by which the ATO can make a director personally liable for those unpaid group taxes, and certain other taxes.[3]

These new provisions apply to a number of provisions within the ITAA. The provisions apply to the collection of instalments of tax on persons other than companies (group PAYE tax), tax file number withholding tax, withholding tax on dividends and interest and prescribed amounts payable.

Directors must ensure that a company that becomes liable to remit an amount to the for PAYE deductions under Div 2 of the ITAA either remits that amount or pursues one of four options (s 222AOB and s 222APB of the ITAA). Under s 222AOB(1) of the ITAA those four options are to:

- remit the amount due;
- enter into an agreement with the Commissioner to pay the amount due over a specified period of time;
- become subject to voluntary administration;
- be wound up.

If one of these four options is not taken, the Commissioner may impose a penalty on the director for an amount equal to the unpaid amount after a number of steps have been taken.

The liabilities of a company under a remittance provision are deemed to be debts for the purposes of the insolvent trading provisions: s 588F.

Directors should also be aware of the provisions of s 588FGA of the Law under which directors can be obliged to indemnify the ATO if a payment made

2 See *DCT v Dollymore Pty Ltd* (1993) 93 ATC 5212.
3 *Income Tax Assessment Act* 1936 (Cth), Div 9, Pt VI.

by the company to the ATO is deemed to be a voidable transaction.[4] For example, if PAYE taxes are remitted by the company to the ATO and this is later found by a Court to be a voidable transaction because it constitutes an insolvent transaction, uncommercial transaction, unfair preference or any one of the other possibilities under s 588FE of the Law, and the ATO has to repay this PAYE remittance to the company by virtue of an order under s 588FF, each and every director is personally liable to indemnify the ATO for any loss or damage suffered by to ATO. This amount will usually be the same amount as the company's PAYE remittance which the ATO was made to repay: s 588FGA(2). This amount is a debt due to the Commonwealth and payable to the ATO and may be recovered by legal action: s 588FGA(3).

[20.1.1] PENALTY NOTICE

Before the Commissioner can impose a penalty on a director, a notice must be sent to the director setting out the details of the unpaid amount, or an estimate of that amount: s 222 AOE of the ITAA. The notice must be sent to the director at the address shown on the records of ASIC to be the director's place of residence or business: s 222 AOF of the ITAA. This notice must also state that unless one of the four options outlined above is entered into within 14 days of the notice being given, the director will be liable to pay to the Commissioner, by way of penalty, an amount equal to the unpaid amount: s 222 AOE of the ITAA. The notice is "given" when it would be delivered to the director's address in the ordinary course of post and does not have to personally be served on the director.

[20.1.2] ESTIMATE OF AMOUNT OWED

It is important to note that the Commissioner can make an estimate of the unpaid amount, and does not need to articulate the precise amount owing in order to impose a penalty on a director: s 222 AGA.[5] This shifts the onus onto the director to make the Commissioner aware of the actual liability outstanding.

[20.1.3] PERSONAL LIABILITY FOR DIRECTORS

Directors are made personally liable for a penalty equal to the amount of the unremitted tax deductions or for the amount of the estimate made by the Commissioner.

The director can avoid this personal liability if within 14 days of the notice being given to the company to remit the unpaid amount, the company enters into an agreement with the Commissioner regarding payment, enters the company into voluntary administration, or causes the company to be wound up: s 222 AOE(b) of the ITAA. This is the case even if the director had nothing to do with one of those options being taken. However, if the company fails to pay

4 See, for example, *SJP Formwork (Aust) Pty Ltd (in liq) v DCT* (2000) 34 ACSR 604.

5 See E A Slater and J Edstein, "Unpaid Group Tax – Directors' Liability".

under a payment agreement made with the Commissioner, the director can be subjected to a penalty equal to the balance payable under the agreement. The Commissioner does not have to provide a notice for this liability to be imposed: s 222 AWA of the ITAA.

It should be noted that there is no prescribed order for these provisions to be applied and it is arguable that the Commissioner could serve an estimate, notice, and penalty at the same time.

[20.1.4] DEFENCES FOR DIRECTORS

A number of defences to liability are provided for directors. These defences are essential due to the personal liability than can arise from a breach of the provisions. As Mason argues:

> The Insolvency Amendments have cut a dangerously large hole in the corporate veil through which the Commissioner may reach into the pockets of directors to recover certain taxation liabilities of the corporate entity. Not surprisingly, those amendments therefore include significant defences which a director may seek to raise in order to avoid personal liability.[6]

A director will not be personally liable if:

- the director took all reasonable steps to ensure that the company would do one of the four options;[7]
- there were no reasonable steps that the director could take to ensure that the company complied;[8] or
- the director did not participate in the management of the company for illness or some other good reason.[9]

These defences are analogous to the defences under s 588H of the Law for a breach of the insolvent trading provisions.

In determining what is "reasonable", regard may be given to:

- when, and for how long, the person was a director and took part in the management of the company; and
- all other relevant circumstances.[10]

Under the "reasonable steps" defence, a director cannot claim that he or she was unaware of the unremitted tax deductions because of the notice procedure. The

5 See E A Slater and J Edstein, "Unpaid Group Tax – Directors' Liability".

6 C Mason, "Directors of Australian Companies Liable for Unpaid Group Tax – Australia Benefits from Canada's Legislative Pioneering" (1994) 12(1) CSLJ 23 at 25.

7 *Income Tax Assessment Act* 1936 (Cth), ss 222AOJ(3), 222API(3) and 222AQD(3).

8 *Income Tax Assessment Act* 1936 (Cth), ss 222AOJ(3) or (4), 222API(4) and 222AQD(3).

9 *Income Tax Assessment Act* 1936 (Cth), ss 222AOJ(2), 222API(2) and 222AQD(2).

10 *Income Tax Assessment Act* 1936 (Cth), ss 222AOJ(3) and (4), 222API(3) and (4) and 222AQD(3).

notice procedure also means that it is unlikely that the Courts will find that a director who made no inquiry took reasonable steps. It may not be sufficient for a director to rely on an accountant or other professional adviser in dealing with the unremitted tax deductions,[11] but rather positive action on behalf of the director is required.

The Court will have regard to the circumstances of the particular director, their experience and expertise and role in the management of the company in determining what is "reasonable". Different standards of "reasonableness" will be applied to executive and non-executive directors.

If the company has failed to comply with an agreement entered into with the Commissioner, the director cannot rely on any of the statutory defences unless it is proved that at the time the agreement was entered into, the director had reasonable grounds to expect, and did expect, that the company would comply with the agreement.[12]

[20.1.5] RIGHT OF INDEMNITY

A director who is personally liable has a right of indemnity against the company (s 222 AOI of the ITAA) and a right of contribution against other directors on the basis of joint and several liability: s 222 APH of the ITAA.

[20.1.6] PARALLEL LIABILITY

A director's liability for a penalty is parallel to the liability of the company or other directors for that penalty: s 222AOH, s 222AQB and s 222APG of the ITAA. This means that although a penalty may have been imposed, the underlying liability to remit unpaid deducted amounts still remains. However, any amount paid to discharge either the penalty of the unremitted deducted amount reduces other related parallel liability to the extent of that amount.

[20.1.7] NEWLY APPOINTED DIRECTOR MAY BE LIABLE

A newly appointed director appointed after the due date can be made liable for an unremitted tax deduction if one of the four options is not taken within 14 days of her or his appointment: s 222AOD and s 222APD of the ITAA.

---

11 *Buist v Commissioner of Taxation* (1988) 90 FLR 72 at 75 where Kelly SPJ stated:

"In my opinion, this is not the case of the appellant merely failing to make an inquiry which, had it been made, must have shown that the returns would not be prepared in sufficient time to comply with the Commissioner's requirements. On the contrary … he did not care whether this would be done or not. He knew that the final notices had been issued requiring the lodgment of returns for a number of companies for a number of years and he simply left the matter in the hands of his accountants without following it up … the appellant's assumptions that everything in relation to the taxation affairs of the companies concerned was properly done by [the accountant] had little foundation and the fact that it was necessary for the Commissioner to send final notices ought to have raised a doubt in his mind that this was so."

12 See Mason, "Directors of Australian Companies Liable for Unpaid Group Tax", p 25.

[20.2] Philosophy/rationale

The rationale of the amendments to the ITAA to recover the deductions made from employee's salaries by employers and to reduce the incidence of insolvent trading by companies. By sending a notice to company directors notifying them that their company has failed to remit tax deductions by the due date, an "alarm system" is effectively triggered for companies to pay the unremitted deductions as soon as possible or enter into voluntary administration or liquidation in order to avoid insolvent trading. It aims to preserve the assets of a company in financial difficulties so that creditors, including the Commissioner, can have their claims satisfied.

In the second reading speech to the *Insolvency (Tax Priorities) Amendment Act 1993* (Cth), Senator Bob McMullan stated that:

> The main objective of the new regime is to recover the actual deductions made. Ample opportunity will be provided to the person who did not remit the deductions, as required under the tax legislation, to inform the Commissioner of the actual amount deducted. This measure will ensure solvency problems are confronted earlier and the escalation of debts will be prevented. The amendments proposed will result in a company either meeting its obligations to pay the amounts deducted to the Commissioner or going into voluntary administration or liquidation. Directors will only become liable for unremitted amounts when their company does not take those options.[13]

This rationale is further supported by s 222ANA of the ITAA, which was introduced with the new provisions outlined above. Section 222ANA(1) of the ITAA states:

> The purpose of this Division is to ensure that a company either meets its obligations under Division ... 2 ... or goes promptly into voluntary administration under Part 5.3A of the *Corporations Law* or into liquidation.

[20.3] History/former law

Prior to the amendments to the ITAA made by the *Insolvency (Tax Priorities) Amendment Act* 1933 (Cth), the Commissioner enjoyed a statutory priority over other creditors during a bankruptcy or insolvency in relation to unremitted tax deductions. However, it was necessary for the Commissioner to obtain a criminal conviction of a director under s 8Y of the *Taxation Administration Act* 1953

13 Senate, 19 May 1993, p 880.

(Cth) and s 21B of the *Crimes Act* 1914 (Cth) before any unpaid group tax could be recovered. Once convicted under these provisions, the director could be made liable to pay to the Commissioner reparation equal to the amount of the unremitted deduction.[14]

This regime still applies to deductions made by an employer prior to 31 May 1993.

Section 221P(1) of the ITAA provided that when an employer deducted payroll tax from an employee they must be remitted to the ATO within a specified time. It is an offence not to remit by the specified time.[15] Under s 221P(2), this liability was transferred to the trustee where the property of the employer was vested in a trustee, for example as a result of insolvency or liquidation.

However, a number of problems were associated with these provisions:

- The criminal prosecution of the director for failing to remit the tax deductions had to be proved beyond reasonable doubt. In the absence of books or records, this proved particularly difficult.
- To recover all unremitted amounts, prosecutions had to brought in relation to each unremitted deduction. This meant that a multiplicity of actions were required rendering proceedings costly and time-consuming.[16]
- Where the company entered into a type of insolvency administration where a trustee was not appointed to the property of the company, the Commissioner did not have statutory priority to require the trustee to pay the unremitted amounts. This was particularly problematic if a receiver was appointed to the company because receivers are not trustees in control of the property within the meaning of s 221P of the ITAA.[17]
- The provisions as a whole failed to provide a sufficient incentive to directors to avoid insolvent trading and ensure that the company complied with its obligation to remit tax deductions.

[20.4] Notable cases

[20.4.1] *WOODHAM V DEPUTY COMMISSIONER OF TAXATION*

Woodham v Deputy Commissioner of Taxation[18] considered ss 221F, 221R, 222ANA, 222AOB, 222AOC, 222AOE, 222AOH, 222AOI and 222APC of the *Income Tax Assessment Act* 1936 (Cth). In *Woodhams v Deputy Commissioner of Taxation*, the

14 For a discussion of these provisions see C O'Donnell, "Should the Director Pay? Directors' Liabilities to Pay Reparation for Federal Taxation Offences Committed by Corporations?" (1996) 26(2) ATR 56.
15 *Hookham v R* (1994) 181 CLR 450.
16 See P Morrow, "Dynamite for Directors" (1993) 7(4) *Commercial Law Quarterly* 19.
17 See *ASC v Macleod* (1994) 94 ATC 4061.
18 1997) 97 ATC 5119; CA, Vic, 14 November 1997 per Tadgell, Phillips and Batt JJA.

Court rejected the argument that the new provisions of the ITAA relating to unremitted tax deductions imposed a tax on directors rather than a penalty and were thus unconstitutional by virtue of s 55 of the Commonwealth *Constitution*. This decision accepts the purpose of the provisions.[19]

The appellant was director of a company which had failed to remit group tax deductions from the salaries and wages of its employees. The Commissioner had sought to recover these unpaid amounts relying on s 222AOC of the ITAA. The Commissioner was successful at first instance in obtaining judgment against the director.

However, the director appealed the decision, arguing that s 222AOC imposed a tax and was therefore contrary to s 55 of the Constitution. This argument was based on the assertion that s 222AOC merely compensated the Commonwealth for the revenue it had lost as a result of the company's failure to remit the tax deductions. The director further argued that because the exaction on the director could be avoided by following one of four options in s 222AOB, it is not a penalty in the true sense of the word.

The Court rejected this argument, deciding that the obligations imposed under s 222AOB of the ITAA were imposed directly on a director and not the company itself. It is for a breach of the director's obligations under s 222AOB that a penalty is imposed under s 222AOC. Because the penalty is not imposed on the company itself it is not a tax. The fact that the amount of the penalty is equal to the amount of the loss to the Commonwealth as a result of the failure by the company to remit tax is not authoritative in any regard and does not make the penalty a tax. Merely because the exaction can be characterised as recoupment of lost revenue, it doe not follow that it must be a tax because recoupment is consistent with either a tax or penalty.

[20.5] Interesting quotes

[20.5.1] PENALTY PROVISIONS AND STATUTORY PURPOSE

In *Woodhams v Deputy Commissioner of Taxation*[20] Phillips JA emphasised that the penalty notice system and personal liability is entirely consistent with the philosophy of the provisions:

> ... it can be concluded that there is a continuing obligation on the directors to see that the company does one of [the four options in s 222AOB], and if it does

19 See F Farrow and E Power, "Directors' Liability to Unremitted PAYE tax: A Constitutional Defence?" (1997) 71(11) *Law Institute Journal* 55.
20 (1997) 97 ATC 5119.

> not do any of them then what s 222AOC calls a penalty may be recovered from one who is a director after he or she has been given a 14-day notice, warning of the consequences of that non-compliance. This merely reinforces the purpose already described – of ensuring that the company does either make the payment to the respondent which ought to have been made in the first place (or enters into an agreement for that payment) or submits promptly to administration under the *Corporations Law* or goes promptly into liquidation so that what is owing by the company may be recovered out of the assets – and all of this is surely but part of the one elaborate process of collection and recovery.[21]

[20.5.2] CONSIDERATIONS IN "REASONABLE STEPS" DEFENCE

Although passive directors cannot plead ignorance as a defence due to the penalty notice system, subjective factors will be considered by the Courts in determining whether the steps taken by a director to ensure the company complies with one of the four options in s 222AOB are "reasonable":

> The service of the statutory notice will be likely to be seen as something of a 'leveller' as between the various directors, to the extent that a non-executive director could not deny knowledge of the tax remittance problem. The question will then become whether the particular director, given her or his experience and role in the company's management and any other relevant circumstances, has taken all reasonable steps to ensure that one of the four relevant events occurred. Clearly those steps will be different as between executive and non-executive directors, but a court is unlikely to allow a director who makes no inquiry following receipt of the statutory notice to hide behind a classification as a 'non-executive' or 'passive' director.[22]

[20.6] Timeline and checklist

[20.6.1] TIMELINE

A timeline of events is useful for a practical understanding of the operation of these provisions:

(a) Due date for prescribed amount

A company does not remit a deduction to the ATO by the due date for the prescribed amount.

21 (1997) 97 ATC 5119 at 5126.

22 Mason, "Directors of Australian Companies Liable for Unpaid Group Tax" p 26.

(b) Giving of penalty notice

The Commissioner issues a penalty notice to a director of the company for breach of s 221F(5) of the ITAA. This is "given" to the director when it would be expected to arrive at the registered address in the ordinary course of post. In most cases, this will be 2–3 days after the Commissioner issues the notice.

(c) 14-day period after notice is given

After the notice is given to the director, he or she has 14 days to ensure that the company takes one of the four options outlined in s 222AOB(2).

(d) Expiration of 14 days after giving penalty notice

If, after the expiration of 14 days after the notice has been given to the director, the company has not taken one of the four options, the Commissioner will issue the director with a penalty. This penalty will be equal to the amount of the unremitted deductions.

[20.6.2] A DIRECTOR'S CHECKLIST

To avoid personal liability under these provisions, directors should take a number of precautions:

- Stay involved in and informed of the financial affairs of the company, including its position on taxation.
- Ensure that the company is deducting PAYE tax from the salaries of its employees under s 221C(1) of the ITAA.
- Ensure that the company is remitting these deductions to the Commissioner by the prescribed due date under s 221F(5) of the ITAA.
- Make sure the company's business address registered with ASIC is correct for two reasons. First, so that the company receives its tax notice and, second, for any penalty notice purposes. This is because if a penalty notice is given, it is deemed to have been "given" when it would arrive at the postal address of the director in the ordinary course of post and does not need to be personally served.
- Directors could consider changing their registered address with ASIC to their residential address to avoid a penalty notice being misplaced at the office.
- If a person is considering accepting a board appointment as either an executive or non-executive director he or she should make sure that he or she is are fully aware of the company's assets and liabilities, including its situation regarding remitted and unremitted tax deductions.
- If a director receives a penalty notice that has estimated the amount of the unremitted tax deductions, the director should ensure that this estimate is accurate. If it is not accurate, the director should inform the Commissioner of the actual liability outstanding.

- If a director receives a penalty notice, he or she should make sure that this is brought to the attention of all other directors and noted in the minutes of a meeting of directors.
- If a director receives a penalty notice, he or she should immediately call a meeting of the directors. This should be done as soon as possible but must be done within 14 days of the notice being given.
- If a director receives a penalty notice, he or she should not merely expect an accountant or other qualified professional to handle the matter. The director should take positive and unequivocal action to deal with the problem of the unremitted tax deductions.
- If a director receives a penalty notice, he or she should make sure that within 14 days of the notice being given the company pays the unpaid amount, enters into an agreement with the Commissioner for payment, enters into voluntary administration, or is placed into liquidation.
- A director should oversee the progress of the company towards one of these four options and take an active role in the progression of the company towards one of these ends.
- If an agreement in entered into with the Commissioner for payment, the director should make sure that he or she has reasonable grounds to expect, and does expect, the company to be able to fulfil the terms of this agreement. To achieve this, the director should be involved in the negotiation of the agreement and require a financial analysis of the company's financial position and a prediction as to its future ability to pay.
- If the company does not enter into one of the four options and the director is made personally liable for the amount of the unremitted deduction, he or she should seek to be indemnified by the company or other directors that the Commissioner could have sued.

Multiple and Interlocking Directorships

21

"*The practice of interlocking directorates is the root of many evils. It offends human law and divine. Applied to rival corporations it tends to the suppression of competition … Applied to corporations which deal with each other it tends to disloyalty and to violation of the fundamental law that no man can serve two masters. In either event it leads to inefficiency for it removes incentive and destroys soundness of judgment.*"[1]

"*Not surprisingly, although there is general consensus that interlocks [and multiple directorships] should be regulated, there is considerable difference of opinion as to the extent to which they should be regulated and whether the existing legislation is sufficient.*"[2]

1 Judge Louis Brandeis "Breaking the Money Trusts" *Harpers Weekly*, 6 December 1913.
2 R Carroll, B Stening and K Stening, "Interlocking Directorships and the Law in Australia" (1990) 8(5) CSLJ 290 at 299.

OBJECTIVES

This Chapter will:

- discuss the general nature of interlocking and multiple directorships;
- analyse the ways in which such directorships are regulated;
- assess the issues arising from such directorships, consider whether such directorships should be permitted, discuss the arguments both for and against such directorships and the method of regulation of such directorships;
- discuss the statutory ability of directors of wholly owned subsidiaries to take the interests of the holding company into account when making decisions in the best interests of the subsidiary;
- consider recent suggestions to allow directors of partly owned subsidiaries to take the interests of the holding company into account when making decisions in the best interests of the partly owned subsidiary.

[21.1] General overview

A multiple directorship occurs where an individual is a director of more than one corporation. When the corporations involved are in competition with each other this practice is called an interlocking directorship. Multiple and interlocking directorships create connections between the corporations of which the individual is a director. The links created are termed "corporate interlocks", referring to the link between company A and company B by virtue of director X being a director of both.

It is not a breach of directors' duties merely to hold a multiple or interlocking directorship.[3]

Multiple and interlocking directorships are deemed largely inevitable in Australia. In 1989 the Senate Standing Committee on Legal and Constitutional Affairs concluded that it is common for many directors to hold multiple directorships, largely as a result of the limited pool of talent available in Australia.[4] There is no legal limit on the number of directorships able to be held by an individual director.

The regulation of multiple and interlocking directorships in Australia is achieved through the imposition of a number of duties on directors. These are both contractual and fiduciary in nature.

Subject to s 187 of the Law which allows directors of wholly owned subsidiaries to take the interests of the holding company into account (see para 21.1.3), directors who hold multiple and interlocking directorships should give consideration to the separate and independent interests of each company when making a decision that relates to them both.

[21.1.1] CONTRACTUAL DUTIES

The ability of directors to hold multiple directorships will largely be determined by contractual arrangements between the individual director and their corporation. These can arise in three ways: from the articles of association, express contract of service, or by implication from the nature of the relationship between the director and the corporation.[5] The nature of the directorship held by the individual director will often be determinative.

Executive directors will often be precluded from holding a directorial position on another company under an express contract of service or by the

---

3 *London Mashonaland Exploration Company Ltd v New Mashonaland Exploration Company Ltd* [1891] WN 165. See also *Bell v Lever Brothers Ltd* [1932] AC 161 at 194–196 per Lord Blanesburgh; and *Berlei Hestia (NZ) v Fernyhough* [1980] 2 NZLR 150 at 161. See also P D Finn, *Fiduciary Obligations* (Law Book Co Ltd, Sydney, 1977), pp 238–242 and p 253.

4 Senate Standing Committee on Legal and Constitutional Affairs, *Report on the Social and Fiduciary Duties and Obligations of Company Directors*, AGPS, Canberra, 1989, paras 4.37–4.39.

5 R Carroll, B Stening and K Stening, "Interlocking Directorships and the Law in Australia" (1990) 8(5) CSLJ 290 at 294.

corporation's articles of association. In any event, the nature of their relationship with the corporation, and the managerial position they hold, implies that they are unable to enter into any other employment that may give rise to a conflict of interest.[6]

Non-executive directors are often subjected to less strict contractual obligations than executive directors. In most cases, neither the articles of association nor their contract of service will preclude them from holding directorial positions in other corporations or other types of employment. They are not in an intimate relationship with the corporation in the way that executive directors are, and the nature of their relationship with the corporation is unlikely to prevent multiple directorships. In fact, the breadth of experience and skills accumulated by a non-executive director by virtue of their directorial positions on other corporations may serve as an incentive for their recruitment. In the words of Carroll, Stening, and Stening "...the attraction of the non-executive appointee will often be the experience and expertise that person brings to the company by virtue of other directorships held by that person".

[21.1.2] FIDUCIARY DUTIES

All directors are bound by fiduciary duties. These centre on the need to remain loyal to the company they are appointed to serve. In general, fiduciary duties require a director to avoid a conflict of interest between their personal interests and the interests of the company, or between the interests of one company and the interests of another company. Individual directors holding multiple directorships must be particularly careful not to breach their fiduciary duties.

The two main situations in which a conflict of interest may arise are interlocking directorships between competing corporations, particularly those in the same field, and a takeover bid where the director is on the boards of both the bidder and the target.[7]

It is not per se a breach of a director's fiduciary duties to be a director of more than one company even when the companies are in competition with each other.[8] The mere potential for a conflict of interest to arise is not enough to warrant a breach.[9] In this sense, the law grants a wide degree of latitude to company directors in the performance of their duties, in contrast to the strict position imposed on other fiduciaries such as trustees and partners who are prohibited

6 See *Hivac v Park Royal Scientific Instruments Ltd* [1946] Ch 169. See R Carroll, B Stening and K Stening, "Interlocking Directorships and the Law in Australia" (1990) 8(5) CSLJ 290 at 294. See also H A J Ford, *Principles of Company Law* (5th Ed, Butterworths, Sydney, 1990), p 466.

7 See J Lawrence, "Multiple Directorships and Conflict of Interest: Recent Developments" (1996) 14(8) CSLJ 513 at 516; and R Carroll, B Stening and K Stening, "Interlocking Directorships and the Law in Australia" (1990) 8(5) CSLJ 290 at 295.

8 *London Mashonaland Exploration Company Ltd v New Mashonaland Exploration Company Ltd* [1891] WN 165. See also *Bell v Lever Brothers Ltd* [1932] AC 161 at 194–196 per Lord Blanesburgh; and *Berlei Hestia (NZ) v Fernyhough* [1980] 2 NZLR 150 at 161.

9 *Berlei Hestia (NZ) v Fernyhough* [1980] 2 NZLR 150 at 161.

from putting themselves in the position of a possible conflict of interest.[10] There is a great difference between:

> ... asking a director to account for a profit made out of his fiduciary relationship, and asking a director not to join the board of a competing organisation in case he should, at some future time, decide to act in breach of his fiduciary duty.[11]

A breach of fiduciary duties will only arise where there is a "real and sensible possibility of conflict",[12] or a "real, an actual, conflict in some present matter and not simply a theoretical conflict of duty".[13] A breach will only occur where a director actually gains information or insight into a company's affairs.[14]

If a director faces a conflict of interest, they should:

> ... consider whether to refrain from participating in the debate and/or voting on the matter, whether to arrange that the relevant board papers are not sent, or in an extreme case, whether to resign from the board. In any event, full disclosure of the conflict or potential conflict must be made to the board. In considering these issues, account should be taken of the significance of the potential conflict for the company and the possible consequences if it is not handled properly.[15]

Bosch argues that once a conflict of interest has been declared it is possible for the board to deal with it in a number of ways:[16]

- If it is a minor issue, and/or the Board decides that the director's contribution is likely to be so important that it overrides the conflict, the director can participate in the discussion and in making the decision.
- Alternatively the director concerned can receive the relevant papers, participate in the discussion, but refrain from taking part in the decision making.
- Alternatively the director can receive the relevant papers but absent herself or himself from the discussion and the decision.

---

10 See R Carroll, B Stening and K Stening, "Interlocking Directorships and the Law in Australia" (1990) 8(5) CSLJ 290 at 295.

11 R Carroll, B Stening and K Stening, "Interlocking Directorships and the Law in Australia" (1990) 8(5) CSLJ 290 at 295.

12 *Phipps v Boardman* [1967] 2 AC 46 at 124 per Lord Upjohn.

13 P D Finn, *Fiduciary Obligations* (Law Book Co Ltd, Sydney, 1977), p 253.

14 *Glavanics v Brunninghausen* (1996) 14 ACLC 345; and *Byrnes v The Queen* (1995) 183 CLR 501 at 516–517 per Brennan, Deane, Toohey and Gaudron JJ.

15 Working Party of the Australian Institute of Company Directors et al (Bosch Committee), *Corporate Practices and Conduct* (3rd ed, Pitman Publishing, Melbourne, 1995), p 44. Cited in J Lawrence, "Multiple Directorships and Conflict of Interest: Recent Developments" (1996) 14(8) CSLJ 513 at 515.

16 H Bosch, *The Director at Risk: Accountability in the Boardroom* (Pitman Publishing, Melbourne, 1995), pp 228–229.

- Alternatively the Board may decide that the relevant papers should not be sent to the director, in which case the director should also absent herself or himself from the discussion and any decision making.
- Alternatively the director may resign from the Board.

The director can initiate the decision as to which alternative to pursue, he or she may consult the Chair, or the issue may be referred to the board. The significance of the matter giving rise to a possible conflict will also be an important consideration. In any event, declaring any possible conflict of interest and refraining from voting on a particular issue that may cause such a conflict will usually avoid a breach of fiduciary duties. The use of an alternate director in such a circumstance is warranted. However, it is always possible for a director to innocently influence her or his fellow directors by other informal means.[17] In addition, dealing with conflicts of interests and other potential problems raised for directors who hold multiple or interlocking directorships arguably does not effectively deal with the possible problem of insider trading. This problem is discussed in para [21.7.3].

[21.1.3] DIRECTORS OF WHOLLY OWNED SUBSIDIARIES CAN TAKE INTERESTS OF HOLDING COMPANY INTO ACCOUNT

Section 187 of the *Corporations Law* provides that directors of wholly owned subsidiaries take act in the best interests of the holding company without breaching their duties to the subsidiary. In order to do this, the constitution of the subsidiary must expressly authorise the director to act in the best interests of the holding company. In addition, the subsidiary must not be insolvent at the time the director acts in the interests of the holding company or become insolvent because of the director's act.

The provision requires that the wholly owned subsidiary is not insolvent at the time of the director's act and does not become solvent because of the director's act. This:

> ... is intended to remove the protection for a director whose actions do not precipitate an immediate insolvency, but instead lead to a protracted insolvency, that is, the director acts in a way that, while it may be in the best interests of the holding company, effectively runs the subsidiary down, leading to its eventual insolvency.[18]

17 See Senate Standing Committee on Legal and Constitutional Affairs, *Report on the Social and Fiduciary Obligations of Company Directors*, AGPS, Canberra, 1989, para 4.43.

18 Senate Standing Committee on Legal and Constitutional Affairs, *Report on the Social and Fiduciary Obligations of Company Directors*, AGPS, Canberra, 1989, para 2.36.

The director's act does not have to be the sole cause of the subsidiary's insolvency. It can merely be a contributing cause. This aspect of s 187 is intended to include those directors whose acts do not merely trigger an inevitable insolvency but which effectively run the subsidiary into insolvency itself, despite such an insolvency being in the best interests of the holding company.[19]

CASAC has outlined that a major benefit to accrue from s 187 is that it may assist external lenders to corporate groups.[20] In some corporate groups a subsidiary will provide a guarantee or third party mortgage in favour of the holding company. At common law such a guarantee or third party mortgage may be unenforceable because it is not in the interests of the subsidiary providing it. In addition, at common law the external lender may be held to be a constructive trustee for any benefit it derived from the transaction if the directors of the subsidiary breached any one of their fiduciary duties in entering into the transaction and such a breach was known or suspected by the lender. The effect of s 187 is that such challenges to the enforceability of guarantees or third party mortgages provided by a wholly owned subsidiary are less likely as the directors of the wholly owned subsidiary may be deemed to have acted in the best interests of the subsidiary despite the guarantee or mortgage being provided mainly for the benefit of the holding company.[21]

It has been suggested that this ability to act in the interests of the holding company should be extended to directors of partly owned subsidiaries.[22] This will be considered below in para [21.8.2].

[21.1.4] SIGNIFICANCE OF MULTIPLE AND INTERLOCKING DIRECTORSHIPS

Carroll, Stening, and Stening have outlined that the role of the law in relation to multiple and interlocking directorships will depend on the perspective adopted by the legislator as to their importance.[23] They highlight four models of the significance of multiple and interlocking directorships.[24]

The management control model does not regard the practice as important as it perceives outside directors as virtually powerless as against the corporation's senior management.

19 See CASAC, *Corporate Groups: Final Report* (2000), para 2.33.
20 See CASAC, *Corporate Groups: Final Report* (2000), paras 2.31–2.32.
21 See CASAC, *Corporate Groups: Final Report* (2000), paras 2.31–2.32.
22 CASAC, *Corporate Groups: Final Report* (2000), pp 63-64 [Recommendation 3].
23 R Carroll, B Stening and K Stening, "Interlocking Directorships and the Law in Australia" (1990) 8(5) CSLJ 290 at 291–292.
24 See also T Koenig, R Gogel and J Sonquist, "Models of the Significance of Interlocking Corporate Directorates" (1979) 38 *American Journal of Economics and Sociology* 173. Cited in R Carroll, B Stening and K Stening, "Interlocking Directorships and the Law in Australia" (1990) 8(5) CSLJ 290 at 291.

The reciprocity model regards the practice as beneficial as it sees multiple and interlocking directorships as entered into with a consciousness as to the mutual benefits to the corporations linked.

The finance control model sees the practice as a method of facilitating financial institutions supervising their investments.

The class hegemony model regards multiple and interlocking directorships as a dangerous practice allowing small upper-class elite, who are interested in a high degree of consensus and stability within the economic system, holding a substantial power. They see this as a disincentive for innovation.

[21.2] Philosophy/rationale

[21.2.1] REASONS FOR HAVING MULTIPLE OR INTERLOCKING DIRECTORSHIPS

Individual directors often have multiple or interlocking directorships due to the limited talent pool available in Australia. As the number of individuals suitably qualified to manage corporations is relatively low, those who are suitably qualified and skilled may need to spread themselves between more than one corporation. When recruiting for board positions, it is often desirable to recruit someone with a broad range of management experience and in some cases this may only be obtained from someone who is already practicing as a director.

[21.2.2] INDIRECT OR DIRECT REGULATION?

Regulation of multiple and interlocking directorships in Australia is currently achieved though indirect means, particularly the use of directors' fiduciary duties. Debate often ensues over whether the law should directly regulate both the number of directorships able to be held by any one individual, and the type of corporations a director is able to be involved in.

The main objection to multiple and interlocking directorships is the potential for anti-competitive behaviour to occur. Concerns over such collusive behaviour as "... price fixing, market division, exchange of competitive information and other forms of antitrust violations ... [such as] discriminatory treatment in the supply of materials and credit"[25] abound. In this way, it is possible that the real cost of the effects of such director's action may not be accounted for due to their wide impact on the economy at large.

In 1989 the Senate Standing Committee on Legal and Constitutional Affairs concluded that statutory regulation of such matters would be ineffective and self-regulation guided by ethical standards is preferable:

25 R Carroll, "Trade Practices Implications of Director Interlocks" (1990) 18(6) ABLR 395 at 396–397.

> Directors need to understand the ethical considerations involved in multiple directorships and must embrace them ... It is not useful for the law to set limits on the number of directorships a person may hold. The wide differences in the capacity of directors and in the work required to direct different companies make it pointless to do so. The law should clearly set down the required standards of conduct, and directors must then judge for themselves whether their commitments allow them to meet the standards.[26]

Lawrence suggests a number of arguments both for and against direct regulation of multiple and interlocking directorships.[27]

(a) Arguments for direct regulation

1. Interlocks have the potential to facilitate anticompetitive behaviour, conflicts of interest, and the risk of directors making improper use of their position.
2. The restraint of competition resulting from corporate interlocks cannot be regulated under the *Trade Practices Act* because the conduct involved may not involve conscious collusion.
3. Multiple directorships reduce the opportunities for other equally qualified people, and those with divergent views, from obtaining board positions.
4. The quality of services provided by directors with multiple board appointments may be less than optimal.
5. Multiple directorships permit an unacceptable concentration of economic power in the hands of an elite few.
6. Multiple directorships reduce innovation and competition by promoting commonality of action.

(b) Arguments against direct regulation

1. Many corporations perceive it as "ideal" to recruit ex-CEOs to their Board. Due to the limited number of such individuals, ex-CEOs need to be spread amongst numerous Boards.
2. The existence of interlocking directorships does not prove the existence of a power relationship or actual abuse of position.
3. Interlocking directorships can increase corporate productivity through the pooling of resources.
4. Directors will be under-utilised if they cannot hold more than one Board position.

---

26 Senate Standing Committee on Legal and Constitutional Affairs, *Report on the Social and Fiduciary Duties and Obligations of Company Directors*, 1989, paras 4.48-4.49.

27 J Lawrence, "Multiple Directorships and Conflict of Interest: Recent Developments" (1996) 14(8) CSLJ 513 at 514–515.

5. As management and executive directors largely control corporations, the prevalence of interlocking directorships amongst non-executive directors is unlikely to produce anti-competitive behaviour.
6. The *Trade Practices Act*, statutory duties, and equitable fiduciary duties are sufficient to prohibit anti-competitive behaviour.
7. Shareholders should be permitted to decide for themselves whether their Board comprises directors with multiple or interlocking directorships.

[21.3] History/former law

Debate over multiple and interlocking directorships has been alive for many years. The first case to deal authoritatively on the issue of multiple and interlocking directorships was *London and Mashonaland Exploration Company Ltd v New Mashonaland Exploration Company Ltd*.[28] Chitty J held that an individual director is able to hold directorships in other companies, including rival companies, subject to two qualifications.[29]

1. The articles of association of any company can restrict the ability of a director to hold multiple or interlocking directorships. This can be achieved by a clause expressly prohibiting this practice, or by expressly requiring a director to devote all of her or his working time to the affairs of the company.
2. An implied contract may hinder the ability of a director to engage in this practice. A prominent example is the relationship between the company and an executive director.

These qualifications on the ability of a director to hold multiple and interlocking directorships still form the basis of the law in this area.

The reasoning in the *London Mashonaland Exploration* case was further extended in *Bell v Lever Brothers Ltd*,[30] where it was held that the reasoning developed by Chitty J in relation to two competing companies also applies in the situation of a director privately competing with the company.

The latitude that this grants directors was noted in *Berlei Hestia (NZ) v Fernyhough*.[31] In this case, the Board of one company sought to deny access to three directors of the company books because they were directors of a rival company. Deciding that it is not a per se breach of fiduciary duties merely to be a director of a rival corporation, the Court allowed the directors to access the company's books. This case firmly implanted the notion that an actual conflict of

28 [1891] WN 165.
29 For a full analysis of this case see E Boros, "The Duties of Nominee and Multiple Directors: Part 2" (1994) 11(1) *The Company Lawyer* 6 at pp 6–7.
30 [1932] AC 161 at 195.
31 [1980] 2 NZLR 150.

interest or a real possibility of conflict of interest must be established before the Court will find a breach of fiduciary duties and thus limit the capacity of the multiple or interlock director.

The Australian judiciary reasserted these conclusions on two important occasions. Firstly, in *Mordecai v Mordecai*[32] the Court decided that two brothers who set up a new company in order to reduce the potential claim of their dead brother's estranged widow on the other company were in breach of their fiduciary duties. This was because they had actively solicited the clients of the other company in establishing business for the new company, thus making use of information and insights gained in their capacity as directors of the other company. This was a clear case of conflict of interest and improper use of information. Secondly, in the high profile case of *State Bank of South Australia v Marcus Clark*[33] the Court confirmed that directors must disclose any possible conflict arising out of a multiple directorship.

Statutory and legislative discussion of multiple and interlocking directorships has been minimal in Australia. In 1989 the Senate Standing Committee on Legal and Constitutional Affairs recognised that there are many problems involved with multiple and interlocking directorships:

> Holding multiple directorships can give rise to conflict of interests which would breach fiduciary duties. If two companies are in direct competition, or if one is buying something from the other, a director cannot participate in the management of both without running into a clear conflict of duties. The companies' interests, and the director's duties to the companies, could also clash if their businesses were in related fields, or indeed in any situation where the activities of one company were likely to affect the interests of the other.[34]

Despite the recognition of the potential problems arising from these practices, including possible conflict of interest and breach of fiduciary duties, the Committee concluded that the advantages of having people with broadly-based backgrounds contributing to the management of corporations far outweighs the disadvantages. Arguing for a dilution of strict fiduciary duties and the need for self-regulation, the Committee resolved that the law should not seek to impose arbitrary restrictions of the number of directorships able to be held by an individual, but rather enforce ethical standards as a means of self-regulation.[35]

---

32 (1988) 12 ACLR 751.

33 (1996) 14 ACLC 1019.

34 Senate Standing Committee on Legal and Constitutional Affairs, *Report on the Social and Fiduciary Duties and Obligations of Company Directors*, 1989, para 4.40.

35 Senate Standing Committee on Legal and Constitutional Affairs, *Report on the Social and Fiduciary Duties and Obligations of Company Director*, 1989, paras 4.47–4.49.

[21.4] Notable cases

[21.4.1] *MORDECAI V MORDECAI*

Mordecai v Mordecai[36] is Australian authority for the proposition that a conflict of interest will seriously damage the standing of multiple and interlocking directors. It states that a director who holds directorships on two competing companies cannot actively solicit the clients of one company for the use of another without breaching her or his duties to the first company.

In this case, three brothers carried on a business. After the death of one of the brothers, his estranged widow brought a claim against the company (Company A). In order to defeat the widow's claim, the remaining two brothers set up a new company (Company B) that carried on the same business as Company A. They informed all the clients of Company A of this change. As a result, Company A ceased to trade whilst Company B traded with the clients of Company A.

The brothers argued that they were not in breach of their duties to company A because they had not used the property or confidential information of Company A for use in Company B. The Court did not agree with this assertion, concluding that because they brothers had actively solicited the business of Company A for the use and benefit of Company B they had breached their duties to Company A.

Clearly, directors of two companies who are in competition with each other cannot actively solicit the clients and customers of one company for the benefit of the other company. Such an action is a clear breach of the rule against conflict of interest and use of confidential information.[37]

[21.4.2] *BERLEI HESTIA (NZ) V FERNYHOUGH*

In *Berlei Hestia (NZ) v Fernyhough*[38] the New Zealand Supreme Court strongly concluded that being a director on the Boards of two competing companies is not per se a breach of fiduciary duties.

This case concerned the actions of the directors of a New Zealand company. In accordance with its articles of association, three directors nominated by an Australian company that held 40 per cent of its shares constituted its Board, and the other three directors were appointed by its New Zealand shareholders. The company began exporting to Australia in competition with the Australian company. An "irretrievable breakdown" arose between the Australian company and its directors on the one hand and the New Zealand company and its directors on the other. As a result of this dispute, the New Zealand directors refused the Australian directors access to the company's books and premises.

---

36 CA, NSW, 4 March 1988 per Hope, Samuels and Priestly JJA. (1988) 12 ACLR 751.

37 See *Aubanel and Alabaster Ltd v Aubanel* (1949) 66 RPC 343.

38 Sup Ct, NZ, 7 March 1980 per Mahon J; [1980] 2 NZLR 150.

The Court held that this action was unjustified. Finding in favour of the Australian directors, Mahon J argued that holding directorships on the Boards of two competing companies does not per se amount to a breach of fiduciary duties. His Honour noted the "... latitude which the law seems to extend to the practice of a director holding office in two companies which might wholly or partly be in competition"[39] in concluding that:

> ... there [is] a wide distinction between asking a director to account for a profit made out of his fiduciary relationship, and asking a director not to join the board of a competing organisation in case he should, at some future time, decide to act in breach of his fiduciary duty.[40]

Accordingly, because they was nothing on the part of the Australian directors to indicate that they intended to breach their fiduciary duties to the New Zealand company, they must be allowed continued proper participation in the affairs of the New Zealand company.

[21.4.3] *STATE BANK OF SOUTH AUSTRALIA V MARCUS CLARK*

In *State Bank of South Australia v Marcus Clark*[41] the Court reaffirmed that a director who is on the boards of two competing companies must disclose any possible conflict of interest to both Boards. It also highlighted that if a possible conflict of interest may occur, a multiple or interlocking director should refrain from voting on the particular matter.

In this case the defendant, Mr Clark, was a Managing Director and Chief Executive Officer of the State Bank of South Australia. He was also a director of Equiticorp Holdings. As a director of the bank he allowed the acquisition of a company called Oceanic (APA). On completion of this acquisition, Oceanic would be able to repay debts outstanding to Equiticorp Australia, a subsidiary of Equiticorp Holdings. An independent evaluation of the value of Oceanic was not completed. As a result, the bank paid $59m for Oceanic when its real value was between $17m and $21m.

The Court held that Mr Clark could not have simultaneously discharged his fiduciary obligations to the bank and Equiticorp in such circumstances. It was in the bank's interests to obtain a reasonable purchase price for Oceanic whilst it was in the best interests of Equiticorp to have all of its debts repaid. The Court decided that in such circumstances Mr Clark should have disclosed the possible conflict of interest to the boards of both companies:

39 [1980] 2 NZLR 150 at 161.
40 [1980] 2 NZLR 150 at 181.
41 (1996) 14 ACLC 1019; Sup Ct, SA, 29 March 1996 per Perry J.

> ... Mr Marcus Clark, as a director of Equiticorp Holdings and as a director of the bank, owed duties to two companies ... whose interests did not necessarily coincide. Equiticorp Holdings had an interest in securing the timely repayment by APA of the $27m loan by Equiticorp Australia to APA. The bank, on the other hand, had an interest in acquiring the Oceanic shares owned by APA at a price that was not excessive after a proper valuation could be made and considered. Mr Marcus Clark owed a duty to ensure that no more was paid by the bank to APA, if a transaction for the acquisition of the shares was to proceed, than they were worth. However, as a director of Equiticorp Holdings, he had an interest in securing a position where the bank paid to APA ... the highest possible amount which it could be persuaded to pay for the Oceanic shares. The larger the payment to APA, the more effective would be the enhancement of APA's ability to discharge the loan due by it to Equiticorp Australia.[42]

Mr Clark did not disclose this possible conflict of interest to the Boards of either companies. In the circumstances, such a disclosure was necessary to avoid a breach of fiduciary duties to the bank.

[21.4.4] *EQUITICORP FINANCE LTD (IN LIQ) V BANK OF NEW ZEALAND*

Equiticorp Finance Ltd (in liq)[43] considered s 229 of the *Companies (NSW) Code*. The position of multiple and interlocking directorships within corporate groups has always been contentious. This case indicated that directors holding multiple or interlocking directorships within a corporate group must consider the separate and independent interests of each company when making a decision regarding the interests of the group as a whole. However, the decision also highlighted that in many cases directors may consider that the affairs of other companies within the group of companies may be so intricately tied up with the affairs of the relevant company. In such circumstances it is possible that steps taken to protect the group as a whole may be of benefit to individual companies and, as long as separate consideration is given to the interests and affairs of each individual company in making such decisions, directors may not breach their fiduciary duties.

If this case were decided under the current law, it is likely that the outcome would be the same. This is because s 187 would be applied thus allowing the directors of the subsidiary to act in the best interests of a wholly owned subsidiary if taking the interests of the holding company into account.

---

42 (1996) 14 ACLC 1019 at 1039.

43 (1993) 11 ACLC 952; Sup Ct, NSW, 5 October 1993 per Kirby P, Clarke and Cripps JJA.

The facts of this case are complex. Mr Hawkins was the Chairman of Equiticorp Holdings Limited (EHL), the ultimate holding company within a corporate group. He was also the director of a number of other companies within the group, including Equiticorp Financial Services Limited (EFSA). The Bank of New Zealand (BNZ) was the principal banker for the Equiticorp group.

In June 1987 BNZ extended a loan facility to a company within the Equiticorp group. By November 1987 BNZ was exerting pressure on the Equiticorp group to reduce its exposure. By January 1988, the loan facility had been substantially reduced. An extension for the repayment of the loan facility was negotiated and a guarantee was taken from another company in the group as additional form of security. Financial troubles continued, with both BNZ and Equiticorp sharing concerns about the liquidity of the Equiticorp group. A liquidity reserve was established by BNZ for the finance branch of the group. BNZ continued to exert pressure on Equiticorp to repay the original loan facility, indicating that a complete lack of credibility would result from failure to repay the facility prior to the next board meeting. This was communicated to Mr Hawkins.

As it became clear that repayment of the loan facility would be difficult to achieve within this time frame, Mr Hawkins entered into discussions to use the liquidity reserve for the purposes of repayment of the facility. Those consulted agreed with Mr Hawkins that the liquidity reserve should not be used for this purpose because it had been created for use by the financial branch of Equiticorp. However, Mr Hawkins finally decided that he no choice but to use the liquidity reserve to repay the loan facility, emphasising that the "overall considerations of the group are important and I've got to weigh those considerations up". Companies in the finance group, including EFSA, received shares in another company in return for the provision of the liquidity reserve. These shares were never delivered to EFSA.

EFSA and Equiticorp Finance Limited (EFL) brought proceedings against Mr Hawkins, arguing that he had breached his fiduciary obligations to EFSA by authorising use of the liquidity reserve for other purposes. Mr Hawkins claimed that his primary concern was the effect that the loss of support by BNZ would have on the entire group, including EFSA. Clarke and Cripps JJA concluded that Mr Hawkins had not breached his fiduciary obligations to EFSA and had taken its best interests into account when making the decision to use the liquidity reserve to repay the loan facility. They agreed with Mr Hawkins that the loss of BNZ's support would have been disastrous for EFSA and the entire Equiticorp group. However, they stated that:

> A particular difficulty arises when the directors of the particular company enter into the transaction on behalf of that company because they consider that the transaction is of benefit to the group as a whole and do not give separate consideration to the benefit of the company.

Thus, separate consideration must be given to the interests of each company when a multiple or interlocking director is making a decision that will affect more than one company of which he or she is a director. The majority concluded that Hawkins seemed to have given independent consideration to the interests of both EFSA, EHL and the entire Equiticorp group.

In a strong dissenting judgment, Kirby P argued that Hawkins had not given independent consideration to the interests of both EFSA and EHL. His Honour held that:

> No intelligent and honest person in a position of a director of …EFSA could, in the circumstances described, have considered that it was in the best interests of [that company] to authorise the deployment of their liquidity reserves for the purposes for which they were used.

Clearly, under the law as it then stood directors holding multiple or interlocking directorships within a corporate group were obliged to consider the separate and independent interests of each company when making a decision in relation to the interests of the group in order to avoid a breach of fiduciary obligations.

As suggested above, if decided under the current law, including s 187, it is likely that the outcome in this case would be the same. If the constitution of EFSA had allowed its directors to take into account the interests of Equiticorp Holdings, it is likely that the use of the liquidity reserve for the benefit of the holding company and the group as a whole would also not have been held to constitute a breach of fiduciary duty.

[21.4.5] *GAMBLE V HOFFMAN*

Gamble v Hoffman[44] considered s 232 of the *Corporations Law*. The facts of this case are straightforward. Mr and Mrs Hoffman were the only directors and shareholders of Tallimba Pty Ltd (Tallimba), a wholesale fruit and vegetable shop. They were also the director and secretary respectively of Sunhaven Nominees Pty Ltd (Sunhaven), a company operating a retail fruit and vegetable shop. Mr and Mrs Hofman were the sole shareholders of Tallimba.

Sunhaven was operating at a substantial loss. A deed of surrender of lease was negotiated in consideration of a payment of $80,000. Mr and Mrs Hoffman directed Tallimba to make this payment for Sunhaven, effectively creating a loan to Sunhaven. Due to the financial situation of Sunhaven, it could not be reasonably expected that this loan could be repaid. As a result, Tallimba suffered loss and damage.

44 (1997) 24 ACSR 369; Fed Ct, Aust, 25 July 1997 per Carr J.

The Court held that Mr and Mrs Hoffman had breached their fiduciary duties to Tallimba. Carr J decided that their fiduciary duty to Tallimba required them to take two steps when deciding whether or not Tallimba should offer the loan:

1. Assess what benefit, if any, Tallimba would derive from making these payments on behalf of Sunhaven.
2. If there were any benefits so to be derived by Tallimba, to assess whether there was any reasonably foreseeable prospect of detriment to Tallimba.

Carr J concluded that Mr and Mrs Hoffman had not considered the interests of Tallimba when directing it to make a loan to Sunhaven. Accordingly, there were held to be in breach of their fiduciary duties to Tallimba.

[21.5] Interesting facts

The research of Carroll, Stening and Stening into the incidence of multiple and interlocking directorships in Australia was groundbreaking.[45] Using the revised analysis of their data offered by Alexander and Murray,[46] one can see that there is a marginal increase of both practices between 1979 and 1986, and a decrease between 1986 and 1991. Alexander and Murray suggest this decrease may have been a result of the inclusion of State-owned and private companies in the 1991 data, or of a change in board practices following the corporate crashes of the late 1980s.

For explanatory purposes, network links are created when a director sits on the boards of two or more companies. Each director that holds two or more directorships creates links. In this way, a person holding two directorships (in Company A and Company B) creates one link (between Company and Company B), whereas a person that holds four directorships (in Company A, Company B, Company C, and Company D) creates six network links (between Company A and Company B, between Company B and Company C, between Company C and Company D, between Company A and Company C, between Company B and Company D, and between Company A and Company D).

The data of Carroll, Stening and Stening, as revised by Alexander and Murray, is as follows:[47]

45 See R Carroll, B Stening and K Stening, "Interlocking Directorships and the Law in Australia" (1990) 8(5) CSLJ 290.

46 M Alexander and G Murray, "Interlocking Directorships in the Top 250 Australian Companies: Comment on Carroll, Stening and Stening" (1992) 10(6) CSLJ 385.

47 Reproduced from M Alexander and G Murray, "Interlocking Directorships in the Top 250 Australian Companies: Comment on Carroll, Stening and Stening" (1992) 10(6) CSLJ 385 at 390.

MULTIPLE DIRECTORSHIPS AND NETWORK LINKS, 1979 (CORRECTED), 1986 AND 1991

Number of Director-ships	Number of Network Links Created	Number of Directors 1979	Number of Directors 1986	Number of Directors 1991	Number of Network Links 1979 Col 2 x Col 3	Number of Network Links 1986 Col 2 x Col 4	Number of Network Links 1991 Col 2 x Col 5
1	0	1341	1320	1538	0	0	0
2	1	168	201	153	168	201	153
3	3	66	69	33	198	207	99
4	6	33	30	13	198	180	78
5	10	5	13	13	50	130	140
6	15	4	7	3	60	105	45
7	21	4		1	84	0	21
8	28	1		1	28	0	28
9	36				0	0	0
		1622	1640	1755			
Total Network Link					786	823	554
Total Interlocks					1572	1646	1108
Interlocks per Firm					6.3	6.6	4.43

Research by Stapledon and Lawrence[48] indicates that as at mid-1995, in the top 100 listed Australian companies, directors had an average of 1.29 directorships, 19 per cent of directors had more than one directorship, and 13 per cent of the total 690 directors had two directorships. In addition, in mid-1995 an average of 5.74 interlocks existed between any top-100 company and the remaining top 100 companies.

Carroll, Stening and Stening point out that the practice of multiple and interlocking directorships is not uniform across the industrial sector:

48 G P Stapledon and J J Lawrence, *Corporate Governance in the Top 100: An Empirical Study of the Top 100 Companies' Boards of Directors*, Research Paper, Centre for Corporate Law and Securities Regulation, University of Melbourne, June 1996. Cited in J Lawrence, "Multiple Directorships and Conflict of Interest: Recent Developments" (1996) 14(8) CSLJ 513 at 517.

> Using the Australian Stock Exchange's industrial classification, the results for 1986 indicate that seven of the 23 categories record an average number of interlocks for companies within those sectors in excess of eight: transport (8.5), oil and gas (8.6), other metals (8.9), diversified resources (10.7), banks and finance (10.9), entrepreneurial investors (11.9) and paper and packaging (14.5).[49]

They also point out that the prevalence of interlocking is considerably less than in Canada,[50] New Zealand[51] or the United States.[52] It is higher than in the United Kingdom.[53]

Hall has also studied the incidence of multiple and interlocking directorships in Australia.[54] His sample was based on 1200 companies. He commented that:

> ... the average company has a thirty-five percent chance of being linked to another company in the same industry group, a twenty-six per cent chance of being linked to a company in an industry which supplies it, and a twenty-two percent chance of being linked to a financial institution of some sort.[55]

Commentators and theorists dispute the policy implications of the above research. Carroll, Stening and Stening conclude that levels of multiple and interlocking directorships are high and warrant concern.[56] Alexander and Murray dispute this, claiming that general levels of multiple and interlocking

---

49 R Carroll, B Stening and K Stening, "Interlocking Directorships and the Law in Australia" (1990) 8(5) CSLJ 290 at 293.

50 See M D Ornstein, "The Boards and Executives of the Largest Canadian Corporations: Size, Competition and Interlocks" (1976) 1(4) *Canadian Journal of Sociology* 411.

51 See M Firth, "Multiple Directorships and Corporate Interlocks in New Zealand Firms" (1987) 23(2) *Australian and New Zealand Journal of Sociology* 274; and G Fogelberh and C R Laurent, "Interlocking Directorates: A Study of Large Companies in New Zealand" (1973) 3(2) *Journal of Business Policy* 16. For recent data see D Blackmore, M Fox and G Walker, "Potential Corporate and Director Interlocks: A Study of the Top 200 New Zealand Companies" (1997) 15(8) CSLJ 510.

52 See M P Allen, "The Structure of Interorganizational Elite Cooperation: Interlocking Corporate Directorates" (1974) 39 *American Sociological Review* 393; and J M Pennings, *Interlocking Directorates: Origins and Consequences of Connections Among Organizations' Boards of Directors* (Jossey-Bass, San Francisco, 1980).

53 See P J Johnson and R Apps "Interlocking Directorates Among the UK's Largest Companies" (1979) 24 *The Antitrust Bulletin* 357.

54 C Hall, "Interlocking Directorates in Australia: The Significance for Competition Policy" (1983) 55(1) *Australian Quarterly* 42. Cited in R Carroll, B Stening and K Stening, "Interlocking Directorships and the Law in Australia" (1990) 8(5) CSLJ 290 at 293.

55 C Hall, "Interlocking Directorates in Australia: The Significance for Competition Policy" (1983) 55(1) Australian Quarterly 42 at 50.

56 R Carroll, B Stening and K Stening, "Interlocking Directorships and the Law in Australia" (1990) 8(5) CSLJ 290 at 294.

directorships are not high, but rather that the concentration of directorships holding in the hands of a few is high.[57]

[21.6] Checklist

Before accepting a position as a multiple or interlocking director, a director should consider the following:

- Is the Board of the company offering the director a Board position aware of the directorship/s the director already holds?
- Is the company offering the director a Board position in the same industry as the company/companies on whose Board/Boards the director already serves?
- Is the appointment likely to give rise to a conflict of interest?

Upon accepting a Board position that gives rise to a multiple or interlocking directorship, a director should do the following:

- Immediately notify the Chair of each company of the directorships held in other companies.
- Immediately notify the Chair of each company of any other interests held in other companies.
- Notify both the Chair and the board of each company of matters on which the director is unlikely to vote due to possible conflict of interest (this will give notice of the possible need to appoint an alternate director).

When making a decision, a multiple or interlocking director should consider a number of factors. These factors should also be considered by insolvency practitioners when seeking to prosecute a director who holds multiple and interlocking directorships for breach of duty:

- What is the nature of the matter at hand?
- How will this matter affect the company in question?
- Could this matter possibly affect the interests of any other company in which the director holds a directorship?
- How would the interests of any other company the director holds a directorship in be affected by the director's decision on this matter?
- Is the decision the director intends to make in accordance with the interests of Company A? Is the decision the director intends to make in accordance with the interests of Company B?

57 M Alexander and G Murray, "Interlocking Directorships in the Top 250 Australian Companies: Comment on Carroll, Stening and Stening" (1992) 10(6) CSLJ 385 at 393.

- Has the director notified the Chair and the Board of any possible conflict of interest on this matter?
- Have the Boards of both companies given the director permission to vote on this particular matter?
- If the Board of one company on which the director serves has decided it would be a conflict of interest for the director to vote on this matter, has the director notified the other board of this?
- If the Board of another company on which the director serves has decided that the director should not vote on this matter, has the director notified the Chair of her or his inability to vote on this matter?
- If this situation has arisen before, should the director consider resigning from the Board of this company?

[21.7] Loopholes/deficiencies/tricks/ hints

[21.7.1] LACK OF EMPIRICAL RESEARCH

There is an evident lack on empirical research into the effects on multiple and interlocking directorships on the economy in general. The work of Carroll, Stening and Stening has been significant in determining the prevalence of these practices in Australia and providing an international comparison. The revised data offered by Alexander and Murray is also important in this regard.[58] However, the ability to determine the type and extent of regulation required will be hampered in the absence of fresh data on the wider effects of these practices. For the purposes of competition policy, it would be useful for a body to collect data, using the same methodology, on the incidence and types of multiple and interlocking directorships every five years.

[21.7.2] INABILITY OF THE TRADE PRACTICES ACT TO PROHIBIT POTENTIAL ANTI-COMPETITIVE EFFECTS

Some commentators and legislators have argued that existing regulatory devices are sufficient to regulate the potential anti-competitive effects of multiple and interlocking directorships. It is argued that contractual obligations, fiduciary duties and other indirect statutory devices are effective in themselves.

The anti-competitive aim of the *Trade Practices Act* 1974 (Cth) is often cited as a statutory device sufficient to hinder anti-competitive conduct potentially resulting from multiple and interlocking directorships.

---

58 M Alexander and G Murray, "Interlocking Directorships in the Top 250 Australian Companies: Comment on Carroll, Stening and Stening" (1992) 10(6) CSLJ 385.

The purpose of the *Trade Practices Act* 1974 (Cth) has been described as being "to strengthen the competitiveness of private enterprise at the various levels of production and distribution of industrial and consumer goods and services",[59] both for the benefit of the public as ultimate consumers and the benefit of business in general. If the primary purpose of the *Trade Practices Act* is to preserve and enhance competition, then consideration should be given to the effect that interlocking directorships have on competition and whether the Act adequately assesses this issue.[60]

However, as Carroll points out, the *Trade Practices Act* does not expressly prohibit or regulate multiple or interlocking directorships. In fact, the claim that it sufficiently and effectively regulates the potential anti-competitive effects of multiple and interlocking directorships is severely hindered when it is analysed more closely. Carroll documents three main deficiencies in this claim. First, a mere directorial appointment is unlikely to be sufficient to prove that the purpose or effect of the appointment was the "substantial lessening of competition". Secondly, in the absence of a "contract, agreement or understanding" it would be difficult to attribute any breach of s 45(2) of the *Trade Practices Act* to the existence of a multiple or interlocking directorship. Thirdly, although a multiple or interlocking directorship may in fact lie behind the types of behaviour prohibited by the *Trade Practices Act*, in itself it does not amount to a contravention.

Carroll argues that although the *Trade Practices Act* has the potential to prohibit anti-competitive behaviour arising from multiple or interlocking directorships, it has never been used in this way. This is largely as result of the lack of specific regulation provided, the need for proof of anti-competitive effect, and the lack of available empirical date on the effects of multiple and interlocking directorships on the economy in general.[61]

For these reasons, the argument that the *Trade Practices Act* is sufficient to prohibit and regulate the potential anti-competitive effects of multiple and interlocking directorships is seriously deficient.

[21.7.3] MULTIPLE AND INTERLOCKING DIRECTORSHIPS SHOULD NOT BE ALLOWED

Christie has vigorously asserted that multiple and interlocking directorships should not be allowed.[62] He argues that the common law doctrine of conflict of interest places the highest standard of required conduct on company directors and that the practice of multiple and interlocking directorships blatantly abuses this standard of conduct. He calls for the Courts to acknowledge that previous

60 R Carroll, "Trade Practices Implications of Director Interlocks" (1990) 18(6) ABLR 395 at 397.

61 R Carroll, "Trade Practices Implications of Director Interlocks" (1990) 18(6) ABLR 395 at 397–398.

62 M Christie, "The Director's Fiduciary Duty not to Compete" (1995) 55(4) *Modern Law Review* 506.

cases that decided that these practices should be allowed were wrongly decided as they dangerously relax the concept of good faith and hinder commercial morality.

There is some merit in this argument. Multiple and interlocking directorships pose a challenge to the common law rule of conflict of interest. Whilst the Law seeks to deal with this problem by safeguarding statutory directors' duties and allowing for some commercial flexibility through the introduction of s 187, such provisions do not adequately deal with the potential insider trading problems posed by multiple and interlocking directorships. For example, a director X may be a director of Company A which is secretly examining buying Company Z and may also be a director of Company B which has also indicated internally that it may examine the possibility of buying Company Z. In such a situation it may be extremely difficult for director X to know when to absent him or herself from voting. Even if he or she says nothing he or she may still breach her or his duties regarding conflicts of interests. Such considerations may suggest that being a director of two competing companies, particularly in the same industry, may be just so fraught with conflict as to be completely untenable. As discussed below in [21.8.1], s 8 of the United States *Clayton Act* 1914 prohibits interlocking directorships between companies competing within the same industrial sector subject to certain conditions. Arguably this may provide a basis on which the Australian legislature may seek to regulate multiple and interlocking directorships within the same industry.

[21.8] Proposals for law reform

[21.8.1] REGULATION OF NUMBER AND TYPE OF DIRECTORSHIPS

The Senate Standing Committee on Legal and Constitutional Affairs has decided that it unwise for statutory limitations to be placed on the number of multiple or interlocking directorships held in Australia:

> It is not useful for the Law to set limits on the number of directorships a person may hold. The wide differences in the capacity of directors and in the work required to direct different companies make it pointless to do so. The Law should clearly set down the required standards of conduct, and directors must then judge for themselves whether their commitments allow them to meet the standards. If ethics cannot deliver proper conduct, the Law must.[63]

63 Senate Standing Committee on Legal and Constitutional Affairs, *Report on the Social and Fiduciary Duties and Obligations of Company Directors*, 1989, para 4.49.

This reasoning is persuasive in regard to the number of directorships able to be held. There are large differences between the workload required of different companies. In many cases, the more directors that are sitting on the Board the more likely that each director has a specific role and function to fulfil. Depending on the nature of the company and the management structure, directors in such circumstances may have a heavy or light workload. Because it is impossible to determine the aptitude or workload of any given director, the Law should not set limits on the number of directorships able to be held.

However, as indicated above, there are strong arguments in favour of regulating multiple and interlocking directorships within the same industry. The potential risks posed by the possibility of insider trading and the impossible situations directors may find themselves in with regards to conflicts of interests may simply make such intra-industry directorships untenable. The Australian legislature should arguably consider regulating the number and type of directorships held within industry sectors.

It should be noted that interlocking directorships between industrial companies are regulated in the United States. Section 8 of the *Clayton Act* 1914 prohibits interlocking directorships between industrial companies subject to four statutory requirements:[64]

(i) At least one of the interlocks must involve a company with capital, surplus and undivided profits aggregating more than $1,000,000.
(ii) Both interlocked corporations must engage in interstate trade and commerce.
(iii) The interlock must involve corporations "other than banks, banking association, trust companies and common carriers".
(iv) The interlocked companies must be competitors "by virtue of their business and location of operation … so that the elimination of competition between them would constitute a violation of the antitrust laws". Thus, the two corporations must be real competitors in practice.

In addition, ss 1, 2 and 3 can be used to prohibit interlocking directorships on the grounds that it is a restraint of trade or an attempt to monopolise.[65] Weinfeld J of the United States District Court summarised the reasons for the introductions of statutory regulation of interlocking directorships as follows:

> Congress had been aroused by the concentration of control by a few individuals or groups over many gigantic corporations that in the normal course of events should have been in active and unrestrained competition. Instead, and because of

64 Cited in R Carroll, "Trade Practices Implications of Director Interlocks" (1990) 18(6) ABLR 395 at 399.

65 R Carroll, "Trade Practices Implications of Director Interlocks" (1990) 18(6) ABLR 395 at 400.

> such control, the healthy competition of the free enterprise system had been stifled or eliminated. Interlocking directorships on rival corporations had been the instrumentality of defeating the purpose of the antitrust laws. They had tended to suppress competition or to foster joint action against third party competitors. The continued potential threat to the competitive system resulting from the conflicting directorships was the evil aimed at. Viewed against this background, a fair reading of the legislative debates leaves little room for doubt that, in its efforts to strengthen the antitrust laws, what Congress intended by section 8 was to nip in the bud incipient violations of the antitrust laws by removing the opportunity or temptation to such violations through interlocking directorships. The legislation was entirely preventative.[66]

The Australian legislature could use such arguments to introduce statutory regulation of the number and type of interlocking directorships held.

[21.8.2] DIRECTORS OF PARTLY OWNED SUBSIDIARIES

CASAC has recommended that the directors of partly owned subsidiaries be afforded the same rights as directors of wholly owned subsidiaries are afforded under s 187.[67] The New Zealand *Companies Act* contains a similar provision which it may be possible to adapt to apply to upstream financial transactions within a partly owned corporate group.[68] The *Corporate Law Economic Reform Draft Bill* (1998) originally contained a provision similar to s 131(3) of the New Zealand *Companies Act* 1993 but which was deleted from it for further review by CASAC. This draft provision would have allowed directors of partly owned group companies to act in the best interests of the holding company provided that a number of specified conditions were met.[69] These conditions included independent shareholder approval and a requirement that the partly owned

---

66 *United States v Sears, Roebuck and Co* 111 F Supp 614 per Weinfeld J. Cited in R Carroll, "Trade Practices Implications of Director Interlocks" (1990) 18(6) ABLR 395 at 398–399.

67 CASAC, *Corporate Groups: Final Report*, 2000, pp 63-64.

68 Section 131(3) of the *New Zealand Companies Act* 1993 provides "A director of a company that is a subsidiary (but not a wholly-owned subsidiary) may, when exercising powers or performing duties as a director, if expressly permitted to do so by the constitution of the company and with the prior agreement of the shareholders (other than its holding company) act in a manner which he or she believes is in the best interest of that company's holding company even though it may not be in the best interests of the company".

69 Section 8(2) of the Corporate Law Economic Reform Draft Bill provided:
"A director of a corporation that is a subsidiary, but not a wholly-owned subsidiary, of a body corporate is to be taken to act in good faith in the best interests of the subsidiary if:
(a) the constitution of the subsidiary expressly authorises the director to act in the best interests of the holding company; and
(b) a resolution passed at a general meeting of the subsidiary authorises the director to act in the best interests of the holding company (no votes being cast in favour of the resolution by the holding company or an associate); and
(c) the director acts in good faith in the best interests of the holding company; and
(d) the subsidiary is not insolvent at the time, or immediately after, the director acts."

company be solvent at the time that the director takes the relevant action. These conditions were intended to protect minority shareholders and unsecured creditors.[70]

The possible benefits suggested by CASAC for this extension include:[71]

- protecting directors of a subsidiary group company who wish to act in the interests of the holding company but without any clearly discernible direct or derivative net commercial benefit to their own company;
- improving efficiency in some corporate groups by overcoming some of the possible legal restrictions on intra-group financial transaction;
- better protecting lenders to a corporate group, particularly where they seek guarantees or third party mortgages from partly owned group companies.

Some possible detriments identified by CASAC include:[72]

- eliminating the need for directors of partly owned group companies to consider whether their company will receive any benefit from entering into the transaction, which could provide too much protection for these directors, compared with the possible detriment to the group company and its minority shareholders;
- permitting those directors to act even when they had a personal interest in the holding company, given that the test of good faith in the draft provision only refers to acting in the best interests of the holding company;
- reducing the rights of minority shareholders – it would be doubtful whether dissenting minority shareholders would still be eligible to initiate an oppression action concerning a resolution under the draft provision what was approved by a majority of that minority.

It is more easy to justify the ability of directors of wholly owned subsidiaries to take the interests of the holding company into account than it is for directors of partly owned subsidiaries because in the case of wholly owned subsidiaries the owners are ultimately the same. In the case of partly owned subsidiaries the owners will sometimes come from a diverse range of people with often competing or conflicting interests. In such a situation it is important to protect the rights of minority shareholders and, arguably, any such extension would need to contain a provision to protect minority shareholder interests.

CASAC has sought to incorporate protection for minority shareholders. Their recommendation provides that:[73]

70 See CASAC, *Corporate Groups: Final Report* (2000), para 2.37.

71 CASAC, *Corporate Groups: Final Report* (2000), para 2.38.

72 CASAC, *Corporate Groups: Final Report* (2000), para 2.39.

73 CASAC, *Corporate Groups: Final Report* (2000), pp 63-64 [Recommendation 3].

The *Corporations Law* should permit directors of a solvent partly-owned group company to act in good faith and in the interests of the parent company where the minority shareholders of the former company pass an ordinary resolution, in accordance with its constitution, that approves the directors so acting.

That provision should:

- not stipulate what information is necessary for minority shareholders to make a fully-informed decision
- permit minority shareholders to give retrospective, as well as prior, approval to the directors' actions
- permit minority shareholders to give general approval
- make it clear that the proposal is additional to, not in substitution for, the current common law principles permitting directors to act in the interests of their company and permitting shareholder ratification
- not stipulate a statutory time limit on the operation of any minority shareholder resolution, but leave that to the terms of the resolution
- apply the principle, found in the capital reduction provision (s256B(1)(b)), that the action of the directors in exercising the power should not materially prejudice the company's ability to pay its creditors
- permit all minority shareholders who have not voted in favour of the resolution (that is, dissenting shareholders and shareholders who failed to vote) to exercise buy-out rights
- not impose any additional liability on a parent company for the actions of the directors of a partly-owned group company
- not extend to sibling group companies
- stipulate that the oppression remedy should not apply to any resolution passed in accordance with this proposal.

It is possible that such a provision could be abused by the holding company of a partly owned subsidiary and that this risk suggests that such a provision should not be enacted and, should the holding company want the partly owned subsidiary to act in the best interests of the holding company, it should acquire the shares of the minority shareholders. However, if minority approval for the directors' actions is provided it is difficult to see how the interests of the minority shareholders would be prejudiced by such action.

Whilst CASAC's recommendation will be considered by the legislature, arguably there are some aspects of the recommendation which could cause problematic. In particular, it is possible that in the absence of the provision expressly stating what information is necessary for minority shareholders to make a fully informed decision minority shareholders may not make a fully informed decision. Arguably the provision should, at the least, provide that the notice of the relevant meeting should contain all the information which the minority shareholders need to make a fully informed decision and that this should be at least all the information known to the company. Against this however, the common law principles of disclosure and provision of information may already provide adequate safeguards. Another problem area within the recommended provision may be the recommendation to allow minority shareholders to give general approval for particular types of conduct. This may be particularly problematic if resort to the oppression remedy is precluded. Although general approval would prevent the need for multiple requests for approval for essentially the same conduct, minority shareholders would not be given the chance to scrutinise the director's intended action in each particular factual circumstance and, if they deemed such action inappropriate in one situation, would have no ability to recourse under the oppression remedy.

It is yet to be seen what sort of considerations the legislature will have reference to in considering CASAC's recommendation.

PART E

Liabilities and Practicalities

Directors' and Officers' Liability

22

"... *there needs to be taken into account the clear policy of the [Companies] Code that companies must be accountable and be seen to be so by the public.*"[1]

1 *Commissioner for Corporate Affairs (WA) v Ekamper* (1987) 12 ACLR 519 at 524.

OBJECTIVES

This Chapter will:

- outline the various categories of liability which may be imposed for a breach of duty;
- discuss the various remedies available for a breach of a civil penalty provision and set out those duties which are subject to a civil penalty;
- analyse the nature of criminal offences and consider the various penalties which may be imposed for a criminal offence;
- outline the relationship between civil and criminal liability;
- consider the utility for insolvency practitioners of the penalties which may be imposed on directors or other officers.

[22.1] General overview

The liability that follows a breach of the insolvent trading provisions or a breach of other statutory duties is largely the same. Although only directors can be liable under the insolvent trading provisions, both directors and officers can be liable under many other statutory duties.

A breach of duty will result in either primary liability or secondary liability. Primary liability includes civil penalties, criminal offences, and liability for compensation. Secondary liability includes disqualification from managing a corporation, personal liability for managing a corporation whilst disqualified, personal subjection to external administration, and other miscellaneous sanctions.

There is a clear separation of liability between civil penalties and criminal offences. Each section specifically states whether a breach of it constitutes a civil penalty offence or a criminal offence.

[22.1.1] PRIMARY LIABILITY

(a) Civil penalty orders

A civil penalty order can only be made if a director or officer breaches a civil penalty provision.

Subsection 588G(2), the duty to prevent insolvent trading, is a civil penalty provision. Only directors are bound by the duty to prevent insolvent trading under subs.588G(2), and so only directors can be liable under the provisions.

The statutory duties of care and diligence, good faith and use of position and information are also civil penalty provisions (see s.180, s.181, s.182 and s.183). Both directors and other officers can be liable for a breach of these duties.

Section 9 of the Law defines a "civil penalty order" to mean any of the following:

(a) a declaration of contravention under section 1317F;
(b) a pecuniary penalty order under section 1317G;
(c) a compensation order under section 1317H;
(d) an order under section 206C disqualifying a person from managing a corporation.

Each of these is considered separately.

(i) Declaration of contravention

Only ASIC can apply for a declaration of contravention: s 1317J(1). It is not necessary for private plaintiffs to seek a declaration of contravention in order to seek redress under the insolvent trading provisions.

Section 1317F states that when the Court makes a declaration of contravention, it is conclusive evidence that a person has contravened a civil penalty provision. ASIC can not seek a pecuniary penalty order or a disqualification under s 206C unless it has obtained a declaration of contravention.

A company may intervene in an application by ASIC for a declaration of contravention: s 1317J(3) and s 588J(2). It can be heard on all matters except whether than declaration of contravention should be made: s 1317J(3).

A declaration of contravention must specify the following by virtue of s 1317E(2):

- the Court that made the declaration;
- the civil penalty provision that was contravened;
- the person who contravened the provision;
- the conduct that constituted the contravention;
- the corporation or registered scheme to which the conduct related.

An application for a declaration of contravention must be made within six years of the contravention (s 1317K), which acts as a limitation period for commencing an action under the insolvent trading provisions by ASIC. When hearing proceedings for a declaration of contravention, the Court must apply the rules of evidence and procedure for civil matters: s 1317L. This means that the burden of proof will be on the balance of probabilities.

(ii) Pecuniary penalty order

After the Court has made a declaration of contravention under s 1317F: s 1317F(1)(a), ASIC can apply to the Court for a pecuniary penalty order: s 1317J(1). The company can intervene in the application for a pecuniary penalty order: s 1317J(3) and s 588J(2). It can be heard on all matters except whether the pecuniary penalty order should be made: s 1317J(3). The application for a pecuniary penalty order must be made within six years after the contravention: s 1317K. When hearing proceedings for a civil penalty order the Court must apply the civil rules of evidence and procedure: s 1317L.

The pecuniary penalty order will not be made unless the contravention:

- materially prejudices the interests of the corporation or scheme, of its members;
- materially prejudices the corporation's ability to pay its creditors; or
- is serious: s 1317G(1)(b).

A pecuniary penalty order can be made of a sum up to A$200,000 for each breach: s 1317G(1). There are a number of factors the Court is likely to consider when deciding the amount of the pecuniary penalty order. In relation to the predecessor provision of s 1317G, s 1317EA(3), the Court held that the object of pecuniary penalty orders is:

> ... to protect the public by preventing a corporate structure from being able to be misused to the detriment of the company, its shareholders, creditors, investors and other dealings with the company.[2]

In *Re Tasmanian Spastics Association: Australian Securities Commission v Nandan*,[3] Merkel J took the following factors into account in making an order under the predecessor provision to s 1317G, s 1317EA(3):

- The contravention involved a deliberate, systematic and unauthorised misuse for personal or private purposes of the funds and facilities of the Association on a regular basis.
- The conduct engaged in constituted an abuse of trust and confidence placed in the respondent by his employer.
- The contraventions were camouflaged from discovery in a manner which gave rise to serious concern of the respondent's honesty and integrity.
- The respondent attempted to justify his conduct and failed to display any remorse or contrition in respect of the contravention.

Section 1317G(1)(b)(iii) states that a pecuniary penalty order must not be made unless the contravention is serious. It is unclear what the precise meaning of "serious" is in this context. It is interesting to note that fraud has been described as a serious offence.[4]

Arguably, the sorts of factors the court will take into account are:

- the nature and extent of the contravening conduct;
- the amount of loss or damage caused;
- the circumstances in which the conduct took place;
- the size of the company;
- the degree of power the company has, as evidenced by its market share and ease of entry into the market;
- the deliberateness of the contravention and the period over which it extended;
- whether the contravention arose out of the conduct of senior management or at a lower level;
- whether the company has a corporate culture conducive to compliance with the Law, as evidenced by educational programs and disciplinary or other corrective measures in response to an acknowledged contravention;[5]

---

2 *Re Tasmanian Spastics Association: Australian Securities Commission v Nandan* (1997) 23 ACSR 743.
3 *Re Tasmanian Spastics Association: Australian Securities Commission v Nandan* (1997) 23 ACSR 743.
4 *Neat Holdings Pty Ltd v Karajan Holdings Pty Ltd* (1992) 67 ALJR 170.
5 See, for example, the range of factors the Court will take into account in assessing penalties under the *Trade Practices Act: TPC v CSR Ltd* (1991) ATPR at 41-076.

- whether or not the company has shown a disposition to co-operate with the authorities responsible for the enforcement of the Act/Law in relation to the contravention.

A pecuniary penalty order is a civil debt payable to ASIC.[6] It is not money payable to the company.

(iii) Compensation order

ASIC or the company can apply to the Court for a compensation order: s 1317J(1) and (2). In most cases, the liquidator will make an application for a compensation order on behalf of the company. ASIC or the company does not need a declaration of contravention in order to make an application for compensation. Proceedings for a compensation order must be begun within six years after the contravention: s 1317K.

The Court may order a person to compensate a company or registered scheme for damage suffered by the corporation or scheme if the person has contravened a civil penalty provision and the damage is a result of the contravention: s 1317H(1). When determining the damage suffered by the corporation or scheme, the Court is to take into account any profits the person made from the contravention or offence and any diminution in the value of the scheme property: s 1317H(2) and (3).

The amount of the compensation to be paid must be specified within the compensation order: s 1317H(1).

A compensation order may be enforced as if it were a judgment of the Court: s 1317H(5).

If the civil penalty provision that has been contravened is s 588G(2), the insolvent trading provision, an additional right of compensation is available under s 588J: ss 588G(4) and 588P. If ASIC makes an application for a compensation order, the liquidator of the company has the right to intervene: s 588J(2). The liquidator is entitled to be heard only if the Court is satisfied that the person committed the contravention and only in regards to whether or not the Court should order the person to pay compensation to the company: s 588J(3).

Where an application is made for a civil penalty order to be made as a result of a contravention of s 588G(2) the Court may order the person to pay compensation to the company equal to the amount of loss or damage caused if it is satisfied that:

- the person committed the contravention in relation to the incurring of a debt by a company; and
- the debt is wholly or partly unsecured; and

6 Section 1317G(2).

- the person to whom the debt is owed has suffered loss or damage in relation to the debt because of the company's insolvency: s 588J(1).

This compensation order under s 588J(1) can be made whether or not the Court has also made a pecuniary penalty order under s 1317G or an order under s 206C disqualifying the person from managing corporations: s 588J(1). An order to pay compensation under s 588J can be enforced as if it were a judgment of the Court: s 588L.

It should be noted that s 588J(1) includes the phrase "loss or damage" as the measurement of compensation to be paid. In contrast, s 1317H only includes the term "damage" and this is specified to include any profit the person who contravened the civil penalty provision made as a result of the contravention: s 1317H(2). However, it is unclear what is included within the ambit of "loss and damage" within the insolvent trading provisions. The meaning of "loss and damage" has been considered in relation to other early statutes. Many decisions under the *Trade Practices Act* 1974 (Cth) have indicated that it can exceed the amount of the debt that caused the contravention and include the entire disadvantage suffered by a person or corporation.[7] It is likely that this interpretation will also be relevant to the assessment of compensation under s 588J(1). It is likely that the Court will also include any profit made by the person who contravened the provision as a result of the contravention, in a similar fashion to the determination under s 1317H(2). However, in practice there will not often be circumstances in which a profit is made.

(iv) Disqualification from managing corporations

After the Court has made a declaration of contravention under s 1317F (s 206C(1)(a)), ASIC may apply to the Court to disqualify a person from managing corporations for a period that the Court considers appropriate: s 206C(1).

"Managing a corporation" is defined under s 206A. It includes:

(a) the making, or participating in making, decisions that affect the whole, or a substantial part, of the business of the corporation;
(b) exercising the capacity to affect significantly that corporation's financial standing;
(c) communicating instructions or wishes (other than advice given by the person in the proper performance of functions attaching to the person's professional capacity or their business relationship with the directors of the company) to the directors of the corporation:
    (i) knowing that the directors are accustomed to act in accordance with the person's instructions or wishes; or
    (ii) intending that the directors will act in accordance with those instructions or wishes.

7 See *Demagogue Pty Ltd v Romensky* (1992) 39 FCR 31 at 47–48.

The Court can only disqualify a person from managing corporations is it is satisfied that the disqualification is justified: s 206C(1)(b). In determining whether the contravention is justified, the Court will consider:

- the person's conduct in relation to the management, business or property of any corporation; and
- any other matters that the Court considers appropriate: s 206C(2).

This provides the Court with a very wide scope of factors to consider when determining whether or not a person should be disqualified.

In the case of *Commissioner for Corporate Affairs (WA) v Ekamper*,[8] decided under a predecessor provision to s 206C, Franklyn J identified a number of factors the Court will consider when determining whether or not a person should be disqualified from managing corporations. It is worth quoting his Honour at length:

> … the defendant, having regard to his professional background, demonstrates an incomprehensible lack of regard by him for his obligations both as a director and a secretary … His evidence reveals a lack of concern for the observance by a company and its officers of prescribed obligations under the Code and discloses a positive refusal by him to accept the responsibilities which appointment as secretary and/or director of a company carry … His admissions show him to have quite deliberately decided that the companies the subject of these proceedings … should ignore their respective statutory obligations … despite the fact that to do so was clearly a breach and an offence. They also decided that he deliberately decided that he would ignore his own obligations as secretary … These decisions were arrived at for reasons which have no validity, being based on a personal view contrary to the requirements of the law that compliance with the provisions of the [Companies] Code was 'unnecessary' … In my opinion … there needs to be taken into account the clear policy of the [Companies] Code that companies must be accountable and be seen to be so by the public. To that end in the public interest they are obliged to comply with specified requirements and to place on public records prescribed information. The Commission and the public have an interest to ensure that such obligations are complied with. Quite apart from the question of penalties which may be imposed for failure to comply with statutory obligations there is a public need to ensure that only suitable persons act as directors, secretaries and otherwise in a managerial capacity so that compliance with the statutory requirements can be assured and that persons so acting in fact so comply.[9]

8 (1987) 12 ACLR 519.
9 (1987) 12 ACLR 519 at 524.

Franklyn J accepted that a number of matters should be considered, but indicated that this list was not exhaustive:

- the character of the defendant;
- the nature of the offence;
- the structure of the companies concerned and the nature of their business;
- the interests of shareholders, creditors and employees;
- the risk to those persons or to the public of the defendant continuing in his present function;
- his honesty and competence;
- hardship resulting to him, his personal and family business interests;
- his appreciation that future breaches could result in fresh proceedings for the Court to disqualify.

The Federal Court considered the application of the disqualification provisions to a passive director. In *ASC v Roussi*[10] a husband and wife were the only two directors of a succession of failed computer retail companies. The couple had been previously convicted of a number of offences against the Law but had continued to flout their obligations as directors in other ways by "failing to co-operate with liquidators and denying creditors their entitlements". The evidence indicated that they had done this willingly and knowingly and not exhibiting an appreciation for the gravity of their conduct. Einfield J considered the phoenix nature of the companies established successively by the couple and held that this suggested "a deliberate course of conduct designed to serve and enrich the [couple] at other people's expense. In the circumstances this activity cannot be characterised in any other way than intentionally dishonest and a reckless disregard of the Law and [their] legal obligations."

The wife contended that she was a passive director and was a mere "puppet" of her husband who merely did what she was told. The Court did not deny this. Einfield J considered the protective rather than punitive rationale and purpose behind the disqualification provisions. His Honour disqualified the wife for a period of 10 years starting from the time at which her husband was discharged from bankruptcy. He concluded that:

> [The wife] accepted the position of director time and again when she must have known that the multiplication of companies was brought about by their indebtedness and at least incompetent management. Yet there is no evidence to suggest that she gave even a moment's thought to needed changes, still less to the victims of this manipulation of her and her husband's corporate empire. In any case, a

10 Unereported, Fed Ct, Aust, Einfield J, 11 May 1999.

director cannot take the rewards of her companies while disowning her responsibilities to them and the community.

Clearly, in applying the disqualification provisions the Court will consider their purpose and whether the director has systematically breached the Law or acted in total disregard of her or his obligations and duties as a director. In this way where a director is passive and does not take an active role in the control and financial management of a company they can be subjected to disqualification even though he or she may not have acted with dishonest intent.

ASIC is required to keep a record of persons disqualified from managing corporations: s 1274AA.

A person who is disqualified from managing corporations under s 206C can apply to the Court for leave to manage corporations, a particular class of corporations, or a particular corporation: s 206G(1). The person must lodge a notice in the prescribed form with ASIC at least 21 days before commencing the proceedings: s 206G(2).

When considering an application for leave, the Court is likely to take into account the factors listed above.

If leave is granted by the Court, the order granting leave can be expressed to be subject to exceptions and conditions as determined by the Court: s 206G(3). The person must then lodge with ASIC a copy of any order granting leave: s 206G(4). This must be done within 14 days after the order is made: s 206G(4). ASIC can then apply to the Court to revoke the leave: s 206G(5). The order revoking leave is not effective until it is served on the person: s 206G(5).

A person commits an offence if they manage a corporation whilst disqualified from managing corporations: s 206A. The penalty is A$5000, one year imprisonment, or both: Sch 3 of the Law. It is a defence to an offence under s 206A if the person had permission to manage a corporation.

(b) Criminal offences

Where a breach of a provision is intended to have criminal consequences, this will be clearly stated within the provision itself. This means that the requirements for an offence to be committed are different and will depend on the nature of the duty breached. Similarly, the penalty for committing an offence differs throughout the Law. As a result, the nature of criminal offences within the Law is tailored to meet the specific requirements of particular duties and obligations and the policy and philosophy behind each particular provision.

Subsection 588G(3) outlines when a breach of the insolvent trading provisions will constitute a criminal offence. A person will commit an offence under the insolvent trading provisions where:

- the person is a director of the company when it incurs a debt;

- the company is insolvent at that time, or becomes insolvent by incurring that debt, or by incurring at that time debts including that debt;
- the person suspected at the time when the company incurred the debt that the company was insolvent or would become insolvent as a result of incurring that debt or other debts; and
- the person's failure to prevent the company incurring the debt was dishonest.

Section 588G(3) virtually mirrors s 588G(1), which outlines when the insolvent trading provisions apply. The crucial difference is that s 588G(3) imposes an additional requirement of criminal intent. The criminal intent required is that of dishonesty. Although the exact meaning of "dishonesty" is not clear in this context, it is likely to mean an intentional, willed, or deliberate act.[11] It is likely to involve an element of deceit or fraud. In this way, a reasonable but mistaken director would not be at risk under s 588G(3).

A director found guilty of a criminal offence under s 588G(3) will suffer a penalty of A$200 000, five years' imprisonment, or both: Sch 3 of the Law.

Section 73A of the Law defines when a Court is taken to have found a person guilty of an offence. An Australian Court finds a person guilty of an offence if the Court convicts them of an offence or if the person is charged with an offence, and is found to have committed to offence, but the Court does not proceed to convict the person of the offence.

In addition to this penalty (s 588P), where a person is found guilty of a criminal offence under s 588G(3), the Court may order the person to pay compensation to the company under s 588K. The Court may order compensation to be paid whether or not it has imposed a penalty under s 588G(3). Compensation can only be ordered if the Court is satisfied that:

- the debt is wholly or partly unsecured; and
- the person to whom the debt is owed has suffered loss or damage in relation to the debt because of the company's insolvency: s 588K(1)(b).

The amount of the compensation to be paid is equal to the amount of loss or damage suffered.

An order to pay compensation under s 588K can be enforced as if it were a judgment of the Court: s 588L.

If a person is convicted of an offence under s 588G(3), they are automatically disqualified from managing a corporation: s 206B(1)(b)(i) or (ii). The period of automatic disqualification starts on the day the person is convicted and lasts for:

- five years after the day on which they are convicted, if the director or other officer does not serve a term of imprisonment; or

11 See *Chew v R* (1991) 173 CLR 626.

- five years after the day on which they are released from prison, if the director or other officer serves a term of imprisonment: s 206B(2).

A breach of many other provisions of the Law will constitute a criminal offence.[12] Although it is not within the scope of this book to discuss all criminal offences, it should be noted that breach of many of the statutory directors' duties constitutes a criminal offence. Section 184 states that breach of the duty of good faith, breach of the duty of use of position, and breach of the duty of use of information constitute a criminal offence. It should be noted that the prime element of criminal intent within these provisions is dishonesty. The meaning of dishonesty has been discussed earlier in this section.

Breach of s 184 results in a penalty of A$20 000, five years imprisonment, or both. If a director or other officer is convicted of an offence under s 184 they are automatically disqualified from managing a corporation: s 206B(1)(b)(i) or (ii). The period of automatic disqualification starts on the day the person is convicted and lasts for:

- five years after the day on which they are convicted, if the director or other officer does not serve a term of imprisonment; or
- five years after the day on which they are released from prison, if the director or other officer serves a term of imprisonment: s 206B(2).

(c) Relation between civil and criminal proceedings

Where a person has been convicted of a criminal offence under the Law, the Court can not make a declaration of contravention or a pecuniary penalty order: s 1317M.

There is nothing precluding criminal proceedings being commenced after proceedings under a civil penalty provision have already begun: s 1317P. Criminal proceedings can be commenced against a person for conduct that is substantially the same as conduct constituting a contravention of a civil penalty provision regardless of whether a civil penalty order has been made: s 1317P. However, proceedings for a declaration of contravention or a pecuniary penalty order are stayed if:

- proceedings for a criminal offence begin, or have already begun; and
- the offence is constituted by conduct that is substantially the same as the conduct alleged to constitute the contravention (s.1317N).

The proceedings for the declaration or order can be resumed if the person is not convicted of the offence. Otherwise, the proceedings for the declaration or order are dismissed: s 1317N.

12 A quick way to determine which sections are criminal offence sections is to consult Sch 3 of the Law, which contains a full list of the criminal offence provisions and the penalties associated with each.

(d) ASIC may require person to assist

ASIC may require a person to assist it in an application for a declaration of contravention, a pecuniary penalty order, or criminal proceedings: s 1317P(1).

(e) Compensation

Compensation can be awarded for a breach of a civil penalty provision: s 1317H. Where the civil penalty provision that has been breached is s 588G(2), the insolvent trading provision, an additional ground for compensation arises: ss 588G(4) and 588P.

Section 588J provides a ground for compensation where a person has breached s 588G(2). Section 588K provides a ground for compensation where a person has breached s 588G(3).

Where either s 588G(2) or (3) has been breached, a further ability to claim compensation is granted to liquidators and creditors under s 588M. This action is not affected if the director has been convicted of a criminal offence or a civil penalty order has been made in relation to the contravention: s 588M(1)(e) and (f). Compensation paid under s 588M does not preclude proceedings from being instituted for a breach of either s 588G(2) or s 588G(3). However, provision is made to avoid double recovery from a director: s 588N.

The liquidator has the primary right to recover compensation from a director under s 588M. This is intended to ensure equal sharing between creditors. The liquidator can recover, as a debt due to the company, an amount equal to the loss or damage where:

- the director has contravened s 588G(2) or (3); and
- the creditor has suffered loss or damage because of the company's insolvency; and
- the debt was wholly or partly unsecured; and
- the company is being wound up: s 588M(1)(a), (b), (c) and (d).

Proceedings must be brought within six years after the beginning of the winding up: s 588M(4). Amounts recovered from directors are paid to the company for distribution to all creditors. Unsecured creditors have priority over secured creditors during the distribution of compensation received: s 588Y(1).

However, creditors have a secondary right to bring an action under s 588M(3). A creditor can proceed directly against a director to recover the debt owing to that creditor if the creditor has the written consent of the liquidator: s 588R(1). A creditor can bring an action for compensation without the consent of the liquidator if the liquidator does not take action within three months after a notice procedure is complied with and the Court grants the creditor leave to proceed: ss 588S and 588T. However, a number of matters prevent a creditor from taking action under s 588M(3) (s 588V), including if the liquidator has intervened in an application for a civil penalty order for a contravention of s 588G(2) in relation to the incurring of the debt: s 588U(1)(c). Proceedings by a creditor must be commenced within six years of the winding up: s 588M(4).

[22.1.2] SECONDARY LIABILITY

(a) Disqualification from managing a corporation

Directors can be disqualified from managing corporations in a number of ways. Managing a corporation is defined in s 206A.

If a director is bankrupt or has been convicted of certain criminal offences, including insolvent trading, he or she is automatically disqualified from managing a corporation without leave of the Court for five years after conviction or release from prison: s 206B.

If a director has breached a civil penalty provision and the Court has made a declaration of contravention under s 1317E the person may be disqualified from managing corporations for a period that the Court thinks appropriate: s 206C. The Court must be satisfied that the disqualification is justified: s 206C(1)(b).

A director may be disqualified from managing corporations for up to 10 years if they have been involved in the insolvencies of at least two corporations within a seven-year period and poor management was wholly or partly responsible for the insolvency of the corporation: s 206D. The Court must be satisfied that the disqualification is justified: s 206D(1)(b)(ii).

Disqualification may also result where a director is repeatedly involved in breaches of the Law: s 206E. A director is deemed to have repeatedly breached the Law is the director has contravened two provisions or on two occasions: s 206E(1)(a)(i) and (ii). The Court must be satisfied that the disqualification is justified: s 206E(1)(b).

ASIC also has the power to disqualify a person from managing corporations for up to five years where the director has been involved in the insolvencies of two or more corporations within a seven-year period and the liquidator of each corporation has lodged a report about the inability of the corporation to pay its debts: s 206F(1)(a). ASIC must give the person notice of its intention to disqualify them and an opportunity to be heard: s 206F(1)(b). ASIC must be satisfied that the disqualification is justified: s 206F(1)(c).

Unless the person was disqualified by ASIC under s 206F, the person may apply to the Court for leave to manage corporations, a particular class of corporations, or a particular corporation: s 206G(1). The person must lodge a notice in the prescribed form with ASIC at least 21 days before commencing the proceedings: s 206G(2). If leave is granted by the Court, the order granting leave can be expressed to be subject to exceptions and conditions as determined by the Court: s 206G(3). The person must then lodge with ASIC a copy of any order granting leave: s 206G(4). This must be done within 14 days after the order is made: s 206G(4). ASIC can then apply to the Court to revoke the leave:

s 206G(5). The order revoking leave is not effective until it is served on the person: s 206G(5).

Under s 206A, a person commits an offence if they manage a corporation whilst disqualified from managing corporations: s 206A. The penalty is A$5000, one year imprisonment, or both: Sch 3 of the Law. It is a defence to an offence under s 206A if the person had permission to manage a company: s 206A(1).

(b) Personal liability if managing corporation while disqualified

Under s 588Z, if a director has managed a corporation whilst prohibited from managing a corporation, personal liability can be imposed on that director for as much of the company's debts and liabilities as the Court thinks appropriate, after an application by the company's liquidator.

(c) Personal subjection to external administration

A director who cannot pay any order against him relating to his management of a company can be personally declared a bankrupt. When a person is declared a bankrupt, all his or her property vests in a trustee[13] who has a number of powers to administer and distribute the property.[14] The Law provides for a number of arrangements which could be entered into with creditors to settle the payment of debts in order to avoid bankruptcy.[15]

Even if a person is declared bankrupt, this does not extinguish civil penalty orders remaining to be paid. Subsection 82(3A) of the *Bankruptcy Act* 1966 (Cth) states that a pecuniary penalty order is not provable in bankruptcy. This means that despite the bankruptcy, the person is still liable to pay the pecuniary penalty order (subs. 553B(1)).

(d) Miscellaneous sanctions

Other sanctions include injunctions (s 1324) and fines: s 1311. Section 589 provides for the Court to make a summary judgment against a delinquent director or officer for a breach of any duty in the Law under which it can make any order it thinks appropriate in certain cases.

(e) Removal of directors

The members of the company can remove directors.[16]

---

13 *Bankruptcy Act 1966* (Cth), s 58. Some property is exempted.

14 These powers include those to sell any part of the property, make compromises with creditors and bring or defend any legal proceedings in relation to the administration of the bankrupt's property. See *Bankruptcy Act 1966* (Cth), s 134.

15 *Bankruptcy Act 1966* (Cth), Pt X.

16 For a discussion see J De Plessis, "Some Peculiarities Regarding the Removal of Company Directors" (1999) 27(1) ABLR 6.

Directors of a proprietary company can remove a director through a resolution and appoint another director by resolution: s 203C.

A public company can by resolution remove a director from her or his office: s 103D. However, a notice of intention to remove must be given to the company at least two months before the meeting is to be held, the company must give the director a copy of this notice, and this director can argue their case to members.

[22.2] Philosophy/rationale

There is a wide range of sanctions resulting from a director's breach of duty or obligation. The Cooney Committee stated:

> It is appropriate that there be a range of sanctions available to enforce company directors' duties and obligation. A range of sanctions provides a means whereby sanctions may be tailored to the circumstances.[17]

Civil penalty provisions were introduced into the Law for breaches of its provisions in 1992. Prior to this time criminal sanctions were the main method used to ensure compliance. The introduction of civil penalty orders was clearly intended to increase the chance of successful actions against directors by lowering the standard of proof to the balance of probabilities. The high civil penalties that can be imposed, including fines ranging up to $200,000, and the threat of disqualification act as a strong disincentive to directors to breach a civil penalty provision.

The Law has progressively been decriminalised. The criminal offences that remain in relation to breach of duty only relate to dishonesty, and not recklessness. Due to the hefty civil penalties, criminal offences are only possible for very serious and dishonest breaches. However, as civil penalties will not always be a sufficient deterrent, criminal sanctions are still necessary to a certain degree. This means that criminal liability will only be imposed where the relevant conduct is genuinely criminal in nature.[18]

Criminal proceedings can be commenced even if proceedings for a civil penalty order have already begun. However, evidence given in the course of proceedings for a civil penalty order is not admissible against the same person during prosecution for a criminal offence constituted by substantially the same conduct. This is designed to protect the defendant's right of a fair trial, and to

17 Senate Standing Committee on Legal and Constitutional Affairs, *Company Directors' Duties*, AGPS, Canberra, 1989, para 13.27.

18 See the Senate Standing Committee on Legal and Constitutional Affairs, *Company Directors' Duties*, AGPS, Canberra, 1989, para 13.12.

ensure that ASIC has incentives to commence civil penalty proceedings without forfeiting its further ability to bring criminal proceedings.

The liquidator has the primary right to bring recovery compensation proceedings in relation to the insolvent trading provisions: s 588M(3). The intention behind this to ensure equal sharing between creditors during the winding up of the company and avoid a multiplicity of actions by creditors.[19] Because the duty to prevent insolvent trading is owed to the company, rather than individual creditors, it is also appropriate that the liquidator, acting on behalf of the company, have the primary right to seek compensation.[20] This is a worthwhile provision as it puts litigation in the hands of the person with the greatest access to the evidence and it provides benefits to all unsecured creditors if recovery is successful.[21] However, strong arguments have been made against the liquidator's primary right to bring compensation proceedings. In particular, Dabner argues that this provision is superfluous as the recent broadening of joinder rules in most Australian jurisdictions means that provisions already exists for individual creditors to join their actions and reduce the incidence of costs borne individually and the inconvenience of multiple actions.[22]

The disqualification provisions, providing for a director to be disqualified from managing corporations, is intended to protect the public by ensuring that only suitable persons are able to manage corporations in which ordinary people invest.[23]

[22.3] History/former law

The Cooney Committee initially recommended that civil penalty provisions be introduced into the Law where no criminality is involved.[24] Civil penalty provisions were introduced with the *Corporate Law Reform Act* 1992 (Cth). Prior to the introduction of the *Corporate Law Economic Reform Program Act* 1999 (Cth), the civil penalties that could be imposed were a pecuniary penalty of up to $200,000 or an order prohibiting the person from managing corporations: see the old s 1317EA(3). However, these were extended to include disqualification and a declaration of contravention.

19 A Herzberg, "The Metal Manufacturer's Case and the Australian Law Reform Commission's Insolvent Trading Recommendations" (1989) 7(3) CSLJ 177.

20 ALRC, *General Insolvency Inquiry* Vol 1 (1988), para 313.

21 See S Worthington, "Recent Developments: Legal and Administrative" (1992) 10(3) CSLJ 214.

22 J Dabner, "Trading Whilst Insolvent – A Case for Individual Creditor Rights Against Directors" (1994) 17(2) UNSWLJ 546.

23 See *Commissioner for Corporate Affairs (WA) v Ekamper* (1987) 12 ACLR 519 per Franklyn J.

24 Senate Standing Committee on Legal and Constitutional Affairs, *Company Directors' Duties*, AGPS, Canberra, 1989, para 13.15.

Under the predecessor criminal provision, s 1317FA, a person would be liable of a criminal offence if they contravened a civil penalty provision:
(a) knowingly, intentionally or recklessly; and
(b) either:
  (i) dishonestly and intending to gain, whether directly or indirectly, an advantage for that or any other person; or
  (ii) intending to deceive or defraud someone.

The structure of the old criminal provisions was complex and was structured so that both the elements in paragraph (a) and either subparagraph (i) or (ii) of paragraph (b) must be established in order to satisfy the provision. This complex structure led to considerable difficulties in enforcing criminal sanctions. In particular, the interaction of the mental elements was often problematic. For example, it is difficult to imagine a person doing an act recklessly with the intention to deceive or defraud someone. The mental elements in paragraph (a) were arguably redundant. The use of knowingly in paragraph (a) made little sense when connected with dishonestly intending to gain or deceive and defraud. These deficiencies were removed with the new approach to criminal offences which has dishonesty as its emphasis.

The nature of the compensation provisions has also changed in recent times. Under the old s 592, for debts incurred prior to 23 June 1993, the amount of compensation that could be claimed was equal to the amount of the debt. However, such liability was criticised by the Harmer Report:

> ... the court [should] have a very broad power to give judgment in favour of the company in such amount as is just having regard to the interests of the creditors. This formulation [should] ensure that the damages recovered do not simply reflect some nominal damage to the company. The damage suffered by creditors is the relevant measure. It is not sufficient simply to provide that the measure of damages should be an amount equal to the sum of the unpaid debts which were incurred during the relevant period of insolvent trading.[25]

As a result, the Law was amended to include "loss or damage" as the relevant measure of compensation. This measure of damages is still retained in the Law, although the new s 1317H states the measure of compensation under a contravention of a civil penalty provision to be the amount of damage suffered by the corporation including any profits the director made because of the contravention. Although it is presumed that the meaning of "loss and damage" includes consequential loss, profits made by the director as a result of the

25 ALRC, *General Insolvency Inquiry* Vol 1 (1988), para 317.

contravention, and other damage suffered, this is not made clear in any Explanatory Memorandum.

The predecessor provisions to the current s 1317M, s 1317N and s 1317P dealing with the relation between civil and criminal proceedings were s 1317FB, s 1317GA, s 1317GB and s 1317GC. These predecessor provisions stated that where civil proceedings were initiated in respect of a particular contravention, no criminal proceedings could be brought in relation to the same contravention: s 1317FB. This was seen as necessary due to the lower standard of proof and the more liberal rules of evidence in civil proceedings. Also, it was argued that allowing a criminal prosecution to follow a civil action could seriously disadvantage a defendant: ss 1317GA and 1317GB(1). Under the predecessor provisions, civil proceedings could be brought in relation to a contravention for which criminal proceedings had already begun,[26] thus allowing the Court to proceed straight from an acquittal in relation to the criminal offence to the imposition of a civil penalty order. However, these provisions provided a serious disincentive to ASIC to commence civil penalty proceedings, as once begun this would effectively bar later criminal proceedings.[27] For this reason, this bar was removed by the new provisions and instead they provide that evidence given in the course of proceedings for a pecuniary penalty order is not admissible against the person in proceedings for a criminal offence constituted by the same conduct. This is intended to ensure the right of the defendant to a fair trial. In addition, the current provisions provide that where a criminal prosecution has failed, ASIC must commence fresh proceedings in relation to a civil penalty order.

The disqualification provisions under s 206 differ from their predecessor provisions in a number of ways. In contrast to the old provisions that were located throughout the Law in s 229, s 230, s 599 and s 600, the current provisions are all located within s 206. In addition, the old provisions did not contain an automatic disqualification provision that is now contained in s 206B.

The primary right of the liquidator to sue for compensation under the insolvent trading provisions was introduced by the *Corporate Law Reform Act* 1992 (Cth). Prior to this time, standing to commence an action was extended to creditors only. An insolvent company's liquidator had no standing to bring a claim on behalf of all creditors affected.[28] Consequently, creditors owed only a small amount were unlikely to risk legal action. Further, a multiplicity of actions had to be brought if all creditors were to recover which often meant that the First Creditors to take action would exhaust the assets of the directors.

26 Sections 1317GA and 1317GB(1).

27 The Parliament of the Commonwealth of Australia, House of Representatives, *Corporate Law Economic Reform Program Bill 1998 (Cth): Explanatory Memorandum* Circulated by Authority of the Treasurer, the Hon Peter Costello MP, 1998, para 6.129.

28 See *Ross McConnel Kitchen Pty Ltd (in liq) v Ross* (No 2) (1985) 9 ACLR 532. See also A Herzberg, "Insolvent Trading" (1991) 9(5) CSLJ 285.

To remedy this situation, s 588M was introduced into the Law to provide a primary right to the liquidator to bring an action of behalf of all creditors, whilst retaining a secondary right for creditors to bring an action.

[22.4] Deficiencies

[22.4.1] LOSS OR DAMAGE

The current s 1317H of the Law states the measure of compensation to be paid by a director as an amount equal to the "damage" suffered by the corporation. This is in contrast to the special actions for compensation provided for as a result of a breach of the insolvent trading provisions, s 588J, s 588K and s 588M, which measure the compensation to be paid as the amount equal to the "loss or damage" suffered. Although s 1317H attempts to provide some meaning as to the term "damage" by providing that it includes profits made by the person as a result of the contravention and any diminution of the value of property of a registered scheme, the other provisions lack such guidance. It is unclear what is meant by the phrase "loss or damage". In the context of s 588J, s 588K and s 588M, the provisions do not indicate whether "loss or damage" is limited to the amount of the debt that caused the contravention or can include consequential loss and profit made by the person contravening the provision.

[22.5] Proposals for law reform

[22.5.1] CLARIFY MEANING OF "LOSS OR DAMAGE"

The Law should be amended to clarify the meaning of "loss or damage" in the context of compensation proceedings under the insolvent trading provisions.

23 Practicalities

OBJECTIVES

This Chapter will:

- discuss directors and officers (D&O) insurance and analyse the benefit which D&O insurance may have for insolvency practitioners seeking to bring an action against a delinquent director or officer;
- provide an overview of litigation funding arrangements and consider their usefulness for insolvency practitioners seeking to bring an action against a director other officer for breach of duty;
- consider the appropriate Court in which to institute an action for breach of duty;
- analyse the most appropriate plaintiff to bring an action for breach of duty;
- consider applicable time limits;
- discuss other practicalities of bringing an action for a breach of duty.

[23.1] General overview

There are a number of practicalities involved in bringing proceedings against a delinquent director which are worthy of note.

[23.1.1] D&O INSURANCE AND INDEMNIFICATION

(a) D&O insurance

A problem for many insolvency practitioners is that when a company goes into voluntary administration or liquidation there may be little value left within the company itself for distribution to creditors if an action is brought for the recovery of funds. A source of claims may be against a director or officer of the company for insolvent trading or other breaches of the Law.

However, like many professionals who may be faced with personal liability in the future, many directors take steps to ensure that they have few if any assets in their own name. So there may be little benefit to a practitioner or creditors in successfully pursuing a director, unless of course the director is covered by D&O insurance giving the practitioner and creditors access to the funds of an insurance company (and hopefully not an insolvent one).

Given the increasingly onerous duties placed on directors and officers and their vulnerability to proceedings and financial exposure, the role of D&O insurance and indemnification has become more important in recent times.

Typically a D&O policy contains two separate insurance components. The first usually consists of a company reimbursement component which provides for the company to seek reimbursement for those amounts which it is obliged (or in some cases permitted), under its articles, to indemnify its directors and officers. The second usually consists of a direct cover component which provides indemnification to directors and officers where the company itself is unable to do so.

Sections 199B and 199C of the Law provide that a company (and a related body corporate) is prohibited from paying, or agreeing to pay, the premium for insurance of an officer (including a director) or an auditor of the company against a liability (other than for legal costs) arising out of:

- conduct involving a wilful breach of duty in relation to the company; or
- a contravention of s 182 or 183 (which relate to directors' use of position and use of information).

Provided that there matters are excluded from the cover under the D&O policy, which they usually are, there are no restrictions on the ability of a company to pay for an insurance premium for their directors and officers.

There are also a number of standard exclusions from D&O policies which significantly restrict the ambit of their operation. These include:

- **prospectus-type liability exclusion** which will often be of importance to directors of companies who propose to embark on a public offering;
- **professional indemnity exclusion** which excludes cover for claims alleging a breach of duty other than the professional duties owed by a director;
- **insured versus insured exclusion** which excludes claims brought by one person covered by the insurance against another, including by the company against a director. This is a significant exclusion because a director's duties are owed to the company itself and actions thus brought by the company are a significant potential source of liability. Many D&O policies contain an exception to the insured versus insured exclusion. This is to prevent the manufacturing of a claim for example by the directors of a company breaching a duty and voting to sue themselves to get damages for which the company is insured. D&O policies normally include an exclusion to extend cover to claims brought in the name of the company:
  - (i) as a shareholder derivate action;
  - (ii) by ASIC; or
  - (iii) at the instigation of a receiver, administrator or liquidator.

Unless the policy contains such an exception, a D&O policy is unlikely to provide relief for an action brought by the company/liquidator against a director or officer for insolvent trading or any other breach of duty as the action would be brought on behalf of the company.

(b) Can the liquidator find out if there is D&O insurance?

The Law confers on a liquidator the power to question relevant persons as to the "examinable affairs" of the company in liquidation. Examinable affairs includes the property of the company which extends to choses in action. The Courts have held that information concerning the company's prospects of successfully litigating a claim and the likelihood that any judgment obtained would be met by payment, is information about the "property" of the company in liquidation.[1]

The examination powers under the Law effectively places the liquidators in a special position compared with the "normal" plaintiff. This was recognised by the High Court of Australia in *Hamilton v Oades*[2] in that:

> The very purpose of [the examination provisions under the Corporations Law] is to create a system of discovery. This ... gives to the liquidator rights not possessed by an ordinary litigant.

1 *Grosvenor Hill (Qld) Pty Ltd v Barber* (1994) 48 FCR 301; *In the matter of Interchase Corporation Ltd and in the matter of an Application by Barber*, unreported decision of Kiefel J Qld registry of Fed Crt, 2 August 1996

2 (1989) 166 CLR 486 at 497-498.

This advantage granted to a liquidator offsets the disadvantages faced by a liquidator when contemplating commencing proceedings. As the Queensland Court of Appeal in *Adler Group v Quintex Group Management Services Pty Ltd (in liq)*[3] observed:

> In the nature of things, liquidators when they are appointed labour under the particular disability of not knowing as much about the examinable affairs as former directors and officers, and that they often cannot obtain reliable information about suspicious transactions. Generally the only source available to them is the records of the company such as books and documents if still available, and the information they contain is always vulnerable to contrived explanations and even to distortions to persons not anxious to disclose what they really know about events which took place when they were in charge of the company's affairs.
>
> A plaintiff in civil proceedings is bound to prove his case and generally must do so by oral evidence. Directors and senior officers of the company in liquidation, even if they have not absconded, are often unwilling and uncooperative witnesses … Few other litigants suffer to that disadvantage, or to the same extent, as liquidators.

A party is entitled to claim legal professional privilege on an examination.

Access to the insurance documents allows a liquidator to assess the merits of proceeding with (most likely costly) litigation.

(c) D&O indemnification

As well as paying for a premium for D&O insurance, a company can indemnify a director or officer for certain liabilities incurred. The provisions which deal with the indemnification of directors and officers (s 199A) deal separately with when an indemnity for liability for legal costs, and one other than for legal costs, will be allowed.

A company, or related body corporate, is prohibited from providing an indemnity, other than for legal costs, in a number of circumstances. This prohibition applies to an indemnity against liability incurred as a director, officer or auditor of the company which is:

- owed to the company or a related body corporate;
- for a pecuniary penalty order or a compensation order for a breach of certain provisions (including the insolvent trading provisions); or
- owed to someone other than the company (or related body corporate) and arose out of bad faith.

3 (1996) 22 ACSR 446 at 449.

A company must not indemnify a director, officer or auditor for legal expenses incurred:

- in defending proceedings in which the person is found to have a liability for which the company could not indemnify the person;
- in defending or resisting criminal proceedings in which the person is found guilty;
- in defending or resisting proceedings brought by ASIC or a liquidator for a Court order if the grounds for making the order are established; or
- in connection with proceedings by the person for relief under the Law which are denied by the Court.

In all other cases the company is able to indemnify the director, officer or auditor for her or his legal costs.

Interestingly, these provisions allow an indemnity for legal costs to be provided before the outcome of the proceedings is known. If an indemnity is advanced but an adverse decision is given by the Court the costs already paid must be refunded. In addition, a company can provide a loan or advance to a director, officer or auditor in respect of legal costs. Again, if an adverse decision is reached such a loan or advance must be repaid.

(d) How useful will D&O insurance be in the context of insolvent trading claims?

Sections 199B and 199C of the Law provide that a company must not pay an insurance premium of the company against a liability arising out of conduct involving a wilful breach of duty. So long as the D&O policy excludes such claims from its ambit a company is able to take out effective D&O insurance for its directors and officers.

As indicated earlier, there are a number of sanctions which may be imposed on a director by the court for insolvent trading. These fall into two categories: civil penalty provisions and criminal penalty provisions. Basically a criminal offence is committed by insolvent trading where it is done with wilful deceit.

Section 199A of the Law prevents a company from indemnifying a director against liability incurred for a pecuniary penalty order or a compensation order under s 1317H. This is because such a fine or compensation is payable to the company as a result of wrongs committed against it. It would be against the policy of the Law to allow a company to indemnify a director or officer in such circumstances. As a result it will often be difficult, if not impossible, for a company to indemnify a director or officer for liability incurred for insolvent trading and to then seek reimbursement itself from its insurer under its company reimbursement policy. In such circumstances a director or officer will usually seek direct cover under the D&O policy.

However, because D&O policies must not cover a director or officer for liability incurred as a result of a wilful breach of duty (s 199B), a D&O policy will not cover a director or officer for liability incurred for insolvent trading or other breach of duty where such a contravention is a criminal offence. This is because a criminal offence is committed as a result of a wilful reach of duty, or wilful deceit.

Accordingly, most D&O policies will only cover the liability of directors or officers which is incurred under a civil penalty provision, such as an imposition of a fine or the requirement to pay compensation to the company. Whilst this could be seen to restrict the effectiveness of D&O policies in the context of insolvent trading or other breach of duty, a criminal offence is difficult to prove and thus will rarely be made out. Most insolvent trading actions will seek civil penalty remedies and would thus be covered under the direct cover component of a D&O policy.

However a far greater risk to the effectiveness of D&O policies is the "insured versus insured" clause which was discussed above. Many D&O policies provide that the policy will not respond to claims brought by or on behalf of the company or any of the company's directors or officers against any other director or officer. Most such policies however provide an extension which means that the exclusion will not prevent cover for claims bought by a shareholder, ASIC or an insolvency practitioner appointed to the company.

[23.1.2] LITIGATION FUNDING ARRANGEMENTS

(a) Ability of liquidator to bring proceedings in the name of the company

In addition to the primary right of the liquidator to bring proceedings for insolvent trading, a liquidator has the general ability to bring or defend proceedings in the name of the company: s 477(2)(a). Generally the liquidator will seek the approval of the creditors before commencing proceedings, particularly where it is likely to involve substantial expense.

There are usually insufficient funds left in a company to commence proceedings. If this is the case and there are substantial prospects of success the liquidator may seek an advance or indemnity from creditors. If a creditor provides such finance the liquidator can seek orders from the Court to permit her or him to treat the funds creditor more favourably than other creditors in the distribution of any property or funds that are recovered by the proceedings because of the risk assumed by them in financing the proceedings: s 564. The liquidator may also seek litigation funding or insurance from a third party as part of her or his ability to sell or assign the "property of the company": s 477(2)(b).

When a liquidator is defending proceedings brought against the company he or she is not usually liable for legal costs. However, where the proceedings are commenced by the liquidator he or she may be held liable for legal costs if the proceedings are ultimately unsuccessful and there are insufficient funds within the company to provide for reimbursement. Usually a liquidator will not commence proceedings unless there are large prospects of success or there is available funding.

(b) Significance of litigation insurance funding for liquidators by third parties

Until the mid-1990s funding of insolvency litigation by third parties was prevented by the rules known as "champerty and maintenance". These rules made it illegal to financially assist a party to litigation without lawful justification. In particular it made it illegal to provide such funds in return for a share of the proceeds of any successful action. This effectively precluded insurance companies and other private funders from providing funds to liquidators to commence proceedings in the case of insolvency. If there were not enough funds available within the insolvent company to commence proceedings liquidators would simply be unable to do anything about it.

However, in 1982 the position began to change in England where the House of Lords decided that a liquidator could assign a cause of action which the company possessed, such as an action against directors for insolvent trading, to a third party if the assignee had a genuine commercial interest in accepting the assignment and enforcing it for its own benefit.[4] The "genuine commercial interest" in the litigation had to be an interest separate from the benefit that the outsider would seek to gain from supporting the litigation, such as making a profit. This decision opened up the possibility of liquidators assigning a cause of action held by the company to a third party, such as an insurance company, who would receive a cut of any proceeds recovered.

Liquidators began to see that they could commence proceedings and recover funds for the benefit of creditors if they were able to receive financing from outside sources. This led to the development of litigation insurance funding arrangements between an insolvency practitioner, usually a liquidator, and an insurance company where the insurer funds the relevant action, indemnifies the liquidator for any cost orders made against her or him in return for a share in the proceeds of a successful action. In this way, the liquidator is not exposed to any liability for legal costs if the action is unsuccessful and the insurer will be liable for the amount of any legal costs order which outweighs the proceeds recovered.

4 *Trendex Trading Corporation v Credit Suisse* [1982] AC 679 (HL).

Generally, a liquidator will prepare a proposal for the insurance company outlining the nature of the relevant action, the risk and the proceeds which are likely to be recovered. The liquidator then gives the proposal to the insurer for consideration. Further negotiations may take place, but when the proposal is accepted in the final form the liquidator will usually, and is well advised to, seek the approval of creditors before accepting the proposal. Much of the law relating to litigation insurance funding arrangements have resulted from liquidators applying to the Court to get its "okay" that such arrangements do not breach the rules of champerty and maintenance.

In 1996 the liquidator of Movitor Pty Ltd sought a direction from the Court as to whether or not he was able to enter into a litigation insurance funding arrangement to bring an action against Movitor's directors for insolvent trading.[5] Although some of Movitor's creditors were willing to provide funding to the liquidator they were not willing to indemnify the liquidator if that action was unsuccessful. Under the arrangement the insurer would pay half of the legal fees, indemnify the liquidator for half of any costs order awarded against him and allow the liquidator to instruct the solicitors regarding the conduct of the action. If the action was successful the insurer would receive 12 per cent of the share of the proceeds received.

The Court considered that such an arrangement would in fact breach the rules of champerty and maintenance because the insurer had no "genuine commercial interest" in the litigation other than the share of the proceeds it would receive if the action was successful. However, the Court looked beyond these principles and considered the liquidator's powers of sale under s 477(2)(b) of the Law. The Court decided that a right of action possessed by a company, such as the right to bring an action for insolvent trading, fell within the definition of "the property of the company" and, accordingly, the liquidator had the right to sell the right of action to an insurance company despite that fact that it would otherwise breach the rules of champerty and maintenance. The power of the liquidator to sell the property of the company is conferred by statute and it did not matter that the property could include either the "fruits of the action" (such as a share in the proceeds recovered) or the action itself so long as the action was a genuine asset of the company. The Court suggested that if the insurance company made a grossly excessive profit out of the litigation then the sale may not be a "bona fide" exercise of the liquidator's power of sale and any such agreement may be valid. The Court will look to the particular circumstances of each case and the magnitude of the risk assumed by the insurer in deciding whether or not the profit made is "grossly excessive". Of course such complications can usually be eliminated if the liquidator has the approval of creditors to enter into the arrangement.

5 *Movitor Pty Ltd (in liq) v Simms* (1996) 14 ACLC 587.

These sentiments were reiterated by the Court in 1997 when the liquidator of Tosich Construction Pty Ltd applied to the Court for permission to enter into a litigation insurance funding arrangement.[6] Originally the arrangement would not have involved the actual sale of the action to the insurer but this was later amended to incorporate a sale of the action to the insurer in return for the insurer funding the proceedings and indemnifying the liquidator against any legal costs order. Without this amendment the arrangement would not have fallen within the Movitor principle of the liquidator's power of sale of the property of the company. The Court decided that the liquidator was able to enter into the arrangement. The Court also commented that the purchaser of any action should not be allowed to intervene in the conduct of the proceeding as this may affect the "bona fides" of the proceedings.

These, and a number of subsequent, cases clearly provide for a liquidator to sell a right of action possessed by the company to a third party, usually an insurance company, in consideration for the insurer funding the proceedings and often providing an indemnity to the liquidator in return for receiving a reasonable share of the proceeds recovered.[7] In order for the arrangement to be valid, some or all of the action must be sold to the third party, the third party should not have a role in the actual running or conduct of the proceedings and the arrangement must generally constitute a bona fide exercise of the liquidator's powers. If these steps are not taken the liquidator runs the risk of having the arrangement declared invalid and having to finance any legal costs incurred herself or himself. This development means that liquidators are now more likely to bring an action against directors of an insolvent company for insolvent trading and that this trend is likely to continue well into the future. Of perhaps equal importance liquidators can now threaten such proceedings more forcefully as a director can no longer simply assume that a liquidator of a company without funds of its own is a "toothless tiger".

In 1998 there were media reports of the possible establishment by entrepreneur Rene Rivkin of the so-called "Justice Corporation" which would fund all forms of civil litigation. Such a development may well be quite a development in litigation funding, providing funding in cases other than insolvency, but the Courts seem reluctant to allow such a development at this stage. Whilst many judges see the benefits in litigation funding for all actions due to the inability of many companies and persons to bring actions for lack of resources, the Courts are hesitant to condone trafficking in litigation. The Court's current position could well change in the near future.

What then are the policy and practical implications of litigation insurance funding arrangements in the context of insolvency? The main benefit is obvious

6 *Re Tosich Construction Pty Ltd* (1997) 23 ACSR 126.
7 See, for example, *Ultra Tune* (1997) 1 VR 667.

– it allows the recovery of funds for the benefit of creditors in circumstances where recovery would otherwise not be possible. By encouraging liquidators to take action against rogue directors without incurring further expense for creditors it may relieve creditors from a substantial financial burden in circumstances where they have often already lost funds. Litigation insurance funding potentially increases the number of actions to be taken against delinquent directors and may act as a greater deterrent. It is possible that it may also increase the likelihood of settlement as the plaintiff is less involved emotionally in the proceedings. Settlement may also occur earlier if the plaintiff has sufficient funds as the plaintiff could continue the litigation until the hearing itself and thus, if the defendant wants to settle the litigation he or she may have to make a realistic offer of settlement earlier than he or she would otherwise have to if the plaintiff had no prospects of being able to continue the litigation in any event. It also has a considerable benefit for liquidators and insolvency practitioners themselves, allowing for a recovery of remuneration, costs and fees in cases where there would not otherwise be any funds to pay them.

There are, of course, concerns over litigation insurance funding arrangements. The main concern is that in practice the liquidator's control over the conduct of the proceedings could be thwarted if he or she, as a practical matter, feels inclined to take the interests of the insurer into account when making decisions as to the conduct of the proceedings. This is no more obvious than in relation to settlement negotiations where the liquidator may feel obliged to reject offers of settlement which may cover her or his costs and fees and provide a minimal return for creditors but not a substantial return to the insurer. In this case the liquidator may wish to settle if there is little chance that more proceeds would be recovered for creditors if the litigation continued, however the insurer may wish to make a greater profit out of the litigation. Whilst taking such considerations into account could arguably mean that the liquidator is not exercising her or his powers bona fide, it is not yet known what effect such pressures may be having on liquidators in their conduct of proceedings. Another concern is that liquidators may feel obliged to enter into funding arrangements as part of their duty to realise all the property of the company for the benefit of creditors, even where there is no prospect of a substantial return to creditors, and thus inadvertently 'line the pockets' of the insurance industry.

Regardless of these public policy considerations, litigation insurance funding arrangements are becoming a tool increasingly utilised by liquidators and other insolvency practitioners. This trend is resulting in a growing number of actions taken against rogue directors for insolvent trading.

[23.1.3] APPROPRIATE COURT

The remedies available under Pts 5.7B and 9.4B for a breach of duty are expressed in terms of "the Court", rather than "the court". Section 58AA of the

Law defines the meanings of the terms "the Court" and "the court" and the difference between the two. The use of the term "the Court" means that jurisdiction to hear proceedings for a breach of duty is not extended to the lower courts. Jurisdiction is restricted to the:

- the Federal Court;
- State Supreme Courts;
- The Family Court of Australia; and
- A court to which s 41 of the *Family Law Act* 1975 (Cth) applies because of a Proclamation made under s 41(2) of that Act.

Actions for breach of duty by a director will usually be brought in the Federal Court of Australia or the relevant State Supreme Court.

[23.1.4] PLAINTIFFS

If remedies are sought by way of civil penalty orders under Pt 9.4B of the Law, only ASIC can apply for a declaration of contravention, a pecuniary penalty order or a disqualification order: s 1317J(1) and s 206C. Both ASIC and the company can seek a compensation order under s 1317H: s 1317J(1) and (2). A liquidator can intervene in an application for a declaration of contravention or a pecuniary penalty order and is entitled to be heard on all matters except whether the declaration or order should be made: s 1317J(3). In this way a liquidator has standing to sue for a breach of a statutory duty where a compensation order is sought. If a compensation order is sought under Pt 5.7B for a breach of the insolvent trading provisions, standing to sue is primarily in the hands of the liquidator. Under s 588M(2) the liquidator can directly recover from the contravening director compensation for the loss and damage sustained by the company as a result of the insolvent trading. Creditors have a secondary right to bring an action under s 588M(3). A creditor can proceed directly against a director to recover the debt owing to that creditor if the creditor has the written consent of the liquidator: s 588R(1). A creditor can bring an action for compensation without the consent of the liquidator if the liquidator does not take action within three months after a notice procedure is complied with and the Court grants the creditor leave to proceed: s 588T(2).

A liquidator may also bring proceedings for a breach by a director of an equitable or fiduciary duty owed to the company.

[23.1.5] BURDEN OF PROOF

Section 1317L states that the rules of evidence and procedure for civil matters must be used when hearing an application for a declaration of contravention or a pecuniary penalty order. This means that that the Court need only be satisfied on the balance of probabilities.

[23.1.6] TIME LIMITS

Limitation periods for most actions in Australia are set out in statutes of limitation in each State and Territory. Generally, the limitation period commences to run on accrual of the cause of action rather than discovery of the basis of the cause of action by the potential plaintiff[8] except in cases of fraud or deceit. A number of limitation periods are considered below, covering a wide range of actions directors can be subjected to.

(a) Contract and negligence

Generally the limitation period for actions for breach of contract or negligence is six years.[9]

(b) Misleading and deceptive conduct

The limitation period for an action for damages for breach of s 52 of the *Trade Practices Act* 1974 (Cth) for misleading and deceptive conduct is three years,[10] as is the period for breach of s 12DA of the *Australian Securities and Investments Commission Act* (s 12GF of the ASIC Act) and s 42 of the *Fair Trading Act* (NSW).

(c) Civil penalty orders

An application for a civil penalty order can only be made within six years after the alleged contravention: s 1317K.

(d) Compensation for insolvent trading

Proceedings for the recovery of compensation for loss under s 588M resulting from insolvent trading by a director must be commenced within six years after the beginning of the winding-up of the company: s 588M(4).

(e) Criminal proceedings

Under the Law, criminal proceedings must be commenced within five years after the alleged act or omission constituting the offence or at any later time with the Minister's consent: s 1316.

[23.1.7] JOINT AND SEVERAL LIABILITY

Where only one director is sued under the insolvent trading provisions and a judgment is entered into against that director, the director can then seek to obtain redress from the other directors on the basis that they are jointly and severally liable.[11]

---

8 *Hawkins v Clayton* (1988) 164 CLR 539.
9 See, for example, *Limitations Act* 1969 (NSW).
10 *Trade Practices Act* 1974 (Cth), s 82.
11 *Australian Securities Commission v Snellgrove* (1992) 10 ACLC 1542.

[23.2] Philosophy/rationale

Briefly, this primary right of the liquidator to seek compensation for a breach of the insolvent trading provisions is a result of the fact that the duty to prevent insolvent trading is owed to the company rather than individual creditors. It also seeks to put litigation in the hands of the person with the greatest access to evidence.[12]

[23.3] History/former law

The primary right of the liquidator to sue for compensation under the insolvent trading provisions was introduced by the *Corporate Law Reform Act* 1992 (Cth). Prior to this time, standing to commence an action was extended to creditors only. An insolvent company's liquidator had no standing to bring a claim on behalf of all creditors affected.[13] Consequently, creditors owed only a small amount were unlikely to risk legal action. Further, a multiplicity of actions had to be brought if all creditors were to recover. This situation was remedied with the introduction of s 588M.

[23.4] Checklist

[23.4.1] A CHECKLIST FOR BRINGING AN ACTION

- Is there a need for a litigation funding arrangement to be made in order to bring the action?
- In which Court should the action be instituted?
- Who is the appropriate plaintiff to bring an action? Does the liquidator have standing to bring an action?
- Is the creditor seeking to bring an action for compensation under s 588M(3)? Within six months of the beginning of the winding-up of the company, has written notice been given the liquidator of the intention to sue and asking for a written notice to be given by the liquidator seeking consent to sue or the reasons for withholding consent? Has this written notice of consent been received within three months? If not, has the Court given leave to begin proceedings? If the liquidator has given a written notice of the reasons why proceedings should not be commenced, has application been made for leave of the Court to begin proceedings and the Court been supplied with the notice from the liquidator?

---

12 See S Worthington, "Recent Developments: Legal and Administrative" (1992) 10(3) CSLJ 214.

13 See *Ross McConnel Kitchen Pty Ltd (in liq) v Ross* (No 2) (1985) 9 ACLR 532. See also A Herzberg, "Insolvent Trading" (1991) 9(5) CSLJ 285.

- Has the time limit for proceedings passed?
- Is there evidence to prove civil matters on the balance of probabilities?
- If ASIC seeks to bring criminal proceedings, is there evidence to prove a criminal offence beyond reasonable doubt?

Table of Cases

Table of Statutes

Queensland

South Australia

Victoria

Imperial

New Zealand

United Kingdom

United States

Index